Catching Shrimp
with Bare Hands

Catching Shrimp
with Bare Hands

A Boy from the Mekong Delta

∼

Michelle Robin La

ViewPort Publishing
Santa Barbara, CA

Published in the United States by ViewPort Publishing
www.viewportpublishing.com

ISBN (paperback): 978-0-9909177-7-9
ISBN (ebook): 978-0-9909177-8-6

Library of Congress Control Number
2014959224

Cover Design by Sabina Funk
Map by Sabina Funk
Photographs courtesy of Lê Thị Rở
Author Photograph by Dot Salogga

The montage on the cover uses a photograph taken by the
author of the traditional hand embroidered painting *Bến Chiều*
by XQ Việt Nam. The artwork is owned by the author and her
husband and used with permission from XQ Việt Nam.

FIRST EDITION

To Má—without you there would be no story.

To Lượng—your name means generous which you are.

To catch shrimp in the Mekong Delta is to wade along a stream, the brown water flowing around you. Hands and arms disappear into a muddy cloud searching hidden places along the bank. You don't know what you'll find until you clasp it in your hands.

As told to me by my husband, Lượng La.

Contents

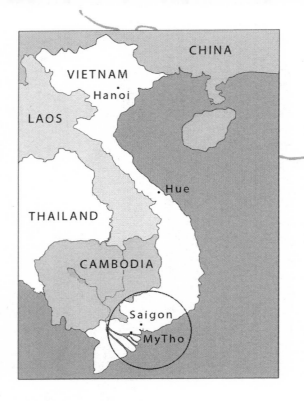

Mỹ Tho

Đồng Tâm
Military Base

Tân Long

Phoenix Island

Quới Sơn

Giao Long

Cồn Tàu

An Hóa

Bến Tre

Sài Gòn ↑

Ocean

Mekong Delta

3 km

Lượng's Family

Ba* = father
Má = mother
Anh = an older brother (or male the age of an older brother)
Chị = an older sister (or female the age of an older sister)
Em = a younger sibling (or person the age of a younger sibling)

Note: Younger siblings call their older siblings by their rank. In the South, the oldest has the rank of two. Neighbors and relatives are also referred to by their title and family rank.

Lượng's family by birth order:

First Name**	Family title	Rank
Thanh	Chị Hai	2 (Hai)
Lan	Chị Ba	3 (Ba)*
Huệ	Chị Tư	4 (Tư)***
Thơm	Chị Năm	5 (Năm)
Vân	Anh Sáu	6 (Sáu)
Thượng	Anh Bảy	7 (Bảy)
Lượng	Anh Tám	8 (Tám)
Young	Em Chín	9 (Chín)
Hằng	Em Mười	10 (Mười)
Sang	Em Út	Last (Út)

Ba means father and also means three. Bà means old woman.

**In this book, formal names are usually given in Vietnamese and nicknames in English*

***Tư translates as fourth. Bốn is four. The other numbers don't have a different ordinal form.*

Lunar New Year (Tết) 1964 in front of the house in Quới Sơn. Má holds Lượng (6 months). Siblings from left to right: Huệ (Chị Tư), Lan (Chị Ba), Thanh (Chị Hai), Thơm (Chị Năm), Thượng (Anh Bảy), and Vân (Anh Sáu).

A Moment of Clarity

The sound of heavy footsteps comes down the dirt road in front of our house. I look up from the hole I'm digging with a stick in the shade of the tamarind tree. The tamarind tree leaves and our neighbor's tall red flowers hide the person coming. I hope it's the big man who carries roast pig in a flat basket on his head. He usually stops for tea and asks if we want to buy the leftover pieces. He'll give my brothers and me a piece of the crunchy skin. I'm not allowed up by the road, so I listen for him to call "roast pig, roast pig," as he walks past our neighbors.

A woman walking barefoot comes from the other way, the baskets creaking on her shoulder pole. Coconut and pomelo trees cover the tin roof of the market behind her. The heavy footsteps get closer. It's too many people to be the roast pig seller. I move toward the muddy line where water comes up from the canal on the side of our house and go back to digging. I don't know why the roast pig seller doesn't come every day. My older brothers aren't around. If he came today, I'd get all of the skin.

Boots stomp nearby. I stand up and look around the tamarind tree. Captain Can of the Army fort and three soldiers with guns walk toward me. The grenades hanging from their shirt pockets and belts sway with each step. The captain's dark brown dog follows, its pink tongue rolling out of its mouth. I drop the stick and run into the house.

My father sits on the floor in front of his desk fixing a bicycle. "Ba, guests are coming," I say.

Ba puts his tools on his desk and winds through parked bicycles and past his moped toward the open door. "Come in. Have some tea," he calls out to the captain.

"Are you well?" Captain Can says. He enters and turns toward the lean-to and calls to Grandfather. "*Chào,* Bác. Are you well?"

Grandfather nods from the chair in the lean-to and goes back to looking out his window at the dirt road.

One of the men stays in the road and takes out a cigarette. The captain and the others pull chairs up to the small table in the front room. The dog comes in too.

"Thơm!" Ba calls toward the kitchen for my sister. "Offer the captain and his men some tea and cookies."

I follow Chị Năm to the table in the hallway. My sister pulls the teapot out of a coconut husk warmer and pours tea into cups. I stand next to her and stare at the rectangular tin of Holland cookies. I wish they weren't just for visitors and customers. Maybe I'll get one since my brothers aren't around.

"Lượng, go away," Chị Năm says as she counts the cookies onto a tin plate. She sets the tea and cookies on the small table. I stay nearby hoping Ba or one of the men will offer me one. The dog sits by them. It looks as big as me. It doesn't wag its tail. It sits and waits like it's in the military, too. I move away from the dog and sit on the dirt ledge that goes up to Grandfather's lean-to.

Captain Can turns to my father. "Is the repair business going well today?" His pistol and holster tilt forward when he reaches for his cup.

"Just enough." Ba points toward his desk on the other side of the room. Bicycles and parts line the walls. A cabinet holds radios he put together to rent. "Only a few bicycles and a clock to fix. How are things at the fort?"

"Getting worse." The captain picks up a round cookie. I imagine how it tastes.

"It could get active around here soon," says one of the captain's men. The men pick up cookies and eat them piece by piece. I wonder if there'll be any left.

"It's hard to have enough customers with all the fighting around here." Ba sighs. "Quới Sơn gets smaller all of the time."

Everyone seems so worried. I used to be able to go outside more. Now, as soon as it's late afternoon, even my brothers have to stay close to the house. I wish we would win the war, so I could have fun playing and slingshoting birds like my brothers used to.

"We had it better under Diệm," the captain says. "Now the Việt Cộng are everywhere."

Ba nods. Việt Cộng come to our house at night sometimes. My parents always push us into the back room when they do.

A soldier leans forward and takes another cookie. There's only one left. I stare at it, hoping it will magically appear in my mouth. Usually Ba puts the extras back in the tin, but maybe, since there's only one left, he'll give it to me.

Captain Can picks up the last cookie and stands up. "Well, if you see anything you don't like," he says, "tell one of my men or come by the fort."

He looks at me and holds the cookie out.

"Thank you," I mumble. I take the cookie and put it in my shirt pocket.

The captain calls the dog and walks out with his men. I follow them out and sit on the dirt foundation of our house. I look to make sure no one is around before I pull out the cookie. Then I bite off a small piece and eat it slowly so it lasts.

~

"My Dear People . . ."

I wake up in the dark. What's going on? It's so loud. The voice seems like it's in the room with us.

"My Dear People, the current regime is corrupt. It is a puppet for the evil American imperialists."

Má and Ba wake up on either side of me.

"They have murdered our people in . . ."

My baby sisters sleep next to me in the middle of the bed. I wonder if the noise will wake them up.

"We are the People's Liberation Front of the South. Communism is the clear light that will lead you out of poverty and oppression—"

Rầm. Rầm. Rầm. The Army fires the machine gun on the side of their fort.

The wood frame of the bed moves as Má shifts. "Those Army soldiers don't know what they're shooting at in the dark," she says. "I can't believe Anh Bảy has started his speeches again."

It's my uncle out there?

"Why doesn't he start his propaganda somewhere else?" Ba asks. "Why always under the tamarind tree out front? Talk to your sister about her husband and his Communist brother before we get killed because of his speeches."

Râm. The Army fires again. Are they going to hit our house?

Ba and Má argue. I try to go back to sleep. I toss and turn trying not to wake up my baby sisters, wondering if my older brothers and sisters in the next room are awake like me.

≈

"My Dear People . . ."

I hate that megaphone. I hate my uncle. I wish he'd quit waking me up in the middle of the night.

". . . the Army is a corrupt puppet for American imperialists determined to steal our country from the people. Remember—"

Râm. Râm. Râm. My uncle stops talking. Sometimes he starts shouting again from a different place after the Army fires at him. I'm not scared the Army will hit us. I just wish they'd hit him so he'd stop.

≈

People hurry down the dirt road in front of our house calling out that someone's going to get carried through town.

Má runs up to where my brothers and I play under the tamarind tree. "Get inside, kids," Má says. "Get inside. They're going to carry a dead person through town. It's going to be scary, don't look."

I hurry in behind my brothers. Má closes the door but stays outside with Ba and some neighbors.

My brothers peek through the long, sideways gaps between the wood planks of the front wall of the house. Vân turns to Thượng. "Are you going to watch?"

"No. It's too scary," Thượng says.

I stay toward the back of the room with my older sisters. I'm not going to look.

"None of you should watch," Chị Tư says. My brothers move away from the front wall. My sister looks at me. "Especially you, Lượng."

Shouting comes from down the street. My brothers run to the gaps in the wall. I have to find out what it is. I run over to my brothers and peek between the boards.

Má stands by the tamarind tree. A crowd lines up along the road across from us, stretching out away from town. Everyone looks toward the market. Two men appear through the pomelo and banana leaves with a pole over their shoulders carrying a burnt body in a hammock. A couple of men follow. The man in the hammock seems small, shrunken from the fire. His bent arms stick out from the straw mat wrapped around his body. The skin pulls tight over his bones, golden and crisp, black in places like a roast pig. The tamarind tree blocks my view as the men carry him past our house. I strain to look. The hammock comes out on the other side. I see the man's face now. His hair is burnt off. Oil drips down his cheek from a crack under his eye. Little drops. Roast pigs don't have a crack like that. The smell of burnt fat, skin, and hair mixes together. The men carrying the hammock disappear behind the concrete grave and flower bushes in Mr. Three Xuyên's front yard.

I stay by the gap in the boards, breathing in the strange scent, imagining the man's face with the oil dripping out under the eye. I turn away. My sisters and brothers all stand by the cracks in the wall.

Vân pulls away. "That's the first time I smelled something like that."

"It smells so strong," Chị Tư says.

"He was burned up," Chị Năm says. "I had my eyes closed. I wasn't going to look, but . . ."

"Who do you think it was?" Chị Tư asks Chị Năm as they go back to the kitchen.

Chị Năm shakes her head. "I don't know."

∾

A half hour later, Mr. Fourth Farmer comes to the front door. Ba puts down the wrench he's using to fix a bicycle. "Come sit down, have some tea."

"No thank you, I've had some already," Mr. Fourth Farmer says.

Thượng and I stand quietly in the shadow of the hallway. I want to know if they'll say anything about the burnt man.

Mr. Fourth Farmer sits in the chair. "Did you hear who they carried through town?" he asks.

"No." Ba's voice sounds quiet. "I don't know anything about that."

I wait as still as I can.

"The Communist propagandist."

The burned man was my uncle?

"What happened?" Ba asks.

"The Army found him near that shack by the river where all the Việt Cộng hide."

"How?"

"The American Special Forces helped. The Army took him into the shack and beat him for information while the Americans watched. Then the Army tied him to one of the posts in the shack and burned it down with him in it."

Ba shakes his head. "It was bound to happen. He was crazy to stand out there at night spouting propaganda."

Mr. Fourth Farmer leaves, and Ba goes back to work on the bicycle. I stay in the hall and think. All I can think is that I'm glad it will be quiet tonight.

~

We must be winning the war. It's quiet at night, and I don't have to stay inside as much. I run after my brothers through a row of banana plants up to a barbed wire fence. On the other side, Mr. Three Xuyên lives alone in a French-style house made of concrete and white plaster. He's the only one whose yard has an iron gate facing the road and flowers next to the front door. The mangoes on Mr. Three Xuyên's tree dangle from the branches, almost touching the ground. They're still green, but we can dip green mangoes in salt mixed with chili pepper or sugar and fish sauce.

Vân peeks out from the bananas to see if Mr. Three Xuyên's dog is hiding in the doorway under the birds of paradise and canna lilies. "No one's there," he says. Everyone sleeps during the hot sun in the middle of the day.

Vân and Thượng start scraping away the sandy dirt under the barbed wire fence to make room to crawl under.

"Thượng, you go and get them this time." Vân lifts the lowest wire up and Thượng goes into Mr. Three Xuyên's yard.

We crouch behind the banana plants while Thượng creeps up to the mango tree. Behind the tree is a grave with a concrete roof where Mr. Three Xuyên's father-in-law is buried. My brothers get in trouble for climbing on the grave, but I'm too scared to go near it.

"That's enough, toss them back," Vân says.

Thượng tosses a mango toward us. Mr. Three Xuyên jumps out from behind a tree. "I caught you." He reaches out to grab Thượng.

My heart pounds. Thượng drops the mangoes and runs around the yard. He can't get out because of the fence and the iron gate.

Vân runs. I can't keep up. I race after him into the house and hide in a corner of my parent's bedroom. It's the darkest place in the house besides the bomb shelter—but I don't want to go in there.

Thượng cries outside. I peek out of the bedroom. Mr. Three Xuyên drags him into our house by the ear. "Your boys were picking my mangoes again," he says as Má comes out of the kitchen.

Má looks at Thượng. "What did you do?"

Thượng doesn't say anything.

Mr. Three Xuyên lets go of him. "Don't you boys know not to take things that don't belong to you?" he asks. My brother runs over to stand by Má.

Mr. Three Xuyên reaches both hands into the big pockets in front of his *áo bà ba* shirt and pulls a mango out in each. "What am I going to do with green mangoes?" He sighs and hands them to Má. "Here, maybe you can cook something with them."

⁓

"It sure would be nice to have some mango in my belly," Vân says.

"I'm not going this time," Thượng says. "I can't get out fast enough. Lượng is small. He can fit under better."

"Lượng." Vân looks at me. "We'll lift the wire up. You get the mangoes."

My heart starts to beat faster, but my stomach hurts from being empty. I don't know when Má will get home from farming and we'll eat. I nod and follow Vân and Thượng to the banana plants. We check that Mr. Three Xuyên's dog isn't out and then dig under the fence to make more space.

Vân lifts the wire up. I look at the pointy barbs, then over at the mango tree. I wriggle under the fence and glance up at the white concrete side of Mr. Three Xuyên's house. The shutters on the windows are open, but I don't see him inside. I crawl to the tree and search through the leaves for fruit.

I pick a mango and throw it toward the fence. Vân steps out and

grabs it. I snap another mango off the tree and toss it. Thượng gets it
and waves for me to come back.

I look at the house—all clear. I creep back to the fence as fast as I
can. Thượng lifts up the wire, and I scurry under. I try to stand up and
run. *Ui!* A barb sticks my butt and catches my shorts. I pull my shorts
off the wire and race home. We try not to make a sound as we peel the
green mangoes and dip them in salt mixed with a chili pepper.

~

Vân and Thượng grab their slingshots. "Từ Ba's kids have been chasing
us and shooting at us," Vân says. "It's time to get back at them."

"Every time we walk by they attack us," Thượng says.

"Make me a slingshot." I've heard my brothers talking about war
with the crazy woman's sons. It's more exciting than stealing mangoes.
My brothers said they've even shot at the pots and pans inside the
crazy woman's house.

"Later, Lượng," Vân says as he heads out the door with Thượng.

"Let me help."

Thượng turns to look at me. "You can hold the ammunition and
hand it to us when we need it."

I run after them. We're going to have a battle. Someone could even
get hurt.

"Let's go get Dũng and his brothers to join us," Vân says. "Then,
we'll outnumber them."

We walk down the dirt road toward Dũng's house.

"We're going to have a shoot 'em up with the sons of the crazy
woman," Vân whispers to Dũng at the door of the house. "Get your
brothers and slingshots and come with us."

Dũng, Tẻo, and Tẹc follow us over to the edge of the ditch on the
side of the road. My brothers break off the corners of dirt pieces with
their hands and rub them against a coconut tree trunk to make them
round. I hold out my shirt to collect them.

"We'll get Từ Ba's kids this time," Vân says. "They won't bother us
again."

"That woman is so crazy," Dũng says as he looks for clumps of dirt,
"she talks to herself all the time and you can't understand what she's
saying."

I nod. I've seen Mrs. Từ Ba talking to herself in the road, her hair all tangled. She screams and throws pans around in her shack.

"I heard she's so crazy," Vân says, "that she picked up a grenade and brought it to the market. A soldier had to grab it away from her before she pulled the pin."

Thượng nods and laughs. "That's right."

"Má says she thinks they're fruit," Vân says. "That's why she picks them up. Who would think a grenade is fruit?"

I run over to my friend Tẹc. "Look how much I have." I hold out my shirt with the dirt clumps in it.

"It's starting to rain," Dũng says. "The dirt's getting too wet. Let's find some young coconut fruits to use."

Tẻo points to three boys in the path behind the widow Bà Bảy's house across the road. "There they are."

"Let's get them," Vân says.

"You're crazy sons of a crazy woman," Dũng calls. "When your mother is crazy what else can you be?"

"You sons of dogs," the oldest enemy boy calls. He's bigger than Vân or Dũng. "We're going to teach you to stay away from our house."

My brothers and their friends load their slingshots. "We've got you outnumbered," Dũng calls. We chase them back toward their shack and hit them with dirt and coconut fruit.

"Get out of our yard!" the oldest boy yells, aiming at Dũng.

"Make us!" Vân shouts. He fires his slingshot.

"Lượng, we're running out of ammunition," Thượng says. "Grab some dry dirt."

I look for clumps of dirt or coconut fruits while my brothers hit the wood boards of the house with their slingshots. It starts to rain harder.

"We'll get you good this time," Vân says, loading up. "This'll teach you to attack us when we walk by."

The boys run into their shack. My brothers and their friends fire inside. We're right at the entrance. They don't have a door to close. We've won.

Mrs. Từ Ba steps out. Everyone stops firing. She stands in front of her house. "I know you think I'm crazy," she says looking past us, "but in the rain I can see what's happening and my mind is clear. I know what my sons do, and I know what you do."

She doesn't sound crazy.

She drops to her knees and looks at the ground. Grown-ups aren't supposed to do this. "Please, in this moment of clarity, please, I beg you . . . quit tormenting us."

She calls to her three sons. "Get down on your knees." The sons kneel down on the wet dirt in front of us. The rain patters. "Apologize for fighting," she orders.

With their eyes on the ground, her sons whisper, "Sorry."

"My sons only act to protect me," Mrs. Từ Ba says. "Please forgive them and leave us in peace."

I thought they were bad—that it was good to get even. They were just protecting their mother. I walk home with my brothers in the rain. No one talks.

Chapter Two (1967)

The Bomb Shelter

B efore dinner, I go out to check the cashew tree that leans against the back of the house. I like the fruit the cashews grow out of. Yesterday one was close to ripe. I look up into the leaves for it. I can almost taste the sweet and sour juice. There's only one small, green fruit hanging from the branches. Where's the other one? The big, yellowish-red one. My face gets hot and tears come down. I run into the kitchen. "Who took the cashew fruit? It was mine."

"How did it become yours?" my older sister Chị Tư asks. She squats next to the rice pot, fanning the fire with a betel nut pod. Smoke drifts through the water coconut leaf roof.

"I watched it every day."

My sister laughs. "The one who finds it eats it."

Chị Tư puts the pot of rice on the table and takes some food to Grandfather in the lean-to. We crowd around the long wood table. I sit on a bench with my brothers. Ba sits in a chair at the end. When Ba begins to eat, everyone reaches their chopsticks for pieces of salty meat and stir-fried water spinach. I have a spoon and can barely reach the top of the table. Má puts some food in my rice bowl. I wander to the corner and sit down on the floor away from everyone jostling me.

Ba puts his rice bowl and chopsticks down. He's already done eating. "Children, you need to be ready to run to the bomb shelter if you hear a shell whistle. Or gunfire or airplanes. Run, don't wait."

I glance away from him to the dark entrance of the bomb shelter at the end of the kitchen. It's dug halfway into the dirt.

"The first one in should roll out the mats, so we can sit on them," Má says. "Then stay as low as you can."

"I'm too old to go into anything that looks like a grave," Grandfather calls out from the lean-to.

"Grandfather will be safe in his room," Ba says. Grandfather has a shallow hole in the dirt floor of the lean-to that he can dive into during an attack. "The rest of you get into the bomb shelter as soon as you hear fighting."

I don't see how the bomb shelter can protect us. It's dug into the dirt, and dirt is soft. The coconut logs making the walls are white and soft in the middle. The sandbags around the outside are soft, and have sand pouring out. The coconut husk roof is soft, too. We even burn some of the husks when our pile for cooking runs out. How can soft things stop a bomb?

∽

I wake up to shouting. What's going on? It's black. I close and open my eyes again. It's still black. "Run! Run!" Ba tosses me out of bed and pushes me toward the bomb shelter. *Âm.* It sounds like thunder. I start to run. *Kum!* I crash into a coconut log pillar holding the roof up. My head hurts. I start to run again. *Kum!* My shoulder hits another pillar. Where am I? There's only supposed to be one pillar. Skin and clothes brush against me. I run in a circle until someone grabs my legs and pulls me into the shelter. *Ui!* My head hits the top of the entrance. The dirt floor feels cold and damp, not clean and hard like the packed dirt floor in the rest of the house. I squat down and walk with my knees bent to avoid splinters and spiders in the wood above. I feel somebody and crouch next to them on the straw mat in back.

"Lượng?" Ba says.

I sit down on a matcurler bug and flick it away. "I'm here."

"I have Young and Hằng," Má says.

Ba calls the rest of my siblings. They each answer.

"The fighting sounds nearby," Má says. "Less than a kilometer away." A flash of light comes through a crack. It's quiet. A whistling noise comes overhead.

We wait for a while. My head and shoulder hurt from hitting the coconut tree pillar and the top of the door. There's a *xè xè xè* right above us. "If you hear the fuse burning, it means it's close," Ba says.

We sit hunched down with our heads in our knees. I get tired and lean into Má. For hours, we listen to shells. The air smells like the stuff matcurler bugs make when you touch them. The noise stops, but no one moves. After half an hour of silence, Ba leaves the shelter. He comes back and whispers to Má. Then he says, "Back to bed."

In the morning my head hurts. I rub it with my fingers and feel two big lumps. When I walk into the kitchen, Chị Năm hands me a bowl of rice with some shrimp. "Lượng! Look at the lumps on your head," she says. "Well, everyone has to hit the top of the entrance at least once. Then you learn." She grabs an extra shrimp from the pot with her chopsticks and puts it in my bowl.

After breakfast, I go outside with my brothers to look for shrapnel stuck in the trees. Vân points to a banana plant with one stem crumpled over. I get down on my hands and knees, but I can't find the piece of metal that lopped it off.

"Let's see if we can find any pieces stuck in the coconut trees," Vân says. We walk around the canals behind our house searching for wounds on the tree trunks.

Before dinner, I go over to check the cashew tree. The one green fruit on it has a few streaks of red now. I get a stick and poke it down. It tastes bitter and spongy.

～

Má and Ba push me out of bed toward the bomb shelter. "Run! Run!" My head knocks into the pillar. Tears start in my eyes. I move around the pillar and run. Someone shoves me toward the shelter. I put one hand to the side and the other hand over my head and crouch down. Ba calls our names. We wait. My head throbs. I hope we don't have to stay here for hours like last time. After a while, Ba and Má tell us we can go back to our beds.

I have another lump on my head in the morning. I promise myself I'm not going to hit the entrance or pillar again. I go to the room I sleep in and count the steps from the end of the bed to the pillar in the hallway. Then I count steps from the hallway to the door of the shelter. Standing in front of the shelter, I kneel down and see how low I have to bend to get in without hitting my head. I go back to the bed and practice sliding off it and running to the shelter counting steps.

At night I stay up listening for sounds in the sky. At any moment, shells could start falling, and Ba will tell us to run.

∼

In the afternoon, I lie in the hammock in the front room with Vân. We have to stay in the house most of the day, except for Má and my sisters who take the boat out to our island farm. I want to sleep during the day, so I can stay awake at night and not hit the pillar if we have to run to the bomb shelter.

The *rồ rồ rồ* of Má's boat comes up the stream. I go out with Vân to see what kind of fruit she brought back. Usually she brings back bananas, guavas, and soursops. My brothers grab the handle of a basket filled with guavas and try to lift it—it's too heavy. Má hands us some empty baskets to carry. After we bring them in, Vân goes to play marbles with Thượng in their bedroom. I go back to the hammock in the corner. I'm tired, but I can't sleep. I close my eyes and pretend.

Má takes her *nón lá* off and stacks it on the other palm leaf hats. "My soul ran away from me today," she says to Ba. "When I turned off the river onto our stream to head home, I heard a whirl of blades. A helicopter, the big kind with guns pointed out the open doors, was right above our boat."

I open my eyes a little. Ba puts the spokes back on a bicycle rim while Má talks. It seems like so much work to straighten them and put them back in. "I heard a big chopper a while ago," he says, "and some gunfire. What happened?"

"Well, I stopped the motor right away and let the boat drift. Then I told the girls to take off their *nón lá* to let their long hair show and wave their hands in the air. I picked up the Southern flag and waved it. The helicopter went on its side toward us. It leaned over so far I thought it was going to crash. But then it pulled up and went away. Before I turned on the motor, I heard two bursts of fire from the helicopter . . . I'm not sure what they were shooting at."

"We'll find out if it's anything," Ba says. "We have to be careful. At least the Americans check before they shoot, not like the Việt Cộng or Army who shoot at everything."

I get out of the hammock and go to the kitchen to see what my sisters are cooking for dinner. Maybe they saw the helicopter. My sisters talk while they chop lemongrass. "I could see the American gunner looking right at me," Chị Tư says.

"I saw his hand on the trigger," Chị Ba says. "I was so scared he was going to squeeze it."

~

People stand inside Mr. Fourth Farmer's house talking. Coconut trees and shadows block our view. "What's going on?" I ask Thượng.

"Maybe they're having a party."

"I hope so. I'm hungry."

Chị Ba carries a teapot through Mr. Three Xuyên's yard. She enters Mr. Fourth Farmer's house from the back. If our sister is at the party, then maybe it's alright for us to go over. We're too scared of Mr. Three Xuyên to take the path through his yard, so we make crooked turns around the canals until we stand on the edge of the canal that runs on the side of Mr. Fourth Farmer's house. A large group stands to the side of the house talking about Mr. Fourth Farmer. A few people gather around the washing slab that hangs over the canal. It looks like they're washing a large piece of meat, long with pale skin, maybe a pig for a special day. The meat on the slab looks raw and shredded. A man pours a bucket of water over it while a woman washes it with her hands.

"I can't see anything from here." Thượng jumps across the canal. He wobbles on the other side, before climbing up. I wade out of the water and mud and scramble up the bank to catch up with him.

The man and woman clean the meat, rubbing their hands slowly over it. A few other people stand nearby watching. Something is wrong. No one laughs or talks like they usually do when they butcher a pig for a feast. A red streak of fresh blood runs over thick, darker blood down the concrete slab and into the canal. The meat looks too bloody. They're supposed to drain it. Why would they waste all the blood? I see an arm. It's not a pig.

One of the women looks up. "Get away from here."

Thượng turns around and leaps across the canal. I make a running jump. I fall in. I'm covered with mud. And there's blood in here. I have to get out. I have blood on me. I run to the canal on the side of our house to wash it off.

I wring out my shorts the best I can without taking them off. "Maybe we can find out what happened in the market," Thượng says.

When we walk under the tin roof of the open market, people are gathered in front of the pork seller. "Poor Fourth Farmer's wife," the pork seller says, "floating all night in a boat with two dead bodies."

The pork seller squats next to a pig spread open with its rib cage showing. I knew the meat we saw wasn't pig. I thought nothing would scare me after I saw my burnt uncle. But Mr. Fourth Farmer's blood was on me in the canal. It was all over me.

"She's lucky to be alive," a woman says, putting a piece of pork into her basket. "Can you imagine waking up in a boat covered with your husband's flesh and blood?"

I had his blood on me. I won't go in that canal again.

"I heard guns firing yesterday," a woman selling guavas and pomelos says. "Why didn't Fourth Farmer stop? The Americans usually fire warning shots before they send a helicopter out."

"His wife said they were tired after working all day," the woman who bought the pork says. "Fourth Farmer thought he'd turn off into a stream before the patrol caught him. Those boat checks can take a long time. You have to go all the way across the river to the patrol boat and then back again."

"Better wait than dead," the fruit seller says. "When we go out on the river we always bring a Southern flag and make sure not to wear black. You don't want to give them any reason to mistake you for Việt Cộng."

"You have to be so careful." The woman shakes her head and sighs.

We follow people going to the stream to look at Mr. Fourth Farmer's shot-up boat. Má sees us. "Don't go there," she says. "You're not allowed over there."

"That could have been us," Má says at dinner, "but when I saw the helicopter I stopped and waved the flag. You have to be smart."

That night I lie awake, waiting to run to the bomb shelter. When I finally fall asleep, I have nightmares of people walking around with their bodies shot into pieces.

~

I try to sleep with my eyes halfway open. My eyes get used to the dark, and I can see in the moonlight. When it's time to run, I'll be ready. A shell whistles overhead. I jump out of bed before Má and Ba call. The shell explodes and everyone wakes up. One, two, three, four, five, six steps to the pole. One, two, three steps to the shelter. The mats lie on the floor from last time. I go to a high spot in the corner. It's dry. Outside, my family shouts and runs into each other and the coconut tree pillar.

"Where's Lượng?" Má says when she gets inside.

"I'm here already," I say.

Ba calls out the rest of the names. Then we wait. Time goes faster in my dry spot in the corner. After a half hour of silence, Ba tells us it's safe to get out. I curl up in bed, but I don't close my eyes in case we have to run again. I can see in the dark if I don't fall asleep. I won't ever hit a pillar again.

I lie half asleep for an hour or so. A shell whistles over the house. I jump out and count the steps to the shelter. Then I crouch down and crawl to my spot in the corner. The rest of my family stumbles in after me, half asleep. More shells screech overhead. Ba calls to check if we're all here. A burst comes from a rifle. Shells whistle by one after another and explode. *Rầm.* An explosion shakes the ground. "That was close," Ba says. "Probably only a hundred and fifty meters away."

Grandfather screams from his room. He must be hit. There's nothing covering the top of his hole.

Ba's voice trembles. "We all stay here until the shelling stops." He moves toward the entrance to the shelter.

Grandfather moans from his room. Who's going to help him? We sit and wait. "I think the shelling has stopped," Ba says. He crawls out and lights a kerosene lamp. Then he disappears down the hallway. After a few minutes, he comes back toward us. From the shelter, we can see his light in the bedroom moving around. "A bullet scratched Grandfather's leg. I need to get something to wrap the wound."

"How bad is it?" Má sits in the doorway of the shelter.

"Not that bad. It grazed his calf, but there's a lot of blood." Ba and the light move back to Grandfather.

~

Captain Can and his men come to visit in the morning. "We heard screaming from your house last night. What happened?"

Ba fixes them tea since Má and my sisters are at our island farm. I stand back by the kitchen listening.

"A bullet came through the wall and scratched his calf." Ba points to the side of Grandfather's lean-to that faces the street.

"Why wasn't he in the shelter?"

"It's too far to run in the dark. I dug a hole for him next to his bed, but he had his legs sticking out over the edge."

The captain and his men laugh. Grandfather shrugs in his chair.

"Don't be lazy," Captain Can says. "Dig a bigger hole."

"Of course," Ba says. "Of course."

"Put some antiseptic on the wound and bandage it," the captain says. One of his men takes out a kit and puts some medicine and cotton on Grandfather's calf. Ba and the captain talk about how the war is going. They always say the same things.

As soon as the soldiers leave, Grandfather tears the bandage off his leg and throws it on his table. "Get me some real medicine," he tells Ba. "None of this Western treatment. What do they know?"

Ba leaves to see the Chinese doctor. I come along because I might get a medicine ball to chew on.

We walk down the dirt road away from the market to the doctor's house. The doctor listens to Ba while his son takes down glass jars from the wooden shelves behind the counter to mix the medicine. The doctor's wife comes up to me and smiles. Her short hair puffs out around her face. It's so different from Má's long, tied back hair. "Lượng, have you eaten yet?" she asks. "I have some salty pork in the kitchen you could have."

The Chinese doctor and his wife are like an uncle and aunt to us. I think it's because Ba and Grandfather are Chinese like the doctor. I point my eyes up to a glass jar filled with dark brown medicine balls.

"Ô, I see what you want," the doctor's wife says. She smiles and turns back to the kitchen. Only the doctor can give out medicine balls.

The doctor mixes herbs in a stone bowl, then puts the paste in a piece of wax paper and gives it to Ba. After Ba pays, the doctor smiles at me and hands me two medicine balls. I take a small bite of one, sucking out the licorice and cinnamon flavor as we walk home.

"It's about time I got some care," Grandfather calls out as we come in the door.

Ba sets the medicine on the small table in the lean-to. "Lượng, stand back," he says. Grandfather puts on his glasses and spreads the paste on the wound on his calf. Then he puts some leaves on it and wraps it with an old shirt. He doesn't need the Chinese doctor to come and fix him. Grandfather can fix himself because he was a Chinese doctor before he came to live with us.

~

That night, I hear people or maybe ghosts walking around outside. There's a soft knock on the front door. A voice whispers for Ba, "Chú Tám, Chú Tám."

Ba opens the door. Two men hurry inside and pull the door closed behind them. The lantern in the front room flickers. I peek out of the bedroom at the dark outlines of the men. They must be Việt Cộng. They only come when it's dark. Má says the Communists aren't scared of ghosts because they're ghosts themselves.

"Did someone get shot here?" one of the men asks. He acts like the leader.

Ba motions toward the entrance to the lean-to. "My father had his leg sticking over the edge of his hole last night during the fighting. It got scraped by a bullet."

"What?" The men laugh and walk into Grandfather's room. "You have a hole to lie in and don't know enough to get down?"

I sneak out into the front room and hide behind Ba's desk.

"What's that you've got on your leg?" The second man points to the shirt tied around Grandfather's calf.

"You need to put some antiseptic on that wound and bandage it up," the leader says. "Do you need bandages or medicine?"

Grandfather scowls at them from his bed.

"No. We're fine," Ba says.

"Luckily it wasn't a head sticking out." The men laugh and move toward the door. They become silent and open it a crack. The leader peers out. After a moment, they slide out into the dark. I sneak back into the bedroom.

The next day, Ba has some men dig a bigger hole in Grandfather's room and put an oil drum in it for him to climb down into when there's shelling. Má buys new reed mats for the bomb shelter and puts a lantern inside it. She makes my brothers sweep the bugs away.

We run to the bomb shelter most nights. I can't fall asleep. One night two shells land right behind the bomb shelter and make big holes in the row of banana plants between our house and Mr. Three Xuyên's. In the morning, my brothers and I go out to inspect the fallen banana plants and holes and look for shrapnel. We find lots of broken leaves and fresh wounds in the coconut trees. Ba tells us to come in—it's too dangerous to be outside now.

Chapter Three

Tết 1968

At dinner, Má and Ba say Việt Cộng are going through town telling everyone that the Army is going to do a major sweep—bombs, artillery, everything. "The Việt Cộng say we should all run for the rice paddy when it happens," Má says.

The next morning helicopters and airplanes fill the sky. Gunfire and artillery start. "Run," Má says. "Grab the children and run to the rice paddy."

"I don't see how running to an open field is going to help," Grandfather calls from his chair in the lean-to. "I'm too old to run."

"You need to come. We'll help you." Má turns to Ba, "Anh ơi, please talk to your father. Make him come."

"I'll stay here and watch the house," Grandfather says. "If everyone leaves it will get looted."

Ba helps Grandfather move from his chair over to the oil barrel dug into the floor. Grandfather sits on the edge of the hole with only his legs in the barrel.

"Stay all the way down," Má says.

"I'll get in all the way when the fighting is closer."

Ba bends down and talks softly to Grandfather in Chinese.

"Come on. We need to get out now." Má picks up one of my baby sisters and herds us out into the bright sun.

Ba carries my other little sister. Neighbors run down the dirt road. Má and Ba follow them. We run toward the market and then along the trail toward Mrs. Từ Ba's. I can't keep up. Their long legs move so fast. Other families push around us. I didn't know this many people still lived in Quới Sơn. The sun is hot, and I'm thirsty. My lungs feel like they're going to burst.

The grown-ups slow down when we reach the narrow strips of land that cross through the fruit farm and canals behind Bà Bảy's house. We have to go two at a time. Small helicopters with wire frame tails pass overhead toward the rice paddy. Old queen planes circle high above on the far side of it. The old queens come first. The big airplanes that drop bombs come next. We should hide in the bomb shelter. If a bomb fell now, everyone in our village would be killed.

We pass Mrs. Từ Ba's house and come up to a wide canal with a bamboo pole across it. People run into each other trying to cross the pole bridge one by one. A girl falls off into the canal. She gets stuck in the mud trying to climb up and cries. Her mother jumps into the ditch to pick her up. So many people push to get over that I'm scared I'm going to fall into the canal too. We cross two more pole bridges and reach the edge of a coconut grove.

It's shady under the coconut trees. If we stay in the middle of the grove we'll be safe—the trees can protect us. I don't want to leave the trees, but the grown-ups push me through. We come out on the edge of a narrow dike running along the rice paddy. After the shade of the coconut grove, the open field is like a fire. Planes buzz overhead. There's nowhere to hide.

I'm hungry and thirsty. I wish I could drink the water in the rice paddy, but it smells bad and it's a rusty color. "It's *phèn* water," Má says. "Don't drink it or you'll get sick."

On the other side of the rice paddy, helicopters and airplanes roar, bombs explode, and machine guns fire. Everyone halts. Some people start to turn around and go back into the coconut grove.

"What's going on? Why did you stop?" someone behind us calls.

"You're running toward the fight," a man says. "Everyone go back to your house and hide in your bomb shelter."

We run back through all the bridges and canals. The explosions get farther behind us. When we get home, we rush to the rain barrel in the back and take turns using the coconut ladle to gulp down water. Má stands in the back door calling for us to hurry into the shelter.

Grandfather sticks his head out of the oil drum. "What's happening out there?"

"It was a trick," Má says. "The Việt Cộng were using us as a shield for their base on the other side of the rice paddy."

We wait in the bomb shelter. The fighting continues, but it's not moving closer. Má and Ba whisper to each other. "I'll make rice," Má says.

"Careful. Don't make a lot of smoke when you start the fire," Ba says as she climbs out.

A pot clangs in the kitchen. Rice grains spill *rạc rạc* against the metal. Smoke drifts over to the bomb shelter. "Watch the smoke," Ba says. I lean against my older sister. Finally, Má calls us out of the shelter to eat rice with only a little fish sauce sprinkled on top.

~

Everything is quiet and hushed. We're not supposed to go far from home anymore. Vân whispers to Thượng on the side of the house and points to the row of banana plants. "Why do you think they buried it there? Do you think they rigged it with grenades?"

Buried what? I pretend I'm not listening and wait for them to leave. I go over to the row of banana plants and search for sand that's been turned over. I pull a few handfuls back and hit something hard. I push the sand away. A cloudy plastic bag filled with large bullets lies in a hole. I quickly fill the sand back.

I run over to my brothers. "What do you think is in the sand?"

"You found it, too?" Vân says.

We go to the banana plants and dig with our hands. I help push sand off more bags of bullets. Vân lifts up a bundle of papers wrapped in clear plastic. The papers are stamped with a red and blue flag with a gold star—the Việt Cộng flag. The same flag that's painted on the coconut trees along the stream on the way to my aunt's house by the rice paddy. More bundles of papers cover something large wrapped in plastic.

"Guns," Vân says. "A lot of flyers and guns."

"They didn't hide them very well." Thượng points to freshly dug sand. "You can see where everything is by the mounds."

Vân and Thượng go inside to tell Ba. I stand in the back door where Ba can't see me. "Don't go and dig up other people's things," Ba says. "You don't mess around with military things."

My brothers come outside. A few minutes later, Má calls us into the kitchen. "Did you move or touch anything?"

"We only looked," my brothers say.

"If anything is missing and the Communists find out, we're dead," Má says. "If the Army finds this by our house we're dead. Do you understand?"

We nod.

"Did you take anything or move it?"

"No."

"Are you sure?"

"Yes."

All afternoon, my brothers and I keep going back to inspect the piles of sand. The next morning before breakfast, we go out to check again. The sand is smoothed over and dips where the mounds used to be. There are footprints near the edge. My brothers push the sand away. There's nothing there.

～

A man wheels a faded yellow bicycle up the ramp to our house.

"*Chào*. Have some tea," Ba calls from behind his desk. He sets down the watch he's working on.

"How much to get this bicycle tuned up and painted before *Tết*?" the man asks.

Ba gives him a price.

The man wheels the bicycle to the side of Ba's desk and puts the kickstand down. "Is bicycle fixing going well today?" he asks.

"It's going well." Ba waves toward several bicycles on the side of his desk. "I've got all these bicycles to fix and paint before *Tết*."

"I heard that there's going to be a cease-fire for *Tết*," the man says. "We may have a peaceful New Year's. A lot of soldiers are coming home on leave."

Ba nods. "I've been hearing that too."

When the customer leaves, Ba calls us all over to get a Holland cookie. He smiles when he hands them out. He's been smiling a lot. All the grown-ups seem less worried. There hasn't been any fighting for a while. I eat my cookie slowly. I'm glad the war isn't going to ruin *Tết*.

～

I watch the neighbors sweep leaves in front of their houses while I play on the edge of the canal. They cut dead branches from trees and bushes and take the brown leaves off the banana plants. Everything is supposed to look new for *Tết*. Inside, Má works on her sewing machine making us new clothes. My sisters dust the furniture, sweep the house, and wash all the bed mats and blankets. They even put new rice in the urn for incense on the altar. But our family doesn't have to cut the old leaves from our banana plants. We've already cut them for using in the outhouse over the canal.

A *bẹc bẹc bẹc* comes down the dirt road. Ba comes toward the house on his moped. He has on the white dress shirt he only wears when he goes to the city. I run to see what he brought back.

Ba with his moped by the side of the house in Quới Sơn. The coconut husks stacked under the eaves provide fuel for cooking and protect the bedroom on the other side from stray bullets. The banana plants separate the yard from Mr. Three Xuyên's house. The low sandbag wall of the bomb shelter is hidden behind the moped.

Ba wheels the moped up the packed dirt ramp into our house. I follow him in, stopping to check the greenish-yellow buds on the branch of *mai* we cut from Great Aunt's tree and planted in the dirt by our front door. When all of the yellow blossoms open it will be *Tết*.

The duffle bag tied to the back of the moped bulges out. Ba flips down the moped stand and parks it near the cabinet filled with radios for rent. He unties the duffle bag and places it on his desk. My brothers come in from the back of the house with their slingshots and my older sisters poke their heads out of the kitchen.

When Ba goes into the bedroom to change clothes, my brothers and I peek into the bag. We can't see anything besides bicycle parts. Má walks up and pulls a tin of cookies and some dried fruit and watermelon seed *mứt* treats out of the duffle. Underneath is a red string of firecrackers. She leaves the firecrackers and puts some of the cookies and *mứt* treats on the altar next to the vase of cut *mai*.

Ba comes back in a tank top and shorts and counts out five firecrackers to each of my older sisters and brothers. I reach out my hand. "Watch your brothers," he says and gives Vân my firecrackers.

Vân gets an incense stick and lights it in the oil lamp on the family altar. I follow him out. "Not by the house," Má says. "We don't want to set it on fire."

Vân sinks a firecracker into the mud near the stream by the side of the house and lights the fuse. "Stand back," he calls.

"I want to see," I say. "It can't get me here."

"Lượng, get out of the way." Vân pushes me. "I can't back up with you right behind me."

Bùm! The firecracker blows a little crater in the mud.

Thượng lights one. *Bùm!* "That fuse is too short. It nearly got my hand," he says.

"Let me light the next one," I say.

"No. We don't have that many," Vân says.

But he has mine.

"Give him this one with the short fuse," Thượng says. "Maybe then he'll leave us alone."

I push the firecracker halfway down into the mud.

Vân hands me the incense stick. "Angle it away from us."

I stand as far back as I can and put the tip of the incense next to the fuse. *Bùm!* I turn to my brothers. "It didn't get me."

My brothers finish and wander off. I look for duds. There's one by the tin can Chị Năm was blowing in the air with her firecrackers. I run to the altar to get an incense stick and then back outside.

"Ba! Ba!" Vân says. "Look at Lượng trying to light the duds."

"Lượng, come here," Ba calls.

I go inside. Now I won't get to light firecrackers anymore. Ba finishes painting a pinstripe on a bicycle and goes over to his desk. I stand to the side and look down at my feet. "Don't play with the duds," Ba says. "You don't know when they'll explode." Ba unlocks the top drawer of his desk. Inside is the red string of firecrackers. He separates five and puts them in my hand. "Play with these."

I run out to make craters in the mud.

The next day I get five firecrackers like everyone else.

~

On the day before *Tết*, we each get a handful of firecrackers. I save some in the can where I keep my marble and a big coin with the old president on one side and bamboo on the other. For dinner, we eat Ba's favorite dish, pork belly and boiled eggs stewed in coconut juice. Má puts a chunk of pork and one boiled egg on my rice. Then she uses her chopsticks to cover the top of my rice with the pickled mustard greens she makes for *Tết*. Afterward, we sit around eating the *mứt* candy Ba brought home from Mỹ Tho.

"Lượng, you should start making up wishes to get *lì xì*," Chị Tư says.

My belly tightens. "I don't know how to make up good luck wishes." I pick out the dried coconut *mứt* to eat and leave the ginger. Ginger makes me too hot.

"You wish people good health and good luck for the New Year. Then they'll give you *lì xì* money, and you can buy more firecrackers in the market."

I worry all evening about what I'm going to say the next day. I want it to be *Tết*, but I don't want to stand up in front of everyone saying wishes. I hope I'll get *lì xì* anyway. At night I crowd into bed with my brothers—I sleep with them instead of my parents now. My older sisters sleep in the bed next to us. I wish it were already morning.

Firecrackers crackle in the distance. Midnight. The New Year will be here in the morning. I wake up when my brothers and sisters do. When we walk out into the front room, the door is only open a crack, not all the way like it usually is. "Quiet," Má says. "Go out and pee and then come right back in."

Ba sits next to Grandfather's bed listening to the radio. The volume is so low I can hardly hear it. "There's a large attack going on in many cities in the middle," Ba tells us. "You need to stay inside. Otherwise if it erupts here you won't be able to get to the bomb shelter fast enough."

The middle of the country is so far away. If the fighting isn't here, will we still get to play with firecrackers?

"Be as quiet as you can and no firecrackers," Má says.

I look down to hide my burning eyes. Maybe the fighting won't get here and Má will change her mind.

After breakfast, we put on our new clothes and line up by age to give New Year's wishes to Grandfather and my parents. My belly tightens again. My older sisters carry my baby sisters, so I'm last. I try hard to think of what to say. I listen to my older brothers giving wishes, but the words go too quickly.

"Lượng, be respectful," Chị Tư whispers to me when it's my turn. "Fold your arms and bow your head."

Grandfather looks stern sitting in a chair in front of his lean-to. I cross my arms and bow. "Grandfather, *chúc mừng năm mới*." Happy New Year is all I can remember. Ba and Má look at me, waiting. Grandfather is old and sick. "Health and long life, Grandfather." I bow.

"Be obedient to your parents," Grandfather says. I wait to see if he'll give me some *lì xì*, but he stares straight ahead.

"Lượng, go to Ba and Má." Chị Hai nudges me over. Everyone looks at me. I move over to where Ba and Má sit in chairs by the side of the altar. Bicycles line the wall behind them.

"Ba Má, *chúc mừng năm mới*." I try to think of more wishes. What did Thượng wish? "Long life and happiness," I say in a low voice.

Ba hands me a gold envelope. "Be good and obedient this year."

I nod and run to the back room where Vân and Thượng sit counting their *lì xì* money at the dining table. My brothers put the bills back in their envelopes and ask if we can go outside. We still have our new clothes on so we can't play in the dirt, but we could visit the neighbors. "No," Má says. "And don't play in the front room. Stay in the back of the house."

After a while Má lets us go outside to pee again. "There's a hump right in the road in front of our house," Vân says. I follow Vân and Thượng over to the side of the house and look at the street. A coconut log covered with dirt and thorny lemon and lime tree branches blocks the road in front of Mr. Three Xuyên's house.

How can we get to my friend Tẹc's house or the Chinese doctor's house and get more *lì xì* with this blocking the road? Why did the Việt Cộng put it by our house this time? Usually they put it by the Chinese doctor's house and after a while the Army comes and tears it up. Then they put up another one. People complain to my parents that the Việt Cộng make them help build it.

We go back inside and sit around the dining table. A man calls, "Happy New Year" from outside our house. Ba steps out. "The market is open," the man says, "but there aren't any customers."

Through the crack in the door, we see other people walking on the street. It looks safe. "We should go out to get some more *lì xì*," Vân says.

"Bà Bảy gives a lot and she's closest," Thượng says. "Let's go to her house first."

"Where are you going?" Má calls.

"Only across to Bà Bảy's," Vân says.

"Don't go near that hump in the road," Má says. "The Việt Cộng hide grenades in them."

I stare at the coconut log as we walk across to Bà Bảy's house. It doesn't look scary in the bright sun. Why do the Việt Cộng block the road anyway? Nothing big comes down it.

Bà Bảy's door is closed. "Bà Bảy, Bà Bảy," we call. Doors are supposed to be open for greeting people on the New Year.

Bà Bảy opens the door. She has a kind face, but I'm still scared. What should I say? Thượng elbows me. I cross my arms and bow my head down like my brothers. "*Chúc mừng năm mới,*" I mumble along with them. "May you have health and happiness in the New Year."

Bà Bảy smiles at us. "This year, be good boys for your family. Be healthy and smart." She hands us each folded up money. It's much thicker than the money from Má and Ba. "Go home now."

We walk back to our house and hide our *lì xì*. "I wish we could go to Tẹc's," I say.

"Má didn't say we couldn't go *around* the hump," Vân says.

We walk in the ditch around the coconut log. Tẹc's door is closed, too. "We came to give you a wish for *Tết,*" Vân calls.

Tẹc's mother lets us in and then goes into a back room. When she comes out, Vân starts to wish her good luck. I worry about what to say, but Tẹc's mother puts envelopes in our hands before Vân finishes his wish. The envelope feels thick. Not as thick as Bà Bảy's stack of bills, but more than Má and Ba's. "You'd better go home," Tẹc's mother says.

We go back out on the road. Vân says we should walk to the Chinese doctor's house. He only lives a little way up from Tẹc. I'm not scared to wish the Chinese doctor—he's like our uncle. When we get to his house, he gives us more *lì xì* than Tẹc's mother, but not as much as Bà Bảy. On the way back we pass Tẹc's house. It looks dark and quiet.

I go to the bedroom to hide my *lì xì* in my can. I stare at the firecrackers in it. "When can we play with firecrackers?" I ask Vân.

"I don't know," Vân says. "Nothing seems to be happening."

"No more firecrackers," Má says. "They sound too much like gunfire."

I hope tomorrow everything will be back to normal so we can play with firecrackers and go to the market to spend our *lì xì*.

Nothing happens the rest of the day. It doesn't seem like the fighting will get here.

~

I wake up to a string of firecrackers going off. The sky is dark, but an oil lamp glows in the hallway. The firecrackers explode over each other. A long, loud explosion drowns them out. It must be a big firecracker. My brothers move in bed next to me. The small firecrackers stop, but the other explosions get louder and sharper.

"That sounds like gunfire," Ba calls from the other room. "Run to the shelter."

I run. Má takes the oil lamp in with us. Ba brings in some mats and blankets. He leaves again and comes back with a radio. He tries to find a station, but we only hear *rẹc rẹc rẹc*.

Grandfather's radio whistles in the lean-to. "Something is wrong," he calls. "The radio stations aren't broadcasting."

Explosions and gunfire come from the side of the shelter facing Mr. Three Xuyên's house. "It's coming from Mỹ Tho," Ba says. "There isn't any firing from the fort." He starts to climb out of the shelter. "Stay and see if you can get a signal."

We pull blankets around us and sit on mats around the lamp listening to the battle in Mỹ Tho and the *rẹc rẹc rẹc* on the radio. At least we have blankets and a light this time. Má sends one of my sisters out to see where Ba went. "He's with Grandfather," she says when she returns. "He said to go back and wait."

Ba peeks down into the bomb shelter at us. "You can come out. The fighting seems to be away from here."

My sister brings the lamp out to the kitchen table. We huddle around it. Finally, Má sends us to bed. I lie awake listening to the battle. Someone knocks and calls from outside. Ba and Grandfather step out the front door. "Did you hear anything on the radio?" the Chinese doctor asks.

Grandfather says something in a low voice. Gunfire covers up his words.

"I wonder when the fighting is going to get here," the doctor says.

I fall asleep to guns firing in the distance. In the morning, the fighting sounds louder. It's still coming from the direction of Mr. Three

Xuyên's house. I hurry to the kitchen.

Má comes in from talking to a neighbor. "Mỹ Tho is under attack," she says. "Someone came by and told us that the Việt Cộng took over Sài Gòn."

I knew *Tết* would be ruined when I heard the fighting. Now I have to wait a whole year to play with firecrackers again.

Má hands us bowls with a little cold rice and leftover pork. "We shouldn't cook," she says. "An airplane might mistake the smoke for something, and the sound of pots and pans rattling could be mistaken for support for the Communists."

Thousands of guns fire in the background. There's no sound besides the pounding noise of the battle. "Stay inside," Má says. "Anyone on the road might get shot."

∼

"Let's go to Bà Bảy's and wish her again," Vân says when Má isn't looking. "Maybe she forgot about the first time."

We open the front door and hurry across the empty road. Nothing is happening here. The fighting is all the way over in Mỹ Tho.

Bà Bảy's door is still closed. We call, and she lets us in. I'm scared to stand in front of her and make another wish, but I want more *lì xì*. I try to say what Vân and Thượng say. It's hard to hear. Big and small guns fire constantly.

Bà Bảy gives us each another bunch of folded bills. Thinner than the first time, but it's extra.

We run back home. The gunfire stays in the distance. In the late morning, we ask if we can go to the market to buy treats with our *lì xì*. Má says our sister can take us since the market is in the opposite direction of the gunfire and we don't have to go near the hump in the road. Besides firecrackers, I want to buy boiled duck eggs with the baby ducks inside or fried bananas and a coconut milk and bean drink.

No one else is out. The Army fort next to the market is empty. Usually there are firecrackers and dragon dances in the market during the New Year, but when we get to the market, it's empty too. The only sound is gunfire in the distance. If we can't get firecrackers today, we might have to wait a whole year until they sell them again.

We go home and lie around. We can't play with firecrackers, and we're not supposed to leave the house. "We could try to wish Bà Bảy one more time," Vân says after lunch. "Maybe she forgot again."

I follow my brothers across the street. I'm nervous Bà Bảy will remember. "*Chúc mừng năm mới*," Vân says. "May you have health and . . . a long life and . . . may all of your children be successful and happy."

"*Chúc mừng năm mới* to you as well," Bà Bảy says. "I appreciate the wishes, but I have already given you *lì xì* two times and have no more. You children should stay home. It's not safe."

We run home. "It's too bad Bà Bảy remembered," Vân says.

"What were you doing?" Má says. "Stay inside and stop trying to do multiple wishes."

Vân says we should play marbles with Dũng, Tẻo, and Tẹc. I go to the bedroom and pick my marble out from under the firecrackers in my can. We sneak out the back door and walk around the hump in the road. Dũng, Tẻo, and Tẹc come out and sit with us on the hard dirt under the longan tree in front of their house. It's the best place to play because we can bank marbles off the tree roots sticking out of the ground. A gunshot rings out above the pounding in the distance. We stop and look around. It's not close enough to worry. We go back to playing. Tẹc's father comes out. "Go home now. Don't come over here anymore. It's not safe."

Late in the afternoon, a neighbor stops by. "A lot of people are leaving the village," he says. An explosion booms over the sounds of shooting.

Where are they going? No one left when we had to run to the bomb shelter. Toward evening, my brothers and I walk around our yard to see whose house has a light on or smoke from cooking coming out. Bà Bảy's house is dark. So are all the others.

～

The next day Thượng and I sneak out the back to visit Tẹc's family again. Their door is closed. It's quiet and no smoke from cooking comes out. We walk around their house peeking through the cracks in the boards. No one is inside. We shoot marbles under the longan tree, bouncing them off the roots. After a while, we go home.

In the early afternoon, the Chinese doctor and his wife come over. Grandfather turns off the radio. Má and Ba stand near the lean-to talking with them.

"You should flee the chaos," the doctor says.

"Where would we run?" Ba asks.

Run? I don't want to leave Quới Sơn. The shelling was closer before and we stayed.

"We're going to Tân Long," the doctor says. "A lot of people have moved there to get away from the fighting."

"You should come too," his wife says. "You can stay with us."

"The fighting is over in the city," Grandfather says, "not here."

If the fighting is far away, what's there to be scared of?

"There's no fighting in Tân Long," the doctor says. "It's just a small island. I heard on the radio the Army is pushing the Communists to the city outskirts. The fighting will get here soon."

"The gunfire *is* getting closer," Ba says. "But what's there to fight over here?"

"You don't want to get caught in the crossfire," the doctor's wife says. "At least consider it."

~

The gunfire gets closer and more spread out. We can't leave our yard. A rumble comes from the direction of the rice paddy land. Má says it's by Bến Tre. I sit in the front room and listen to Grandfather and Ba talk about how the cease-fire was a trick—that the Communists must have been planning the attack for a long time. "I heard on the radio that the Việt Cộng had weapons hidden in the city before *Tết*," Grandfather says. "That's what those weapons by the side of the house must have been. The Communists were going to use us as a human shield. That's how they fight."

We run out of food except for the clay vat Má filled up with rice for *Tết*. The market is closed, but people stop by the house to sell pork or rice. My sisters pick some yam leaves in the backyard and water spinach growing in the canals. We even eat Grandfather's dried Chinese cabbage. Mr. Three Xuyên moves away, but it's not mango season, so we don't try to sneak over to his house. I wonder when things will go back to the way they were.

Ship Island

"Wake up, wake up." Má stands in the faint daylight coming in the bedroom door. She opens the dresser drawers and puts clothes into a pillowcase. "Get dressed and eat breakfast. We're going to the island."

I get to go to our farm on the island? I wonder what it's like. Má took my older sisters there yesterday.

I go to the kitchen and eat on the bench next to my brothers. Ba silently scoops rice into his mouth with chopsticks while Má fills baskets with food.

"Pack your things and get in the boat," Má calls.

I put a few pair of shorts, some shirts, and my *dép* sandals into a grass-weave basket. I reach into the can for my marble, the big coin, and the firecrackers I saved. I put them in my pockets. When we go out the door, Ba stays at the table.

Má hides the pillowcases full of clothes under the empty baskets heaped in the center of the boat. My cousin Anh Chín Phát reaches out his hand to help me on. He's Chị Tư's age and he helps Má with the farm. The boat wobbles when I step in. I get down on the floor with my brothers and baby sisters and the empty baskets. We wait. I expect Ba to come out, but he doesn't. "Keep down. Don't make any noise," Má says. She starts the motor. I guess the boat is too crowded and Ba will come next time.

Anh Chín Phát stands in front of the boat in his shorts pushing away fronds of water coconuts that arch over the stream while Má steers in back. The small stream empties into a wider one. A man in a green nylon uniform steps out of the bushes where the streams meet. He motions to Má, and she cuts the motor. As our boat drifts forward, four more men dressed in green nylon come out of the bushes and stand barefoot on the mud bank. I look down at my feet.

"Where are you going?" the first man says to Má.

"To Cồn Tàu to farm," Má says from behind me.

The other men peer into the boat. Their eyes move over us and the baskets heaped in the center. They glance at each other and back at the first man. He nods to Má and waves us through. Anh Chín Phát gets down on the floor with us. His long, narrow face is expressionless. No one says anything. The stream ends. Brown water stretches in front of us as far as I can see. I look back to make sure we're not on the ocean.

Once we're all the way out on the river, Má lets us get up. Anh Chín Phát and Vân move up to the edge of the boat to sit. Thượng and I sit on stools, and our little sisters lean against our legs. The water curls as Má steers the boat. She looks straight ahead, her hand on the handle of the motor, moving the shrimp-tail propeller back and forth.

Water coconuts and cheap trees grow along the river edge closest to us. I can't see the other side of the river. Every now and then we meet another small boat. Except for the loud *rồ rồ rồ* of the motor it's quiet. Má turns the propeller to avoid tangling it in clumps of purple water hyacinth floating by. I'm tired, but I don't close my eyes. Má said it would take two or three hours to get to Cồn Tàu. I don't want to miss anything.

After a while, Anh Chín Phát gets out an aluminum pot of cooked rice and scoops it into bowls. He hands me a spoon and a bowl of rice with fish sauce and steamed water spinach. We eat while we move down the river. When we finish, Anh Chín Phát dips the bowls over the edge of the boat to clean them and stacks them back in a basket. Bubbles spin off the propeller blade and rise to the surface. A stream of water squirts out the side of the motor. I wonder why it's there. It would be fun to stick my hand in it.

Má points to an island in front of us that's surrounded by cheap trees. The trees look like they're growing out of the water. Their roots stick straight up around the trunks like reeds. "That's Cồn Tàu," Má says above the noise of the motor. "Ông and Bà Năm say that a freighter sank here and the land collected around it to make the island. That's why it's called Ship Island."

We head toward the trees like we're going to run into them. Cồn Tàu doesn't seem solid. It floats like a raft of cheap trees. Má slows the boat and enters a small stream that cuts into the island. We glide past a hut and turn into a smaller stream, passing under a bamboo pole bridge. Each time we head toward a hut, I think it will be ours. Má turns at a three-way fork. The stream gets narrower and water coconut fronds crash into us from the sides. Anh Chín Phát gets in front to push the fronds away. When it feels like we can't go upstream any farther, Má stops near a hut.

The boat drifts under guava trees toward two posts with hinged boards and a long bamboo basket between for catching shrimp. My sisters come out of the hut as Anh Chín Phát takes a rope and ties the boat up to a water coconut frond. "Get out and help carry something in," Má says. Anh Chín Phát hands me a basket.

I put the basket inside and go back out and look around. One side of the roof of the hut is so low I could climb on it. On the other side a steel cable runs from the roof to the ground to keep it from leaning over. Guava trees dangle ripe fruit over the canals on the farm and fallen fruit lies on the muddy banks. I want to bring all of the fruit back to the hut to eat or sell.

When it's time for dinner, Anh Chín Phát's older brother Handsome Boy Six and a man helping on the farm go to the back of the hut where sugarcane rots on strips of land. I follow. They pour water down rat holes, and when the rats come out they club them with a stick. They each come back to the house holding a handful of rats by their tails and drop them in the kitchen. Handsome Boy Six cleans the rats by the cement block over a canal. After he has enough for dinner, he throws the rest into the stream. Má cooks the meat with lots of fish sauce and scallions. It's chewy, like an old chicken. We haven't had this much meat in a long time.

～

A few days later, someone says that Ba is coming. I go out of the hut and stand downstream from the shrimp catcher. Ba walks toward us with an older man and woman. He's wearing shorts and a tank top. His gold watch shines in the sun. Everyone comes in to greet him.

"Where's your father?" Má asks.

"He's watching the house." Ba looks down at the blue plastic basket he's carrying. "I was only able to bring a few small tools." He nods to the old man he came with. "I had to borrow farm clothes to wear on the boat. I didn't want Việt Cộng checking at the river to get suspicious."

At dinner, Ba says that the shelling is close to our house in Quới Sơn. "Mrs. Seven Silkworm got killed by a shell, almost right across the street from us at Tám Bình's. I left right afterward."

The Chinese doctor was right. We did need to leave.

"It's lucky we left early," Má says.

I wonder if a shell has already hit our house.

Má looks at Ba. "What about your father?"

"He refuses to leave. He says he'll watch our house until we get back."

"He's not safe. We need to go back and get him."

"He says if he leaves everything will be stolen. We won't be able to repay everyone."

"You use possessions to shield yourself, not yourself to shield possessions," Má says. "I'll go back with Chín Phát tomorrow. I'll get your father to leave."

~

Má returns with Grandfather sitting in the boat with his arms crossed and his head down. He has a white cloth bandage covering the top of his head. A little blood shows through the top. Anh Chín Phát steps out to tie up the boat. Ba comes out of the hut and helps Grandfather out. "So you decided to leave?" Ba says. "It must be really bad."

"Your crazy wife picked me up like a sack of rice and carried me out here to this swamp." Grandfather leans on Ba. Even though Grandfather's hunched over he's still taller. "No one is watching the house. You're going to lose everything now. All your customers' things. Everything."

Ba guides him into the hut. "How is the shelling? Who's still around?"

"It's everywhere. I don't know which houses got hit, but it's close."

My older cousins and sisters crowd around Grandfather. "What happened to his head?" Ba asks Má. "Is it serious?"

Grandfather walked into the house. He must be alright.

"He didn't get down far enough in the oil drum," Má says. "A piece of shrapnel took the skin off the top of his head, clear from the front all the way to the back."

Má gets the antiseptic. Grandfather looks at her and says loudly, "Now everything will get stolen."

Ba helps Grandfather to a bed in one of the bedrooms. "Sit down and rest."

Everyone gathers around. I can't see through their backs.

Ba walks toward Má and lowers his voice. "How did you get him here? Did anyone see you?"

"I don't think anyone saw us," Má says. "I told Chín Phát to stay in the boat and be ready to leave. Your father was sitting on the ledge between his lean-to and the front room with his legs and arms crossed. His head was bleeding, but he wouldn't move. I picked him up and carried him out to the boat. It's good he's scared of water so he didn't jump out."

"At least he's safe now."

Grandfather calls out, "I'm not a sack of rice to be picked up and carried around."

Má smiles and goes outside to unload the boat. Ba takes the antiseptic over to Grandfather and hands it to Chị Tư. I stretch up onto my toes trying to watch. Grandfather grabs the bottle from my sister. "Here, give me that."

~

I try to sleep in the bed with Anh Chín Phát and his older brother Handsome Boy Six. It's too hot. I crawl onto the end of a small bed that sticks out under the eaves through an open wall where my two brothers and Chị Năm and Chị Ba sleep. It's cooler under the open sky.

I wake up with the full moon shining on me through the mosquito net. I look out from under the eaves of the roof at the sky. There's a faint hum. I feel like I'm still dreaming while the moon glows. The humming sounds far away. Something's not right. I search the sky. An old queen makes a big circle high above. The old queen comes first—the next airplane will drop a bomb. I push my sister's arm and whisper, "An old queen is circling in the sky."

People shift around in bed, but no one gets up. There's no bomb shelter to run to. I lie waiting next to my brothers and sisters. A motor whirls and blades chop. An attack helicopter comes into the sky.

"Run," Má says. "Run."

Run? Where are we supposed to run?

"Get outside!" someone says. "Run toward the mango trees." More helicopters and airplanes appear in the sky. I run with everyone behind the hut and across a pole bridge to a strip of land with a cluster of mango trees.

"Stay on the opposite side of the tree from the airplane," someone calls.

I press against the tree trunk with my body and hands. I feel safe behind it. Ba, Anh Chín Phát, and Handsome Boy Six splash into the canal and hide behind the mud bank.

"Hug a tree or stay underneath, so they can't see you," Ba says. "The pilots can see at night, just like day." I scoot around the tree when the helicopter comes back the other way. Do the pilots have something like a cat's eye so they can see at night?

The helicopters circle, firing machine guns and rockets in the distance.

"Where's Grandfather?" someone asks.

"He's in the house," Ba says. "He wouldn't leave."

A helicopter swoops down, and we circle the tree. Ba and my cousins move to the other side of the canal. An airplane drops a sunburst that dangles from a parachute and lights up the sky. I try to stay in the shadows, but the helicopters move too quickly. Rockets and guns fire. The helicopters and airplanes make larger and larger circles. After a long while, it's quiet. Ba and my cousins climb out of the canal, and we run back into bed under mosquito nets, muddy and full of bites. I lie awake listening to the sky.

∼

In the morning, attack helicopters fly over us. They fire cannons and rockets at another part of the island. Ông and Bà Năm, the old couple who helped Ba get here, come over. They farm nearby, but they're from Quới Sơn like us. Ông Năm sits on a stool in the hut and digs into his shirt pocket. He pulls out a plastic bag of tobacco and a paper and starts rolling a cigarette.

Má tells them about running from the helicopters last night.

"What were you doing running around outside at night?" Bà Năm says. She goes out to get a betel leaf from a vine. Then she sits down on a stool next to her husband. "Only mysterious misters run around at night. You don't want the Army to mistake you for them."

Bà Năm takes out a little jar from her *áo bà ba* shirt pocket and uses a betel nut shell to scoop white powder out and spread it on the leaf. Then she wraps a quarter of the meat of a betel nut in the leaf and puts it in her mouth. Má doesn't chew betel like all the other women and Ba doesn't smoke like all the other men, so whenever someone visiting does either, I watch to see how.

"They had helicopters circling over us," Ba says.

Ông Năm finishes making his cigarette and lights it. He's thin and doesn't talk much. Mainly he rolls cigarettes on everything and smokes. "The Army is after the Việt Cộng base at the head of the island," he says.

"You're safer inside," Bà Năm says, chewing on the betel. She has a wide, friendly face and talks a lot. "Don't worry."

Ông Năm puts the cigarette to his mouth, draws in, and blows smoke out. "The base is far away. The Army won't take out homes. They know a lot of villagers have fled here."

"There's nothing to fight over on this island." Bà Năm turns and spits red onto the dirt outside the open door. "Our daughter should leave Quới Sơn. It's not safe there with so many Việt Cộng all over. Remember how there used to be so many Liberation Front meetings?"

"Until people figured out it could be *them* coming back without a head," Má says.

"If you suspect it's your turn you need to make sure you aren't around or leave for good," Ông Năm says.

Má glances at Ba. "Whenever Anh Tám was invited, he hid," she says. "I told the Việt Cộng that my husband was in the city."

Ba nods. "It's better if you can make an excuse not to go."

"The first time Anh Tám was invited," Má says, "he hid at Mr. Three Xuyên's house."

I wonder what it would be like to stay in Mr. Three Xuyên's French-style house with the concrete walls and tile roof. But how could Ba hide there? The Việt Cộng come into your house whenever they want.

"After the meeting, Việt Cộng came to our door and asked where my husband was," Má says. "I told them he had to go to the city for parts."

Bà Năm spits out her betel. "In the end, only women and old men came to the meetings."

"At the last meeting I went to, the Việt Cộng didn't wait for the person on trial to come." Má shakes her head. "They arrested him and brought him to the meeting blindfolded."

In the afternoon, two helicopters appear in the distance. They shoot their front cannons and fire side rockets at something near the top of the island. The helicopters disappear and reappear behind the trees. I climb up on the roof where it almost touches the ground and a *mướp* vine runs up the side. The vine covers the roof with leaves and long, green squash. I crawl toward the center, trying to make sure I don't fall through the water coconut leaves. Another helicopter comes toward the target and shoots. The side rocket comes out with a puff of smoke. Silence. Then the sound of the rocket firing, right before it hits the target and explodes. As soon as one helicopter empties its rockets, another shows up. Why don't they carry more so they don't have to leave so often?

Thượng climbs up to the roof to watch with me. Vân does too, but Má yells that he's too big. I stay there all afternoon. Helicopters come to the same area at the top of the island for two more days. "The Việt Cộng must be in shock after all this stirring and attacking," Má says.

～

My seventh aunt, Dì Bảy, and her four children come to stay with us. Their house is on the rice paddy land in Quới Sơn, near the Việt Cộng headquarters. We sit around the fire telling stories after dinner. Outside the hut, shadows move with the firelight. "You left just in time," Dì Bảy says. "The shelling in Quới Sơn is worse now."

She sits on a wooden bed with my parents. My older sisters and cousins sit on another bed with the mosquito net pulled tight around them. There's no room, so my brothers and I and Dì Bảy's three sons move around the fire trying to stay in the smoke so the mosquitoes don't eat us.

"It's because of the dream I had," Má says. "I dreamt a Việt Cộng was carrying an injured comrade past our house to the canal. The injured man was missing his legs and the man carrying him kept whispering, 'Quiet, quiet, or you'll wake up the bicycle repair man. We'll get you medicine soon and make you whole.' It was a sign for us to leave."

Má saw ghosts by the canal near our house in Quới Sơn? Where I played?

Dì Bảy laughs. "All those Việt Cộng in Quới Sơn were reprimanded for letting you slip through right in front of them."

Má frowns. "They can't use us as a human shield now."

A fish gulps a water bug on the surface of the stream out front. My brothers and I try to guess from the splash whether it's a bass or a snakehead fish. If it's a snakehead, my older sisters will try to catch it in the morning so we can eat it for lunch.

"What's happening to our house?" Ba asks. "What's still there?"

"Only the desk and beds," Dì Bảy says. "The bicycles and radios keep disappearing one by one."

Why are people taking our things? Everyone knows it's our house.

"The Army came by to check on your house. They didn't take anything, but I heard that the soldiers were squirting each other with air from the bicycle pump for fun." Dì Bảy laughs and Má gives a little laugh too. I liked playing with the bicycle pump. We'd put it under our knees and pump down to make farting sounds.

"Can you go there and get some of my tools?" Ba asks.

"If it's safe, I'll take a look when I get back," Dì Bảy says.

"We'll have to get new tools, if we need those tools at all," Má says. "Fixing electronics is better than bicycles."

"What are you going to do to pay people back?" Dì Bảy asks.

"Losing the bicycles isn't that bad," Má says. "We owned a lot of them and were trying to sell them. But the radios . . . There were fifteen, maybe seventeen, of them in the house when we left. We'll have to sell a piece of land . . ."

Gnats swarm us. I try to beat them away with my hands. Má steps out of the hut to get a bunch of guava leaves. Smoke billows up when she puts them on the fire. "Get smoky," Má says. "Then the gnats won't bother you."

When it's time to sleep, I lie on the floor side-by-side with my brothers and younger cousins with a mosquito net canopy over us. I like the outdoors here and all the fish and shrimp to eat, but it's crowded. When will we be able to go back home? Will there be anything left in our house when we do?

~

After Dì Bảy and my cousins leave, Thượng and I sit playing marbles in front of the hut. An airplane hums high up in the sky. We look for it through gaps in the guava leaves above us. It's small, like an old queen.

It disappears behind the trees. I stand up, but I can't find it. I glance down at my marble to make sure it doesn't roll off into the stream. When I look at the sky again, the airplane has turned and is going back in the direction it came from. It flies back and forth above us while we play. The smooth hum of the engine stops. It stutters. Thượng and I look for it again. It stutters again, and a cloud of black smoke appears.

We move over to the area between the hut and the shrimp catcher where there aren't any guava trees. The engine sputters get further apart. The airplane glides down at an angle, then spirals until it vanishes below the trees. I look for a parachute but don't see one.

"Did you see that?" I say. "That old queen started to smoke and came down."

Thượng nods. "I didn't hear any guns."

We run into the hut to tell someone. Má and the others are cutting grass under the newly planted tangerine trees on the other side of the stream. We find Handsome Six in the hut and tell him about the old queen smoking down. "Ồ, is that right?" he says and goes back to cooking lunch.

After lunch we play marbles between the hut and the stream again. The sky fills with helicopters. Small wire cage helicopters buzz around while an Attack helicopter flies in a big loop. Airplanes zoom above us. Two big, gray troop carrier helicopters hover over our land. One starts to come down. With each thump of its blades, my heart beats outside of my chest. How can something that big fly? It disappears behind the guava trees and the water coconuts in the stream in front of us. We only hear the grinding and whistling of the engine.

Thượng and I climb onto the roof to see where it is.

"Get down," Má says as she walks over the pole bridge toward the hut. My cousins and two workers follow her.

Handsome Six comes over the bridge last. "There're six soldiers surrounding the helicopter," he says. "The rest are coming toward us."

Má and the others stand by the shrimp catcher. Three soldiers walk across our land toward them. When they cross the bamboo bridge their heavy boots bend the pole. The last soldier to cross seems larger. His cap covers his hair and shades his face, but I can tell his nose is pointy and tall, and his skin is whiter than ours. I've never seen an American—he must be one.

The first soldier goes back to the other side of the bridge and joins three men with machine guns who've spread out along the stream.

The American and a Vietnamese soldier stand in front of Má and the others. They have pistols. My brothers and I stay off to the side, in front of the hut. The American towers over everyone.

Má and the others move between us and the soldiers. The Vietnamese soldier asks for the owner of the house. Má steps forward. The American speaks and then the Vietnamese soldier asks, "Did you see or hear anything?"

"No, just us cutting grass and doing farm work," Má says.

Everyone stops talking. Another helicopter comes out of the sky. It pounds the air as it lands over by Ông and Bà Năm's land.

The Vietnamese soldier talks to the American. Then he asks Má, "How about two or three hours ago? Did you see or hear anything unusual then?"

"No. It's quiet here except for some birds and us talking."

I call from behind them, "We saw an airplane."

"Come here." The Vietnamese soldier motions with his hand for my brother and me to come over. Má and my cousins step back so we can come closer to the soldiers. "Tell me what you saw."

Everyone looks at me. I look at the soldiers' uniforms and boots. They wear a lot of clothes. "We were playing marbles, and we looked up and saw the airplane," I say. "Then the airplane started to sound funny, and we saw smoke come from it."

The Vietnamese soldier makes hissing sounds when he speaks with the American. Their words sound leaky, like a bicycle tire losing air. Are they talking or just making sounds?

"Did anything come out of the airplane?" the Vietnamese soldier asks us. It's hard to hear because of all the helicopters and airplanes around.

"No. We watched it fall until it went below the trees," Thượng says.

"What did the airplane look like?" the soldier asks.

"One of the old queens that fly really high and quiet," Thượng says.

The Vietnamese soldier talks to the American again. Why do they waste so much air when they talk? Do they really need all that *shhhshhhing*? Are they making real words or communicating in another way?

The Vietnamese soldier turns back to us. He wants to know exactly where the airplane was when it started to sputter.

"Maybe over there." I point toward the center of the island.

"Where was it when you saw the smoke?" he asks.

I point in the direction of the helicopter he came in, toward the banyan trees just beyond our land. "Over past that coconut grove."

The Army swarms around our farm and the neighbors' looking for the plane the rest of the day. At night, airplanes fly close above. "It was right there by the coconut grove," Thượng says when they're still searching the next day. "Why can't they find it? Did it go into the water?"

~

The planes stop searching after a few days. It's low tide and my brothers and I play near a shallow canal. Two men in black nylon clothes with AKs walk toward our hut. Việt Cộng are coming in the day? My brothers and I try to cross the canal to find out why they came. I thought the Việt Cộng wouldn't be here after all the fighting. My older sister waves us away. Another sister goes to the field to get Má. Ba comes out of the hut, and Má comes over the bridge.

"Did the soldiers in the helicopter give you a hard time?" one of mysterious misters asks. My brothers and I stand on the other side of the canal trying to listen.

"They were looking for something," Má says.

"What did you tell them?" the mysterious mister asks.

"I didn't hear anything or see anything," Má says. "What do you think they're looking for?"

"They're looking for something." The mysterious misters turn and leave.

"They're looking for an airplane," Thượng and I say when the men disappear.

"Don't talk about it with anyone," Má says. "The frog dies because of its big mouth."

A few days later a caterpillar helicopter comes and lifts a small scouting airplane out of the trees. It looks like it has four seats instead of two—bigger than an old queen. I wonder if they found the pilots or if the Việt Cộng ambushed them.

The men in black nylon come back. They call the adults out of the hut one by one and talk to them across the canal. Má and Ba seem scared. I don't feel safe anymore.

Chapter Five (Summer 1968-1969)

Owing Buddha a Chicken

The red and white eyes painted on the front of the new boat look down at the river watching for water spirits. I sit next to my sister wondering what our new house in Tân Long will look like. Everyone else is already there. Má slows the boat down near a net strung between two coconut log posts in the stream. She calls up to a water coconut leaf hut on the bank, "Anh Tư, do you have anything good today?"

Mr. Fourth Post steps out of the hut onto a dock made of tree trunks. "I just emptied the net and got a good catch." He pulls a rope up and a basket rises out of the stream. "Take a look."

Má hands him money, and he empties his catch into a bamboo basket on our boat. The fish and shrimp flop around as we head out to the wide Mekong. Má nods toward wooden buildings and huge barrels straight across on the other side of the river. "That's the fish sauce factory." We head diagonally to the other side, then Má steers the boat straight upriver. I look at the coconut, mango, and cheap trees along the shore to see if they have any fruit. Blue and red fishing ships pass us on their way to the ocean. Their painted eyes look down at the water too.

"Look, Lượng," Chị Tư points to the far side of the river. "That stream goes toward Quới Sơn. We're halfway there."

The stream to our old village looks like a tiny gap in the trees. I miss our old house and neighbors. I wish we didn't have to leave it. If everyone in my family is in Tân Long now we must not be going back.

When we get to a sunken metal barge on the edge of the river, Chị Tư says that we're two-thirds of the way there. We start to see the tail-end of an island in the middle of the river. "That's Tân Long," Chị Tư says. The name means New Dragon Island.

Má turns the boat toward the island. Tin and water coconut leaf roofs crowd together on the edge. Boats tied to posts and docks line the shore. An Army fort with a concrete cylinder watchtower juts out into the river halfway up the shoreline. "That's the Round Fort," Má says. "The Việt Cộng aren't stupid enough to come around here."

I haven't seen a round fort before. I look for big guns pointing out like on the fort in Quới Sơn. Two soldiers look out of the watchtower, but there aren't any guns sticking out.

Má points to the right of the fort. "Do you see that sign?" A wood sign sticks out from the tin roof of a two-story house. "That's where our house is."

"What does it say?" I ask. The sign is painted white with red letters. No other house has one.

"Prosper Going Forward TV and Radio Repair." Má points to the shore across from the island where there are even taller buildings and more ships. "That's Mỹ Tho. People there can see our sign from across the river."

"Does Ba still fix bicycles?" I ask.

"There are too many bicycle repair shops in Mỹ Tho. Electronics are more difficult, not many people know how to do it."

Má steers the boat around the fort toward a narrow dock made of boards on stilts. Anh Chín Phát ties the boat up to one of the stilts. A small boat ferrying people from the city across the river comes in behind us. The boards bend as Má and my sister walk ahead carrying baskets, but they're easier to walk on than bamboo pole bridges. The ferry passengers get off and walk along on the boards behind us.

I follow Má across a concrete path to the two-story house with the red and white sign. A balcony runs along the front. My brothers come out and lead me inside. I run up the stairs after my brothers. The large, flat boards making up the second floor spring with each step. They can't be from trees—how could you get a tree with a trunk that wide across? My brothers point to the mats where they sleep. The tin roof above us seems sturdier than water coconut leaves.

Grandfather sits in a bed next to a balcony. "*Thưa*, Grandfather." We all bow to him. "I just arrived," I add.

We go out on the balcony and look across the river to Mỹ Tho. Below us, the Round Fort is its own island with a moat separating it from the land in front of our house. A brick wall with a barbed wire fence on top surrounds it. Soldiers patrol with cigarettes and guns. It's like having our own private guard.

At night, instead of the pitch black of the countryside, lamps flicker inside houses. Across from us, the fort glows with dim lights. Strings of blinking lights crisscross above the tables of an outdoor café down the street. It looks like New Year's.

~

Grandfather spits on us from the balcony when my brothers and I play marbles in front of the house. He yells for us to be quiet. Thượng and I go over to the side yard and dig in the dirt with sticks. "This would be a good place to plant something," Thượng says.

"I want to plant yams," I say. In the countryside we can go outside and get a yam whenever we want—it would be nice to have them here.

Bà Ba walks up to the wire fence that separates our yard from the alley. Thượng and I stop digging and look up. Má says to stay away from Bà Ba because her husband was a shaman. "Her husband only taught her how to talk to the dead," Má said, "but she might be able to do some magic on you." Bà Ba's son Thọ stands by her. He's Thượng's age but a lot bigger.

"If you uncover anything strange," Bà Ba says, "let me know."

Thượng and I sweep the dirt back into the hole and leave. What could be buried there? When no one is around, we come back. We uncover shards of clay pottery in the dirt and poke at them with a stick. Just garbage.

The next day, Má takes me and Thượng over to the window in our house that faces the alley. She points outside. "Have you kids been digging over there?"

We nod.

"Did you find any pots?" Má asks.

"We only found broken pieces," Thượng says.

"Don't go digging around breaking pots," Má says. "They're filled with the ghosts Bà Ba catches. She used to bury them there before we built our house. So many angry ghosts floating about—it's not good."

Thượng and I dig a bigger hole looking for one of the clay pots. We try to dig carefully so we won't break anything. "Wouldn't it be scary if we broke a pot and the spirits flew out?" Thượng says. "It must have a magic seal to keep the ghost inside."

"What kind of seal do you think it has?" I ask. Some neighbors hang mirrors with magic symbols on their doors to keep ghosts out. Má got red papers with yellow symbols from the temple and stuck them to all our doors, windows, and rafters with rice paste.

Thượng shrugs. "Maybe ones like in comic books."

We dig faster and harder. All we find are clay pieces. The spirits have already flown out. "The workers who built our house must have broken all the pots," Thượng says.

I pick up a clay piece and throw it. Why would Bà Ba put dangerous spirits in something that breaks?

~

Má takes me to the tailor. "You need to get ready for school," she says. A few days later she brings home new blue shorts and a white shirt with pockets and tells me to put them on. I drag behind as she walks downstream to sign me up for school. I've seen Vân and Thượng going off with books—it doesn't look fun.

We pass an alley that goes into the middle of the island. At the corner of a vacant lot next to the alley, street vendors sell boiled green bananas, yams, tapioca roots, and sweet rice. Past them, under a covered area in front of a house, kids my age sit in rows of desks stretching out to the path. All the boys wear clothes like me. The girls wear black pants and white *áo bà ba* shirts. This isn't the school my brothers go to.

"The teacher used to work at the elementary school until he retired," Má tells me. "Now he teaches in his home. In the fall, you'll go to first grade at the same school your brothers go to, but you have to learn to write first."

"*Thưa*, Thầy Đóc Liển," Má says to a man wearing glasses and a suit. He looks tall and skinny like Grandfather, except his hair isn't all white.

"*Thưa*, Thầy." I bow. He holds a strip of wood in one hand. His wife wears a regular *áo bà ba* pajama shirt and pants and looks friendlier. Má hands the teacher's wife money, and she writes my name in a book.

The next week, Má takes me back to the teacher's house. I find a seat in the back corner, next to the concrete path. There's an empty outdoor café on one side of the teacher's house and an open space with a ditch on the other side. I reach into my cardboard case and take out a pen, inkwell, and paper, and line them up on my desk. Thầy Đốc Liển taps the strip of wood against his pants as he walks through the rows of desks. His wife walks around on the other side of the room.

The other students already have the rows of boxes on their papers filled with letters. I dip my pen in the ink and put it against the paper. I'm not sure how to hold it. I try to write a letter in one of the boxes. It's hard to fit it inside. *Quúc!* The teacher stands over a boy ready to hit his knuckles again. I look at the teacher's wife to see if she'll do anything. She walks through the rows of desks without looking. I slump farther down in my seat and pretend I know what to write.

The next morning, I take the same seat in back. I look over at the open space on my right. There's a ditch—maybe there'll be some mud-skippers. I wish I were at the canal in back of my house or back at our hut in Cồn Tàu. The teacher walks toward me. I crouch down and move my head behind the boy in front of me. Thầy Đốc Liển stops at my desk. I bend over my paper and pretend I don't know he's there.

"Lượng, tell me what the lesson is about," Thầy Đốc Liển says.

I don't know what to say.

"What's that mess on your paper? Have you been paying any attention at all?"

I look down, hoping he'll walk away.

"Write *a*, *b*, *c*," Thầy Đốc Liển says.

I pick up my pen and try to figure out how to hold it.

"Now!"

I dip my pen in ink and press it into the paper. The tip splits. I reach into my case for another tip. I hope Thầy Đốc Liển will leave, but he stands and watches me put it on. I dip the new tip in ink and try to make a letter. It doesn't look anything like an *a*.

The piece of wood comes down on my hand. "Try harder." The teacher points to the board in front. "It looks like that."

It's harder to write with my hand throbbing. I try to make an *a*. I know what it's supposed to look like, but I can't make it. Thầy Đốc Liển leaves my desk for the next student.

When Má comes to pick me up, I run to her side. Thầy Đốc Liển hands Má back her money. "I can't teach this boy."

Má stares straight ahead with her mouth set while he talks.

"I've never seen anyone so stupid. He shows no capacity to learn."

I'm not stupid. He doesn't know me.

When we walk out onto the road, Má says, "You don't have to go to school, Lượng. Go and play. In the fall you'll go to first grade."

I don't have to go back? I don't care what the teacher thinks about me as long as I'm free.

~

I thought I'd be able to play all day, but Má takes me back to our farm in Cồn Tàu. Má steers the boat past Mr. Fourth Post's net and follows the stream through the island. A Việt Cộng dressed in black nylon stands on a cheap tree stump on the stream bank. I don't remember anyone guarding the stream when we left. Má stops the boat. "Who are you?" he asks.

How can he not know Má?

"I'm Rở, the wife of Tám Chan," Má says. "I farm next to Ten Sea and Six Soybean."

"I need to check. Stay here."

After an hour, the man comes back and says we can go to our land.

~

The hut leans more than when I left. A second steel cable holds it up. My head is closer to the top of the door than it was before. Long green *mướp* squash cover the water coconut leaf roof and dangle inside. It makes me happy having them hanging above me. We can make stir-fry and soup out of *mướp* squash, vines, and flowers.

I stay in the hut alone while they farm. When Má goes back to the city to sell fruit, she usually leaves me with my cousin or sister. But sometimes we all go with her. On our way back out to the countryside, the tide is too low for the boat to go all the way upstream to our hut. Má ties the boat at Bà Năm's land. Chị Mộng gives me some empty baskets to carry, and we walk toward Bà Năm's hut.

When we step into the door, a man in black nylon growls at us. "What are you doing here?" He sits on the wood bed next to the hammock with two other men in nylon uniforms. They have their hands on the guns leaning against them.

Má greets the men. I look at the ground, trying hard not to be disrespectful and meet their eyes. Why are they at Bà Năm's house?

Her son is in the Army.

Má gives Bà Năm some food someone sent down from the city. The men pick up their guns and leave. I look up and see them walking away through the coconut grove. They only carry small backpacks. How do they fit everything they need inside? They disappear into the water coconuts growing along the edge the stream. "Don't look where they're going," Má says. "And don't stare at Ông Five One-Eye. He doesn't like people looking at his missing eye."

Who had one eye? I was too busy looking down.

∽

A storm comes. The thatch sides of the hut lift up and sideways rain blows through. We stand near the door so we can run out if the hut collapses. Má has us put pots and pans to catch the leaks, but there are so many she gives up.

"We need a new hut," Má says.

"Why not just string more cable?" I ask.

Má and my sisters shake their heads.

"We need to wait for the *mướp* to finish," I say. There are still so many squash dangling down to eat.

Má sends me back to Tân Long while she has a new hut built. I'm glad to be with my brothers and not alone in the countryside.

"Ready?" Vân says. We're not supposed to be playing upstairs, but it's raining.

"Not yet." Thượng smiles at me in the tent our heads make under an itchy, old Army blanket. I crouch between my cousin and sister. We put pillows on our heads.

"I'm starting." Vân walks around outside the blanket, stopping to feel our heads through the cloth. If I didn't have the pillow, my flat head would give me away. "This is Lượng." Vân touches Thượng's head, "this is Young—" Young squeals and tries to move away. "Quit moving. I need to guess who's who."

Quíc! Something hard hits my head. I cry and I cover it. *Quíc!* "I'll tell you who's who," Grandfather says.

I scurry out from the blanket holding my pillow as a shield. My little sisters run away crying. Grandfather swings the handle of the feather duster at us. "You devilish kids make too much noise and give no respect!"

◇

Má takes me back out to the countryside. The new hut is tall and drafty. I miss the *mướp* vines growing all over the old hut's roof and the long green squash hanging inside. The front faces away from the stream and the six strips of land on the other side, so I can't see Má working from the door anymore. My sisters and I don't like it, but Má says that this way is better because the sun rises on the front door. Only the dead should have their heads pointing west.

Má sends me with my sister to get the supplies we left in Bà Năm's house. We walk along the path to the back of her house. Before we get to the door, Five One-Eye rushes out.

"What are you doing here?" His one eye stares at me. The hammock swings behind him. There's a net print from it around his patched eye. I try not to look at him but his one eye follows me. It seems bigger than a normal eye. How could he have been sleeping? I thought Việt Cộng were always alert.

"They're Chị Tám's kids," Bà Năm says. "They're getting their things."

I glance up at Five One-Eye's patch. What does his eye look like underneath? Before he looks at me, I look back at the ground.

We pick up the cooking oil and rice we left in the corner of Bà Năm's house. The men quickly leave.

"You need to be careful," Bà Năm says. "Make lots of noise and come in the front way. You don't want to surprise any mysterious misters staying here. Ông Five One-Eye is dangerous."

"I know, I know," Chị Năm says.

I'm glad that he doesn't stay with us.

Five One-Eye and his men walk through the coconut grove. The bushes move ahead of them. Then, they're gone.

When we tell Má we met Five One-Eye, she asks, "Were you *very* respectful?"

We nod.

"What did he say? Was he angry?" Má asks. "Don't ever do anything to get him upset."

◇

I spend most of the day alone in the new hut. A breeze shakes the leaf walls like a spirit flying through. The *nón lá* hanging by cloth straps lift away from the wall and flutter. Sleeves on the indoor clothesline wave. I rush outside. Water splashes against the mud bank of the stream. Guava and water coconuts hide Má and the grass cutters on the other side. If our boat were tied up here instead of at Bà Năm's, I could hop on it to get across. If the tide were lower, it wouldn't matter if I slipped on the bamboo pole bridge and fell in.

I go back inside. The breeze comes through again. Is it spirits or the wind? I look out the door to see if the leaves on the trees move. I stare at the rafters and the water coconut leaves in the roof. Are spirits up there watching me? Do they know what I'm thinking? I stand near the stove in front of a vase filled with rice and incense for the cooking god. "Buddha, I'll offer you a chicken if you bring someone back."

No one comes. The sun gets hot and the cicadas start to buzz. I go back to the stream and wait. The bamboo pole bridge bends as Chị Bảy Kim walks across. When she gets close to the other side, the end of the pole slips and spins. She hops onto the bank before she falls. I wish I could cross like her.

"Ê! Lượng." My cousin takes the *nón lá* off her head and hangs it on the wall. "Go pick some yam leaves from the side of the hut."

She starts a fire and puts a pot of rice on it. Even though I'm hungry, I hope she takes a long time to cook. The house doesn't feel cold and haunted with someone else here.

After lunch, the sun moves to the other side of the hut making it dark inside. I'm all alone again until dinner. I wish our land was like the countryside in the TV show I watch in Tân Long. *Bonanza* comes on after dinner and the news. A bunch of boys come over to watch with me and my brothers. There's the father cowboy, the skinny cowboy, and the fat cowboy. We don't understand English, so we argue about what happens on the show.

"That man killed that other man I'm sure."

"That girl likes that boy."

"He's the father of that one."

But we know what will happen at the end. We wait for the fat cowboy. He's stronger and draws his pistol faster. He'll get the bad guy.

The sun sinks farther. It grows darker inside the hut. It would be lighter if I lived in the big house made of logs in *Bonanza* because the pine trees are spread out. And I wouldn't be trapped if I lived there— there aren't any canals, just rolling hills in back. I'd even have a horse to ride and a dog. I offer Buddha another chicken, but no one comes.

The next day I start to offer Buddha a chicken again. But I already owe him so many. Where will I get one? Will he strike me down if I don't keep my promise? Even when he didn't make anyone come? I wait. Usually someone comes back to make lunch when the sun is high and the cicadas start to buzz.

∾

I'm happy when it rains and everyone stays inside with me. Or when Má and the other grass cutters take a break from farming. Even Mr. Six Soybean's mother, Bà Bảy, who works for us cutting grass, stays and talks with us instead of going home.

"Someone was up on the moon walking around," Anh Chín Phát says one day while they squat by the stream sharpening their knives. He seems to know a lot about it.

"I don't know if it happened or not," Má says.

My sister and other cousin don't say anything. Did it happen? Someone brought out a newspaper with a picture of a man walking on the moon. The moon looks so small and faraway it's hard to believe someone went there.

Bà Bảy puts some water on the stone and rubs the knife back and forth against it. "You have to keep straight what's real and what's not real." Her teeth look red from betel when she talks. "The grass, that's real. Up above us might be real, but the moon is in the heavens, it's not part of this world."

Bà Bảy says that Hằng Nga, the moon fairy, is on one of the dark spots on the moon. There's also a tree, the moon man, and the old shepherd who watches over things. I can't even see people across the river. How can I see them on the moon when it's farther away?

"They used a rocket to send people there and have special suits to protect them," Anh Chín Phát says. "The Americans have more advanced technology than we do. Look at all the big ships and airplanes they have. They can go places we can't."

Bà Bảy frowns. She grates the knife *xẹc xẹc xẹc* across the stone as she talks. "All my life I hear people claim this and that about things outside of our world, but you can't cross between our world and the heavens."

"I saw it on TV," Anh Chín Phát says. "I saw the men step out."

"You believe too easily," Bà Bảy says. "It could be a show."

I don't know what to think. Ba tells us that there's a lot we don't know. He says to look at how radios work. We can't see the waves, but they're there.

They finish sharpening their knives and leave me alone in the hut until dinner. I wait for the tide to go down so I can go out and catch shrimp. The gray sky makes it feel like ghosts are all around. If there are other worlds we can't cross over to, then how do ghosts cross over to ours?

∽

Má and my sisters get in the boat. I follow them along the bank as they push it downstream. "Take me with." There's so much going on in the city that I don't know about. I want to see the men walking on the moon on TV and find out what else is happening. I don't like being out in the countryside with just my cousin.

"Stay here, Lượng," Chị Tư says. "We're just moving the boat down to Bà Năm's so when the tide goes down we aren't stuck."

It seems like a week before they come back. The next time my sisters and Má load fruit, I pack my clothes in a bag and sit in the boat. Má and my sisters get in with me. "Lượng," Chị Tư says, "go back into the hut and ask Chị Bảy Kim to come out."

I run back into the hut to get my cousin. The motor starts. I turn around and run after them. Chị Tư tosses my bag onto shore. "Go back to the hut. You can come next time."

I run ahead of them to a bridge. Could I run onto it and jump onto the boat? The boat passes underneath and disappears around a bend. The sound of the motor fades downstream. I turn back. They won't trick me next time.

∽

"Where's the starter?" Má calls after she's done loading the boat. Má's belly looks big and uncomfortable. She can't squat to cut grass, but she still works all day.

"I don't know, I'll look for it," I say. They can't leave without the starter.

"Did anyone see the starter?" Chị Tư calls.

I poke my head in an empty wicker basket in the hut. "It's not here."

Chị Tư comes up to me. "Did you take it, Lượng?"

I shake my head. "I didn't see it."

"We really need to go before the tide gets too low. I know you want to come, but we're not ready for you yet. Stay here with Chị Bảy Kim. Maybe next time, we'll take you."

I look down. "I don't believe you."

Chị Tư puts her hands on her knees and bends a little so she can look right at me. "Lượng, I know you're really smart—smarter than a lot of kids your age. If you get me the starter, I won't try to trick you anymore when we're leaving. You'll get to come soon."

I go to the back bedroom and get the starter from under a pile of blankets in the corner. Má and my sisters don't come back the next day or the day after.

~

Aunt Curly comes to the door when Má gets back. "I saw your boat come by." She looks at Má. "What are you doing here? You're about to have a baby."

"Work has to get done," Má says.

After a few days, Má and my sisters start toward the boat. I follow them to Bà Năm's house. Every time Má leaves, I wonder what I'm missing. Grandfather Lê just died—I only remember seeing Má's father once. Only Má and one of my sisters went to the funeral because it's dangerous to go to the Việt Cộng side of the river near our old home. So much is changing without me seeing it. I want to be with them in the city when the baby comes.

"Lượng, go back," Má says, "We have to move the boat out before it gets stuck."

My sisters push the boat out past Bà Năm's house and stick the bamboo pole in the mud to tie it up before they go back to get the fruit. I stay out by the boat. I'm tired of waiting all of the time, never knowing when Má will be back, and worrying we'll run out of rice. My sisters keep moving the boat farther downstream. I follow them on land around different houses and fruit farms and across bamboo pole bridges over canals.

They tie the boat where two streams meet. Ahead is the cheap tree stump the man in black nylon stood on when he stopped us. My sisters and Má get into the stream to push the boat into deeper water. I jump in and wade after them. "I want to come too."

Chị Tư turns around. "Go back."

"I don't know how." They'll have to take me with—I can't find my way back.

"You'll be fine, Lượng. Go back to Chị Bảy Kim."

My sisters push the boat and pull themselves in. I run after it. How can I be fine when I don't know how to get back?

Má gives the boat a push. "Help me up." She holds her belly. "The baby's coming."

Chị Ba and Chị Tư pull her into the boat and help her sit down. They all talk at once. "Lượng, we need to take Má to the clinic," Chị Tư says. "We can't take you with us."

I wade to the bank and climb up on the cheap tree stump. How can the baby be coming now? I thought Má would know ahead of time.

"Má, lie down here," Chị Ba says. "The baby can come out on these clothes, they're clean."

"No," Má says. "These are Dì Hai Temple's monk clothes. They're holy—we can't use them. Get some banana leaves."

"Wait. Wait." Chị Ba jumps off the boat with a knife and goes to the bank across from me.

"It's alright if the leaves are green," Má calls.

Chị Ba lays the banana leaves on the bottom of the boat. Má lies down near the motor. My sisters gather around, and she tells them what to do. I stretch up onto my toes on the cheap tree stump, but I can't see anything. Má makes some murmuring noises. She grunts. A baby cries. It's here already?

Chị Tư gets out and pushes the boat. "It's stuck,"

"Go and get a canoe from Mr. Fourth Post," Má says. "You can bring me and the baby down to their house. We can borrow their boat."

Chị Năm and Chị Tư climb onto shore and head toward Mr. Fourth Post's house.

Chị Ba looks up at me. "Go back to the hut, Lượng."

"I want to go to Tân Long," I say.

"We're not going to Tân Long, we're going to the clinic in An Hóa. Do you know the way back?"

"Yes." I'm not sure I do. I turn to go home. It's late afternoon and trees block the light. I hurry across the pole bridges and canals. If I fall in, I'll jump on the mud bank and climb up.

Chapter Six (Summer 1969)

Invitations

"I want to stay," I say when Chị Tư comes back to pick me up. "I like being down here."

"Why?" my sister asks. "You wanted to leave before."

"I can cross all the bridges now, and I learned how to swim better and catch shrimp." After I walked home myself, I felt like I could explore the whole island. I'm not stuck in the hut anymore.

"No one is here to watch you," Chị Tư says.

We load the boat and make our way out of the island. Chị Tư swerves to avoid Mr. Fourth Post's net. The tide is high, so he's put it out between the two posts. I'm sad to leave the countryside behind.

When we get to Tân Long, our house is full of my aunts. Má and my new baby sister, Sang, lie on her bed. The baby's name means "wealthy person."

"Look at this baby, she's so dark," Dì Hai says bringing a bottle in, "not like any of her brothers or sisters." My aunts all look tall and thin like Má, except for Dì Hai who's fat and the best cook.

"It's because of all the Chinese medicine I took," Má says.

The baby is dark, but I'm probably darker. I move away from the hot bed. Every time Má has a baby, she has to lie in bed for a month with an urn full of coals underneath to keep her body warm and eat lots and lots of ginger. I don't know why. It's so hot already.

I go to the cupboard and steal a piece of pig heart Dì Hai roasted for Má to eat. When I come back, Má is talking to Dì Hai and Ba about her dream. "My father warned me. He stood there calling, 'Rở, Phải! Run!'"

Which aunt is Phải? Má has eight sisters. I know Phải is Dì Ba, aunt number three, but what does she look like?

"Did you have this dream more than once?" Ba asks.

"Just when I was in the clinic after the baby," Má says. Could Má's father talk to her in her dream because he died right before the baby was born? "I thought the Việt Cộng were going to attack the clinic. That's why I left when the nurse wasn't looking. But I didn't warn my sister when she came to visit the baby. I thought father meant she was supposed to take medicine for her miscarriage. Now I know he meant for us both to get away from the countryside."

How does Má know which dreams to do something about when we have so many?

Má's parents: Grandfather and Grandmother Lê.

∼

Seven of Dì Ba's children, all but the two oldest, come to our house. Má gets out of bed and sits at the head of the dining room table. Dì Ba's children gather around. "As all of you have heard," Má says, "your mother is missing and probably won't return."

My brothers and I sit on the stairs. Má says her dream warned her that my aunt should have run. She's upset she didn't figure it out in time to tell her sister. But where do you run to get away from the Việt Cộng if you live in the countryside? They're everywhere there.

Chị Bảy Kim cries softly. Chị Mộng sits without showing anything. Everyone else is sad and quiet. I'm not sure which aunt Dì Ba is and what "missing" means. I know it's their mother, but I don't remember what she looks like. Chị Bảy Kim and Chị Mộng have poufy hair. Which aunt looks like them? Most of my aunts have long, flowing hair they tie behind their head like Má.

"According to tradition, in your mother's absence I'll look out for you," Má says.

How can they live without their mother? I can't imagine anything happening to Má. What about their father? Is Dượng Ba still around?

"Listen to my guidance," Má says. "If you need anything at all come and ask me like you would your mother."

Chị Bảy Kim looks up from crying. "Yes, Dì Tám."

"Yes, Dì Tám," Chị Năm Hộ says.

Má stands up and my cousins leave. They're going to live up the street from us now. I wonder if the cousins closest to my age—Trực, Bảnh, and Dearest—will be fun to play with.

My brothers and I wander outside to the washboard sticking out into the stream in back of our house. "What do you think?" Thượng asks. "Do you think Dì Ba is dead?"

Vân moves the cover of the clay vat near the washboard and looks inside. "Yes, she has to be for Má to tell our cousins to listen to her. It's official."

"Má didn't say Dì Ba died," I say. "She said she's missing." Why would the Việt Cộng kill her? Má says our aunt should be one of their martyrs because she lost her two oldest sons to their cause. And Chị Năm Hộ's husband and my cousin Anh Sáu Triệu were working for them. "Maybe she didn't die," I say. "Maybe the Communists sent Dì Ba to a prison in the North." That's what Ba said.

Vân takes the metal bucket on the washboard and dips it in the stream. "All we know is the man tied up next to Dì Ba said they were going to die. He got away, but Dì Ba didn't."

Vân pours water into the clay vat. I imagine men in black nylon tying my aunt up to a post and the water rising with the tide. I'm not sure which aunt to imagine it happening to. The man next to her pulled up the pole he was tied to and floated down the river until someone dragged him out. Could I pull up a post if I was tied to it? Maybe not now but when I grow up? "Maybe she floated away and someone pulled her out like the man with her," I say.

Shouldn't someone look for my aunt? If you lose something, aren't you supposed to search for it until you find it?

~

Dì Hai, Má's oldest sister.

Dì Hai stays to help Má with the baby after all my other aunts leave. "Look at how big you are now, Lượng," Dì Hai says at dinner. "You were so tiny when you were born." She moves her hands together to show me. "Only one and a half kilo."

Ba finishes eating and goes back to his desk to work. I wish I could leave too.

"Lượng's bigger than his brothers were at this age," Má says.

I don't want Dì Hai to tell my story. I look at my brothers. They used to treat me like I wasn't as strong and smart as them, but they don't anymore.

Dì Hai looks straight at me. "You're so lucky. The nurse almost threw you out." I look away. "When you came out she asked, 'Should I lay the baby by the side or take it away?'"

"I was too sick to answer," Má says. "All the blood moved out of me when you were born. You should show Dì Hai how much you appreciate her. Without her, you wouldn't be here."

Dì Hai smiles at me. "I told the nurse, 'The baby still looks healthy. Why don't you put it down at the feet?'"

Má looks at me to make sure I'm listening. "Usually the baby goes next to the mother. The nurse put you by my feet and said, 'I'll come back to see if the baby is cold.' She put you there so they could throw you away if you died."

I imagine myself thrown away in a trash bin. Tears start in my eyes. I push them down.

"The hospital didn't have anything small enough to feed you with," Dì Hai says. "I had to go to the market to buy a betel nut. You wouldn't suck, so I took a piece of the skin and made a scoop to drop a little bit of liquid in your mouth." Dì Hai puts her lips together and makes a sucking noise. "Poor boy. It's a good thing I got you to suck otherwise it would be over."

Tears drip into my rice bowl.

"Look at him, so sad," Dì Hai says. "*Hì hì.*"

I don't want to cry. I hate that they always talk about this.

"When I took you home on the ferry," Má says, "I held you with one arm like a thermos. People said, 'I thought you had a baby? Where is it?' When I showed them, everyone said, 'But he's so tiny.'"

The tears keep coming. Why can't I stop them?

"I put you in bed with a hot water bottle and fed you mashed up oranges," Má says. "Look at you now. You're bigger than your brothers at this age . . . I should have turned you more so your head wouldn't be flat."

I don't care that I have a flat head—I can sleep without a pillow—I just don't like being called flathead or snakehead fish.

"You were two months early. You're lucky you're alive," Dì Hai says.

"I know." I just don't want them to remind me all of the time.

∾

"Can I come with?" I ask Má as she packs to go to the countryside. I haven't been back since I learned how to cross bridges and explore. I want to catch shrimp and try to slingshot birds.

"No," Má says. "You need to stay and get clothes made for school. Try to make friends."

There's still a little time left before school. Thượng and I walk up-stream toward the market to where my missing aunt's family lives. We turn left on a path that goes deeper into the island. "Do you think Anh Sáu Triệu will tell us how he escaped?" I ask. I know there's a program for Việt Cộng to defect because planes drop leaflets about it. We pick them up and save them because they smell like the new money we get on *Tết*. But I've never known anyone who defected.

Thượng swoops his hand around. "Think of a standing face boat crashing into the shore and lowering its ramp."

I imagine a boat with a ramp in front for unloading soldiers zooming up to rescue my cousin. I wish I could have seen the ramp lowering and my cousin walking into the boat's mouth. Why don't more people tell the Army when the Việt Cộng have head chopping meetings? They could call the Navy and get them to take their standing face boats and pick people up so that they don't get killed.

We run across a wooden bridge over a canal into what looks like a shack for storing things. My cousins Bảnh and Dearest come out. Trực stays inside reading. The four of us run back and forth over the bridge, trying to step down hard in the middle to bounce the person behind us off.

The sun gets too hot, so we go inside. I look around their house. They have dishes for cooking and mats for sleeping—nothing else. Anh Sáu Triệu sits at the table smoking and drinking tea. Chị Năm Hộ's husband had to go to the Army after he defected, but Anh Sáu Triệu is too young. I'm glad my cousin is on our side now, but won't the Việt Cộng kill the rest of my aunt's family who stayed in the countryside?

"Tell us how the standing face boat picked you and Anh Năm Nô up," Thượng says.

"That story's already been told," Anh Sáu Triệu says. He takes a puff from his cigarette in one hand and picks up the tea cup in the other.

"But how did you get to the boat?" Thượng asks.

Anh Sáu Triệu puts down his cup. "The Việt Cộng had us under house arrest when they took Má. We had Chị Ba Chẳng take a note to the Army for us and then snuck out." He raises his voice. "What were they thinking? Anh Năm Nô and I were helping them."

"What's it like to be on the other side?" I ask.

Anh Sáu Triệu stares ahead. "When they took Má away everything changed."

I look at him out of the corner of my eye. I wonder if the Communists are going to send people to kill him in the night. He doesn't seem afraid. It must be safe here with the Round Fort nearby.

~

Mr. Three East walks in the door with a green uniform and a pistol on a holster around his waist. He used to be a soldier, but now he guards the town hall. My parents offer him tea and sit with him at the table in the front room. "I heard that your sister is missing," he says.

I sit near the door pretending not to notice them talking. Even though my parents told us to keep quiet about my missing aunt, everyone seems to know.

"We'll have to find out exactly what happened," Má says.

"She's probably dead," Mr. Three East says. "The Việt Cộng don't keep prisoners."

"We won't know until we find the body," Má says. "My sister wasn't the enemy of anyone."

"Maybe the Việt Cộng didn't drown her," Ba says. "Maybe they just tied her to the post to scare her. Why would they want to kill someone who was with them?"

"It looks like they'll kill you without a clear reason," Mr. Three East says. "Your sister lived among them and participated and they still killed her." He takes a deep breath and looks toward Má. "Chị Tám, I know you farm in an area with a lot of Việt Cộng. You have to protect yourself. It's safer to have someone else with you. It's harder for them to operate if you have others around, even children."

"It's because my sister wouldn't allow her young son to join the Việt Cộng." Má shakes her head. "Even though he joined against her will anyway." Her voice gets higher. "I detest those women who get up and cheerfully testify about your crimes at those meetings."

Mr. Three East looks at Má. "If you get invited to a meeting you won't come home."

"I make sure someone always knows where I'm going," Má says.

～

Má comes back from the farm early. At dinner she says, "I left before the tide got too low so I could stop by and talk to Mrs. Fourth Post. I saw her husband early in the morning on the way in."

How could Má see him? Mr. Fourth Post is missing like my aunt.

"He was standing on the cheap tree stump past his house. I told Mộng to stop the motor and went up to the front of the boat to talk to him. He looked sad and pale. I asked him, 'Anh Tư where have you been? A lot of people have been looking for you.'

"He said, 'I'm very cold, and I'm sad that I can't take care of my family.'

"It was foggy." Má shivers. "I was scared because the boat drifted closer, and I could see he wasn't standing on the stump. He was floating on top of it. I said, 'Whatever happened to you, please don't haunt me.' I thought his ghost might tell me where his body was so I asked, 'Where can we find you?' He pointed downstream and said, 'At the mouth.'"

Má talked with a ghost?

"I was terrified. The boat drifted up to the stump. Mộng kept calling, 'Dì Tám, Dì Tám who are you talking to?' When she came up to the front next to me, Mr. Fourth Post whispered, 'Goodbye.' Then he was gone."

After dinner, Thượng and I find our cousin. "Chị Mộng, did you see the ghost?" Thượng asks.

"I didn't see anything," Chị Mộng says, "but Dì Tám did."

"Why did Mr. Fourth Post's ghost tell Má instead of his wife and children?" I ask.

"Some people are more connected to the otherworld," Chị Mộng says.

"His spirit must be active," Thượng says. "I bet he shows up all of the time."

"Which stump was he on?" I want to see a ghost.

"The big one for tying up your boat," Chị Mộng says. "I knew there was something there. I felt a cold wave over me when Dì Tám was talking to his ghost."

When Chị Mộng walks away, Thượng whispers, "I want to go there early in the morning when it's foggy. If we catch it at the right moment the ghost will show up."

~

Thượng and I go out to play in front of the house. We can play here now that Grandfather has moved to the back part of the upstairs—he doesn't lean over the balcony and spit on us anymore. Thọ, the son of Bà Ba, the medium, walks over from his house next door. I'm afraid of Bà Ba, but not Thọ. Even though Thọ is big, he's gentle and doesn't fight. We ask Thọ if he sees ghosts in his house since his mother talks to them and puts them in clay jars.

"No," Thọ says. "The ghosts are afraid of the statues on the altar and the seals we have on the door to keep them out."

~

When Má comes home from farming she says, "A neighbor's dog found Mr. Fourth Post's body at the stream mouth—right where he told me he would be. His head was chopped off and little crabs were eating him. Any longer and they would have eaten him to the bone."

Chị Năm shivers. "It's scary to know his ghost is out there watching us."

Má's voice gets higher. "What did he do to receive a death like this? He should have left Côn Tàu for a while. He didn't have to stay." She moves her hands while she talks. "The Việt Cộng should have let his family give him a proper burial at least. They don't respect traditions and the spirits of the ancestors anymore—they've become barbaric."

Why does anyone join the Communists then?

"You should stay away from the farm for a while," Ba says. "Once the Việt Cộng get in a frenzy of execution trials it's too dangerous. Wait until they're done with this campaign."

"If I don't come every day," Má says, "they'll take over our land."

Chapter Seven (Fall 1969)

Silence Your Breath

When school starts, I put on a new pair of blue shorts and a white shirt with pockets. Chị Tư walks me up the street to the school my brothers go to. "Can I stay home another year?" I ask Chị Tư. "I don't think I'm ready yet."

"I know you're smart, Lượng." Chị Tư smiles at me. "But you still have to go to school. There are a lot of other things to learn."

I hope I get sent home again—the two days I spent at Thầy Đốc Liển's school seemed so long.

Chị Tư stops at a street vendor and buys two roasted sweet potatoes. "Here's one to eat now and one for lunch."

I drop one in my satchel and start peeling the other as we walk. When we get to the classroom, Chị Tư tells the teacher my name. I can't say it because I can't say the letter *L*. She brings me over to a desk close to the front and leaves. A haze floats around the teacher as she writes letters in the grid drawn on the chalkboard. I dip my pen in ink. The smell of the sweet potato in my bag makes me hungry. I can't copy the letters the teacher writes onto the boxes in my paper and listen to her at the same time. I end up with only half the boxes on my paper filled and ink all over my white shirt.

One of the boys comes up to me at lunchtime. "What happened to your aunt?"

"I don't know," I say. "Ask my cousins."

Some of my cousins say my aunt's missing and some say she's dead.

I don't think she's dead. My other aunts say that if she were, her spirit would have talked to Má like Grandfather Lễ's and Mr. Fourth Post's did.

When we come in from lunch, I move as far back in the classroom as I can. The teacher and other kids don't understand me when I talk, and I can't hold the pen correctly. At the end of the day, the teacher sends me home with a note. I'm sure it says I don't have to go to school.

"It's probably from being born too early," Má says when she reads the note. "No one else in the family has trouble speaking. That part of you must not be complete."

I don't feel any different than anyone else.

The next day, Chị Tư walks me to school. She insists on talking to the teacher. Why can't she just let me stay home? "Lượng's very smart," she says. "He just has a little speech problem. But he's smart."

"There's always next year," the teacher says.

People say that if you can't speak correctly, you're *đần*. But I know I'm not. I'm free.

~

After breakfast, I sit on the foundation in front of our house and watch Thượng and Vân walk to school. How can my brothers do that all day? It starts to rain. Two boys my age walk in blue shorts and white shirts, holding their books and cardboard cases with pens and paper close to them in a plastic bag. They hide under an eave, waiting for the water droplets to be less fat, and then run to another overhang.

I creep upstairs past Grandfather to take my picture cards from the bookcase under the altar. Then I run over to my cousins' house. It's more fun to play without Grandfather chasing us or Ba telling us to be quiet because he has a customer. When I get there, Anh Sáu Triệu lies in a hammock toward the back. I thought he'd tell us what it was like to be on the other side, but he doesn't talk about it. Once, though, when he got drunk with some ex-soldiers at a rice liquor party, he slammed his fist on the table and said, "If the Việt Cộng even touch my family and our land in Giao Long, we're going to come back there with the Army and kill them. I know where they hide." I wish he'd go back and get rid of them.

Dearest goes up to talk to her brother. "Why can't we understand you?" Anh Sáu Triệu says. She sounds like she's choking the words out, like something's stuck in her throat. People say she has a goose throat, but it doesn't sound like a goose to me.

Dearest frowns and shrugs her shoulders. I tell her brother what she said.

"How do you understand her?" he asks.

"I just listen. It's not hard." I say some sounds wrong, but my family understands me.

Bảnh, Dearest, and I each put two cards down on top of each other. We use another card to try to flip the bottom one out so it's on top. The first one to do it wins all of the cards.

My card springs out of my hand into the back part of the room. It lands close to a two-legged table leaning against the wall. Incense burns in front of a picture of my missing aunt. I didn't notice the altar before. In the picture, Dì Ba sits on a chair wearing an *áo dài*—New Year's clothes. I remember that aunt.

Dì Ba used to stop at our house while she waited for the foot ferry on the way home from the market. She had a light blue patch on her shoulder where she carried her shoulder pole and her *áo bà ba* shirt was gray from banana stains. I knew she had to be older than Má because she was so much taller than everyone else, and she talked like she was in the military giving orders. Once I watched her talking with Má, and she called me over. I looked at her pocket hoping she had a sweet in it. She waved me to look into one of the two flat baskets sitting on the floor next to her shoulder pole. "Have one," she said. I reached in and took one of the leftover green tangerines. It wasn't candy, but it was good.

Now I know which aunt is missing.

~

Anh Sáu Triệu and his father sit drinking tea and eating cookies from a tin. I don't see Dượng Ba often. People say he's an officer in the Army and that's why my aunt is missing. It's good Anh Sáu Triệu and his father are on the same side now. Dượng Ba hands Dearest and me each a cookie. We sit and eat and listen to them talk.

I go lie in the hammock. I'm tired of playing here, but my brothers are at school and Ba is working. Má says I should play with Dearest because she doesn't have many friends. But I'm still mad at Dearest for tricking me into eating dog at her brother's rice liquor party. My family doesn't eat dog. Only a few old men who sit around and drink rice liquor eat dog. The neighborhood dogs growl and bark at them all of the time. They know.

Dearest comes over to my hammock. She doesn't look happy.

"Have Lượng tell us what you're talking about," Anh Sáu Triệu says. She repeats what she said, and I tell her brother.

"From now on have Lượng translate what you say for us," Anh Sáu Triệu says.

They should try harder. I'm not around all the time. When she can't make a sound they should know which one she's trying to say.

Anh Sáu Triệu turns to his father. "It's good these two kids can play together. Lượng can understand her. He must have the same brain."

I'm not the same. My problem will go away—I don't know if hers will.

∾

Dearest and I walk along a path tossing dirt into the canal. The canal is filthy. More people live next to Dearest now. They wash in the water and dump their leftover food and trash in it. We pass the house of a woman who raises pigs. "When you grow up you can marry your cousin," she says. "You two *đần* kids are a perfect match."

Is this what everyone means when they say we play so well together? That I'm *đần*? I stop and look at Dearest. Her hair is cut so it makes a square around her face—her brother probably cut it—and her clothes are faded, but otherwise she looks the same as everyone else. She just can't talk so anyone can understand. I know how that feels, but she has to work on it herself. "I'm not like you," I say. "I can't say a few letters and people think I'm *đần*, but I'm not. This is the last time I'll play with you."

"We can still play. Just ignore people." She goes back to tossing dirt in the canal.

The next day, I stay home and play marbles on the step in front of the house. Dearest comes over and looks out of her square hair at me and asks if I'll go over to her house. "No. You're still my cousin, but I won't play with you."

I go back to banking the marble off the track the wood panel doors slide on until she leaves.

Chị Tư calls me over to her desk where she's fixing a radio. "Why won't you play with Dearest?"

"I'm not like her. I don't want people to call me *đần*. I have a little problem talking, not a big one like her."

"You can still be friends with her," Chị Tư says. "It's good for her to have a friend."

"It's not good for me," I say.

～

It's hot in the afternoon. The canals in Tân Long are too dirty to swim in now. Thượng and I walk across the road to the Round Fort. The barbed wire fence and Claymore mines along the wall are gone. Families who moved next to the fort complained that the mines could accidentally go off. The only way to get to the fort is a bridge made of boards on stilts that goes across the moat. It's high tide, so we can reach down and touch the water from the bridge.

Some older boys are there. We jump off the bridge into the moat, swim, climb up, and jump again. We try to avoid splashing the house-boat tied to a post in the moat. An Army soldier sits on the wall of the fort smoking. He wears a full uniform, hat, and boots. When we first moved here there was a whole squad living in the fort, but now only three or four soldiers stay there. Usually the soldiers look out toward the river, but he looks back here at us.

"How long can you silence your breath?" one of the older boys says. "Do you think you can drown yourself?"

What would it be like to drown like my aunt? If I silence my breath underwater long enough will I die? I take a deep breath and plunge into the water. I hang onto one of the bridge posts. As soon as I start to run out of air, I burst up to the surface. Thượng has already given up, but the older boys are still down. They pop up one after another. Then they all climb out. Thượng leaves with them. Only the soldier on the wall watches me.

I go back underwater and wrap my arms and legs around the post as tightly as I can. I want to know what it would feel like to be unable to breathe. I want to see if I can make myself die. My lungs run out of air. I start to panic. No. I'm going to hang on and keep silencing my breath. My lungs calm down. I feel peaceful. I open my eyes, but it's too muddy to see anything. I close them again. It's quiet down here. I hold on. How long can I have this feeling? My body pushes away from the post.

I shoot out of the water gasping. Air rushes into me. I feel wonderful, like I was just born.

"What are you doing, kid?" The soldier from the wall reaches down and grabs me by the neck. "You could die."

I gasp for air. The soldier grabs my arms and pulls me up to the bridge.

"What were you doing?" His face is cold and stern.

"I wanted to know how long I could silence my breath."

"That's dangerous. You could lose control and drown. With this murky water there's no way for me to find you. If I weren't here, you'd die."

I'm not sure what he means. I tried to see if I could die, but my body wouldn't let me.

∽

Má brings me out to the countryside again. She turns the boat into the stream that runs through Cồn Tàu. Mr. Fourth Post's hut looks empty. A rope holds a piece of his tattered net to one of the posts. I look hard at the big cheap tree stump near his house to see if there's an outline of him. Má says he was a white figure. I don't see the shape of a person or even a shadow.

When we tie the boat up at Bà Năm's house, someone's talking inside. I hope it's not Five One-Eye. Má seems more worried about him than any of the other mysterious misters.

A man in black nylon sits on the dirt floor oiling the long barrel of his gun. Another sits on a stool folding something into his backpack. His gun leans against the post next to him. Five One-Eye isn't there. A teenager who looks like one of my older cousins sits on the wooden daybed talking with Ông and Bà Năm like a neighbor. He doesn't have a gun, but he must be a Việt Cộng if he's with them and wearing black nylon.

"Quý, how's your family?" Má asks the teenager. "Is your mother well? How is your grandmother's health?"

Is this the Quý everybody talks about? The one Má says got tricked into joining the Việt Cộng?

Quý gives Má a calm smile. "Thank you, Thiếm Tám, everyone is good. How's the harvest going?"

He looks normal. I thought he'd look stupid.

"Good, good," Má says.

The other two men glance around like they're about to grab their guns and run. Quý just smiles. Could he really have killed someone?

"And Chú Tám? Is your husband's work in the city going well?" Quý asks.

"It's going well," Má says.

Quý goes through the names of all of my brothers and sisters asking how each one is doing. How does he know everyone? When he gets to my name, Má pulls me over. "Lượng, greet Anh Tám."

"*Chào*, Anh Tám," I say.

"You were very little when you first got down here," Quý says. "Now you're big."

He knows me, too? I look at him out of the corner of my eye to see what's different about him. Five One-Eye looks like he wants to kill you, but Quý looks like a neighbor.

Quý stands up and picks up a satchel like the ones my brothers have for school. "Please extend my respectful greetings to Chú Tám."

Why does he want to greet Ba? Ba never comes down here.

"Please extend my greetings to your family with wishes for health," Má says.

The two other men put on their backpacks and pick up their guns. Quý walks out the front door with them. He doesn't have a gun.

I wait until we start walking on the path to our land. "Is that the Quý that used to be Lành's friend?" I ask.

"His mother and sister live across from the old hut on the rice paddy land," Má says.

But is he *that* Quý? When we get to our land, I look for Chị Năm— she and my cousin stayed here overnight. "I saw Quý today," I say. "He looks different and smarter than the other Việt Cộng. He doesn't look like a soldier."

"That's Quý," Chị Năm says.

"Is he the one that killed Lành's father?"

Má glances over at me. "Don't go around saying things like that."

"I know. I just want to know how he got tricked into killing his best friend's father. Did he kill anyone else?"

"The Communists are very tricky," Má says. "They lure young kids. If you go to a meeting, the leader could call your name and tell you to execute someone. If you don't, they'll execute you. Once you kill someone for them you can never leave."

"How many people did Quý chop the head off of?" I ask.

"One too many," Má says. "It's too late for him. Don't *you* get trapped."

I would never get trapped. I'll join the Army like Lành.

~

We only have a little fruit to sell, so instead of going all the way back to Mỹ Tho, Má takes our boat to An Hóa. It's a clear, sunny day. We turn to cross to the Việt Cộng side of the river toward the mouth of the stream An Hóa is on. To get a break from the heat, I stick my hands in the water running along the side of the boat. A terrible stink hits me. Má steers the boat to the right to avoid a body. The buttons on the uniform stretch out to hold the bloated flesh. It floats high like a barrel. It doesn't have a head.

"It has to be an American," my cousin says. "The frame of that person is so big."

"It smells really bad," Má says.

"It's big like a cow," Chị Năm says. "A floating cow."

I try not to breathe. People pull dead bodies of Army and Việt Cộng out of the river all of the time and bury them, but I haven't seen an American soldier's body. Má speeds up to get away from the smell.

A passenger ferry carrying about sixty people comes down the stream. It heads straight toward the body. The driver runs over it, and the propeller chops it into pieces. I can barely breathe.

"It's as if he was aiming right at it," Má says. "He couldn't have missed the smell, and it was so big right in front of him. "

"The driver is probably a sympathizer," my sister says.

"The dead should be buried," Má says, "but there won't be a chance now."

He shouldn't have run over the body. Dead bodies can't fight.

~

When we come back to Tân Long, I find the boy who moved in next door. Sơn's mother is Vietnamese, but his father is an American. Sơn looks like us, but his older sister Simone has light skin and hair and a tall nose. Sometimes she looks Vietnamese and sometimes, when the sun makes her hair glow, she looks like one of the girls in *Bonanza*.

I tell Sơn about the American soldier floating in the river.

"No, that was just a fat Vietnamese," Sơn says. "The Americans track every soldier. They don't let people float in the river like that."

I wonder where Sơn's father is—I haven't seen him yet. What would it be like to have an American father?

~

I sit alone on the cement foundation in front of our Tân Long house and push my marble around. Across the street a soldier sits on the concrete wall that runs around the fort. I don't want to play with Dearest and my brothers are at school. I wish Má would take me out to the countryside again.

Smoke pours over the wall of the fort. It spreads over the moat toward our house. "Run!" someone shouts.

People race past our house and turn into the alley on the side. "Run! Everybody get out of here!"

The smoke hits me. My eyes and nose start to burn like I ate a chili pepper. My throat hurts. I race down the alley with everyone. Wind blows the smoke along with us. I can't outrun it. My face is on fire. Am I going to die? I close my eyes and run without looking. I feel a little better. I put my fingers over my eyes to clear the tears away. I open them, take a peek, and run. Every breath running over my throat burns. Halfway to the center of the island, we stop. There's still a thin haze. I gasp for air. Each breath burns more. I try not to take big gulps of air, but I'm out of breath from running. Finally my lungs catch up. I take as few breaths as I can.

"Look for lemon trees. We need to find some lemons." Someone finds two lemons and cuts them. People start to squeeze them and rub the juice on their face. I look for a piece, but there aren't enough. "Pee and wash your face with it," a neighbor woman tells me.

I pee down the leg of my shorts into my hands. It doesn't seem right, but my eyes and nose feel like they're on fire, so I try washing them with pee. My nose and throat still burn. I pick a piece of squeezed lemon off the ground and rub it on my face. It doesn't help either. More people spill out from the alley. Maybe I should run farther away? People put shirts over their faces and squat under the haze. I squat down and close my eyes. No one is dying. The smoke can't kill us.

Chị Tư finds me. Young and Hằng hold her hands and cry. "I saw

Ba come out, but he went back home," she says.

"Where's the baby?" a woman asks. "There was a baby in that house. Did anyone bring it out?"

Who are they talking about? I look around. Where is my baby sister?

"Whose baby is it?" a man asks.

"Chú Tám's family," the woman says.

My baby sister. We left Sang in the house. Why didn't Ba or my older sisters take her?

The woman calls around. "Does anyone know where the baby is? The baby might not be able to handle this gas. She might be too small."

"We need to go back and get the baby," the man says.

My sister and the man and woman run back down the alley to our house. Mrs. Fourth Fresh, the woman who lives behind us, gives me half a lemon. I hand it to Young and Hằng. "Rub some on your face."

The burning starts to go away. I walk toward our house with my little sisters. What would happen if I were stuck in the house? Could I live in this gas? I want to find out if Sang is alive. The smoke thins near the house. What made it? I hope another blast doesn't come from the fort.

I walk in the back door. Sang has a gas mask over her face with a shirt wrapped around the sides to keep the air out. Her back arches against the hard wood daybed under the stairs. Cậu Tám Tranh, the nurse who lives next door, takes off the mask and starts to clean spit from her mouth. "Fan her, give her some air," he says. "Keep her airways clear and stay around to watch that she's still breathing."

Sang's eyes roll back into her head. Her body tenses up and arches again. She's going to die.

"What's happening to her?" Ba asks.

"Tear gas can cause severe seizures," Nurse Tranh says. "Some kids can die from the pain and seizures—they stop breathing." He cleans the spit by her mouth with a cloth. "Luckily, she can breathe. We have to wait."

A soldier from the fort stands to the side of the room. He holds a gas mask. The huge eyes and the hose coming out of the mouth make it look like he's carrying a strange monkey.

Sang goes limp. Her back drops. Did she die? Her eyes roll back in place. She takes a few deep breaths and starts to cry. Ba picks her up.

The soldier holding the mask sighs. "It was an accident. A terrible accident . . . I was sitting on the wall. I—I sat on a tear gas canister and the pin came loose." He twists the gas mask in his hands. "I heard the baby crying and put the mask on her. I'm really sorry . . ."

"It's a good thing we got her out of the seizure," Nurse Tranh says. "She would have died from it."

Ba glares at the soldier. "What are you trying to do, kill my child and my father?"

I forgot about Grandfather. Where did he go?

Another soldier pokes his head in our back door. He looks toward my father. "Is everyone well here?"

Ba nods his head.

I walk out front. Sơn is by his house. "How come you weren't out back?" I ask.

Sơn steps inside. He comes out with a gas mask and puts it on. "Can I try?"

"Sure."

The mask covers my face.

"My father left these for our family in case anything happened," Sơn says. "He told us what to do."

I remember when Sơn's father came to visit him. He stayed in their house most of the time. He seemed older than other soldiers and wasn't as big as the cowboys on TV. I thought he must work in an office. "Do you have an extra mask I can have?" I ask.

"No, these are special." Sơn turns to go inside. "You can't get them."

Mr. Three East walks toward our house. I follow him in. He's wearing his uniform and pistol. "Where did your father go during this?" he asks Ba.

"I helped him out of the house," Ba says, "but he refused to go past the fishpond. I thought my older daughter had the baby."

"This is unacceptable." Mr. Three East walks across the street and stands on the bridge leading to the fort. "We're soldiers," he yells. "We have responsibility. A baby and an elderly man almost died over here. We have to be careful among civilians."

A few minutes later, the captain of the fort comes over with two soldiers. "It was an accident," he says. "That soldier was bored. Somehow he pulled the pin. It snapped and he couldn't put it back."

"Tear gas is one thing," Mr. Three East says, "but if there is a fight, civilians are going to be the main casualty here, not the enemy. Having a fort in the middle of a civilian population is not acceptable."

"We are well aware of the situation," the captain says.

The captain goes back to the fort and returns with two gas masks. As soon as he leaves again, I tell Sơn to come over.

Sơn picks up one of the masks. "It's probably defective."

"No, it's in working order from the Army," I say.

Sơn puts the mask down. "Mine is from the Americans."

"They all came from the same place."

"Well, mine is new. Yours has been used."

I bend over to inspect the masks. "One of them looks used, but the other looks newer than yours."

Sơn looks at it. "I guess so, but you didn't get to use it when you needed it."

"I have it now."

"Only two. We have one for everyone in our family." He leaves.

I put one of the masks on and chase the neighbor kids, pretending to be a person from outer space or an alien monkey.

Tết 1970. Chị Năm (Thơm) with Hằng, Sang, and Young.

Chapter Eight (1970)

Mysterious Misters

Má sits on a stool cooking a pot of rice on the fire inside our hut in the countryside. "*Chào*, Thiếm Tám," the leader of a group of Việt Cộng calls out. "How is your family? Is the harvest going well?"

It's a new group. Not Quý's or Five One-Eye's. There are nine of them. They used to stay at Bà Năm's house, but after we built the new hut they started to stay here. "We have to be nice to them," Má told us. "We don't want them to think we don't support the cause or we'll be tried for treason and executed."

The men sit down around the table and on the bed waiting for a meal.

"This is all the rice I'm cooking," Má says. The smoke filters out through the wood walls and the water coconut leaf root. "We can't cook rice we don't have. We have to stay down here for two days."

The squad leader sends one of the men to get rice from another farmer. Má sends me to the canal to pick more water spinach. Now I know why the Việt Cộng have such small backpacks—they take everything they need.

Má goes to the big clay jars near the window ledge and spoons *mắm* onto a dish. We eat a lot of *mắm* because pickled fish keeps a long time and is ready whenever you need it. Má puts it out on the table along with the boiled water spinach and rice.

"*Mắm* is only good for eating with green guavas," the leader says. "It isn't supposed to be a meal."

"This is all we have," Má says. "We're too busy farming to catch shrimp or fish."

The men scoop rice into their bowls. They spread out over the wooden bed, stools, and floor. Some reach into their backpacks for small bottles of fish sauce, sprinkle a little on their rice, then put the bottles back. They dip their chopsticks into our *mắm*. "This *mắm* has too many bones in it," the leader says. "You're supposed to get rid of the bones, not chew them up and swallow them."

The men start to pull tins of dried meat out of their backpacks. "Next time buy some pork or something," the leader tells Má.

"If you give me money, next time I'll get some pork for you," Má says. "This is all we can afford."

They hang around smoking and talking after they eat. I wish they'd leave. I wait all day for my family to finish farming so we can sit around the fire and tell stories, but with them here we have to be careful what we say.

Má looks at the men smoking in the hut. "Only women live here," she says to the leader. If the Army comes by and smells tobacco, they might set up an ambush."

The leader tells them to put their cigarettes out. One of the men steps out to throw his in the canal.

"Throw it in the fire," Má says.

"It will break apart in the canal," he says.

Má shakes her head and points to the fire.

At night the men cover the floor with their sleeping mats. One of them rearranges his backpack, taking out a blue and red flag with a gold star in the middle. It's more colorful than the yellow Southern flag with three red stripes. He folds the flag and puts it back.

They leave after breakfast. Má sniffs the air in the hut. "They're not supposed to smoke. It leaves a trail." She takes down the ropes they borrowed and strung up everywhere to dry their clothes. "Look around and see if there's something that doesn't belong to us." Má picks up a pair of black nylon shorts and ties them into a small bundle to hide. "They'll want it when they come back."

My sister and cousin go over to the pile of dishes by the washboard. "They treat us like slaves, expecting us to clean up," Chị Mộng says.

"They always eat more rice than they put in the pot," my sister says.

Chị Mộng holds up a rice bowl. "Look, they chipped it. Why don't they use their own?"

"Let's not make them upset over something small," Má says. "They might report that we're against the cause. Hopefully, they'll go somewhere else. Look at all these footprints. If the Army shows up, lie down and crawl out of the house. They'll throw grenades."

If the Army comes, I'm not going to lie on the floor where I can get shot. I'm going to jump into a canal. The soldiers in Tân Long talk about digging a hole to hide in—a canal is like a big hole.

~

Ba and Má in the spring of 1970 after the birth of their tenth child.

We go back to Tân Long to sell fruit. On the return trip to the countryside, it rains. Má and my cousins put on raincoats and *nón lá*. There aren't enough coats, so Chị Năm and I have to wear military surplus ponchos. I don't put mine on. The ponchos are too big and rain comes in the neck. I stick the ends of a piece of plastic in a crack in the edge of the boat and hold it over me. The boat fills with water and my cousins and sister take turns bailing with a plastic jug cut into a scoop. Halfway into the trip, I stick my head out to look for the stream that goes to Quới Sơn, but it's hard to see across the river in the rain. We usually don't travel along that side. Má says that's the Việt Cộng's side.

When we get to Bà Năm's hut, the wind picks up and rain hits the wood walls. It comes through the doorway and windows. Even though it's raining, the wooden flaps on the windows are propped up on sticks and the door is open. Otherwise it would be dark inside.

Má sets down her plastic medicine basket. "I guess we're staying until the rain slows down a bit." The rain pushes softly on the water coconut leaf roof. It pounds on the mud outside the open door and falls *lụp bụp* into the canal. "Maybe the rain will keep those mysterious misters away from our hut."

My cousin and sister set down the supplies they're carrying. "Those mysterious misters use all our rainwater and want us to serve tea," Chị Năm says.

"First it was just a few of them," Má says, "then five, and now ten."

A kingfisher squawks outside, but otherwise the whole world has stopped. The only time people talk about the Việt Cộng is when it rains too hard for anyone outside to overhear.

Bà Năm puts some wood on the fire. "You'd better be careful. Lành didn't get killed on the front. He's back and he's building a fort. His men could be wandering around, and you don't want to be in the crossfire."

"That's what I heard." Má squats over our baskets, arranging them. "How big a fort do you think the Army is going to build for him?"

Lành must be brave to come back here. I see more Việt Cộng here than I did in Quới Sơn, but I haven't seen any Army since they got their airplane.

"I don't know," Bà Năm says. "The Navy is dumping a lot of supplies for the fort." Smoke from the fire curls around the rice pot and twists up through the water coconut roof, adding more soot on the leaves above the stove. "Those mysterious misters staying with you is an omen," Bà Năm says. "An omen that's going to pull you into a bad fate."

"You keep saying that," Má says. She moves into a hammock. "What do you mean?"

"All the mysterious misters hanging around your house," Bà Năm says. She holds onto her wad of betel and chews on it seriously. "They weren't there before you rebuilt. If you want to have any peace, you need to pray and make an offering to the spirits."

"What spirits are there to offer to?" Má says.

"There are more spirits underneath you than you think," Bà Năm says. "Make sure you make a worthy offering. You should have built across the stream."

"Did something happen on our land before?" Má asks.

Bà Năm doesn't answer.

When the rain stops, we go back to our hut. "Something must have happened here," Chị Năm says. "I don't like to be inside the hut by myself. When I come back to cook and no one's here, I can feel a cold spirit draping around my back."

Má and my sister go out to work, and I'm alone in the hut again. I feel something cold. I turn around to look for a sign of something watching me.

~

A roast pig sits on a wooden tray in the back of the boat next to Má. "Why didn't I pick up what Bà Năm was saying before?" Má says. "I should have known. Why couldn't she just tell me? Now I have to offer a pig every year."

Tết 1970. Lượng (age seven) with Thượng and Vân.

My brothers and I sit in the boat staring at the pig. My burnt uncle looked like that. Every time I see a roast pig or a piece of hair drops into the fire, I think of him. But the smell of roast pig is different. It's so good that I want to break off a piece of crispy golden skin with fat stuck to it.

My stomach rumbles. I move to the front of the boat and try not to focus on the pig. I tilt my head into the wind to get away from the smell and stick my hand in the water coming off the bow.

When we get to our hut in the countryside, Má sets a table up outside. My cousin and sister grab a handle on each side of the tray and carry the pig to it.

I hover near the table with Thượng and Vân. "When will we eat?" Vân asks.

"After the spirits," Má says.

Má goes to the boat to get the incense for the ceremony. My brothers and I each steal a flake of skin. It melts in my mouth. I wonder if the pig tastes as good to the spirits as it does to me. We walk around a little and come back and grab another piece. Má takes some paper gold and silver and burns it on the ground while my cousins light incense sticks around the front of the door to call the spirits. We can't eat until the incense finishes burning.

Thượng and Vân go off with their slingshots. I circle back to the table. The incense burns close to the top of the stick. The spirits take too much time to eat. I wish I were one of them so I could eat now. No one is around. I want to peel off some crunchy skin near the butt, but someone would notice it missing. The curly tail sticks out. I break a little from the tip and stick it in my mouth.

I walk across the coconut log bridge over to a corner of the land where no one is around. I eat the crunchy part and suck on the bone.

"Lượng, what are you doing?"

The bone cracks in my mouth.

Má appears across the canal. "The spirits are going to break your neck for this. You should have waited."

Can the spirits be that greedy? They have a whole pig. They'll understand if I take a little.

~

When the Việt Cộng come back, there are twelve of them—the most I've seen together. After dinner they stand and lie around talking. I try to avoid brushing the nylon shirts and pants hanging to dry from ropes strung all over the house. The only place the men stay out of is the back room where Má and my sisters sleep. I want to get some yams to roast or some guavas to dip in salt and a crushed chili, but if we do, we have to invite them to eat, and there's not enough.

The sound of boot steps come from the east. Everyone stops what they're doing and turns silent. The leader and Má look out the door.

The marching gets closer. The Army is coming. The Việt Cộng push their hammocks and clothes into their packs, grab their guns, and head out the door.

"Clean up all the dishes," Má says. "Make sure they didn't leave anything."

The sound of marching boots surrounds us.

"Go find out what it is," Má tells Chị Mộng. She hands her a basket. "If you meet anyone say you're going to Bà Năm's to pick up sweet potatoes. Sing so you don't surprise anyone, and we can hear that you're safe."

Má gathers up tins of food and cups on the table and jackets hanging on bed posts. She shoves them into a bag and takes them across the canal to hide.

My cousin walks outside singing. Her voice shakes. I look out the door as she crosses the canal in front of the hut. The marching noise stops. She turns toward Bà Năm's house and disappears, still singing.

Má comes in and pulls down shorts and shirts the men left hanging to dry. "We don't have time," she says to my sister. "Wrap them in mud and throw them in the stream."

A pair of shorts float up after my sister throws them in. "Go into the stream and push them down," Má tells Chị Năm.

After a few minutes, Chị Mộng returns. The old couple who live downstream follow her in. "I met Ông and Bà Năm coming over," Chị Mộng says.

"How many Army are there?" Má asks.

"What Army?" Ông and Bà Năm ask together.

"Didn't you hear or see anything?" Má looks from my cousin to the old couple.

"No," Bà Năm says.

"Yes, nothing," Chị Mộng adds from behind. "No boot prints, no trampled plants, nothing."

We sit and wait for the Army. Are they sneaking up on us in the dark? "Maybe they marched the other way?" Má says. She turns to Bà Năm. "Did you see anything at all?"

"I told you the spirits were going to help you now," Bà Năm says.

"Did you hear footsteps or see boot prints?" Má asks.

Bà Năm laughs. "No, it's just spirits chasing unwanted visitors away."

The next morning, Má puts the tin cups and clothes left by the Việt

Cộng in a sack and buries it. I walk all over looking for signs of the Army marching through. Nothing looks touched.

∾

A few days later, we pass Mr. Six Soybean's house on the way to the rice paddy land Má bought. Má pokes her head in the door. "*Chào.*"

Some of the Việt Cộng who fled our house sit inside. I wonder what they found out about the marching noise. "So how many Army came by?" the leader asks. "Were there any Americans with them?"

"I thought you would know," Má says.

"We went the other way. We didn't see anything."

If he knows something why isn't he telling us?

"No one stopped by," Má says. "Maybe they went east?"

"It had to be something. We all heard the troops coming."

"We all heard it, but no one saw anything," Má says. "Maybe it was spirits making a noise."

The leader's face gets red. "I can't report that."

Communists aren't supposed to believe in spirits. Má says they're ghosts themselves because they travel at night.

The leader raises his voice. "We need information so we can protect our people."

It sounds like he doesn't know what the noise was.

"I'm not in the military, so I don't know," Má says. "If you find out, tell me if I'm in danger."

"We left some things behind," the leader says. "We'd like to collect them."

"We threw everything in the stream," Má says.

"Those were our things. You can't just throw them out."

"Your things will get us killed," Má says. "You can go along the bottom of the stream in front of our house and find them. Next time you run bring all of your belongings."

The leader frowns. "Where did you throw them?"

"Between our house and Ông Bà Năm's. It was an outgoing tide."

As we turn to walk down the path, I glance back at the men. Maybe it was spirits that scared them away.

Before Má goes back to Tân Long, she digs up the sack with the Việt Cộng's tin cups, pants, and jackets. She fills it with dirt and puts it in the boat. She says she's going to drop it in the stream on her way out.

Don't Follow the Talking Wind

Kids in my grade sit scattered around the schoolyard eating bread or sweet potatoes for lunch. I sit on the concrete under a tree in the corner. I've given up. I thought the teacher would send me home at the end of the first week, but she didn't. I'm stuck here.

When the other boys finish eating, they tag each other and sit together in the shade of a covered walkway telling stories. Sometimes I join them and talk about living in Quới Sơn before we moved here. I tell them about seeing the neighbors washing the dead body of Mr. Fourth Farmer by the canal and how he was shot to pieces so we couldn't even tell it was him. The other boys don't believe that the helicopter shot him and his helper while they were in the boat: *How could they shoot two people in the boat and not kill the wife? Why didn't the boat get shot up and sink?* But I know it's true. His wife told us what happened, and Má saw the helicopter.

A group of girls starts playing hopscotch near the boys. None of them come to find me, not even Sơn. I hate that people think there's something wrong with you if you can't talk right. I close my eyes. I have trouble sleeping between my brothers under the mosquito net and the hot tin roof. And the grandfather clock Má got when her father died ticks and gongs downstairs all night. Lunch seems too long. I wish we could use the time to finish school and go home earlier.

The bell rings. I'm glad to come in from sitting on the hot concrete. Bellfruit trees shade the windows of the back of the classroom. I take out my notebook and start writing down the lesson on the chalkboard. I'm sure the teacher will make me take first grade over again—so why won't she let me go home?

At the end of the day, I walk home. "Where's Má?" I ask when I walk through the door.

Chị Tư looks up from the radio she's fixing. "Má's in Cồn Tàu."

"Isn't she coming back?" I need to tell Má I want to go out to the countryside with her in the morning. Sunday is our only day off.

"No, she has a lot of work to do. She's staying overnight. How did you get so much ink on your shirt?"

I shrug and go find my brothers.

Chị Tư (Huệ) fixing a radio at her desk. The shutters in back are closed since the window faces Sơn's house less than a meter away. Behind the TV one of the wood panel front doors is pulled open during the day.

∽

Ba gets up and paces around his work area in the lean-to. "This is unreasonable! We already paid the Southern government. Now the Việt Cộng want money? They should only tax land that produces, not rice paddy land chest-high in grass."

It would be nice if we could keep the money. Maybe then, we wouldn't have to worry about having enough rice.

Má stands expressionless by his desk. "Why did you buy that land anyway?" Ba asks, "I only see money coming out of my desk drawer for that land."

Tết 1971. Back: Thơm (Chị Năm), Huệ (Chị Tư), Lan (Chị Ba), Thanh (Chị Hai). Middle: Má, Ba, and Vân. Front: Young, Sang (on Má's lap), Hằng, Lượng, and Thượng. Lượng was told to smile to show his missing tooth.

But I did see Má give Ba a bundle of money once before. "From the land," she said when she handed it to him.

Ba goes back to work at his desk. We have ten days off from school for Tết, but after a few days at home, Má has to go to countryside. "The land doesn't wait. Fruit doesn't wait. Nothing waits," she says as she packs a roast pig to take on the boat.

"Do we have to offer a pig every year?" Ba asks from his desk. "Are the Việt Cộng going to eat the pig too?"

"We don't want bad luck we end up dying with," Má says. "The spirits chased the Việt Cộng away and will keep them away."

When we get to our hut in Cồn Tàu, I stand near the roast pig. I wish I could break off part of the tail again. Vân and Thượng come up. Vân lifts up one of the cut squares on the pig's back, pulls some meat off the bottom, and pats it back in. "You don't break off a piece they can see," he says.

Thượng pulls up a different piece and does the same. "No one notices." He walks off with Vân, trying to hide his chewing.

I search for the fattest piece and lift it up. As I pull the meat off, someone's body and legs flash through the leaves. I pop the meat into my mouth. Quý walks up, his satchel hanging over his shoulder. He's the one coming to collect taxes? I thought Má was going somewhere to pay them.

"Lượng, go get my medicine bag," Má calls.

I nod, holding my mouth so that it doesn't look like it's got anything in it. When Má turns to talk to Quý, I swallow and run into the house. A blue plastic net basket pokes out under the bed in the back room. I grab the handles and bring it back.

Má digs around in the plastic bag inside her medicine basket and pulls out a bundle of money. She hands it to Quý.

Quý sits down on the bed near the door and starts to unfold the bills. How did my parents get that much? Má sits on a stool close by. Quý takes each bill out of the stack and counts it into another pile. All that money would buy a lot of rice. Where is he going to put it? If I had that much money, I'd hide it upstairs in the bookcase under the altar. Then I'd have money to buy rice noodles and tofu dessert for lunch instead of bread or a sweet potato.

Quý counts the bills twice, then opens his satchel and takes out a small pad of paper. The paper has a reddish tint like the paper gold and silver for burning on the altar. Each page is stamped with the Việt Cộng's blue and red flag with the star in the middle.

Quý writes the amount on a page and signs and dates it. Má studies it. Ba told her to make sure Quý writes the whole amount down. That way he'll have a hard time keeping any for himself. Finally, Má puts the receipt in her medicine bag. She stands up and brings out a tin of Holland cookies. "Stay, have something to eat."

Quý takes one. Má hands him a glass of water and pulls up a stool. I stand next to her hoping for a cookie. She closes the lid. "Come back later this evening and have some roast pig."

Why do grown-ups always invite people when they don't really mean it?

"No, no. I have work to do. Thank you, Thiếm Tám," Quý says.

I knew he would say no. If you want to make sure the Communists don't come back to visit you invite them back later. That's what the men who have tea with Ba say. They won't come if they think the Army might be there waiting.

Quý stands up and puts his satchel over his shoulder. That's all he has with him. He doesn't carry an AK like all the other Việt Cộng. "*Chúc mừng năm mới*," he says.

"*Chúc mừng năm mới* to you and your family," Má replies.

How's he going to keep all that money safe? What's he going to do with Lành and the Army chasing him if he doesn't even have a gun?

~

I try to go out to the countryside whenever I can. After dinner, Má decides who's coming to the countryside in the morning and tells us what we're going to carry. I ask to carry the basket with food. I worry someone will forget to bring the rice. At four the next morning, Má wakes us. Chị Tư stays home to help Ba fix radios, but she gets up and closes the door silently after us. Only our bare feet hitting the wood dock make noise until Má starts the motor. I'm glad to be gone from this crowded island for the day.

Má passes the stream that leads to Ông and Bà Năm's house and takes the boat farther up to a stream that cuts into the center of the island. Where are we going? We pass a big mound near the bank of the stream, like someone decided to build a hill. There's a hut on the other side of the stream that has fruit trees behind it. Má pulls the boat up between the mound and the hut. It's the rice paddy land Má bought. I haven't been here by boat. I thought it would be impossible to drain the rice paddy and build planting strips, but Má already has little fruit trees growing. I wish we had kept it a rice paddy. Then, we wouldn't run out of rice. We already have a fruit farm.

I walk around with my slingshot. Near an old hut, Chị Năm squats next to a pot sitting on a fire she's made in a hole. The smell of fresh cooked rice drifts over to me. While I wait for lunch, I go over to a canal that separates our land from the land across from it.

"Ê!" Chị Năm yells at me. "Don't do that!"

"Do what?"

"Pee over there! That used to be where the mysterious misters had meetings. People were killed there. You have to give them respect."

"Here?"

"Yes. Lành's father was killed over there across the canal. Probably lots of other people, too. You don't want their spirits to get you."

I pull my shorts up. "Lành's father was killed next to our land?"

"Yes. His ghost must live around here. If you're innocent and die like that, your soul will stay around and torment people that come near."

I wasn't disrespectful on purpose—ghosts only mind if you know and do it anyway.

Chị Năm points across the stream to a big tree behind the dirt mound. "Lành hid right over there behind a tree and watched Quý kill his father. Their land is right next to ours. Quý will have to pay for his sin."

I knew Lành was our new neighbor, but I didn't know it was *that* Lành.

"You also have to respect that grave over there." Chị Năm points to the dirt mound.

"That's a grave?" It seems more like a hill of dirt than a grave.

"There's a marker on it. You can't see from here."

I run up to where my sister is cooking and stare at the land on the other side of the canal. Quý must have chopped off Lành's father's head over there. And the dirt mound on the other side of the stream must be where they buried him.

After lunch, I wander around while Má and my sister work. I get hungry again and look around for some fruit. There's no ripe fruit on our land, but there's a mango tree over on Lành's land. I go to the boat and get my slingshot and aim a hard clump of dirt at the stem of a green mango. I miss the stem and hit the skin. It tears. The flesh explodes. It hangs tattered in the tree. I pick up another clump of dirt and try to knock down another mango. I hit the stem and it falls down. I jump over the canal to get it. There's nothing around. No breeze, no birds. I stand silent, waiting to see if something will move. Maybe animals can't live here because it's haunted. Where exactly was the head chopping? I pick up the mango and jump back across the canal.

"Lượng, where did you get the mango," Chị Năm says.

I point at the tree across the canal. Chị Năm spots the exploded mango hanging in the tree. Her eyes get wide. "You're going to get in trouble."

It wasn't even a ripe mango. It was green and sour. I try to knock it down before Má sees it.

Má comes up behind me. "Where did your shots hit the ground?" she says. "Was it where Lành's father was killed?"

"No."

"Did anything talk to you over there?"

I shake my head.

"Stay away from there. Don't follow the wind that talks to you."

I can hardly wait to tell the other boys at school that someone was executed on the land next to ours. After I eat lunch, I walk up to the group of boys and lean against the wall in the school courtyard. "You have to hear this."

The boys all look at me.

It takes me a long time to get the story out because my classmates keep interrupting with *what did you say?* and *what was that?* I have to find a way to describe it that doesn't use the letters I can't say. I finally tell them how Lành and Quý were best friends and Quý wanted them both to join the Communists. Lành's father wouldn't let him, though, because Lành was only sixteen and his father thought the Communists shouldn't recruit kids. But Quý joined, and they made him kill Lành's father for his initiation because the Communists have to show everybody you can't say "no" to them. Quý probably didn't even want to kill his friend's father, but if he didn't, they'd kill him. And now Quý can never quit, but he has to hide all the time, because Lành joined the Army and is trying to kill him.

"I saw right where it happened," I say. "It was on our new land."

"It couldn't happen on your land," Tuan says. He sits in front of the class and thinks he knows everything.

"Why not?"

"Maybe it happened, but I don't think it happened on your land."

"It did too! And I know the person who did it."

"You know a person who chopped someone's head off?" Six Chicken asks. I'm not sure why everyone calls him Six Chicken, except that he *is* chicken and his mother treats him like an egg that might break.

"He looks normal . . . just like everyone else. He doesn't even carry a gun. He just runs whenever he sees Lành or someone in the Army."

"You're making this up," Tuan says.

"If someone was chasing me, I'd want the biggest gun ever," Phong says.

"Ask my brothers," I say. Everyone looks up to my brothers at school.

"What do you think Việt Cộng use to chop off heads?" Six Chicken asks.

"They can use anything," Tuan says. "Just keep chopping until it comes off."

"No. Việt Cộng have a special kind of knife just for it," I say. I hear people talking about meetings all of the time. "They need to do it in one cut, otherwise it's a mistake. They practice on banana trunks because they're the same as human bodies." These boys don't know anything.

∾

After school I find Sơn. He usually doesn't talk to me at school. I tell him about Quý killing Lành's father on our land. "You should see the land where it happened," I say.

Sơn stands near his door. He covers his mouth with his hand and brings it down like he doesn't have anything in it. I know he's eating something. He just doesn't want to share.

"It gives you the creepiest feeling. I even saw where Lành hid when they had the meeting. It was just across the stream behind a tree. He saw Quý chop his father's head off. He saw everything."

Sơn covers his mouth again. He's hiding something he got from the refrigerator in his house. No one else has a refrigerator, not even the café down the street. "Is that really true?" he asks.

"*Có!* Lành faked his age and joined the Army the next day. He got sent to the front and everyone thought he'd die. But he came back and now he's got a team on the island trying to hunt down Quý and kill Việt Cộng. Ask anyone in my family. Everyone in Cồn Tàu knows it."

"I don't know," Sơn says.

∾

My sisters complain that Lành's father's spirit is haunting everyone. No one wants to go in the hut on the converted rice paddy land now. Má says Lành's father's spirit is looking for revenge because the Việt Cộng attacked Lành's first fort. She packs some *bánh* and salty pork and rice for the trip to the countryside. "We need to make an offering to Lành's father," she says. "Lượng, you need to come with and ask for forgiveness."

"I don't feel like going today," I say.

"You're coming."

When we get to the converted rice paddy land, Má walks over to the hut and places some incense sticks in the entrance. She puts the platters of food near where I stood and peed and pushes incense into the ground to form a line on our side of the canal. She hands me an incense stick. "Tell Lành's father you're sorry."

I walk up to the edge of the canal and bow with the incense between my hands. "I didn't mean to be disrespectful."

I stick the incense in the dirt bank. The wind moves. It sounds like people whispering, humming in the background where I can't see them or hear what they're saying. I liked it better when I didn't know we passed a grave on the way to the rice paddy land, and Lành's father's ghost didn't seem real. I wasn't scared before. I want to stay in the countryside, but it's hard with all these ghosts.

Chapter Ten (Early 1971)

Death Land

I n the late afternoon, I sit in front of our house and look across at the empty concrete watchtower of the Round Fort. The Army closed it after the tear gas accident, and the sawmill owner bought it and made a dry dock. For a while, every day after school, I watched men carry sand and fill up the moat around it. I still feel safe, though. The Navy has a base right across the river from us in Mỹ Tho.

A crowd of people gather down the road from my house. I hop off the porch and walk toward them. A machine gunner walks along the road with ammunition belts crossed over the front of his uniform. The ammunition chains gleam in the sun. "It looks like he's polished each bullet," a neighbor says.

The gunner is one of the soldiers on leave who come over to Tân Long to drink in the cafés along the river. He swears about how tough he is, how much he's carrying.

"He's not carrying that much," a neighbor whispers. "Maybe ten kilos. Not like the gunner last week who must have been carrying at least fifty."

That gunner had ammunition belts double-crossed over his bare chest. I followed him when he wandered out of a beer-hug place, his muscles bulging out. This gunner doesn't look that strong.

"They walk around like it's the only trophy they have," the veteran who lives behind us says. He's talking with Crazy Two A. I move away.

The machine gunner turns to walk the other way. "Don't go around disturbing the dead," Crazy Two A calls. Once someone asked Crazy Two A why he's so crazy. He said that when he was the bodyguard for an officer, he decided he was going to eat an enemy soldier.

The gunner stops in mid-curse and turns around. He straightens up like he thinks there might be an officer nearby. He looks at the crowd and goes back to cursing.

"I said, don't disturb the dead," Crazy Two A calls out again. He said he tried all parts of the body, the kidney, the liver, the intestines, and cooked them over a campfire. "You have to eat the organs to know what it really tastes like," he said, "because the flesh isn't anything worth eating except the inner thigh."

The gunner comes up to Crazy Two A and the other veteran. "What makes you think you can say that?"

I hope they'll fight. I want to see how tough Crazy Two A is and if he really is crazy.

The veteran nods his head toward Crazy Two A. "He's your superior."

Crazy Two A's body is fit and tough, but his face is thick and his cheeks sag. I heard Crazy Two A goes over to Mỹ Tho to find fights, but all I've seen him do is get drunk and yelled at by his wife.

"What? He's a drunk," the gunner says.

"Ever heard of the bodyguard that got discharged?" The veteran asks. "That's him. Don't take my word for it. Ask someone. You can always come back and find us here."

Crazy Two A snickers. "Come back so I can snack on you." People say he ate the enemy soldier because he wanted to get a reputation, but now everyone stays away from him because who wants to be around someone who eats humans. What will they do to you?

The machine gunner starts walking away from them. He's stopped cursing. I wish they were going to fight. But I guess it's better for him that he walks away. Mr. Three East says to leave veterans like Crazy Two A alone. "The war in his head never ends," Mr. Three East says. "He's just waiting for death." Crazy Two A says his life ended when he was dishonorably discharged.

"He's just fresh meat to be ground," Crazy Two A says.

I look back at the gunner. I wonder if he'll be dead soon. Crazy Two A must know—he was on the front. The news on TV shows the number of soldiers who die on both sides every night. As long as more on the other side die than us, we'll win.

≈

Má veers the boat over to the side of the Mekong we avoid because of the Việt Cộng. My brothers and I sit between our cousin Chị Mộng and her younger sister Chị Châu. "What do you think the land in Giao Long will look like?" we ask each other. People who still live there have stopped by and told us the land we abandoned has been bombed and shelled. It's overgrown like a jungle and the Việt Cộng put a Death Land sign on it.

"That's the stream that leads to Quới Sơn," Má says.

"I know," I say. Someone points it out every time we pass. I miss my old house—I wonder if I'll ever see it again. No one I know lives there anymore.

Má turns the boat into a smaller stream to go to Giao Long. We pass fruit farms with canals and rows of trees. The stream winds through land that looks like a jungle on one side. Vines climb up betel nut trees and over coconut trees tying them together. On the other side, the trees are in neat rows. Má stops the boat near a small clearing on the wild side of the stream. Is this our land? There's a big coconut tree on the edge of the bank with a piece of aluminum nailed to it. It has the faded outline of a skull and crossbones painted in red. DEATH LAND is written underneath in black. Are we supposed to be here?

Chị Mộng points to the sign. "What's that about?"

Má picks up a knife on the rack near the boat engine. "It's taken care of." She steps out of the boat onto the base of the coconut tree and grabs the sign with one hand. With her other hand, she pries it off with the knife. She throws the sign into the bottom of the boat. "The land is safe."

We get out of the boat and follow her along the stream. Má uses a bamboo pole from the boat to brush the ground in front of her. She stops at a big leafy tree. Shrapnel cut off the bottom branches, but it still looks happy. Má twists off two of the huge pods clinging to its trunk. "It's cacao, try it." She hands Chị Năm one and me the other. Chị Năm gets the knife from the boat and cuts open the golden pods. The flesh inside is yellow with big seeds. I bite into the sticky pod.

"Everyone back in the boat," Má says. "I need to talk to Thầy Bi before we walk farther."

We get back in and Má tests the water with the pole. "It's too low to go upstream. We'll wait."

We sit in the boat and wait an hour until the tide floats the boat upstream toward a log bridge. Má sticks the pole into the bottom of the stream, ties the boat to it, and pulls her black pant legs up as she wades out and up the bank. "Thầy Bi?" Má calls as she walks toward a hut.

Thầy Bi comes to the door. He's the retired teacher who came to our house in Tân Long to visit before. He brought us some coconuts he collected from our land. About ten or so. "I didn't see any grenades when I collected the coconuts," he told us. "The coconuts dropping would have set them off if there were any."

Má goes inside. After a few minutes, the teacher's wife steps out. "Come in and eat."

"We ate already," Chị Năm says. We're supposed to say no to invitations unless we know they really mean it.

"Have some tangerines then," she says.

Má and Thầy Bi come out. We step off the boat and bow to the teacher and his wife.

I look in the trees for the ripest tangerine. There aren't many. The teacher picks one and gives it to Má. I wait for him to pick more, but he doesn't.

Má gets the metal Death Land sign from the boat and hands it to the teacher. He puts it in his hut and walks across the log bridge to our land. Má follows. "You can hardly walk with all these vines," she says.

The teacher steps through the brush to a coconut tree right in the middle of a path along the stream. "Do you see this sign here?" He looks at me and my brothers.

We nod. It's another metal sign with a red skull and crossbones and DEATH LAND painted on it. It doesn't look as faded as the one Má took down.

He points to a pile of thorny tangerine branches blocking the path behind the coconut tree. "Don't go over there. If you go over there you'll get stuck by more than tangerine thorns. It's rigged with grenades."

I peer through the bushes. The fort by Dì Hai's house has grenades strung in the trees and along the ground with wires running everywhere. Is it like that? I can't see any grenades—it's just trees and vines.

Má looks at me. "Do you understand? This land is only for death."

I step back. Why do we need this land when it's overgrown and next to the Death Land? We have lots of land in Cồn Tàu. There aren't any warning signs there.

"Remember Mrs. Từ Ba in Quới Sơn?" Má asks. "Picking up grenades and thinking they were fruit? Now she's dead."

Má talks about Mrs. Từ Ba every time someone steps on a grenade. I imagine Mrs. Từ Ba walking through the coconut trees on the path to her shack, picking up a grenade, playing with the pin like it's the stem of a cherimoya with thick square scales. She could think clearly, like on the day she made her sons kneel down in the rain, but one of the times she didn't killed her.

We follow Má into the land. Next to the stream the land seems like a jungle, but inside, only the trunks of shelled coconut trees stand. Everything looks dead and dry.

"Look how clean this crater is." Má points her foot to the edge of a water-filled hole left by a bomb or shell. It's three meters across and surrounded by overgrown grass. "It looks like it's only six months old. When it fills in we can try some okra here."

My brothers and I stomp around the edges of more water-filled craters. We poke sticks in. They're as deep as we are tall. The edges of the craters overlap and are partly washed away by the rain. We try to guess how old they are, but we don't know as much about how long mud takes to move and grass takes to grow as Má.

∼

When we get off the boat on our next trip to Giao Long, there's a milky stain covering all the leaves in one area. It's even on the banana plants—usually everything runs off banana leaves because they're so waxy. "What's going on here?" Má asks. "This looks like some kind of chemical."

She cuts powder-covered leaves off a banana plant growing into the path, until only a few leaves remain at the top. It looks funny. Can it live like that?

"It can't be from a bomb . . ." Má chops milky leaves off another banana plant. "All the coconut trees nearby are still standing . . ." The banana plants only have three bunches instead of ten or more. And the bunches aren't complete: they're like hands with some fingers too small or missing. "Let's stay away from it," Má says. "There are lots of other areas without this powder."

At least the cacao tree doesn't have white powder on it. It's the most beautiful tree. It has so many dark green leaves spread around it. Chị

Năm helps me get another pod. I take a few bites. My tongue finds a hole in my mouth. My loose tooth is missing. Did I drop it? I run down the trail to the boat.

"Lượng, what are you looking for?" Má asks.

"My tooth. Where did it go?"

Má looks at the cacao pod in my hand. "You must have swallowed it."

"But I don't remember chewing it." Part of me shouldn't have disappeared without me knowing about it.

Má shrugs. "Well, where else can it be?" She goes back to work chopping and pulling down vines.

A reddish, brown centipede as fat as a finger rears its pincher up. Má chops it into pieces. My sisters and cousins throw leaves and branches in the stream. Under a pile of leaves, Chị Mộng finds a nest with baby rats in it. "Should we cook them for lunch?"

No one says anything. The hairless rats look disgusting.

A rat scurries out of the bushes. Má points at a long snake with black and orange stripes chasing after it. "Ê. Look! A tiger snake." The rat runs up a coconut tree and the snake follows.

I go to the boat to sit. It's safer here. Land snakes are poisonous, but water snakes aren't. I practice sounds I can't say. "Wa, twa, twa." It feels strange with my missing tooth. Everyone else can say those sounds. Why can't I? "Twa, thwa, thwa, th." I pick a new sound and start practicing.

~

When I come out to Giao Long again, the land is clear enough to walk around on. I haven't been here for a while because of school. I look for the happy cacao tree on the edge of the stream. There's only a stump. "What happened?" I ask Má.

"It was just leaves with hardly any fruit."

I stare at the stump. The cacao tree was the only good thing about this land.

"I'm sorry," Má says. "It blocked the sun from the other plants."

Couldn't Má have trimmed it? Why did she have to chop the whole tree down?

My sister cooks some rice in the small hut in the middle of the land. It starts to rain. Water drips through the leaf roof. There's no place to sit in the hut, and it's full of rats and bugs. When it's time to eat, we sit on the edge of the boat and pull a piece of plastic over us. I put a lot of fish sauce on my rice, but it doesn't taste good cold.

The retired teacher waves to us from his house. "Come in. Get out of the rain."

We sit in Thầy Bi's house eating on the wood bed frame in the front room. Three mysterious misters in green nylon appear in the back of the house. I glance at Thượng. How did they get here? I ask with my eyes. The men come out and stand around the table. Má and my sister and cousins eat without looking at them. Thượng glances toward the bomb shelter in the back of the house and gets up. I follow him. The bomb shelter's door is so tall you can walk right in, but it's too dark to see inside. A radio hisses. Thượng creeps toward the entrance.

"You boys get away from there," Thầy Bi says.

We come back.

On the way home I sit next to Thượng. "Do you think there's a tunnel hidden in that bomb shelter?" I ask.

"There has to be," he says. "Where else did all those mysterious misters come from?"

Má frowns at us. "Keep it to yourself. It's safer not to know."

$\sim$

"Why go back to Giao Long at all?" Ba asks the next time Má packs the boat up. "That land doesn't yield anything. Why not abandon it?"

I think Ba is right. I don't like the land there. Without the cacao plant there's nothing to eat. When we go to Cồn Tàu, our boat seems close to sinking on the way back with all the fruit we pick. But when we come home from Giao Long, the boat is lighter because we ate our lunch.

"It was my father's land," Má says.

"Is there anything there you can harvest?" Ba asks.

"Probably, the coconuts falling down," Má says.

It's low tide when we get to Giao Long. My brothers and I wade in the stream with my cousin and sister, catching shrimp and fish for lunch. Chị Châu rolls up her long pants before stepping into the stream. How can her legs be so white? I'm so brown from being in just my shorts.

Chị Năm walks downstream ahead of us with her pants dragging in the water. She doesn't roll them up because she has a rash on her legs. I'm glad I don't have to wear all those clothes. With their long shirts and pants and *nón lá* on their heads, their skin rarely sees the sun. "*Ê!* Look at this," Chị Năm calls. I hope she found some shrimp. "There's a big bomb here."

We rush over to where my sister stands. The bomb sticks partway out of the mud on our side of the stream, showing fins and a dial.

"Stay away from it," Chị Năm says. "I'm going to tell Má about it."

Chị Châu follows my sister out of the stream. As soon as they leave, my brothers and I go back to the bomb.

"Which way do you spin it to make it blow up?" Vân says.

Thượng spins it to the left. "This way."

"Really? I thought it was to the right, like a watch." Vân spins it the other direction.

"Maybe we can spin it one way and then the other way, so it resets?" Thượng says.

We each take a turn spinning it. When it's my turn, I feel it click *rịc, rịc, rịc* against my hand.

"If it went off, we'd all be dead," Vân says.

"How big do you think the hole would be?" I ask.

"At least as big as the ones by the hut. It would go all the way to that tree." Vân waves to a coconut near the bank closest to us.

We each spin the dial again before my sister comes back.

The next time we go out to Giao Long, Má steers the boat close to the teacher's side of the stream to avoid the bomb. When it's low tide and no one is looking, I wade out to see if the bomb is still there. It has propeller marks on it now. Someone's boat must have hit it. *Rịc, rịc, rịc* I spin the dial.

Shadows and Winds

When Má goes to Giao Long, I try to stay in the city. But when she says she's going to Cồn Tàu, I go along. On the way down to Cồn Tàu, soldiers on an American patrol boat stationed near the end of Tân Long Island wave us over. "Stay calm, don't laugh, don't do anything," Má says. "You don't want to get shot."

My sister straightens the small South Vietnamese flag on a stick on the side of the boat. The big faded-yellow flag in the back of the boat is on a long pole so it stays straight. Má idles the motor. We sit silently around the sides of the boat. I see river patrols all the time, but I've only been in the boat once when it was stopped. Our boat drifts toward them. An American soldier in a green T-shirt calls out. He looks scary standing above us. So strange and white. A South Vietnamese soldier next to him translates, "Where are you going?"

"We're going to Cồn Tàu to work our land," Má says.

"What are you working on out there?" the translator asks. "How many days are you going for?" The American points to my two older sisters. Chị Hai and Chị Ba usually don't come with us because they're at boarding school. "What about the girls?" the translator says.

"They're students," Má says. "They're on break, so they're helping me."

The soldiers look at my sisters. "You're students? What school?"

"Hello," my sisters say. They say something else I don't understand. I wish I could speak English.

Chị Ba (Lan) and Chị Hai (Thanh) wearing school clothes— white traditional long dresses with pants (áo dài). They carry nón lá (leaf hats) and satchels.

The American says a lot of words back to them. It sounds so strange. Not like the cowboys talk on *Bonanza*. My sisters talk shyly and laugh. They turn to the translator. "We don't understand all of the things he said."

The translator tries to explain, but the American keeps talking. Three more American soldiers come out and start talking and laughing. Some of them wear pants but no shirt, and some have a T-shirt and Army shorts. They're all barefoot. When they smile and laugh they seem like anyone else. They're not scary. I like them. They're keeping us safe.

My sisters say a few more words, then stop talking. The Vietnamese translator encourages them to say more. The soldiers smile at them. I want to hear them talk more too. The soldiers all talk at once and laugh. My sisters get quiet. They look down at the boat and then glance back up at the men.

"Come closer," the translator says.

We paddle the boat closer. The Americans lean over and hand down apples and canned chicken. My sister stands up to take it. She says something in English. I think it's "thank you."

We wave goodbye. When we were stopped by a patrol before, they went through all the fruit in the baskets—this time they didn't check anything. Má starts the motor again, and my sisters pass out the apples. Má tells us how a patrol boat tried to stop her once, but she didn't see it. They shot bullets on each side of her boat. We eat the apples while she talks. They're soft. Má laughs. "Finally I stopped. The soldiers asked me, 'Why did you keep going when we were shooting?' I told them, 'I thought it was fish jumping.' *Hì hì.* If they had moved a little, I'd be dead."

Every time someone talks about being stopped by a patrol, Má tells that story and laughs. "You'd better stop," she says. "If I hadn't, I'd be dead."

~

"Five, ten, fifteen, twenty . . ." Chị Năm stands in the stream next to a water coconut with her eyes closed.

"I know where to hide," I tell Thượng. I'm glad to be out in the countryside for the summer. I thought school would never end. Usually we hide in the water coconuts on the side, but I lead him upstream to a caved-in area in the bank. "I saw it when I was catching shrimp," I whisper. We take a stick and poke inside to make sure there aren't any water lizards hiding there. It looks too smooth to be natural and seems deeper today. Like someone has been here before. I wonder who made it.

Chị Năm wades upstream. She turns the corner. "I see you!"

We run in the stream toward the water coconut. Chị Năm spreads out her arms and tags us. "Got you," she says. She points back at the caved-in place where we hid. "Don't erode the land, you'll get in trouble."

"We didn't dig it. It was here before."

"Well, don't let it get any bigger."

It's already bigger than it was the first time I saw it.

~

Chị Năm comes out of the back bedroom in the hut. It's still dark. She lights a small lantern and pours rice into a pot near the bed I'm sleeping in. My cousin sleeps deeply next to me. They want me to sleep in the back bedroom, but it's hot and dark there, so my cousin has to sleep out here with me. Chị Năm lights a small fire on the floor and sets the pot on a stand over it. After the rice cooks, she leaves the embers burning to keep it warm and goes back to bed.

An hour later we get up to eat. The sun still hasn't risen. "Why did you leave the lid on the rice partly open?" Má asks. The fire is out and the rice is cold.

"I didn't leave it open," Chị Năm says. "Why would I do that?"

"I thought maybe you were sleepy," Má says. "This rice tastes bad. Like it got cooked with too much water and then the water was drained off."

"It's bland," Chị Mộng says.

"I cooked it and it was done," Chị Năm says.

"Even if you didn't cook it well, it would still have flavor," Má says. "The ghosts must have eaten all of the flavor while it was sitting out."

My sister tosses the leftover rice into the stream. No one wants to eat food ghosts have eaten.

∾

After lunch, we sit around waiting for the sun to go down a little so it's cool enough to work. My cousins and sisters talk together. Má stands in the door talking to Bà Năm. "We had strange rice today," Má says. "The flavor was all gone. I think the ghosts ate it."

I smooth the dirt floor with my hand and pretend I'm not listening. "Yes. It happened to me too," Bà Năm says.

"There are so many spirits nearby," Má says. "When I'm out here, I dream I see ghosts wandering around."

"There are definitely spirits around," Bà Năm says. She takes some betel out of her *áo bà ba* pocket. "You need to make it so good luck goes toward you and bad luck doesn't stick."

"I heard about those mysterious misters having meetings around here," Má says. "You should have told me what happened on our land before."

Bà Năm looks around the hut as if something might jump out of the water coconut leaf walls. "I told you not to build here, but you didn't want to listen."

"You were talking about luck. I thought you meant something else. What happened here?"

Why doesn't anyone tell you what they mean? Everyone talks in shadows and winds.

"The mysterious misters had a lot of meetings in the banyan trees," Bà Năm says.

"How about here? Where our hut is?" Má asks.

Bà Năm turns and walks across the pole bridge to the strips of land on the other side. Má follows her across. So do I. Bà Năm stares at our hut and chews her betel faster. She whispers, "There used to be a pond where your hut is. The bodies floated down from the banyan trees and stayed there."

"Did someone bury the bodies?" Má asks.

"The mysterious misters wouldn't let anyone get the bodies. They stayed there until they sank."

That's why I felt so scared when I was alone in the hut. I wasn't imagining things

Má stares at the back of the hut. Bà Năm looks at the hut and then at Má. "There was a reason you could buy this land so cheaply."

"If I had known, I wouldn't have built here. I wish you had told me. I can't rebuild now."

"It's bad luck to say it. If I told you, the spirits might have gone after me. If you had built your house on the other side of the stream like I told you, then you would have avoided the bad luck. Now you have to pay respect."

"Why didn't someone build an altar here?" Má says.

"If you build one you might end up on it." Bà Năm spits betel into the canal. "A family put an altar up over by the small banyan tree. Those mysterious misters said the family committed crimes and got them in trouble."

When I go back into the hut I shiver. Can there really be dead bodies underneath?

∼

Thượng and I walk with our slingshots away from the converted rice paddy land. A plump woman walks toward us with two men in nylon with AKs. "Who are you?" the woman calls out. "What are you doing?"

"We're shooting at birds and fish," I say.

"I've been watching you." She has a round face that looks rounder because her hair puffs out around it.

Thượng points to a strip of land where my sister and cousin are pruning our small guava trees. "Our land is right there."

The woman walks up to Chị Năm and my cousin. "Who are you? I haven't seen you before."

I thought plump people should be happy, but she's not.

"I'm Dì Tám Rở's child. We stay at our hut over there." Chị Năm points in the direction of the six strips of land. My cousin stands silently next to her. "Over near Mr. Six Soybean and Ten Sea."

The woman narrows her eyes at my sister. "How did you get over here? How long have you been working here?" The two Việt Cộng wander off.

"We've been working from morning until now," Chị Năm says.

"Not how long have you been working *today*," the woman says. "How long have you been working on *this land*?"

The men with guns drift farther away.

"A long time," Chị Năm says. "We see you sometimes. Maybe you didn't see us?"

"You couldn't have been here. You must have seen someone else. How do I know you're telling the truth?"

"We've been working here, and I know everyone around," Chị Năm says.

The plump woman calls for the men. They ignore her and talk to each other. She scowls and turns back to my sister. "Well, when your mother is around make sure she comes and talks to me. I need to know all the people who work around here."

"Who do I tell Má she's supposed to talk to?"

"Tell her to talk to the lady leader."

"Would Má know who that is?"

"She'd better know." The lady leader looks at my brother and me. "Don't come over here anymore."

When we go back to the hut, we tell Má about the lady leader of the Việt Cộng. "Fort Hag always questions everyone, even kids." Má sighs. "Try to avoid her."

～

My brothers and I run around the young guava trees on the converted rice paddy land using scissors to cut off the leaves with caterpillar cocoons in them. Sometimes we cut a whole branch or sometimes just a bad leaf. We're trying to finish the trees on the last strip of land before it gets dark.

"It's late. What are you doing around here?" Fort Hag says. She's with two men in nylon again. I wonder how she got her name. Did she help attack Lành's first fort?

"Working," Chị Năm says.

"Is your mother around?"

"No."

"Well, who knows you? I need to be sure you're not spies."

I thought she asked us who we were a week or so ago.

"Uncle Six Soybean knows us," Chị Năm says.

"Stay here." Fort Hag turns to one of the men. "Go get Six Soybean."

We go back to clipping off the caterpillars, trying to finish the row. Fifteen minutes later, Mr. Six Soybean and the man in black nylon approach talking and laughing. When they get close they stop. Mr. Six Soybean nods to Fort Hag. "*Chào*, Chị Ba."

"*Chào*, Uncle Six," Chị Năm says.

"These kids showed up without informing me," Fort Hag says. "Who are they?"

"Aren't they your neighbors?" Mr. Six Soybean asks. "Their family owns this land."

"Why don't I know who they are?"

"Dì Tám has a lot of kids," Mr. Six Soybean says. "Ten of them." He looks toward my sister. "Are you kids doing something you're not supposed to?"

"We're working late," Chị Năm says.

"Your mother is supposed to be coming down tomorrow," Mr. Six Soybean says. "I'll make sure I tell her you met the lady leader here."

Fort Hag scowls at us. "You're not supposed to work late without grown-ups. That's enough for today."

"Why's she so difficult," I ask when she's gone.

"I don't know," Vân says. "Are the Việt Cộng being threatened or something?"

"She's just difficult," Chị Năm says.

~

"Where's Má? Why didn't she come?" I ask my cousin. Má was supposed to come back after selling the fruit and getting supplies in the city.

"I don't know," my cousin says. "Dì Tám was supposed to be here."

We're running low on rice. I hear a boat near Mr. Six Soybean's house, but it stops before it gets upstream.

"Please, let's go to Bà Năm's house and ask if anyone knows," I say.

I'd like some *bánh* too. Má usually brings some when she comes.

There's no one home at Bà Năm's. "Maybe the boat motor broke down," my cousin says.

The tide gets too low for any boats to come in, so we go inside for the day.

The next morning the *rồ rồ rồ* of a boat comes toward the hut. I run out to see if it's Má. The noise stops downstream by Mr. Six Soybean's house. I go back inside. The motor starts again. I run out to a canal and stand on a log bridge. Má's boat emerges from the water coconuts and guavas and creeps toward our hut with the incoming tide. Má looks irritated.

My cousins come in from cutting grass. "Did you come down yesterday?" Chị Mộng asks Má.

"Lành stopped us and made us work on his new fort," Má says. "He made us waste a whole day."

Lành can do that? I haven't heard of farmers helping the Army build a fort.

Má has the old *bánh* she bought yesterday and some new *bánh* she bought this morning. She unwraps the banana leaves around the *bánh chuối* and dumps a plastic bag of coconut milk on top of the rectangles of banana tapioca cake. We sit around tearing pieces off a baguette, but I mainly eat *bánh chuối*. Mr. Six Soybean steps in the door. "I saw you come in. I thought you were coming yesterday."

"Lành wouldn't let us leave. We were slave-working the whole day, so we had to head back to Tân Long. All the other boats were avoiding the fort, but we got called. The guavas are getting too ripe to sell. It's lost money."

"I try not to go in and out, so I don't get stopped at that fort," Mr. Six Soybean says.

"Lành is pretty brave to come back and build another fort," Má says.

Mr. Six Soybean nods. "But, unless Lành has some Navy support, those mysterious misters are going to take this one over like they did before."

∽

"Who got *mắm* out and didn't close the jar?" Chị Năm says when we come in for lunch.

Everyone shakes their heads.

"The rice vat wasn't closed either," Má says. "We don't want the flies to get in or the flavor to come out of the rice."

Chị Năm scoops *mắm* out of the big clay jars on the kitchen counter and sets it in a bowl. I look for a piece of meat with my chopsticks. There's nothing but fish bones.

"Someone stirred up the *mắm* so that all the bones are on top." Chị Năm looks at me. "Lượng doesn't know better. Don't stir up the *mắm* looking for the good pieces."

"I didn't do it," I say. "I take it out all the time for lunch, and I don't do that. Why would I want to—there are just bones on the bottom."

"It tastes bad, too," Chị Năm looks at me again. "We need to buy a new batch."

"I can't even reach that high without standing on something," I say.

Má puts her bowl down. "We have to throw this out. The whole thing is bad."

Someone must have done it—ghosts don't take the flavor out of *mắm*—but it wasn't me.

~

"Does anyone take care of the altar over by the small banyan?" Má asks Bà Năm when we stop by her hut. "Should we go and bring an offering?"

"Unless you have a reason to be there, the mysterious misters will hold it against you," Bà Năm says. "And the spirits might not like it."

"Someone should take care of the altar," Má says.

"The mysterious misters don't want it. They sent two people to take it down and both died. One was walking on a pole bridge on his way there. The pole broke and stabbed him to death. The other asked the family to remove the decorations. The next day he was shot by the Army."

Why do the Việt Cộng want to take down an altar?

"Who do we know that died there?" Má asks.

Bà Năm says, "A lot of people from Giao Hòa and Long Phụng got taken over here."

I wonder how many people died and if their bodies are still under our hut. My sister and cousin pretend there's nothing wrong with the hut, but they won't go inside it alone. Whenever they come back from working on the six strips across the stream they either come together or call, "Lượng, are you around?" before they cross the pole bridge over to the hut.

When Thượng comes out to the countryside, we go to the edge of our land and onto the neighbor's land to look at the banyan trees. There are two trees, but we can only see the larger one. The huge canopy touches the ground and covers the land—it's the biggest tree I've ever seen. Má says the small banyan with the altar under it is nearby. She says not to go there because the spirits are active, and if we disrespect them they might end our life. But I think the big banyan tree should be more dangerous. Everyone says that ghosts like to live in big trees. The ghosts of the bodies under our hut must have moved up to it. I wonder if any of them ever drift down toward us.

~

"Not much farming is getting done because of that fort," Má says to my sister on the boat on the way down to Cồn Tàu. When we get over halfway across the river, we can see a dock sticking out. It must be where they're building the fort. "Hopefully we don't get called," Má says.

I hope we do. I want to see Lành's fort.

The soldier on dock shoots his gun into the air and waves. "I saw him," Má says. "Why did he have to shoot?" She steers the boat back toward the dock. After five minutes we get there. "The tide's going out," Má says to the soldier. "We don't have that much time down here."

The soldier has his M-16 slung over his shoulder. Why do they carry their guns over their shoulders? M-16s have a nice handle on top. "You're required to put in your contribution to rebuilding the fort," he says.

"When will we get excused?" Má asks.

"That's not my decision." He waves her out of the boat.

I start to follow.

"Stay here," the soldier says.

Má and my sister and cousins disappear down the path toward the sound of people talking and shovels clanking. I wish I could see what they're doing. I take out my slingshot and scan the cheap tree branches for golden weaver nests hanging over the river. I don't see any. There aren't any mudskippers either. I lean over the boat and look at clumps of water hyacinths floating by on the muddy water.

A boat going along the far shore of the river turns and starts heading across toward us. The soldier should call them now. If they come to help, we can leave. He takes another cigarette out of a pack in his shirt pocket, lights it with his Zippo lighter, and closes the lighter with a click. I look at him, then at the boat coming toward us, and then back at him. I can smell the diesel from the boat motor. "There's a boat," I say.

He blows out some smoke. "They were here yesterday."

I slump back down. I try to take a nap, but it's too hot. A finch hops along the bushes on the shore. I get out and chase it with my slingshot.

"Stop that," the soldier says.

I put my slingshot away and wade into the water to swim.

"Stay out of the water."

"Can I at least go along the bank and look for shrimp and fish?"

He shakes his head. Before he can stop me, I run up the trail. Má and my sister and cousins dig a circular trench, piling the dirt up in the middle. Some men cut cheap trees into logs and stick them into the trench around the dirt foundation. It will take a long time for them to get anything done. Ba said, *Why doesn't the military use machinery and get it done quickly? Why make the people dislike you?* It would be fun to watch bulldozers.

Near the foundation is a tin roof on poles. Grated metal plates for building bridges and bags of concrete sit stacked inside. Sandbags surround it with machine guns sticking out. Where are the piles of grenades and mortars? Where is the watchtower with a big gun?

Some guava trees on the land next door look like they have fruit. Soldiers patrol around the edge of the clearing. They all look the same with their heavy boots and uniforms. Grenades hang from their belts on straps over their shirts. Which one is Lành? I look for someone with a pistol. Only officers carry those.

I walk to the edge of the clearing, trying to avoid the soldiers. I check to see if there are any Claymore mines sticking up around the edge or wires running to grenades before I step into the bushes. I find two crunchy guavas and step out.

A soldier comes out from under the tin roof. He has a pistol in a holster on his belt. He must be Lành. "Do you want to die?" he says. "Don't go wandering around there."

"I was looking for guavas." I guess there are grenades in the bushes.

But I didn't step on one.

Lành turns to where Má is digging. "He shouldn't be wandering around the fort."

If I shot a mudskipper with his gun, I wonder how much of it would be left.

"Lượng, go back to the boat and don't leave," Má says.

"I'm thirsty."

Má waves me toward a clay water vat. I dip the metal cup in. Then I go back to the boat and dig into our lunch supplies for the plastic bag of salt mixed with a crushed chili. I pour some out onto the edge of the boat, then cut a piece from my guava and dip it in. I don't know why Lành wants to build a fort and get attacked like before. It would be better if he had a standing face boat anchored out here. He could move it wherever he wanted.

~

My sister turns the boat to cross over to Côn Tàu. I hope the fort is done—I don't want to wait again. Waves rock the boat, and Chị Năm has to watch out for freighters. A soldier stands on the dock by the fort.

"*Ủa*, not the fort again," my cousins complain. My sister heads the boat toward the dock. Má said we should just go in and work so they don't shoot their gun and alert the Việt Cộng or hit us on accident. When we get closer to the island, the soldier waves us to come over.

"You don't have to work if you were just there," I say.

"That's only if you come down every day and it's the same soldier standing out there," Chị Năm says. "It feels like they call us every time."

There's another boat like ours tied up to the dock, but no one's in it. "We have some work for you," the soldier says.

Chị Năm and my two cousins climb out. The soldier moves off the dock to the shade of cheap trees on the bank. I grab a *nón lá* from the bottom of the boat and put it on my head to block out the sun. It doesn't help. The shadows shrink as the sun gets higher. People get into the boat next to me and leave.

The soldier leans against the tree and lights a cigarette. I think about practicing the letters I have trouble with, but I don't want him to hear me. Why does Lành spend so much time building a fort? Why doesn't he go and shoot Quý since he knows where all the mysterious misters stay? He could come in with a canoe like Five One-Eye and no one would hear him. With a fort, everyone knows where you are.

Another soldier comes down and leans next to the first one and starts smoking. I shoot mudskippers with my slingshot from the boat while they talk. I wonder what they're laughing about.

"Where do you think Six Gecko is?" one of soldiers says. "Do you think he's on the island?"

The Gecko? My sister says the Gecko is the leader of the Việt Cộng. I know Má met with him once, but I don't know why.

"I don't know," the other soldier says. "I heard he might have some new people joining him."

Whenever we see Việt Cộng at Bà Năm's or Mr. Six Soybean's house I look for a man with pockmarks on his face like a gecko. I haven't seen him yet.

The first soldier shakes his head. "You don't want to get captured by Six Gecko. He'll torture you and then kill you."

Chị Năm and my cousins walk down the path toward the dock. I head back to the boat.

"We need to hurry and eat lunch, so we can get to the farm," Chị Năm says as she steps in the boat. She reaches into a basket in the boat and starts passing out rice bowls and chopsticks.

The soldiers leave their guns against a tree and walk over. "Ê, pretty girls, where are you going?" one of them asks, stepping into the boat. Chị Mộng's older sister Chị Tám Thủy giggles and looks away.

"We need to get going before the tide changes," my sister says.

"We can help you get going." The soldier slides next to Chị Tám Thủy. I feel like I should try to protect my sister and cousins, but the men are so big.

The other soldier steps into the boat and sits on the ledge near Chị Mộng. "Why only girls in your boat?" he asks. "Isn't that dangerous?"

How do we get them out of our boat? Should I yell? Or jump out and run? I watch my sister for a sign.

Chị Năm passes out some salty pork and boiled yam leaves. I take my bowl and move to the back. Now I'm behind the soldier next to Chị Tám Thủy. He can't see me. I eat a little and then pick up the paddle. I poke it into the mud and slap it on the water. If he attacks my cousin, I'm going to take the paddle and hit him on the head.

Chị Năm scoops some rice and yam leaves into her mouth. "We have a lot of work to do," she says without looking at them.

The man next to Chị Tám Thủy starts to put his hand on top of hers. "Do you need us to push your boat out? We can help you . . ."

I put my bowl between my knees and pick up the paddle.

"I'm going to tell Lành you're harassing us," Chị Năm says.

The soldier takes his hand off my cousin. "Well, we have work to do, too." He moves to get out of the boat. The soldiers walk away.

Chị Năm lets the boat drift out. "Is Lành strict?" she calls out.

The men turn around. "He'd shoot us," one soldier replies. "He's the boss."

∾

"Do you know what's really funny?" Chị Năm says as I help her and Chị Mộng pick through water spinach and clean it for dinner. "Someone was going through our things and got their hands full of *mắm*."

"I didn't go through the *mắm*," I say. I wish they'd quit acting like it was me.

"I know who it was, and they did it in the middle of the night," Chị Năm says. "But don't tell anyone."

"I won't, but I didn't do it."

"Lành and his men did."

"What? Where?" I look at my cousin and she nods her head.

"They've been hiding around and checking our place."

"Did Lành tell you?" Why didn't I hear them if they were outside our hut? I sleep out by the kitchen.

"Yes, the last time we were at the fort. One of the soldiers told me Lành made him search the *mắm* jars with his bare hands. He said Lành was sure the Việt Cộng had guns and ammunition hidden in them. I told them, 'So you're the ones that spoiled our food. You had your dirty hands messing everything up.'"

My sister and cousin laugh. I wish I had been at the fort with them.

"He said, 'You have the stinkiest jars, how could I spoil that?' *Hì hì.* 'All those bony fish poking my hands and arms . . . My hands smelled for hours. I can't believe you eat that!'"

I laugh. "They won't do that again."

∾

The next day, we walk around the outside of the hut trying to find where Lành's men hid. "They couldn't have hid in the canal because we'd see the tracks," Chị Năm says.

"They must have been scared out there in the dark," Chị Mộng says.

Chị Năm looks at the water coconuts along the bank. "Lành said he had his men here night after night, waiting to ambush the Việt Cộng when they came. "Lành told Má, 'I know you've been harboring Việt Cộng.'"

"How did Lành know they were here?" I wonder what else he said to Má.

"Somebody must have told him," Chị Năm says. "It's a good thing we weren't hiding anything."

I point to the caved-in area where Thượng and I hid when we played five-ten. "That hole wasn't there before." Was Lành hiding there at night while we hid there during the day?

"It probably just washed out from the current," my sister says.

"It must have been where they hid."

~

In the evening, the smoke billows around us to keep the mosquitoes away. "How did Lành and those soldiers deal with all the mosquitoes when they hid in the stream?" I ask.

"I don't know," Chị Năm says. "They must be tough."

"Má, did Lành tell you where he hid?" I ask.

"No," Má says. "But it's a good thing those mysterious misters weren't around or it would have been bloodshed. The spirits under the hut chased them away and saved us."

"I know where Lành's men must have hid." I tell her about the place in the river bank.

"Ố, is that right?" Má says.

"Wouldn't ghosts get them at night?"

"Guns scare ghosts away," Má says.

When I go swimming, I slip into the caved-in place in the bank and stare out at the hut. It's better than a fort.

Stand Up for What You Believe

I look across to where the Round Fort used to be. The sawmill owners ran out of money to fill the moat in. Now the land is covered with grass and bushes. It's good Lành built his fort out in Cồn Tàu. We need one there more than we needed the Round Fort. Everyone can't hide in the city. That's what Mr. Three East says.

Across the street on the foot ferry dock, passengers start to pick up pieces of wood and big cans of gas and lard floating by. Someone yells, "Dumping." People run to their boats. I go out to Six Chicken's house on the end of the foot ferry dock and watch the small passenger ferry boats race upstream toward Đồng Tâm Navy base. The Americans are leaving the base. On TV President Thiệu said the Americans are withdrawing ground troops. We're going to be on our own, so we have to work together to fight the Communists.

I go back to playing on our porch. On the front door by our house number is the aluminum plaque Ba nailed up with thick painted letters that read, DON'T LISTEN TO WHAT THE COMMUNISTS SAY, LOOK AT WHAT THEY'VE DONE. The government decided that everyone should put plaques on their houses to show they're against Communism. Each plaque starts with ĐẢ ĐẢO CỘNG SẢN, DOWN WITH THE COMMUNISTS followed by a different saying.

When the plaques first went up, I ran around reading the sayings on our neighbor's houses. I like our saying the best. Má and Ba talked about which sign to get before Ba went to the town hall to buy it.

Everyone says that Communism sounds like a beautiful dream, but we see what they really do. It's good the government is making people stand up for what they believe.

Boats start coming back to the dock loaded with supplies the Americans are throwing out. People argue as they unload. "I already had it and you pulled it from me." "You took this out of my boat." "Is it garbage?" "Why are the Americans dumping their supplies?" "Some of the things are good, why don't they leave them for the South?"

"They're clearing out the base," a soldier says. "A lot of stuff sinks."

"How do we get the things that sink?"

Mr. Three The, the medium Bà Ba's grown son, unloads pine wood, plastic tarps, corrugated tin, canteens, belts, and clothes from a boat. He uses the wood to build a hut across the street from his mother. Then, he adds on to Bà Ba's house. Next, he makes a scaffold by the foot ferry and builds a boat out of the pine wood he collected. When it's high tide, he breaks the scaffold and launches his boat.

The next time there's dumping, Mr. Three The goes out in the boat he built and comes back with a load of canned goods to sell. He stops by our house and asks if we want to buy anything. He has expired milk in clear pouches, plywood, wood crates, and cans of chicken. The most expensive is American pâté, Spam.

Ba buys a ten-liter pouch of milk. I sit on the porch in front of our house and lift it up and drink out of the valve on the pouch. It tastes like condensed milk except it's not sweet. Ba puts it in a glass and adds sugar. Some of my sisters also get some in a glass, but my brothers drink from the valve like me. We have to finish it all before it spoils.

I ask Ba to buy more, and he buys milk in a different color bag. I drink half a liter and get sick to my stomach. It doesn't taste like the milk he bought before. "It must be spoiled," I say.

I walk with Ba across the street to Mr. Three The's hut to complain. His hut sticks halfway over the canal because there wasn't enough land.

"It's not spoiled," Mr. Three The says, "it's nonfat milk."

∿

Chị Tư is in Sài Gòn in a program for learning how to fix electronics, so I'm in charge of watering and weeding her flower garden. Each morning before I go to school, I look at the flowers. Her favorites, the pink ten o'clock flowers, are just starting to open.

Chị Tư (Huệ) fix-ing a radio.

I walk up the street and through the school gate. Men and women in white nursing uniforms move tables out to the courtyard. Shots. The teacher has us line up behind one of the tables. It's cold standing outside. In front of the line a nurse with a big syringe pushes the needle into a student, pulls it out, and then pushes it into the next. The first time I got a shot I thought they were going to push all the liquid into me. Now I know I'll only get a little bit, but I still don't like needles. A boy cries while he holds his arm out. After injecting ten kids, the nurse picks up a new syringe and starts over again.

I get closer to the front. The kids ahead of me each say their name and a man at the table writes it down. My stomach goes cold. What am I going to do when it's my turn? He won't understand me—I still can't say "L." The line moves quickly. I look for my teacher. Why isn't she here? Last year the teacher wrote our name on a card for us to hand to the nurse. The boy ahead of me moves over to get his shot. I stand in front of the man at a table. I try to make my tongue say, "La Đức Lượng."

He looks up through his glasses at me. "Phượng?"

That's a girl's name. I push my tongue to say "L." I know what it sounds like. Why can't my tongue do it? Someone behind me snickers.

"Phượng?" the man says again.

How can he think that's my name?

The nurse giving shots turns to see why the line isn't moving. The man starts to write down "Phượng" in his book.

"No." I shake my head and reach out for the pen. The man hands me the pen and pushes a scrap of paper toward me. I write my name. As he starts writing it in the record book, my teacher comes up. "His name is Lượng."

I already wrote it down. Everyone treats you like you're *đần* if you can't speak properly.

On the way back to class, one of the boys in my class starts teasing me. "No one can understand you because you talk like a Chinese."

They're stupid. Grandfather and Ba speak Vietnamese perfectly— not like some of the storekeepers in the Chinese part of Mỹ Tho whose Vietnamese you can barely recognize.

When I get home, the pink ten o'clock flowers are closed up for the day. I hate school, but I don't say anything to Má about it. She'll just tell me that I was born too early. I take a bucket made from an oil can and pour water around Chị Tư's flower garden. Chị Tư always treats me like I'm smart. But I don't need her or anyone to tell me. I know it myself, no matter what the teacher or kids at school say.

~

I lie on the beam under our table hidden by the gray tablecloth and listen to Ba and the men in the neighborhood talk about America abandoning South Việt Nam. Their legs dangle around me as they talk about the war and what they heard from the military or about President Thiệu. The men's calves are long and thin, except for Ba's. His come up from his sandals smaller and knottier.

"The Americans are withdrawing for real now," Mr. Three East says. His gun and holster show under the table. "We have to defend on our own." He's the leader of the new Civilian Self-Defense in Tân Long.

I don't think the Americans will really leave. They've been with the South for so long.

Ba curves up his toes and his knees lean forward. His calves have more hairs sticking out, too. "If South Korea can hold onto its own country without much troop support from the Americans, we should be able to hold on too," he says. "You have to be self-reliant or lose."

"We won't make it without America's support," Mr. Three East says.

But we have a big Army—a million troops—we should be able to hold off the North. And the Americans are still helping us with their airplanes.

Mr. Three East leans back to put his boots on the board under the table and pushes against me. He pulls up the tablecloth. I smile at him. He tucks his boots to the side and drops the cloth.

A few days later, Nurse Tranh, Mr. Five Fermented Beancurd, and

Vũ's father, the mechanic, come over for tea. I sit under the table and listen. The men talk about Mr. Three East taking them out to the backside of the river and teaching them how to shoot the guns he gave them. Ba doesn't say anything. It seems like the Civilian Self-Defense gave everyone a gun besides him. But Ba doesn't seem like the type of person to shoot anyone.

"If there's an attack," Nurse Tranh says, "I'm not sure how we're going to use a gun in a crowded place like this."

"Can we actually shoot Việt Cộng if they attack or will we just kill each other?" Vũ's father says.

"If I shot across to your house, Chú Tám, I'd kill you," Mr. Five Fermented Beancurd says. He built a big house on stilts across the street from us after the Round Fort closed.

"Well, now that the Việt Cộng know everyone is armed, they can't scare us with their guns," Nurse Tranh says.

Ba laughs. "When you have a gun you've taken a side."

⁓

"Ăn cơm, ăn cơm!" Má calls.

I rush to the kitchen table and grab a bowl.

"Lượng, bring this tray upstairs to Ông Nội."

I set the bowl down and take the tray from Má. I wish it wasn't my turn to bring dinner to Grandfather.

It's quiet upstairs. Grandfather must be asleep. I take each step slowly. The soup swishes in the bowl. The plates of food slide around on the tray. I hope I can set it down and leave before he wakes up. My head rises above the upper floor. Grandfather's eyes look straight out of their caved-in sockets at me. I trip. The tray drops. Food and soup spill over the stairs. Bowls and chopsticks tumble down.

I glance downstairs at Ba sitting at the table. He pinches his eyebrows together.

"Go help Lượng clean up and bring a new serving to Ông Nội," Má says. One sister gets a rag to clean up the soup. Another sister gets a clean bowl of rice and meat for Grandfather.

The rice spilled out in a bowl shape. I pick it up and put it back in the bowl. This will be my rice. I put the pork back on the plate and try to scrape the dust and lint from the stairs off, but it's too messy to save. I sit down with everyone and eat the spilled rice. I don't take any other food except some fish sauce to drip on my rice. It's my fault we have less.

Má puts a few pieces of meat in my bowl. "Lượng's too young to carry so many things."

I quickly eat the meat. When Vân spills he gets yelled at more.

~

Grandfather holds the railing with one hand. With the other hand Ba leads him downstairs. Chú Tư, my favorite uncle, rushes over to help. Even hunched over, Grandfather stands taller than my uncle and Ba.

Grandfather makes it down the last step and shuffles into the front room. He sits in a chair and talks to the Chinese doctor who has come with his wife for dinner. Instead of pajamas, Grandfather has on a white shirt and pants. Ba wears a brown blazer.

"Lượng," the Chinese doctor's wife says when I come into the room. I like that she always remembers my name. She's wearing a fancy Chinese dress. Má stands next to her in a green Vietnamese shirt and pants. I'm glad they didn't make me dress up for my uncle's visit.

Chú Tư pulls me toward him in a half hug. It makes me feel important. No one hugs in Tân Long. He smiles at me. "Lượng, are you in school now?"

"I'm in first grade." Chú Tư looks a lot like Ba, except that he doesn't have Ba's soft belly and his hair's not greased straight back. How can he and Ba look so much alike and act so differently?

"How are you doing?"

"I'm just trying not to stay behind next year." I'm glad he doesn't ask my class rank. When my aunts ask, I tell them I'm close to wearing the grade book on my head.

"You have to try. You look like a smart boy, so keep trying."

Chú Tư lets go of my shoulders and helps Grandfather to the table. Chú Tư treats Grandfather so nicely. Shouldn't he be mad Grandfather kicked him out of the house when he was a kid? Ba said Grandfather made him and his brother leave so they'd be self-reliant. But the Chinese doctor and his wife didn't send their kids away. Grandfather is just mean.

I follow them back to the kitchen. Grandfather sits in the back corner where Ba usually sits. Maybe Chú Tư will talk about what it was like living on his own when he was young. Or being in jail. Chú Tư isn't even mad about that. It wasn't my uncle's fault that people darted across the road and he hit them. People shouldn't run in front of a bus. "People died so someone had to go to jail," my uncle said. But why did he have to go to jail when he didn't want to hit them?

I lean toward the roast pig. It takes up most of the table.

"People don't like you watching them eat," Má says. "Đi. Đi."

I wish we didn't have to wait for the grown-ups to eat first. My older sisters get to stay to serve the food. Maybe they'll tell me if Chú Tư says anything interesting.

After dinner Chú Tư goes to Mỹ Tho to sleep in his car so it doesn't get stolen. I wish he'd stay and sleep upstairs with us. He says he'll take us over in the morning and give us a ride. He doesn't drive a bus anymore. Now he has his own cars to drive people in.

Chú Tư in sunglasses opening the door to his car parked on a street.

I wake up early and stand on our front porch waiting. I don't want to get left behind with my little sisters. Chú Tư hugs us all when he comes. We follow him onto a foot ferry to the park across the river. We walk along a street filled with restaurants. The smell of fresh bread comes from a bakery. My uncle walks up to a group of men standing around a car. He circles the car looking at the paint and tires, then he hands the men some money for watching it. We pile in the back seats. The smell of gasoline and fresh bread mix together. I like the smell of the engine. Even with all of us inside, there's so much more room than being squeezed on a bus. I stick my head out the window. I hope Sơn or someone from school sees me.

On the way home, Chú Tư buys some bread to bring back. When Má and Ba aren't around, he gives us each some money—more than twice as much as my parents give us for *Tết*. I hide mine in the bookcase under the altar with my cards. He goes upstairs to talk with Grandfather and Ba. My brothers and I listen at the bottom of the stairs. I creep up a few steps and peek up. Ba sits on the edge of the bed. Grandfather leans out of bed toward my uncle who's sitting on a stool. "I've heard it but I don't believe it," Grandfather says. "We fled from the Communists in China and now my son is trying to help them here?"

I hurry back to the bottom step. My uncle is supporting the Communists? But he was in the Army. We have a picture in our album of him standing next to other soldiers and a jeep, holding his M-16 in one hand like a stick.

"The Communists give everyone opportunities to excel, regardless of their background," my uncle says.

How can someone as nice as Chú Tư be with the Communists? Doesn't he know what they do?

"Maybe you can't help it because you were lured by the Communists when you were in jail," Ba says. "But you're not just condemning yourself, you're condemning your children and grandchildren."

"They'll create a better, more equal society," my uncle says.

How can people convince you to believe something just because you're in jail with them?

"The only equality you'll get is the equal ability to starve," Grandfather says. "You'll bring a famine and a curse down on your family."

Ba's voice gets louder. "The Việt Cộng terrorize civilians. They've demonstrated what their belief is."

"Both sides do terrible things," Chú Tư says.

"We ran from China," Grandfather says. "We know what the Communists did there. They took our freedom."

"The Việt Cộng disregard our freedom," Ba says. "They're just going to hurt people in the end—" He stands up. "I need some water to cool down."

Ba and my uncle start downstairs. My brothers and I hurry away. I hope Chú Tư doesn't leave early because of this.

Ba goes to his desk in the lean-to. Chú Tư sits in the kitchen. My brothers and I gather around our uncle. He tries to smile, but his eyes don't. "What are you doing this summer?" he asks. "Come visit me."

I want to visit him in Vũng Tàu. I haven't been to the ocean. I saw a picture of his house and all of the cars and vans he owns in front of it.

On the side was a junkyard with car parts and Army surplus. Someone with an American car can't be a Communist.

Chú Tư smiling with his helmet on while taking a break to eat at a South Vietnamese Army training camp.

Chú Tư points something out in a South Vietnamese Army training exercise. He has a two-way radio on his back.

Late in the afternoon, Ba calls me into the lean-to. His face is set in a frown. "Go and tell your sister to make some new tea."

When the tea is done, Ba comes out from behind his desk and sits down with my uncle. They seem friendly again, but my uncle says he's going home.

"Already?" Ba says.

I wish he would stay.

Má hears and comes out from the kitchen. "Leave the politics and spend time with your father and nephews," she says.

Chú Tư goes upstairs to say goodbye to Grandfather. Grandfather won't talk to him. As my uncle leaves Ba tells him, "When the time comes to face Communism you might decide you don't like it . . . but by then it will be too late."

I hope he'll come back. Maybe he'll change his mind.

~

I sit at the table upstairs reading. My brothers talk on the balcony about "our gun with the long clip." When I come over they stop talking. Do we have a gun? Did they see it?

On a hot afternoon when everyone else is sleeping, I walk through the house thinking about where a gun could be hidden. When I get to the front room, I stare at the top of the glass door cabinets Ba stores radios in. I pull out the drawers on the bottom of the cabinet by Chị Tư's desk and use them as steps. Then I slide the glass door open so I can climb on the wood shelves. The gun is on top, hidden by a ledge.

Chị Tư (Huệ) standing next to the cabinets in the front room. Behind her, plastic strip curtains (later replaced with seashell curtains) cover the entrance to the hallway leading back to the dining table and kitchen. The cabinets form a wall that separates Má and Ba's bedroom from the front room. Generators sit on the floor. A drill press sits on a table at the entrance of the lean-to. The striped basket on the shelf behind the coconut log pillar is a cloth-covered coconut husk for keeping the tea kettle warm. In the evening, Ba places the TV on the drill press table or Chị Tư's desk so neighbors can watch from the street.

Chapter Thirteen (Early 1972)

Inviting Spirits to Eat

Grandfather leans over the side of his bed and coughs into an empty Similac can. I thought I wouldn't have to carry the tray up after spilling, but I still do. "Ông Nội, please enjoy your meal." I bow to Grandfather and wait for him to tell me to set the tray down so I can run downstairs and start eating.

It sounds like he's trying to bring something up from deep inside his lungs. It's hard to believe Grandfather was a Chinese doctor. Má says he rode like a lord on a white horse to see his patients. He came to live with us after he fell off his horse and couldn't work. Má talks about Grandfather with her sisters when they visit. As they knead clothes in a washing tub behind our house, Má tells how Grandfather had a fish sauce barrel full of opium balls in his house. Each ball started out honey-colored, but it would turn black after he smoked it and he'd save the black balls in the barrel to resmoke. "When we first married we had nothing," Má tells her sisters. "He sat there with all those opium balls each worth the same as gold—if he could have given us just one to help us out before he smoked it away . . . Now all that's left is a cough."

Grandfather spits yellow-green into the empty can from his toothless mouth. I wish he'd stop coughing so I could go down and eat. Má says the drugs consumed him and he's spitting out all that's left. Sometimes when one of my aunts is alone with me, she'll say, "Your family wouldn't have to struggle so much if your Grandfather wasn't such a heartless person—look what he did to your uncle, he kicked him out when he was only twelve years old so he'd have more money for his drug."

Grandfather pulls himself straight up on the pillow and points to the coffee table by his bed. "Set it there."

Ông Nội (Grandfather Lưu).

I set the tray down by the radio and hurry downstairs. My brothers and sisters start eating when they hear my feet on the steps. I wish Má would let me fill my bowl ahead of time. I grab a bowl and pack rice into it as hard as I can before I pile food on top—it's the only way I can get enough rice before everyone takes seconds. Ba is the fastest eater—he always gets two. Vân is the second fastest. My little sisters are happy with one bowl, so they take their food and sit out on the foundation in front of the house. But I feel hungry without a second bowl. I carve the food out of my bowl as I eat, watching who's ahead of me and swallowing gobs of rice without chewing.

Halfway through my first bowl, I rattle my chopsticks on the edge of my bowl to make it sound empty. I reach for the rice pot and smash more on top of my uneaten rice. "Stop that," Chị Tư says. "You didn't finish yet."

"But they'll take it all." I try to scoop rice in my mouth as fast as I can. Vân starts packing his second bowl down. "Quit taking all the rice," I say.

"I'm older than you—I need more."

"No more packing rice," Ba says. "You'll all be hungry unless you behave at the table."

Grandfather bangs his tin cup against the wood post of his bed. Everyone stops to listen. His bed is right above the kitchen table.

"Come up and get the rest of the rice," he says.

Vân brings Grandfather's tray down. Ba sets the dishes in front of us. "Eat."

Grandfather's spit must be all over his rice. "I'm not hungry anymore," I say. I don't want to get whatever disease he has. I'd rather find some green bananas afterward.

No one else will eat Grandfather's rice. Ba holds Grandfather's bowl up to his mouth and pushes the rice in with his chopsticks. "Every grain of rice you leave in your bowl will be a maggot to eat in the afterlife," he says.

I don't leave rice in my bowl.

The next time I bring Grandfather his tray, he says he's not hungry.

"Please eat before us." I set the tray down and go downstairs.

After a short time, Grandfather calls for us to get his tray. Ba tries to get us to eat the leftover food again, but no one will.

The next day, Grandfather sends the tray down right after Thượng brings it up. "Ông Nội says he didn't touch it. He says not to send up food unless he asks for it."

~

After dinner everyone comes out to the front of their houses and sits along the edges of the path like birds lined up, talking and watching people meander up and down. A gray bird swoops down and lands on the wood railing of our balcony. It's dark, so it's only an outline with tufts on its head. It tilts its head down. *Cú cú.*

"An owl," a man from up the street says.

It's smaller than I thought, like a bantam chicken.

The man looks at me. "It's an omen that someone in your house will die."

"Who? Grandfather?" He hardly eats and when he does ask for a meal, it seems like he only breathes the vapors like the ancestors we leave food for on the altar.

"It could be anyone," the man says.

I think about Má going out to the countryside all of the time. "But Grandfather is the sick one." If someone is going to die it couldn't be anyone else . . .

Ba goes up to the balcony and opens the doors. The owl flies away.

"You're not supposed to chase them away," the man says. "It won't change the omen, but it might make you unluckier."

In the middle of the night I wake up to a soft *cú cú*. The owl. The door to the balcony is closed, but I know it's on the railing. A faint light comes through the cracks in the wood of the door. The moon is only a sliver. *Cú cú*. What if the omen's not for Grandfather? What if it's for Má and she goes missing like my aunt? Grandfather coughs in his sleep. The omen must be for him. But what if he becomes a ghost and he knows everything my brothers and I thought or said about him? What if he knows what Má says about him to her sisters? He might decide to go after her.

A few days after the owl, Ba goes next door to get Nurse Tranh. They carry Grandfather downstairs to a bed in the lean-to, and Ba sends for the Chinese doctor. Má calls us all in to say goodbye. I stand in a line with my sisters and brothers around the bed. Nurse Tranh talks with the Chinese doctor while Grandfather leans his head over the side of the bed and tries to spit. His neck looks small and white. Strands of hair barely cover his scalp, but his gray eyebrows stand out as he coughs. They're long, like a Kung Fu master's. "The children are here," Má says.

Grandfather spits some pus and blood into an empty cookie tin on the floor. He sits up and looks at us. "Be good students and obey your parents." He coughs. "Grow up and make your family proud."

His eyes look more sunken than usual. I try to stand back—I don't want to catch his sickness. Grandfather stops talking and lies back. Má tells us we can go.

My brothers and sisters leave, and Má goes back to the hospital. She's still bleeding from the baby. I stand back against the plywood wall. I want to see what it's like to die. I see bodies float down the river all the time and people lying in coffins at funerals with their arms folded on top of their chests looking nicer than they did in real life. I want to see what happens for them to get that way. I want to see what happens to their soul when it comes out.

Ba sits in a chair in his shorts and T-shirt next to the head of the bed. Nurse Tranh undoes the latch on his black medical bag and pulls a cuff out. He puts it around Grandfather's arm and bends over to take his blood pressure. "He's very weak." He drops his stethoscope around the collar of his blue short-sleeve shirt.

"Shouldn't my brother be here already?" Ba looks at his gold watch. "I sent the telegram at dawn."

I want Chú Tư to come. He'll be sad because Grandfather is dying, but I hope he'll still give me a shoulder hug and a smile. I want to be like him when I grow up except the part about believing in Communism. I don't know why he believes it, except that people say it sounds like a beautiful dream.

"When Thạch gets here—" Grandfather stops and takes a breath. I move closer to try to hear what he's going to say about my uncle. "He has to promise to give up this craziness he believes in . . ."

"He'll be here soon," Ba says.

I hope my uncle comes in time. If Grandfather can't convince him, I don't know who can. But if you kick your son out of your house, I'm not sure he'll listen.

"I'm so tired. You have to take my place when I'm gone, Chan . . ." Grandfather's breathing gets harder. "You have to get Thạch to promise . . ." He whispers something in Chinese.

"Keep talking," Ba says. "Hold on a little longer."

"I'm so tired . . . too tired to wait." Grandfather closes his eyes.

"Keep talking." Ba taps Grandfathers shoulder. "Keep talking, don't fall asleep." He gently shakes him. "Wake up." Ba turns to the nurse. "Can we get him something to keep his death back a little longer?"

Nurse Tranh shakes his head. Grandfather's chest hardly rises with each breath.

The Chinese doctor takes his glasses out of his shirt pocket and puts them on his round face. He leans over Grandfather and puts his fingers on both wrists to take his six pulses, three on the left, three on the right. "He has very little time. The only possibility is . . ." The Chinese doctor's black eyebrows rise above the gold metal rims of his glasses.

"What?" Ba asks.

"Well, if you were an addict you can sometimes stretch out your death if you take your drug again."

Ba puts his hands on Grandfather's wrist to feel his pulse. Then he checks Grandfather's neck. He reaches into the pocket of his shorts and hands Anh Chín Phát a wad of money. "Go. Buy some."

Where did Ba get that much money? Is he going to spend it all on drugs? Anh Chín Phát puts the money in his front pant pocket. He stands looking down at his sandals.

"Ask anyone in the market—they'll know where you can find it," the Chinese doctor says.

Anh Chín Phát walks out looking at his feet. I wouldn't want to try to buy drugs. What if he gets caught?

Ba looks at his watch. "How long does it take to drive down from Vũng Tàu?"

A half hour later, Anh Chín Phát returns with two packets of twisted wax paper. I thought drugs would be harder to get. Everyone huddles over the packets. I stay pressed against the wood wall, hoping they won't notice me and tell me to leave.

"You can't give him that," Nurse Tranh says. "He can hardly breathe—he won't be able to smoke. If you're going to give him anything, it has to be something I can inject."

"I could only find a little opium to buy," Anh Chín Phát says, "but someone told me that marijuana would be just as good."

"That's not strong enough," the Chinese doctor says. "See if you can get some heroin in the city."

Ba nods. He looks at Anh Chín Phát. "Hurry. We don't have much time."

I go to the kitchen to eat lunch and then swim in the river to cool down. I come back when Anh Chín Phát steps off a foot ferry. Inside the lean-to, my cousin pulls three clear vials out of his shirt pocket like the ones penicillin comes in. It looks like they're filled with white powder, but I can't see through the backs of the grown-ups. Nurse Tranh takes the vials.

Ba looks at the nurse. "Is it heroin?"

"It looks like it," Nurse Tranh answers. "This stuff is bad. It will knock him out, not wake him up. Let me give him some morphine to help him relax into peace."

"We need him to wake up, not put him to sleep," Ba says. "We need to try. If we can just keep him alive until my brother comes."

Nurse Tranh looks at Ba and then turns to load a syringe. What will the drug do to Grandfather? Má and Ba say drugs destroy your mind. The nurse sticks the needle into the inside of Grandfather's elbow. His bare arms are so skinny it's easy to see all the veins running down them. The nurse pushes the plunger down slightly and takes it out. Grandfather doesn't wake up.

"You barely gave him any," Ba says. "Give him the whole dose."

Nurse Tranh puts the needle back in and presses the plunger down. He pulls it out and stands back. Grandfather shakes. His body bows. He kicks and twists his arms with his eyes still closed. "Hold him down," the nurse says. "Hold him down."

Ba holds Grandfather's head and the nurse holds his arms. My cousin and a neighbor try to keep his back from arching. His legs flail in his white pajama pants. "Help keep his feet down," one of the neighbors says.

I grab Grandfather's foot. Even with everyone holding him down, he thrashes. But he doesn't open his eyes. The veins on his temples stand out like they're about to burst and spurt blood. Foam appears in the corners of his mouth. His yellow toenails push out of my hands. I lean my whole body onto his foot. His legs are bones with no muscle. How did he get this strong? What if he dies and becomes a super ghost—one of the spirits that's not just air, but can reach out and grab you? His foot stops pushing against me. He opens his toothless mouth and bloody mucous comes out. Nurse Tranh lifts up Grandfather's eyelids. There's nothing but white. He moves his fingers to Grandfather's wrist and the eyelids drop.

Grandfather draws air in and out slowly. His breath flutters at the end as if he can't finish. Is he dead? His chest barely rises. The nurse keeps his fingers on Grandfather's wrist. When is a person finally gone?

Nurse Tranh puts his hand under Grandfather's nose. "That's it, everything's stopped."

Ba moves to lean over Grandfather. "Wait," Nurse Tranh says. "The body was moving so much—give it a moment." Everyone stands silent, watching the body. Grandfather lies straight with his eyes partway open. His eyes are cloudy, but the pupil shows through. He's so still. Will his soul do anything to us before it leaves? Souls stay around when you die. It's not until the family opens the grave door three days after the burial that the soul knows it's dead. Before that it's lost. I check Grandfather's fingertips, toes, and hair for a sign.

Ba picks up the vials. "We shouldn't have given him the drug."

Grandfather had so much strength before he died. What would he have done without all the people holding him down? Would he have gotten up and grabbed us? I thought a dying person would just drift away.

Nurse Tranh looks at everyone. "You can't give someone a strong drug like that when they haven't had it for so long. His body was too frail to handle it." He turns to Ba. "My sincere sympathy for your loss."

Tears stream down Ba's face. He closes Grandfather's eyes and says something in Chinese. Ba straightens out his father's strands of gray hair, pushing them off of his forehead and behind his ears. Then he leans over his face, passing his fingers through Grandfather's long eyebrows.

After the body has rested, Ba tries to fold Grandfather's arms on his chest so his fingertips touch. They keep falling back down. A neighbor comes over and helps bend them up. Grandfather lies in his white T-shirt and white pajama pants while people come in and out to pay respect.

The Chinese doctor's wife comes in and squeezes Grandfather's bare forearm. His veins are completely flat now. "He's still warm," she says. She means his soul hasn't left his body yet.

An old woman says, "Make sure no cats are walking around."

Nurse Tranh shakes his head and smiles. People say if a cat crosses over the dead, they'll wake up and grab the nearest person. But if everything has stopped how could that be? Grandfather's looks like he's resting. I wonder if he's still there or not. His head leans to one side. I move to the other side so that if he opens his eyes he won't stare at me. When no one's looking, I touch his wrinkled arm. It's still warm, not like a normal person, but like someone who's cool from sleeping.

~

Chú Tư steps off the foot ferry two hours later. He doesn't hug me or anyone else. He bends over Grandfather's face. Tears fill his eyes. "Why didn't he wait?"

"The loss is yours," Ba says. "The dead have nothing to regret."

"He just fell ill," my uncle says. The tears run down his face. "How could he die so suddenly? Did you give him the right medicine? Did you get a doctor?"

"They gave him something to try to stretch his life," a neighbor says, "but . . ."

"Gave him what? What happened?"

Ba gives the neighbor a sharp look and turns to Chú Tư. "If you came sooner you wouldn't have to ask these questions."

My uncle turns away.

When no one is looking I touch Grandfather's arm again. He still feels a little warm. I look for him to make the slightest motion to show his soul is around. There's nothing.

Grandfather Lưu's funeral February 1972. Behind the coffin, Má holds Sang and stands next to Ba. In front are Lượng (now age 8), Thượng, and Vân with their younger sisters Young and Hằng. Behind them, in a row along the curtains, stand older sisters Lan (Chị Ba), Thanh (Chị Hai), Thơm (Chị Năm), and Huệ (Chị Tư). The coffin is in the front room of the house where Chị Tư's desk usually was. The curtains hide the glass cabinets.

Ba (white head covering, front) prays, flanked by Thượng and Vân. Lượng sits behind, and Má behind him. The coffin and altar take up most of the front room, so the wood panel doors are open and the family sits on the front porch and into the concrete path through the neighborhood. Neighbors gather behind to watch. Ba's friends sit having tea at a table that has been moved outside to the front of the lean-to. The gray-haired man facing the camera at the table is Cậu Năm Lộc, the ferryman. In the background, a man walks from the alley to the foot ferry dock.

Má walks behind the coffin as it is carried out to a foot ferry. Behind is the edge of the house and the lean-to. On the second floor, the outline of a wire railing around the balcony is faintly visible. To the far right, a woman sells food under a makeshift shelter for street vendors. The alley is on the other side of her. Behind the shelter is the straight trunk of a betel nut palm and the leaves of the bellfruit trees. The medium (Bà Ba) owns the wood railing in the foreground where she's drying rice paper on flat baskets.

The family in a foot ferry taking the coffin from Tân Long (left) across the Mekong to Mỹ Tho (right). The Mỹ Tho water tower, naval base, and gardens are in the background. Má sits in a flowered áo dài at the foot of the coffin holding one of Lượng's younger sisters. Ba sits toward the middle with a white cloth on his head to symbolize his grieving. Lượng and his older siblings are in another boat.

Chapter Fourteen (Spring 1972)

Buddha and the Coconut Monk

*T*ết comes two weeks after Grandfather's death. On the second day of *Tết*, Má takes all of us to the Buddhist Temple in Mỹ Tho to pray for him. After we cross over on the foot ferry, we cram into two cyclos. We pull up next to a huge concrete structure on a busy road with a crowd of people coming in and out. It doesn't look like a temple. The temple in Tân Long is behind the main road and has trees and ponds with benches where you can sit and reflect. Here, the yard in front is covered in concrete with only a few painted statues scattered around.

Má buys a package of incense from someone on the street, and we walk under a concrete arch to a two-story high wood door. There's a pile of shoes on the side. Má and my brothers and sisters toss their shoes on the stack. I worry someone might take my new sandals, so I put one gray-blue plastic *dép* underneath some city person's expensive leather sandals. Then, I go to the opposite side of the pile and do the same with my other *dép*.

I enter the towering doors. A gold Buddha stands three stories tall. How did people make such a large statue? Buddha looks sternly down, his hand stretched out as if he's ordering us to bow. Do I still owe him all those chickens? He has a rainbow halo of electric lights radiating out in circles and lines, some steadily on and some flashing like fireworks. It must be expensive to pay for the electricity. Ba hardly lets us use the small dim lights we have at home.

Statues of Buddhist saints, taller than any person, line the walls.

On a room on one side of the main hall there's the lady Buddha, *Phật Quan Ân*, who's like the mother. On the other side is a room with the fat Buddha, *Phật Tổ*, who must be the most powerful because he's the oldest. *Phật Tổ* is the one Buddha sends to defend Heaven in the Monkey King plays we watch on TV.

Má lights some incense and gives each of us a stick. "You need to offer something."

I bend down three times like we do at the altar at home. I look at Má. She's still praying, so I keep bowing. I don't mind bringing up food or incense to the hanging altar upstairs with our pictures of the three Buddhas, but I want to do it without someone forcing me. Finally, Má lets us get up. I push my incense stick in the sand in one of the emptier brass pots lined up on concrete steps in front of Buddha and move to the back wall by the door with my brothers. Má stays in front by the altar praying with my sisters. Every once in a while she turns before she bows and glares back at us. We pretend we don't notice.

Smoke from the incense streams up, following huge pillars to the roof where it collects before escaping out a square hole. At least it's not stuffy. I wander around looking for a toilet, but it's closed. Má would get mad if I left the temple, so I peer out a side door looking for a patch of grass or a tree. Everything is concrete. Monks walk around outside the temple and in the hall picking up discarded incense wrappers and food packaging.

I come back to Vân and Thượng and lean back against the wall. Má kneels on a mat with her hands together praying. People walk in with their shoulders and head bowed down. Some drop money in slots in big wooden boxes near the altar and others put offerings of food on the floor in front of the giant Buddha. Ash from the pots of incense on the steps above drops down on the food. People always bring the ripest fruit and freshly made *bánh*, but it will all be overripe and smell like smoke by the time the monks eat it or give it away tomorrow.

My neck feels stiff from staring up at the monstrous Buddha and his flashing electric aura. It's so different from the Buddha in the temple in Tân Long. There, the monks use candles for lights and the plain bronze Buddha has a serene face. He and the other Buddhist saints are human size and it seems as if they're sitting among the monks meditating on square blocks that run along the walls of the temple. Once I watched one of the monks, trying to see if I could catch him moving. I fell asleep and when I woke up hours later the monk was still there. Then someone called that it was time to prepare dinner, and he rose up as if he were sprouting out of the meditation block. He seemed to float on his robes toward the kitchen in back.

The Buddha in Tân Long doesn't seem like he minds about the chickens, but this one does. Why does Má and everyone else think this version of Buddha is alright? Someone made this statue to scare me into doing what they want. If he is a god, why does he let people use him this way? I look around at the other Buddhist saints that I've always been scared of. I think they must be just people, some fat, some thin, some men and some women, who were famous for some reason.

Má finally finishes praying. I dig my new *dép* out of their hiding spots. Instead of taking a cyclo to the ferry, we walk through a tree-lined street of French mansions with huge lawns. My brothers and I stop and paint the sky blue iron bars in front of the governor's house. Everyone always pees along the wrought iron fences because people don't see you when you face the posts.

"Đi. Đi," Má says. I try to catch up and the strap comes out of my *dép*. The base is cracked so I can't wrap anything around the strap to make it stay in.

My older sister turns around to see if I'm coming. "Lượng, why are you wearing those? You should wear formal sandals when we go to the temple—to show respect. Now look what happened."

I run, trying to catch up to my family with one sandal in my hand and one on my foot.

~

On the next day of *Tết*, we take a bus to visit a relative of Ba's who lives down toward the mouth of the Mekong. I wear my hard plastic formal sandals because Má hasn't gotten me another pair of *dép* yet. We're supposed to wear formal sandals when we visit relatives or go on a long trip anyway. I want to visit Ba's relative, because whenever she stops by our house on the way to Mỹ Tho she brings us fresh or dried *cá kèo*, my favorite kind of little fish to eat. When we get to their house, *cá kèo* swim everywhere in the canals and fields. They get trapped when the tide goes out. I wish we had *cá kèo* in Côn Tàu. Why do they have it, when we don't?

We stay overnight. My sister decides she wants to go to Phoenix Island to see the Coconut Monk on the way home. Chị Tư says she wants to find out what her future will be after she finishes the electronics program. One of Ba's customers told her the name of a fortune teller on the island.

"It's beautiful. A great place to get your picture taken," Anh Long says, offering to come with. He's the son of Ba's relative and is entering university next year. I've always wondered what the Coconut Monk's island is like. I see the iron platform and structures on Phoenix Island when we take the ferry to Bến Tre. People say the Coconut Monk's temple is full of otherworldly sculptures and flowers, like the Sài Gòn Zoo. I haven't been there either.

"You can go along, too, Lượng," Má says.

Má at Phoenix Island a year later in 1973. Behind her are some of the buildings and whimsical structures of the Coconut Monk's floating pagoda.

The Coconut Monk is supposed to eat only coconuts, but I don't believe anybody can eat only coconuts and live.

"He has his chicken-flavored coconuts," Má says, "and his shrimp-flavored coconuts."

"He eats white slices of lard and calls it coconut meat," Anh Long says. "He tells his disciples the pieces of beef he's eating are coconut skin."

We take the bus together back to Bến Bắc. When we get there, I crowd onto a boat headed to Phoenix Island with Chị Tư and Anh Long. The rest of my family gets on the ferry for Mỹ Tho. Our boat comes around the east end of Phoenix Island toward a huge platform on stilts with gold and blue painted metal towers and white arches. The Coconut Monk's family must be rich for him to have built this.

As we go around toward a dock on the other side, Chị Tư points back to a tree-covered island across the river. "Look, Lượng, that's Tân Long."

I look at the backside of the island where we live. I didn't realize the Coconut Monk's island was so close. We get out of the boat by an entrance surrounded by blue and gold dragons wrapped around red concrete pillars with pink lotus buds on top. A man dressed in faded plum-red robes and a matching cloth wrapped around his head collects admission like we're going to a show.

Lượng (age ten) at Phoenix Island the next year (1973). Behind are the elaborate pillars with blue and gold dragons wrapped around.

We wander down a walkway lined with potted pink flowers and bonsai trees toward a building. The railings on each side are metal bars twisted and painted into blue vases with yellow flowers. The concrete railing posts are yellow with large pink lotus blossoms on top. Inside the building, colorful fish swim in glass tanks. A sign says they're from all over the world. We watch the fish for a while and then walk to an exhibit of figurines arranged in shallow pits in the floor.

I stretch over the railing of the closest pit. The bottom is painted red. Figurines of people sit in a boiling cauldron while a devil pokes a pitchfork at them. Animals peel the skin off a man hanging upside down from a tree. Signs explain that there are different hells for each type of sin. A person who swears goes to a hell where devils pull his tongue out and cut it off again and again. After paying for a sin in one hell, the dead are taken to the next one. The worst hells are for people who murder.

I step away. It's so violent. I thought the Coconut Monk was about being peaceful and living off coconuts. I move over to the pit for heaven. It looks like the Buddhist paradise where people sit on clouds and lotus blossoms doing nothing all day. That doesn't seem like heaven to me. What if I want to swim and catch fish instead? They won't let you kill animals. I go back to the hell pit. For me the worst hell is the one with people frozen in blocks of ice having hot oil poured on them. I could handle one or the other but not both at once.

"You're sure looking hard at that, Lượng. Are you scared?" Anh Long asks.

"It looks like someone made it up." I don't know what happens to your spirit when you die, but I don't think it's like this.

"Maybe, but you'll still have to pay for your sins," my sister says. "Let's get going. We need to find the Coconut Monk."

We walk toward the end of the platform and lean against a railing surrounding a large circle. Men in light-gray or plum-red robes with cloths on their heads stand in rows among more pillars with colorful dragons swirling around them. A painted metal cutout of the fat Buddha standing on top of a globe sticks up from one pillar straight into the sky.

"Where is he? Which one is the Coconut Monk?" I ask.

"He's up there on his throne." Anh Long points to a gold pagoda set on top of a fake green hill. On top of the pagoda there's a cut-out picture of Buddha and Jesus standing together with a halo over their heads. On the other side of the picture are the Lady Buddha and the Catholic Lady.

I squint at a throne beneath the gold pagoda. "That small man?" He's wearing bright yellow robes and has something wrapped around his shaved head.

Anh Long nods.

He's so tiny. Maybe he does eat only coconuts.

One of the disciples brings a scroll to the Coconut Monk. The followers below take out their scrolls and read. I haven't seen so many men of active age together before. In Tân Long the men are all either too old or young to be in the Army or they're soldiers on leave. People say the Coconut Monk's disciples are *trốn lính* hiding from the Army.

A disciple swings a mallet into a huge metal bell on a platform. The sound echoes. The men bow up and down on their knees toward the Coconut Monk. Does he think he's a god?

"Let's go," Chị Tư says. We walk to the back of the platform to a row of huts made of wood and water coconut leaves. People try to sell us prayer beads, necklaces and bracelets, pictures, and jade statues of Jesus, Buddha, and the Coconut Monk. My sister stops at a food vendor and buys some *bún* for us to eat. The rice noodles here cost a lot more than in Tân Long, but they're vegetarian and bland. I want more to eat or a drink, but Chị Tư says we need to save money for the fortune teller.

Chị Tư leads us through rows of water coconut leaf huts to the shop of a fortune teller. The fortune teller wears a normal *áo bà ba* shirt. She only lets one person in at a time. Chị Tư sits across from her on the floor. The fortune teller looks a little older than Má and has a full face and poufy hair. She closes her eyes. "*Ùm ùm ùm.*"

How does she know someone's not stealing the necklaces and prayer beads for sale on the walls of her hut? I watch our house when no one's home—you can't close your eyes. She opens her eyes and acts like she's in a trance. But when she asks questions, she searches my sister's face for a reaction. She does the same thing when Anh Long has his fortune told.

"It's your turn now, Lượng," Chị Tư says to me.

"I'd rather get something to drink."

"You have to do it so you know what your future will be."

"She's a fake. I watched her. Maybe it's fun for you to spend money on it, but it's not for me."

Chị Tư and Anh Long order me into the shop. I sit down on the wood floor in front of the fortune teller. She closes her eyes. "*Ùm ùm ùm.*" The tone goes up and down like she's chanting without words. I check to see if she's peeking at the souvenirs on her wall to make sure no one steals them. Her eyes are completely shut. Maybe she listens for thieves. She stops chanting and opens her eyes. "I am looking beyond the veil now. What is there to see? I see there is a neighbor girl . . ."

I look down through the slats in the wood floor at the river and think of Thùy, the girl who lives in one of the stilt houses near the foot ferry dock. That's easy to guess—everyone likes someone.

"Tell me more about the girl who has your heart. What makes her so special?"

I picture Thùy with her short hair. I'm not going to tell the fortune teller about her. "It's the long hair all the way down her back," I say.

"Yes. That's right. I can see her long hair swinging when she walks."

I look up at the fortune teller. She believes whatever I say?

"She's a nice girl," the fortune teller says, "sweet and pretty, I can tell, and her name starts . . . somewhere toward the end of the alphabet."

I slump my shoulders to make her think she guessed wrong.

"Ô, it's on the other side of the veil . . . Of course! Her name is fresh like the morning, it has to be near the beginning half."

She doesn't know—she's only guessing. "That's amazing," I say.

"Let us now go further into the future. I see the two of you starting a life together."

What is she talking about? I'm just a kid.

"What will you be doing in your future together? You like to study, yes? Am I opening the right door?" She looks at me and I nod my head. Can't she see how brown I am and realize I spend all my time outside?

"You do well in school." I make my eyes open wider and move my shoulders up to make her think she guessed right. "Very well. Yes. I see you going to university." I pretend to be excited, but I know I won't go to university. I'll go to the Army. "Maybe even a rocket scientist or a nuclear physicist."

I could have used the money to buy a coconut or something else to drink. I stand up to leave. "I don't really want to know my future."

The fortune teller squints at me with hard eyes. "Your parents need to teach you manners."

"You're cheating. You got everything backward."

"You rude boy! Get out of my shop." She glares at my sister. "You have the most misbehaving, illiterate boy I've encountered in all my days."

"Let's go Lượng." Chị Tư pushes me away from the woman. When we get out of sight she says, "You can't say that to people in their shop."

"But she's a fake," I say. "I'm thirsty. I could have used the money to buy a coconut to drink."

Anh Long looks at me with a wide grin. "You devil. That was pretty entertaining." He buys me a sugarcane drink, but I'm still mad we wasted so much money.

Chị Tư hires a photographer to follow us around. She has me pose with her and Anh Long putting our hands on flowers or leaning against the railing overlooking the river. While we wait for our turn to take a picture in front of a fountain, I hide in the shade to catch my breath. I hope we leave before we get hungry again. I don't want to spend any of my *lì xì* on bad food.

I have to pee and don't want to go back to the stinky toilets by the souvenir stands and risk seeing the fortune teller again. I walk to an empty part of the platform and pee down the leg of my shorts through the railing into the river. I hope no one notices the sound. The toilets empty straight into the river anyway.

The waves make a hollow sound as the tide goes out and the brown, muddy water splashes around the metal poles holding up the platform. It's cooler out here. I look over at the Coconut Monk's disciples. We're going to lose the war if everyone hides here. If the fortune teller were real, I'd ask her how long the war will go on and what it will be like afterwards. If I'll go to the Army, and whether I'll come home alive. But she doesn't know anything. So I do what I always do when I want to know how the war is going—I look to see if there are any ghost bodies floating in the water. Only a few boats and clumps of water hyacinth pass by. I haven't seen any bodies for a few days. I guess the war is on hold during the New Year. Another clump of water hyacinth floats by. I wish I could sit on it and float across to Tân Long like the people sitting on lotus blossoms in heaven.

Mùa Hè Đỏ Lửa—Summer of Pouring Fire

Grandfather's spirit stays around like a shadow. If you leave your food alone for a minute, it will be bland and tasteless because his spirit ate the essence out of it. If the steam from a new pot of rice goes against the wind, his spirit is inhaling it.

Ba hangs Grandfather's picture above the bookcase altar next to the picture of Má's parents. My brothers and I take food to his spirit every evening. We set it in front of his picture, light incense, put our hands together, and bow three times. Then we invite Grandfather to eat just like we did when he was alive.

We take the rice from the altar after the incense burns out. It tastes smoky, but even with it, there's still not enough for everyone to have two bowls. I start to take the rice bowl that's a little bigger than the others. If you use it you can only have one bowl of rice because it's equal to a bowl and a half. That's enough rice for me. Instead of trying to gulp my rice down to get seconds I pile meat and vegetables on top of it and wander around behind the house by the fishpond.

But I'm still hungry after dinner. There's not enough to eat at the start of the year when there's only a little fruit to harvest. The other farmers don't have anything to sell either, so they can't afford to fix their radios. I lift off the clay cover of the rice container in the kitchen and push my fingers into the grains to find the mangoes I hid—they ripen faster in rice. We only get the green mangoes or crooked ones Má can't sell. The mangoes are still green, so I cover them up again. It's hard to hide them from my brothers and sisters with the rice so low.

I go to sleep hungry. A burst of gunfire wakes me. It's louder than normal and spaced out too far to be an M-16. Maybe someone drunk is shooting the gun Mr. Three East gave him? I turn to see if my brothers are awake. Vân and Thượng open their eyes and close them again. *Ầm!* Grenades? M-16s fire. Our side. My brothers have their eyes wide open now. We open the balcony door and step out to look for tracers in the night sky. The clanging of guns and grenades and stomping of heavy military boots comes down the street. Two of Mr. Three East's men run past us toward the south end of the island.

The door below us slides open. Ba whispers across the street to Mr. Five Fermented Beancurd. I turn to my brothers. "That first firing was an AK." The gun the Việt Cộng use.

"There was no AK," Vân says. "It was some Army guys shooting like crazy."

Ba looks up at us on the balcony. "Quiet. Get back inside."

I can't sleep, knowing there's a firefight, wondering what's going to happen next. As soon as it's light, I go outside. Ba stands in the street talking to Mr. Five Fermented Beancurd. "Only two men came down," he says. "It looks like the Civilian Self-Defense didn't sign up to fight."

Army men in camouflage uniforms walk up and down the road. They don't seem concerned. It must be safe. I drift slowly south, out of Ba's sight. Then I run down the road in the direction Mr. Three East's men ran last night.

A crowd stands in the road across the canal from an outpost. Mr. Three East and the Civilian Self-Defense put the outpost up after the Round Fort closed. It looks like a tin can with a door and window facing the road. Sand spills out of bullet holes in the waist-high sandbags surrounding it. Two Army men walk a few steps down the road, then a few steps back, talking and smoking. A boy tries to cross over the canal. "Stay put while we chase down the attackers," one of the soldiers tells him.

People standing in the road ask the soldiers. "How many Việt Cộng? What kind of guns? Big? Little?"

The two soldiers laugh. "It's a simple thing. Việt Cộng came in, shot up the side of the outpost, tossed a grenade, then got in a canoe and left." They laugh again. "The Việt Cộng almost killed themselves with the grenade. They threw it at the side of the outpost and it bounced back at them."

"What happened to the men who were in the outpost?" one of the bystanders asks. "Where are they now?"

"They got a few scratches and shot up their post from the inside." The soldier takes out another cigarette. "Good thing they didn't try to throw grenades—they would have killed themselves."

I walk farther down the road to try to see the other side of the outpost. The tin has tears in it from the shrapnel of the grenade and a spray of holes where the guards must have shot out at the attackers. Bellfruit leaves shot down in the firefight litter the ground. Mr. Three East walks around in back with more soldiers. His radio hisses. "Which of the Navy went over to the backside?" he says into the handset. "Why didn't they chase the attackers?"

I come back to the road in front. The soldiers stroll back and forth smoking like they don't have a care in world. Mr. Three East comes up to the soldiers. "These people shouldn't be here. We're still locating the attackers." He waves us away. "Go back to your houses."

The soldiers herd us north up the road to a bridge. Two more soldiers keep people from coming up from the south end of the island. A woman comes with a shoulder pole. "I have to go over there." The guards look at her. "Hurry up. Go."

I head back home to get ready for school.

～

A few days later, Mr. Three East comes to tea. I lean on the beam under the table. He's been staying in the outpost at night. Mr. Three East is brave, but his men sure aren't.

"What happened down there?" Ba asks.

"I radioed my men to meet at the outpost. Only two came." Mr. Three East shakes his head. "The rest refused. I was right there. They were supposed to run down and back me up. I had to call the Navy for support."

"I want to reinforce the outpost," he says, "but only four of my men, the ones who were in active service before, will stay at the outpost at night. The rest make up excuses. I try to show them it's safe." He shakes his head again. "The Việt Cộng were just probing our defenses. They're gone. If we act scared, the outpost will become useless."

A few days later, the outpost is shutdown. Mr. Three East says he asked the Army for regular soldiers for the Civilian Self-Defense. The

Army said no, so he consolidated his men in the town hall and does a foot patrol in the evening. "Most of my men are gutless," he says to Ba at tea. "After eight o'clock I can't find anyone willing to patrol." Mr. Three East sighs. "I can't choose the men I get. I either get rejects from the regular Army or those who pay bribes."

"Every family here has the gun the government gave them," says a veteran having tea with us. "We're all refugees from the countryside or have family in the Army. If Việt Cộng attack us, it won't be easy."

The next time Ba asks me to watch the house, I take our gun down from the cabinet. I look down the sights like I'm aiming at the enemy.

Chú Tư and his family standing next to one of his vans during a family vacation to the mountain town of Đà Lạt. His oldest son, Ngọc Anh, is sitting in the van.

When I come home from school, my favorite uncle, Chú Tư, greets me with a hug. He brought a metal swivel chair and steel case desk for Ba. He also brought binoculars, tins of Holland cookies, and cans of chicken. It's all military surplus from the Americans.

Ba and Chú Tư spend all of their time arguing about Communism. Why is my uncle so nice to us when all he and Ba do is fight? That's what I like the best about Chú Tư. He has all of these things, and he doesn't act better than everyone else like Sơn's family does. Instead, my uncle always smiles at everyone and seems so kind. Sơn's family doesn't have anything compared to my uncle, just a refrigerator and a generator.

After Chú Tư leaves, Ba complains to Má, "How can my brother believe something so stupid? Everyone getting the same money whether they work or not? My brother runs a business. He should know how hard it is."

"A lot of people believe," Má says. "They're fools."

"He's blind," Ba says. "We have to try to open his eyes."

My uncle must not really believe it. He buys things from the Americans and makes money selling them. We went to visit him in Vũng Tàu and he has an air-conditioned room with a stereo in it. He even had sweet water in his refrigerator. He can't really be a Communist.

∽

On TV we hear that the North is attacking. There's a huge firefight at An Lộc, only ninety kilometers from Sài Gòn. The neighborhood men drink tea and discuss how intense the fighting is now that America has withdrawn its ground troops. They talk about towns on the front as if they were close by, but it seems like another country to me. Everyone says An Lộc is on the verge of being lost. Why are they so pessimistic about our chance of fighting back? We should be better than the enemy. When the house is empty, I check to make sure our gun is still on top of the cabinet.

It's burning hot. I go to the foot ferry dock to search for shrimp along the bottom of the logs passengers use to walk up to the dock in low tide. Sơn sits up on the dock by Six Chicken's house watching me. I wade into the brown water until it's up to my neck and then reach down and run my hands along a log, grabbing and squeezing to find shrimp. I touch something. It feels like a cold hand. I let it go. The water is too brown to see, so I reach down to touch it again. I brush the fingers. It is a hand. Not bloated, but freshly dead.

I come out of the water covered with mud. "Ê, Sơn!" I call up to the dock. "There's a dead hand out there at the end of the log."

"No." Sơn looks down and shakes his head.

"I'll go back and check when the tide goes down." I could help bring the body up and bury it.

The mud dries on my skin as I wait on the dock. The hand felt so cold. Is that what would have happened to my body if Dì Hai hadn't saved me? If the hospital threw me out how long would it have been before I died and my body got cold like the bodies floating down the river? I wouldn't have known, anyway.

After half an hour the tide goes down. "I'm going out to find the hand," I tell Sơn.

I wade back into the water. It's only chest high now. Passenger boats come in and out around me. I search along the logs but I can't find the hand or a body.

"I told you that you didn't see anything," Sơn says.

A boat comes in, idling. As it glides past me, something grabs my legs. I stumble. I flail my arms and grab the rudder of the boat so I won't go under. I reach up for the back and hold on hoping to get towed to shore. Something pulls my legs the other direction. The boat stops moving forward and the driver and passengers look back at me trying to figure out what stopped it. The driver gives the engine more gas. Water from the propeller pushes against me. If I let go whatever has my legs will drag me out to the river. The boat pulls against me, but something drags my legs the other way. The boat won't go forward. "Let go, let go," the driver says. He hits me with the engine starter rope.

"I can't let go." The knots on the rope hit the back of my head and my arms. "Something is pulling me." I put my head down between my arms to avoid the blows. "Keep going. Keep going." If I let go, I'll drown.

The driver cranks up the engine. The boat lurches forward. Whatever has my legs releases them. My body drags behind the boat. The boat heads toward the dock and the driver cuts the engine. I glide in behind the boat for three or four meters.

The driver looks back at me. "How did you stop my boat?"

"I don't know. Something had my legs." I let go of the boat and walk in on the logs.

Sơn comes down from Six Chicken's house to where I'm climbing the ramp up to the dock. "How did you do that? How did you stop the boat when he cranked up the engine?"

"Something was pulling me out to the river." I look at my legs. I don't have any marks besides bruises on my arms from the knots on the starter rope.

"It must have been a water ghost," Sơn says.

I shake my head. Water ghosts grab you around the ankle with slimy hands and pull you straight down. I didn't feel hands. A force like a silk blanket covered my legs and held me there, dragging me out to the river.

I stay at Six Chicken's house waiting until the tide goes out eight meters past the end of the dock. I look in the uncovered mud flat for string and rope or a piece of plastic. Anything that could explain what held me down. There's a place where the soft mud was stripped away by the force of the propeller. I search for the ghost body or its hand. Only coconut logs lie in the mud.

~

There are big and small funerals everywhere in Tân Long. At tea, Ba says, "Business is good for the medium." People come with dog tags from a son or husband left in battle to check the spirits to see if he died or is being held prisoner. If the medium can find his spirit, it means he's dead. I thought ghosts decided who to talk to, like Mr. Fourth Post talked to Má, not the other way around.

When I come home from school, incense drifts out of Bà Ba's front door from a séance. In the evening, loud voices and music come out of Bà Ba's open window in the alley. I finish eating and climb the bellfruit tree, but I can't see anything. I get my brothers, but we're too scared to go down the dark alley to look in her window.

Instead, we go inside and peer out our lean-to window into Bà Ba's window across the alley. Ghosts can't get us inside our house. Through the outlines of the bellfruit tree and banana plants, flickering candles and shadows of people move across her window. Someone chants.

"Get away from there." Má stands in the door of the lean-to. "Bà Ba could have ghosts stuck to her on an invisible rope. You don't want the ghosts to see you and drag you away."

My brothers and I go upstairs to bed. Instead of lying on our mats, we look out the window down at Bà Ba's house.

~

At dinner, Ba tells me to take my food to the front room and watch our things. About twenty people sit and stand around watching the news on the TV next to the drill press. I stand near the lean-to making sure someone doesn't wander over to Ba's desk. The old men and women sit on chairs. The rest sit on the floor or stand outside on the steps. People walking by stop to watch. One of Mr. Three East's Civilian Self-Defense guards stands outside the open panel doors looking at the TV. After a while he leaves to patrol.

A talent show comes on. It gets dark and people turn on the lights in their houses. The guard comes back and smokes in the doorway. His M-16 rests on his shoulder as he leans back against the coconut pillar that holds up the balcony. I'm not sure what the Civilian Self-Defense does on patrol except show us they're here.

Đùng! Everyone turns their head toward the guard. He stares at the gun on his shoulder and runs his hand up the side of his head. I follow the barrel of the gun straight up to the balcony. The guard shot a hole in it.

Ba pushes through the plastic strip curtain covering the hallway and steps into the front room. "What happened?"

"I don't know, I don't know." The guard rubs his ear. "My gun fired right at my head."

"How did it fire?"

"I don't know, I didn't mean to . . ."

People turn back to the TV. Mr. Three East arrives. "You're supposed to be walking around patrolling," he says to the guard. "Go back to the town hall and wait for me."

He and Ba get flashlights and go upstairs to look at the balcony for damage. "I can't believe this happened," Mr. Three East says. "How did that guard accidentally unlatch the safety *and* pull the trigger?"

There's a hole in the balcony floor and another in the tin roof overhead.

A week later, the neighborhood gathers around to watch the next episode of the TV show. The same guard stops by to watch and leans on the post. *Đùng!* Everyone turns around.

"I accidently fired—" the guard says.

Mr. Three East comes down from the town hall. "I'll court martial you if I catch you watching TV on duty again."

I go up to the balcony and dig out the second bullet. I'm not going to sit up there when people are watching TV downstairs.

At tea with Ba and Nurse Tranh, Mr. Three East says, "My men don't treat their gun like their life. They're ornamental soldiers." He shakes his head.

The next time Ba tells me to watch the house in the afternoon, I check to see if the gun is still there. I hope the South has more real soldiers than ornamental ones. Maybe all the real soldiers are out on the front. I hope I can grow up fast enough to help.

∽

Passengers stepping off the foot ferry say that on the other side of the river, people have fished a ghost body out. I grab the binoculars from the altar and race outside onto our roof. With the North attacking, we see ghost bodies floating down the river all of the time. The bodies must be cold in the river. When I die, I wouldn't like to be cold like that. When I see myself dying, it's in battle, not in the river.

Usually we smell them first. A few days ago, I smelt a ghost body and came running just in time to see Mr. Three East bending its arms into a bag right across the street from our house. None of them smell as bad as the headless American body did, though.

I focus the binoculars across the river. Some men have pulled a body onto the concrete near the Navy station. It's too far away to smell. It still has pants on, but its bloated chest must have pushed off the shirt. Someone brings out a wood box. The men put the ghost body inside. One arm sticks straight out over its head and the other is bent upward over its chest.

A man puts rice liquor into his mouth and sprays it onto the body. Maybe to make it easier to bend or maybe to make it not smell so bad. He tries to bend the straight arm down and into the box. It springs up and punches him in the face. Everyone around him laughs. The man covers his face and staggers around holding his cheek.

People watching below me on the dock at Six Chicken's house laugh. "That ghost body hit him hard. *Hì hì.*"

A younger man wearing a white tank top comes up to the body. He's probably from the Navy station. He grabs the arm that punched the other man and twists the shoulder. Then he snaps the bone against the wood box and folds the arm into it. The people at Six Chicken's house stop laughing. Across the river, no one's mouth moves. The man in the tank top reaches for the other arm. People motion him away. They put the lid on the box and press the arm down to close it. The man in the tank top washes his hands off in the river.

I go downstairs to find someone to tell about the ghost body hitting the man. Chị Tư sits at her desk fixing electronics. "Dead people can't punch," she says.

～

On Sunday I go with Má out to the countryside. I'm glad to be going back to where the world is only Cồn Tàu. I can forget the war and think of eating fruit and catching fish and shrimp.

Má stops the boat at Mr. Six Soybean's hut to give him something someone sent down from Tân Long.

"I was over by your land and saw a lot of ripe fruit on the ground." Mr. Six Soybean chuckles. "You sure give fruit bats and fish a lot to eat."

"There's plenty more," Má says. "I'll try to get it today, but I'm working over here first."

"Look at my land," Mr. Six Soybean says. "I don't have more than I can farm, so fruit doesn't go to waste." It's true. It's not fun to go on his land because there's only green fruit. "You should sell some of your land and concentrate on taking care of one piece."

That's what Ba says too. I hear my parents fight about it at night.

"When my land produces it will have so much fruit that if I harvest ninety percent and let the rest rot, I'll still have five times more than you will," Má says.

Má tells us she's going to grow a forest of fruit trees so we can eat until we choke to death and still have plenty to sell. Maybe then my parents will stop arguing, and we won't have to worry about running out of rice. Maybe then we can get rid of the land in Giao Long.

～

I walk around the six strips of land in front of our hut while Má and my sisters work.

"Get in the boat," Má calls. "It's time to go home."

Why are we leaving so early? The tide is still high, and we haven't gone over to pick fruit on the converted rice paddy land yet. I grab my slingshot and hop into the boat. My sister and cousin put half-full baskets of guavas and soursops in the middle and Má starts the motor.

When we get past Ông Bà Năm's house into the bigger stream, the outgoing tide makes a fast current. Má guns the motor and yells to Chị Mộng and Chị Năm to be in front ready to push the boat off the water coconuts if it hits the bank. I move to the middle of the boat with the baskets so the cheap tree branches don't hit me. The current pushes the boat from side to side. Má sits in the back steering. Why do we have to go so fast? Why doesn't Má let the boat float down with the current? We turn sideways and careen toward a water coconut, hitting the base of its leaves. The bush shakes. "Push off," Má calls over the motor. Chị Mộng shoves us out toward the middle of the stream. Má speeds the boat toward Mr. Fourth Post's dock. It looks like we're going to hit one of the posts he used to have his fishing net strung between. Má swerves. We barely miss it. I worry we're going to hit the big cheap trees where the stream enters the main channel. Má steers around a curve past the trees, and the boat flies out into the wide channel that cuts through the island.

Má slows down in the main channel. I stick my hand in the water to watch a wave trail behind. We pass Dì Hai Temple's house. If we're not going to Dì Hai's house where are we going? Everyone on the side of the river across from Dì Hai's house is a Việt Cộng or sympathizer. Má banks the boat to the other side of the river and turns the motor off. She aims toward a group of water coconuts meant for tying up boats. She must have an appointment with one of the Việt Cộng. Everyone who farms has to do something for them.

Dì Hai Temple.

Má reaches for some water coconuts stems on the shore. "Tie the boat upstream and wait here," she tells my sister. "I need to see some people over there." Má steps out of the boat onto a dirt trail holding a package wrapped in brown wax paper inside a clear plastic bag. "If I don't come back, go talk to Dì Hai. Keep the boat moving so it doesn't get stuck when the tide goes down." She disappears into the bushes.

"Who do you think Má's going to see?" I ask my sister.

"Someone at a meeting." Chị Năm names a sympathizer who has meetings at his house all of the time.

"Má was nervous trying to be on time," I say. "It must be someone important. Maybe the Gecko?"

"Probably." My sister turns away.

The mud bank rises next to us as the tide goes out. Chị Năm sticks the bamboo boat pole in the middle of the stream and ties the boat farther out. A few mudskippers skip along the bank. I feel my pocket for slingshot ammunition. I only have a few hard, young guavas in my pocket, and I want to save them in case a bird shows up.

Chị Năm moves the boat downstream with the current. I reach into one of the baskets on our boat and find a crunchy guava to eat. After an hour, the boat drifts back in front of Dì Hai Temple's house. If Má only had to drop off a package why isn't she back? I listen for gunfire. What if Má got caught in crossfire?

"I think I should talk to Dì Hai," Chị Năm says.

Chị Năm returns with a handful of water spinach and other greens. "Dì Hai's not home, but I got some *rau*. Let's eat."

Chị Năm and Chị Mộng get out some old rice and salty shrimp, and we eat the greens with it. Then Chị Mộng slices a green mango into a bowl, and we dip it in salt mixed with chili pepper. I lean on the flat front of the boat and look down at the faded red eyes painted on the bow. What if something worse than getting caught in crossfire happened to Má? What if she goes missing like my aunt?

Chị Năm takes the pole and pushes the boat back up stream to where Má got off. The tide is getting low. Soon we'll be stuck.

Má hurries down the trail. "*Đi. Đi.* Let's go. Let's go." She walks straight into the mud toward the boat. "Start the motor."

Má hops onto the back of the boat dangling her mud-covered feet and pants over the edge. Chị Năm starts the motor. Má kicks her feet in the water a few times, reaches over to grab the steering, and pulls on the gas. "Now," she says.

My cousin stands in front and uses the bamboo pole to push the boat deeper into the channel.

Má sits staring straight past us, her mouth slightly open. She seems exhausted and unhappy. I move out of her way to the front of the boat and drag my hands in the water. When we get out to the Mekong, Má asks Chị Năm, "Why didn't you leave when I didn't come back? I was gone for so long. You could get trapped here by the tide. I could have swum across to Dì Hai's or Bà Năm's house if I needed to."

Why is Má so upset? She steers the boat across the river to the Mỹ

Tho side and starts talking to my sister about the meeting. I want to hear what she's saying, but the motor is too loud. I go to the back of the boat and pick up the scoop for bailing so I can listen. "The Liberation Front wants a lot this time," Má says. "They want Huệ."

"Really? They want Chị Tư?" Chị Năm says.

I imagine Chị Tư out in the countryside alone. My older sister who's so skinny she sleeps with a wool blanket in the summer, and every *Tết* people wish for her to gain weight.

"The Front needs her to help fix electronics," Má says. "We'd never see her again."

We reach "sunken barge spot." Má steers the boat away from the barge hiding underneath the water. I finish bailing, so I move up to the front again. The boat starts going faster because it's a slack tide. The water stills when it changes directions.

When we tie up the boat at the dock across the street from our house, it's past dinner. Ba looks questioningly at Má as she unloads the boat. "I had a meeting with Việt Cộng," she says after she finishes stacking the baskets and *nón lá* in the lean-to.

Ba sighs. "What do they want now?"

"They need help fixing radios," Má says. "We have to make sure that you and Huệ are never near an area where they can capture you."

"You should switch to a different means of making a living," Ba says. "It's too dangerous to go out there."

"A lot of people have been forced from farming, so the price for fruit is good," Má says. "I know everyone out there. If there's danger, I'll change."

It's too bad Chị Tư can't go out to the countryside anymore—I sure like going out there a lot. When no one is around, I check to see that the gun is above the cabinet. I take it down and move the safety on and off. I remove the clip, empty the bullets, repack them, and reload the clip. But, I don't pull the trigger, even with the safety on.

∽

The people reading the news on TV start to call the attack from the North "the Summer of Pouring Fire." Every night they show numbers for dead, injured, and vehicles destroyed. So many soldiers from the North come down that the news divides enemy deaths into two types: Việt Cộng and born North died South. Instead of hearing that we lost this town or that town, I like the numbers to be high. It means a big battle is happening. If there's still fighting it means that we're not losing or quitting. I want us to win and push the North back. Then the enemy won't attack again for a while. Maybe we can attack them instead.

No one can afford to fix their radios, so Ba sits around drinking tea with the neighbors all day. When I'm not in school I lie on the beam under the table listening to them. "How can we stop paying these taxes to the Việt Cộng?" Ba asks the other men. His hair is greased back with the Intine hair cream he always uses. "They squeeze you and suck your blood just enough so you don't die."

"The Việt Cộng turn around and use the money to buy guns," Mr. Three East says. "Then they point the guns at you and tell you to pay more taxes. You're giving them the rope to hang your neck."

Mr. Three East leans back. His boots hit me. He moves them without looking under the table. How can he wear boots when it's so hot? The laces look like they pinch his feet.

"Well," Ba says, "between that and abandoning our land, what can we do? If we could afford to abandon it we would, but we have a lot of mouths to feed."

"Lượng," Ba says. "Why don't you take a look and see if we have hot water?"

I crawl out from under the table.

"I thought that was a dog under there," Cậu Năm Lộc, the Giao Long ferryman, says. The men laugh.

Smoke from the fire rises and swirls out of a hole in the tin roof. While I wait for the water to boil, I lift the clay cover of the rice container. A few days ago, I walked up the street with Má to the rice dealer. He dipped a ten liter scoop into his huge pile of rice and filled our bag with a hundred liters. Now it's almost gone. What if someday we don't have money to refill it?

Steam comes out of the kettle. I walk back to tell Ba. He reaches into the middle of the table and lifts the teapot out of the coconut husk holder. The men sitting around the table gulp their tea down before Ba drains the rest of the tea into their cups. "All these Communists are ridiculous," he says. "They don't have regard for age or anything reasonable. They'll make you do anything to recruit you into helping them."

He's talking about my sister.

∾

Chị Năm comes home from Cồn Tau and tells me that the Việt Cộng ambushed Lành. They attacked him when he went to visit his family on their farm next to our converted rice paddy land.

"How many people got hurt?" I ask. Lành's mother and sisters are just farmers. Why would Việt Cộng attack them?

"People got scared, but not many got hurt," my sister says.

"Did they get Lành?"

"No. He's not that easy to get. Lành had his men stationed there ahead of time, and they had a firefight. Lành's sister got a gash from a bullet, though."

Má hears us talking. "Lành's family isn't happy," she says. "That land is their main source of income." Then she laughs. "Those Việt Cộng better watch out. Lành's going hunting."

Someday that's what I'm going to do—go hunting like Lành.

The next time we go out to the converted rice paddy land, Má takes the boat all the way into the land instead of going to our hut and walking over. She says she wants to avoid having to walk past Lành's land. I look across from our land over to his, but I can't see any signs of a fight. How can Lành's family still farm here with all the Communists around? Aren't they scared?

∾

We tie our boat up at Bà Năm's. Quý sleeps in a hammock inside. Every time I see Quý, I think that it's only a matter of time before Lành catches up with him. Lành's even madder now.

"Quý's been staying over at our place," Bà Năm tells Má when he leaves. "Whenever he comes, I just hope he eats and leaves. One of these days we're going to be in the crossfire—hopefully we don't end up getting killed."

Bà Năm says she's seen Lành's family come out and harvest fruit, so Má decides it must be safe for us to walk by his land. She sends me with Chị Năm over to the converted rice paddy land to collect some fruit.

"Don't go over there," Mr. Six Soybean says when we pass his house. "That land is probably rigged with grenades."

"We have to get there to farm," my sister says. "We saw Lành's family harvesting fruit."

"It's dangerous to be there," Mr. Six Soybean says. "Maybe Lành's family knows how to work around things, but you don't."

We keep walking. When we pass Lành's land, we stay on the path, but look around for casings and torn down trees or a Death Land sign. There's nothing. "Maybe they cleaned it up," my sister says.

There are two sides fighting, but I hate the Communists for making an enemy out of the land.

∼

I go out on the tin roof to look out at the river. The water level is lower than I've seen it. The land is rock hard and rice farmers complain that their seedlings are wilting because of the drought. I walk to the edge of the roof to get a bellfruit off the tree in the alley. There isn't much fruit, but the few pieces I find taste sweet from all the sun.

A B-52 hums above leaving a contrail. It's hazy even though it's so big. I don't know why I can't see B-52s clearly. A string of bombs tumble down like pieces of black sticky rice. A few wobble and one tumbles end over end like a Napalm bomb. They're so close together. Won't they hit each other and blow up?

I run into the house and stretch my arms out to hold the sliding glass panels on the two cabinets in the front room. They hold radios Ba's customers haven't picked up because they can't afford to pay. I wait with the glass against my palms. Ba gave me the job of holding the doors so they don't vibrate and shatter during bombings. Almost a minute goes by. A rumbling starts. Cooking pots and pans clatter *lảng cảng* in the kitchen. I stretch to hold the doors on one cabinet, then the other. The radios march toward the cabinet doors with each vibration. The plane is out plowing the countryside, digging up the dirt with bombs. It's like someone's drumming on us. If the enemy is so close that we have to bomb them here, we're in trouble.

In the evening, I go upstairs to the altar and get the Army surplus binoculars Chú Tư gave us. I open the upstairs back door and step onto the roof of the kitchen. The tin roof is cool enough to walk on now. I hang onto our TV antennae pole and climb up into the area where there's a *V* that collects water so that it runs down to our water tank. I walk up to the PROSPER GOING FORWARD RADIO AND TV REPAIR sign attached to the front of our house and sit down to wait for it to get dark.

I look down at the faded yellow of the Southern flags painted on the roof tops so pilots know not to drop a bomb here. The full moon shines across the river above Mỹ Tho. It reminds me of the documentary I saw on TV of the Apollo landing. Americans really did walk on the moon. I focus the binoculars on the dark spot that's supposed to be the moon fairy. In school we learned how far away and large the moon is. Those spots couldn't really be a fairy—if they were, she would be huge.

An airplane appears that looks like it's shooting a red line down at night because of the tracers. When these kind of airplanes come out, people say the cows are mooing because when it fires that's what it sounds like, *ngò* . . . American ground troops have pulled out, but as long as they're still on our side with all their airplanes we'll be alright. It seems like America can do anything.

~

At school I lie with my head on my desk. My tooth throbs. I suck on the hole in it to make the pain shoot up and when I stop it doesn't seem as bad. Má says to wait until summer, and she'll take me to the free clinic. When I get home, I go to the daybed under the stairs and lie down. I reach into my mouth and feel the hole. If I wait long enough it will fall out, then it won't hurt. Lots of people are missing teeth. Before bed, I go out to the canal to brush my teeth—we haven't gotten rain yet to fill up our water tank. I put some toothpaste on my finger to brush and pick at the hole. The next morning the right side of my face turns red and swells up. I don't want to eat. Má says she'll take me to the clinic in Mỹ Tho tomorrow.

Má wakes me up at four the next morning, and we walk to the foot ferry. We get to the Mỹ Tho Hospital before five o'clock, but the line already stretches to the gate of the courtyard. The line grows into the street behind us. Má buys some sticky rice from one of the vendors selling food in the courtyard. I chew it on the other side of my mouth while we stand in line with mosquitoes biting us. After two hours, we get to the concrete entrance. After another half hour we make it onto the linoleum floor in an off-white hallway filled with patients in portable beds. Mosquitoes hover around the patients. One lands on me. I slap it. What if it bit one of the sick people before me? Will I get whatever sickness they have?

We get to another hallway with a long wooden bench running

down one side. Má sits on the bench to wait for our turn. I wander over to a garden area between the hallways. Moans come out of a room. The sound rises up and up, like someone is in so much pain he should be dead already. A nurse walks into the room. "Try to be quiet. You don't want to wake everyone else—they need to rest."

She comes out and talks to another nurse. "These patients need to be in a cold room. The boy in there has a wound from bomb shrapnel. We're not setup for war injuries."

The wails quiet for a few minutes then gradually rise up again. A boy murmurs, "It hurts, it hurts." He must be the one injured by the bomb.

I go back to the bench and sit next to Má until I get called to stand in a line for a numbing shot. There's another line for the dentist. When I get into the dental chair the clock on the wall points to nine thirty. Metal scrapes against my bone as the dentist digs into my jaw to get the tooth out. The dentist sends me back for more numbing medicine. I don't think I need it. The digging doesn't hurt as much as the pain my tooth has been giving me. When I come back, two doctors with sweat on their forehead dig into my bone, pressing down on me with metal tools. I feel like my skull is being dug out.

When they're finally done, I walk out with a big piece of gauze in my mouth and my face numb up to my eye. Before I find Má, I wander past the garden area and look into the open door of a small room. A boy a little older than me lies face down on a mat on a gurney. The flesh on his rear is completely gone. Part of the bone sticks through blood and yellow pus. A woman next to him shrieks like she's a ghost. The boy cries softly. A bullet or a grenade couldn't have done that to him. It must have been something big like a bomb.

I walk down the hall to the next open door. It's larger and packed with more people lying on gurneys. "You can't be here," a nurse says.

I go back to the bench where Má is waiting. "The sound of that digging on your tooth was scaring everyone out here," she says.

It wasn't anything compared to the boy. What would I do if a bomb fell on me? Where would I run?

Pillars from the Sky

We sit around with our rice bowls eating dinner. "Did you know that Tám Quý got ambushed by Lành?" Chị Năm asks.

"Why didn't anyone tell me? Is Quý dead?" I knew Lành would get Quý.

"No," Chị Năm says. "But the mister with Quý was killed. In the canal right outside Bà Năm's house. Quý only got shot in the butt. *Hì hì*."

"How could Quý run away if he got shot?" my brother asks.

Wouldn't the bullet go through his bones and shatter his legs? I think of the boy lying in the hospital. All the soldiers say M-16 exit wounds tear you up. Wouldn't Quý look like that? Guns must not be as powerful as I thought.

"I don't know, he's slippery," Má says. "Once he gets into the stream he's like an otter. Poor Ông Bà Năm. Their hut got shot up with them inside it. Bà Năm has bad luck. If anything bad happens, it happens to her."

I imagine what Bà Năm's hut looks like. "Can you see bullet holes all over the hut from the firefight?" I ask.

Má shakes her head. "No. Only a little around the window."

I don't believe it. If Lành and his men attacked, Bà Năm's hut has to be shot-up more. When I go out to the countryside again I want to look.

⁓

Once school gets out, Má takes us down to Cồn Tàu where it's cooler and we can catch our food. Ba and Chị Tư stay in Tân Long fixing radios. On the way down, there aren't any patrol boats keeping the river safe. Old queens and B-52s fly overhead, and M-16s fire in the distance. "It's comforting to hear the sounds of Southern guns," Má says.

When we pull into the stream that cuts into the island, the trees block our view of the planes. Má steers the boat past Ông and Bà Năm's hut. Why didn't we stop? I want to see what happened to their hut in the firefight. "Is Bà Năm around?" I ask. "Can we go visit?"

"They're not there." Má looks at Thượng and me. "You stay away from there."

Thượng and I take turns asking if we can visit Bà Năm. We want to find the spot where Lành stood when he shot Quý from across the fishpond. But Bà Năm and Ông Năm are always gone.

Finally, Má says we're going over to bring some *bánh* over to Bà Năm. Thượng and I look at each other. Now's our chance. When we walk up, I check to see if there's a big hole anywhere in Bà Năm's hut. The bamboo window frame is splintered and the wood panel that's usually propped open with sticks is missing, but there aren't any holes in the side. The water coconut leaf walls must have swallowed the bullets.

"I keep having nightmares," Bà Năm says putting a big wad of betel into her mouth. Má and my cousin and sister sit next to her on the daybed. Thượng and I sit on stools. The hammock that used to hang above the daybed—Quý's favorite spot—is gone. I used to nap in that hammock, too.

"I see Binh floating face down in the canal with his body full of holes, oozing blood." Bà Năm looks over at the door by her bedroom and chews her betel. "Lành's men left him there in the canal right outside our bedroom window. I don't know if his spirit is around or if it followed his body when the other misters came that night and took it."

Bà Năm shudders. "I'm glad he wasn't killed inside or I'd be too scared to stay here." She sticks her head out of the window and spits. "It was so close. As soon as I walked back to the kitchen to help Ông, I heard *Ầm! Ầm! Ầm! Ầm!* Four grenades went off."

"Lành was probably holding back," Má says, "waiting for you to get out of the way."

Bà Năm sighs. "We saw Quý jump out of the hammock and get

sprayed in the butt."

How could Lành miss if Quý was lying down?

"Where is Anh Năm?" Má asks. We didn't see Ông Năm out working on the land.

"Ông went to Quới Sơn to stay with our daughter," Bà Năm says, "but someone has to harvest the fruit."

Bà Năm starts talking about her son in the Army. He doesn't like his parents being out in the countryside with all the Việt Cộng around. Thượng and I walk out the front door.

"What are you doing?" Má calls after us.

"We're going to the bridge." We head toward the bridge, the outhouse over the fishpond, but swerve away before we get there to look for boot prints and casings. The water coconuts on the side of the fishpond near the house have broken leaves. Some of the coconut trees have nicks from bullets and shrapnel. Dark red clumps of chewed betel lie everywhere around Bà Năm's house. Wherever the mud looks darker, it's probably from Bà Năm spitting.

We get to the side of the fishpond where Bà Năm grows red canna lilies to sell for decorating altars. "I think Lành hid here." I pick up an M-16 casing next to a tangerine tree and hold it up to my lips and blow. It still smells like gunpowder.

"How could Lành miss Quý with all those grenades and guns?" Thượng asks, picking up a casing.

"I don't know." I walk back inside blowing on a casing.

"Where did you get that?" Má asks.

"Over where Lành was shooting."

"Don't go looking around over there. If the Army sees you, you could get shot. If the Communists see you, you could get shot."

The next time we visit Bà Năm's land, she's chopped down all the water coconuts around her fishpond. The banana plants in front of her door are gone. Má and everyone else told her to clear her land so no one can hide there. Now everyone can see straight out her hut to anyone sitting in the fishpond outhouse. I liked the way it was, wild and alive, not clean and lifeless. It's hard to be a farmer if you can't grow anything.

Whenever we tie our boat at Ông and Bà Năm's, we take the path around their hut instead of the short cut through it. We leave our extra baskets in our boat instead of with them. No one wants to be around Ông and Bà Năm's hut, when they're not home. It feels like death.

On the way back from getting supplies in the city, Má ties up the boat near some paddle weeds and a cheap tree by Dì Hai Temple's house. "We're going to meet somebody," she says.

Two men in a canoe glide out of the weeds. Another canoe with three men follows. The man in the middle is darker and has a pocked face. He wears the Việt Cộng's checked scarf around his neck. Is he the Gecko? The canoe with two men moves to the front of our boat, while the canoe with the pocked-face man pulls up to the back. What does he want?

"Go to the front of the boat," Má says. She talks with the pocked-face man. From the front, we can't hear what they say.

"Was that Six Gecko?" I ask when we get back to our hut. Má must have given him something. I think of how upset Má looked when the Gecko asked for my sister to work for him. If you don't give the Việt Cộng your kids, you have to give them something else.

"Yes. But never call him that," Má says. "If he hears you, he'll get upset. His name is Six Stone Brave."

I nod. But when Má isn't around, Chị Năm and I call him Six Gecko. It makes him seem less scary, more like a neighbor like Mr. Six Soybean or Aunt Curly.

It's so dry that we carry water from the canal to the trees. Because of the drought, the canals are low and easy to fish in. At twilight I drag Thượng along with me to put out the poles I made of sticks and fishing line. He hates getting wet wading through canals and coming home hungry, with nothing to eat. Vân only went fishing with us once. Má sent him back to the city after Aunt Curly and Mr. Six Soybean asked, "Isn't he a little old to be out here?" The Việt Cộng might recruit him.

"Don't go there," Mr. Six Soybean calls out when he sees me and Thượng heading over to Lành's land with a stack of fishing poles. "Both sides are stalking around over there. You could end up caught in the crossfire."

"We're going to put the poles on your land," I say.

"Well, stay away from Lành's land. It could have been rigged with grenades."

We put a few poles on Mr. Six Soybean's land. Then we go across the canal to Lành's land. We have a lot of poles to set and need new places to fish. If I don't see a Death Land sign, I'll walk there.

~

When we stop by Bà Năm's hut, Six Gecko is there with his bodyguards. The bodyguards push me and my sister and cousin into the corner. Má stands in front of him.

The Gecko asks Má about everyone in our family by name. He knows that Ba and Chị Tư fix radios and my older sisters are in boarding school. He looks over at Chị Năm. "Your daughter is growing up."

Má answers nervously. It must have been the Gecko who asked for Chị Tư.

After he leaves, Má says. "Six Stone Brave keeps track of everyone. He wants you to know that you can't get away with anything."

"He's scary." Bà Năm shudders. "He's killed a lot of people."

Má shakes her head. "I'd rather deal with him than Five One-Eye or Fort Hag. When he says he'll do something, he will."

"I don't know," Bà Năm says to Má. "Six Stone Brave is high-up and conducts a lot of meetings. A lot of people die."

"Well, if I get invited by him, then maybe it's bad," Má says, "But no one can invite me to meetings without his say now."

Chị Năm whispers to me, "Five One-Eye and Fort Hag are the ones who tried to kill Má. Five One-Eye invited Má to a meeting and put her on trial."

"When? Why?"

"A long time ago. Fort Hag was accusing her. We all know Má didn't do anything wrong."

I knew Five One-Eye was a killer, but why would anyone put Má on trial? All she does is farm. I don't worry about Má. If the Việt Cộng had wanted her dead she already would be. And Lành is starting to get more control.

~

I keep fishing on Lành's land. Lành's family hasn't been taking care of it since the ambush, so the grass has grown thick in the canals and that's where all the snakehead fish hide. The mature tangerines have shrapnel and bullet wounds on them and the betel nut trees are shot-up. There are basket-size holes in the mud from grenades. I pick up some M-16 casings and wrap them in my shorts. In the morning, when my brother and I go to pick up the poles, we run into a couple of misters. They see us and leave. One of the misters comes back with Fort Hag. "Quit fishing over here," she yells.

Lành should get Fort Hag. That would shut her up. When I come back later, half of my poles are missing. Then Má sends Thượng back to the city. He's too old to be out here now.

～

A mister walks in the distance hunched over. He's going west toward the coconut grove. Má warned us not to go there because that's where the Việt Cộng base is. "Be careful. Don't let the Việt Cộng catch you and force you to become one of them. Then you can't come back," Má always says. But I don't think they're interested in me. While I wait for the mister to disappear, I step into the canal and spread the milfoil out so I can stick my pole in.

The next time I go, I only have time to place four poles because a group of misters are creeping along the path. We used to see them walking around in the day, but now I only see them toward night. Bà Năm, Aunt Curly, and Mr. Six Soybean say it's because Lành's been attacking the Việt Cộng to get revenge. Everyone talks about him beating a pregnant woman with his rifle because she and her husband helped in the ambush on his family's land. Her baby came out stillborn. "Lành's name means peace," Má says, "But he makes silence instead of peace."

The Communists own the countryside, but Lành is taking it back. I feel like our side is winning, that we don't have to be afraid all the time. I hope Lành gets his revenge so I can fish without those mysterious misters bothering me, but Má sends me back to the city before the summer is over. She says it's not safe anymore. When we stopped by Mr. Six Soybean's hut some North Vietnamese were there with the Việt Cộng. People whisper they're hiding after losing a battle. The South is beating the North back.

～

Ba makes us take a nap before lunch every day. If we don't, he won't give us money for lunch. I lie down in the daybed that's under the staircase by the kitchen table. I try not to fall asleep too deeply so I can wake up in time to buy tofu with ginger sauce from the street vendor. I drift to sleep and dream of pillars falling from a gray sky. They're enormous, much bigger than I am. One is right above me. I run to get away. The giant column hits the ground and crumbles. As soon as I escape, there's another. I keep running, but they're falling from the sky everywhere. There are no trees or houses or people. Just pillars. I can't stop to catch my breath. There's always another one about to crush me. I can't rest for even a moment before the next one comes. I jolt awake, covered with sweat. There's a rumble. Pans in the kitchen clatter *lảng cảng*. The B-52s are plowing the countryside again. I get out of bed and run to the front room to hold the glass doors on the cabinets.

When school starts, I sit in the middle of the classroom. I don't feel as lost in third grade. The teacher gives us a week to draw a teapot. After school every day, I sit in the front room at the table and look at the teapot we use to serve customers. I try to draw the outline, but it doesn't look right. I end up erasing again and again until I have holes in my paper.

By Sunday, I still don't have a teapot. It's due the next day, so when I go to Giao Long with Má, I take a notepad and pencil along. The bomb is gone now. I'm glad. Even though I knew it could blow up, I couldn't help spinning the dial. Má said that the propeller on the teacher's boat hit it and it exploded. The teacher wasn't hurt because he had the kind of boat that steered in the front. If our boat had hit it, Má would be dead.

While Má works, I sit on the boat in the canal, trying to stay under the shade of the coconut tree, drawing and redrawing. I tear up a lot of pages, but I'm finally happy that my picture looks a little like Ba's teapot. I trace over the pencil lines with a pen and sign my name.

I put my notepad back in a plastic bag and wander around looking for some fruit to eat. The only trees that have guavas are near the Death Land sign. The sign is still here. I look over the tangerine branch barrier at the land behind it. I don't like that a sign can take away someone's land. I go back to the boat to eat the guavas and practice saying "*L*." It's the only letter I still can't say, but my name starts with it.

The next morning, I put my drawing on the teacher's desk. My picture doesn't look as nice as Thượng's drawings, and the paper looks fuzzy from all the erasing, but it looks like a teapot and has a lot of detail in it. I should get at least a B.

The teacher stands in front and pages through our work. She looks at mine. "Lượng, get up here. This doesn't look anything like a teapot—this looks like a failing grade."

I walk up and stand in front of her. How can it be failing? I tried harder than I've tried before on homework.

The teacher shows the class my picture. "Look at this teapot. It's so ugly." She looks down at me. "You didn't even try."

"I did." I don't care that she thinks it's ugly. I care that she thinks I didn't try.

"You couldn't have. This shows no effort. Stick out your hands."

I stick out my hands. *Quíc!* She hits them with a long, thick strip of wood.

"Go kneel over there." She points to a spot on the concrete floor. I kneel down in front of the class. She hits me with stick. The other boys in class snicker, especially Cường, her favorite.

❧

On TV we see bombs falling everywhere. They're bombing the North. The planes are so powerful. A rain of force comes down like from a god. The Buddhists say we should make peace. Military analysts say we should end the war now by attacking. Every night I dream I'm running from falling pillars. I have to move constantly, looking at the sky or one will hit me. I run all night and feel more tired in the morning than when I went to sleep. I have a hard time staying awake in school. If I wasn't busy trying to keep up copying down the lesson from the board to my notebook, I'd fall asleep at my desk.

After school, Sơn asks me to come over. I haven't been inside his house before—I've only stood in the door and waited for him to come out. We stand around his father's pool table. "Why does the table have holes in it that the balls can fall in?" I ask. The tables at the neighborhood pool hall don't have holes.

Sơn shrugs. "You try to get the balls in them. My father told me that's how they play in America."

He takes out the pool sticks. We start to play. I try to avoid the holes. Sơn insists we need to try to hit the balls into them. "Why are there so many extra balls," I say.

Every shot I make, Sơn worries about the felt getting roughed up. His mother comes into the front room. "Stop that or you're going to ruin the table."

We put the sticks away and push the balls around with our fingers. For a little bit of money we could rent a table at one of the neighborhood halls and have fun.

We go over to his father's bar. The little refrigerator isn't running. Liquor bottles sit on the bar. Why does his father have so many kinds of liquor, but no sweet water? The counter is dusty and the sink is dry like it hasn't been used in a long time. I haven't seen his American father around for a while. I think he's an officer, but I've only seen him a couple of times, and he wasn't wearing a uniform. People talk about whether Sơn's family will go to America when all the troops leave. But Sơn doesn't talk about it, and his father doesn't talk to anyone.

Sơn opens a cupboard just a little, like he's scared of getting caught. It's full of canned vegetables and meat. The labels are in English. "This one is pork, this is chicken, and this is beef," Sơn says. "When Ba comes he gets a lot for us."

"Where does he get it all?" The only canned food we eat are the Moroccan sardines we bring along when we farm.

"He bought it from a store for Americans."

"Can we try some?"

"No. Má would beat me up."

Sơn opens the door of the big refrigerator. It's stacked with yogurt and milk. He takes out a canister and opens it and gives me a small handful of raisins. I eat the raisins one by one, all eight. The cold makes them taste even better.

The next day, Sơn calls me over and offers me a raisin from his curled up hand. It's cold. Straight out of his refrigerator. I suck on the raisin while we walk together back to my house. It's plumper than the ones he gave me the other day.

We reach my porch. "Can I have another one?"

Sơn holds a raisin out in his hand. "Beg for it."

"No."

He looks straight in my eyes. "I know you want it. If you beg I'll give it to you."

"Then we won't be friends."

Sơn waves a raisin in front of me and laughs. "These raisins taste the best. If you want one you have to beg."

"Get off of my porch." I run at him.

He runs back to his house laughing.

Half an hour later, Sơn comes back and asks if I want some raisins.

"We're not friends," I say.

He takes a raisin out of his hand and eats it in front of me, acting like it's the most delicious piece of food he's ever had. I ignore him and go inside.

A couple days later, Sơn comes by after school. "Don't sulk," he says. "I didn't mean it."

He waited this long? "No, you meant it, and I meant it."

∽

On the way to school I walk over to a dock where fishermen are catching giant river prawns. When the bell rings, all the other kids run into the schoolyard. I stay. I'd rather watch people catch shrimp than be in school. After a while, one of the fishermen looks at me. "I think you've seen enough shrimp catching. You should go to school."

I enter the classroom in the middle of a lesson. I know the teacher will hit my hands with her stick, but I'm not scared.

"Lie down on my desk," the teacher says.

What? Lie on her desk?

She calls up Cường, her favorite, and hands him the thick wood stick. "Punish him."

Cường stands over me, hitting my butt in front of everyone. He hits me as hard as he can, harder than the teacher could. It stings. At first I'm embarrassed. Then, it just hurts.

∽

After weeks of running from falling pillars every night, I tell Ba about my dreams.

"Stop dreaming about it. It will go away," he says.

The harder I try not to dream about the pillars, the more they fall.

I tell my brothers I'm tired of running all the time in my dreams, dodging pillars.

"Don't go to sleep until you're really tired," Vân says. "Then you won't dream."

"Sometimes people have the same dream every night," Chị Tư says when I tell her. "They go away after a while."

My nightmares don't go away.

I try to sleep during the day instead. One Sunday after lunch, I lie down in the reclining chair next to the bed beneath the stairs. I'm sleeping deeply in the thick wicker chair. Finally, I'm not dreaming about the pillars.

"*Hù!*" My cousin Bành shakes me.

I begin throwing punches at him. He screams and runs away. He comes back later. "I was just trying to scare you. Why did you get so mad?"

"I haven't slept for so long and you woke me up," I say.

~

I stay home from school sick. I sleep in my parent's bed and dream I'm falling in space. I keep falling and falling. I try to call for help. I can't catch myself or stop falling. I'm going to die and my brain is shutting down. Everything is going blank.

Ba shakes me. "Are you alright?"

At night, I dream about pillars. I don't want to run anymore. I'm done. I wonder how it will feel when the pillar crushes me. I'll only feel it once. I stand still, waiting, looking up at the pillar. It slows down. It falls on me—through me. I'm still here. I'm supposed to be dead. More pillars come, but less rapidly. I stay in place. The first one didn't crush me. The next one won't. They stop before they hit me. I realize I'm dreaming. I can't get crushed. I don't have to run anymore.

Chapter Seventeen (Late 1972)

Catching Shrimp with Bare Hands

At dinner, Má says we're going to Giao Long to clean out the canals in the morning. I don't usually like to come, but Má asked
me to help. When we get there, a thin fog covers everything.

"Here take this," Má says.

I grab the handle of a grass-cutting knife and follow her to the edge
of our land. The skull and crossbones on the metal Death Land sign
stares at me from the coconut tree marking the border.

Má and my sister and cousins roll up their pants and wade into the
canal closest to the sign. They start scooping out blocks of mud and
throwing them up onto the strip of land. Chị Châu climbs out onto the
strip of land and evens the mud out with her white feet. I turn my back
to the metal warning sign and reach down to chop a handful of grass
from the bank on the other side.

It's quiet except for crickets, a few birds, and Má and my cousins
and sister talking. The fog has burned off, so that it's only a haze. "Move
to the other side," Má says. "I don't want to dig too far down next to
that sign. Who knows what might be buried there?"

My feet sink into the cool mud as I move around. The sun heats
up and the dew on the grass disappears. My sister and cousins scoop
out mud and clouds of dirt billow up in the water. A shrimp swims to
the cleaner water at the top, waving its hairlike antennae right below
the surface, trying to breathe. I grab it. Its tail kicks my hand as I roll
it into the waistband of my shorts. I wade through the water searching

for more shrimp. Catching shrimp and fish is my favorite thing to do.

A pregnant woman comes from the neighboring land and walks above me on the strip of land that borders the Death Land. What is she looking for? Usually, people greet you when they come on your land. In Cồn Tàu, people smile and offer food. But the people in Giao Long seem like they're missing something inside. Má says there's so many Việt Cộng everywhere that if you look like you have anything they'll take it away—if you have a smile you hide it or they'll take away your reason for being happy.

I go back to searching for shrimp and tucking them in my waistband. The next time I raise my head the pregnant woman is walking off our land, away from the tree and the sign.

Chị Năm catches a shrimp and sticks its head into the side of the canal. "Lượng, go back to the boat and get the container for catching shrimp," she says.

I get the plastic container and put in the shrimp from my waistband and the shrimp Chị Năm stuck in the mud. A set of antennae flicks. I swish my hand through the water to grab it and toss it in the container floating next to me. The shrimp thumps around. I reach up and break a small twig off an overhanging guava branch and put it in the container to block the entrance.

Shrimp antennae stick out of the water everywhere. Their tails flick away from me as I reach in to pluck them out. Each time I catch one and put it in the container, I begin hunting for the next. Normally, I have to work hard, moving our wicker fishing basket back and forth in a circle while walking in the canal. Today, I can swipe them up with my hands.

My sister and cousins step into the canal and start catching shrimp and tossing them into the container. The container starts to fill up. We have about forty shrimp now and a few small fish. I imagine them sautéed with fish sauce, sugar, and chili peppers for lunch. We race to fill the container before the sun is too high and we have to leave.

Ầm! What's that? Everyone crouches down in the canal. I crawl up the mud bank and poke my head over the edge. Blue smoke spreads out and hangs heavy near the ground. What exploded? Something brown moves back and forth beyond the Death Land sign. A piece of cloth? It's too hard to tell with the tall grass and the smoke and haze covering the ground.

Chị Châu puts her head up to get a better look. "I think I see a dog leg sticking up."

"It must have wandered into that land and set off a grenade," Má says.

Is the dog still alive? How badly would an explosion like that hurt it? I stick my head up farther. I hope it's nothing so we can go back to catching shrimp.

Smoke mixes with the haze in the air, turning it a bluish white. The retired teacher and his wife run across the bridge to our land. My family climbs out of the canal onto the strip of land above us. Cậu Năm Lộc, the man who drives the ferry between Giao Long and Tân Long steps out from the other side of our land where he lives. We all move over to where the coconut tree separates our land from the Death Land. "Did you see what happened?" the teacher asks us.

"I think it was a dog," Chị Châu says.

The ferryman and the retired teacher step up onto each side of the base of the large coconut. Their bodies press against the metal sign nailed to it, as they try to get a better view.

The ferryman steps down from the tree. "It's not a dog." I get a sinking feeling—we're not going to be able to go back to catching shrimp. "I heard a woman moan."

"We have to go in and get her out." The teacher turns to his wife. "Get a hammock." She runs back across the bridge to their house.

"What's the chance there are more grenades in there?" the ferryman says.

"We can't wait," the teacher says. "She's bleeding . . ."

"I don't want to step on a grenade, too," the ferryman says.

"I don't think there would be more than one," the teacher says.

I stand on my toes. I can see someone, but with the blue smoke and the high grass I can't tell who it is. I don't know what to do.

The teacher's wife comes back with a pole in one hand and a folded hammock in the other. The teacher grabs the pole and hammock, and he and the ferryman step over the tangerine thorn barrier into the Death Land.

Nylon pants swish *xộc xẹc*. A man in black appears. "Careful!" he yells at the ferryman and teacher.

The teacher looks down at the high grass around him. "Are there more grenades?"

"Walk back in same footsteps you came in," the man in black nylon answers.

"I can't remember my steps!" the ferryman says. "You come in here and carry her out."

The teacher's wife turns to the man in black. "Are there more grenades? Are there any more?"

"There are more," he says. But he just stands there watching.

The teacher and ferryman have strung the hammock on the pole and are trying to carry someone on it. They have the pole high on their shoulders to keep the hammock above the grass and brush. The pole is short so the person is bent together in the hammock. Another farmer comes across the bridge. "What happened?" he asks.

"Someone stepped on a grenade," Má answers.

The teacher and ferryman come out from behind the big coconut tree and the sign. People move back to make room for them on the narrow strip of land. The pregnant woman lies in the hammock. Her clothes hang ripped by shrapnel. Blood covers the front of her body.

"Ồ. Mrs. Fourth Silk," Má says.

The teacher and ferryman put the hammock on their shoulders. The curve of the hammock presses the woman's body into a *V*-shape with her big belly crushed in the middle. They turn on the strip and my face ends up near the woman on the hammock. "Help me, help me," she cries softly. Her wide white eyes look at me.

Pants swish *xộc xệc*. Another man in black nylon walks up. "Take care of your wife," the teacher says to him. The man gives the pregnant woman a disgusted look and goes to stand by the other Việt Cộng. The woman looks from person to person calling for help, but doesn't look at her husband. Why won't he help her?

"Who are you trying to kill?" The ferryman asks the two Việt Cộng. "All you're doing is killing your neighbors and dogs."

The two men don't say anything.

"The Army will probably send some people out to investigate," the teacher says. The two Việt Cộng walk off.

"Help me, help me." Her skin looks pale. There's blood all over.

"How are we going to get her to the hospital?" the teacher says.

"It's low tide . . . My ferry's stuck, everything's stuck," the ferryman says. "We'd have to carry her over the rice paddy road to get to a bus. It will be the middle of the afternoon by the time we get there and there aren't any buses then."

"She's bleeding a lot. Too much jostling won't be good for her," the teacher says.

"Help me, please help me." She's looking straight at me. What does she think I can do? I can't save her. How can I help when the grown-ups don't know what to do?

"Well, where are we going to find a boat that's not stuck?" the ferryman asks.

Even if they find a boat, it takes too long get to Mỹ Tho. The woman keeps staring at me. "Help me." Blood drips off her clothes and makes wet spots on the mud. I've never seen anyone look like this. She's on her way to being a ghost, but she's still talking.

"Help me, please help me." She'll die if she loses too much blood. Can't someone do something for her? What about a canoe? Maybe we could push her out to the river and hope a boat comes by to pick her up? But what if no boat comes? Please find a boat and take her away from here before she becomes a ghost.

The retired teacher hands his end of the pole to the other farmer and goes to his house across the stream. When he returns, he says that he knows where a boat is, but they'll have to carry the woman half a kilometer over canals and overgrown land to reach it. The men set off to the south, with the woman slung between them.

No one wants to work anymore, but we're trapped until the tide comes in. While we wait to leave, Chị Mộng cooks the shrimp we caught. "Why would she go around us that way?" Má sighs. "Only dogs can't read the sign. I thought she was looking for banana leaves, but her hands were empty . . ."

"I wonder what was wrong," Chị Mộng says. "Her husband wouldn't even look at her."

"If she dies," Má says, "her spirit will haunt her husband—that's for certain."

She'll haunt me, too. She was almost a ghost when they left. Why didn't anyone try to tie up her wounds to stop the blood? She won't be alive by the time they reach the boat. Why didn't her husband care about her?

It's hard to eat. The shrimp are flavorless. How can someone die for no reason? When I die I want it to mean something. I take a stick and start poking it in the mud in the stream. The tide comes in around and under our boat, filling the muddy canals and letting the fish and shrimp breathe again. The minute the tide is high enough for the propeller on our boat to turn, we leave.

Chapter Eighteen (Winter 1972-Summer 1973)

It's Not Peace

"It's not peace. It's stupid." Mr. Three East has come by to tell Ba about the treaty about to be signed in Paris. "The South gets nothing and the North doesn't have to do anything."

Ba nods. He's been saying the same thing. If Northern soldiers stay in the South, then the war's not over.

As Mr. Three East gets up to leave, he tells us the government wants us to fire all but a minimum amount of the ammunition we have for the gun he issued us. Pass the word on. "But don't waste too much," Mr. Three East says. "The government says they'll replenish it, but there's a good chance they won't. With the Americans leaving, supplies are getting low."

When President Thiệu announced the signing of the Paris Treaty on TV, he called it a cease-fire. If it's not peace and not the end of the war, why are we wasting bullets?

I wake up to gunfire. My brothers and I crawl out of the mosquito net and look out the window. Red light from tracers arcs over the dark sky. Out in the river, patrol boats fire their guns.

"Get downstairs," Ba calls up from the stairway. "People are shooting."

I run out to the front of the house. A man holding a big machine gun by its handle stands next to metal boxes and loose chains of ammunition near the foot ferry dock.

"Someone's shooting our house," my sister yells.

Leaves and bits of bark tear off the betel tree next to the balcony and fall down. Tracers come from the foot ferry dock. I run past the man with the big gun to the dock.

"You're supposed to aim high and down river," someone on the dock yells.

"I was aiming at the tree," Six Chicken's father says.

It was just Six Chicken's father. I turn around and go back to help the man with the machine gun. He looks like he's trying to figure out where to set his gun up.

"Put it right there." I point to our house across the street. "I live there."

He moves the gun next to Chị Tư's flower garden. Guns around us fire louder than firecrackers at *Tết*. Bullets spray toward us from across the river in Mỹ Tho. I don't understand why we're wasting bullets if it's just a short break in the war. Won't we need them later?

I pick up a metal box of ammunition. "Can I help?" If they're going to waste bullets, I want to collect the casings.

"Sure." The man sets the gun on a bipod and angles it up with a sandbag. "The bullets will go beyond the island and drop in the river," he says. He shows me how to lift up the flap on the gun, slide the ammunition belt in, and clamp the flap down.

He puts earmuffs on and sits down. Leaning to the side and holding onto the gun with both hands, he starts to fire. I sit on his left and put my hand next to the gun to guide the belt into the feeder. The sound drowns out the other guns around us. The shockwaves thump my lungs.

Casings fly out as he shoots. They're bigger than the M-16 ones I have. When the chain gets close to the end, I go to the other side and push the empty casings into a pile. "Can you scoop them close?" I can barely hear my voice. "I want to collect them." I don't want one of the neighbor kids to come and try to pick them up while I'm busy helping.

The man stops firing. "Go get a basket."

I run inside and grab a large basket and place it where the casings fly after the gun ejects them. He starts firing again. The smell of gunpowder is everywhere, a haze of smoke in the dark. Dust flies. Every ten bullets a tracer with an orange tip fires. It glows red when it gets thirty meters away. I pay attention to the firing rate so I'll know what kind of gun it is when I hear it again. Someone fires a gun like the one Mr. Three East gave Ba. The firings are further apart than those of the other guns. The Army must have given the Civilian Self-Defense their old equipment.

When the muzzle gets red hot, the gunner takes a break. As he loads a new chain, he tells me his name and where he's from. After the last chain is gone, he folds up his bipod. I struggle to lift the basket of casings up the steps to our front door. I come back to help him carry the empty ammunition boxes to the dock. The sun still hasn't come up, but there's less gunfire. I go into the house to put my casings on the balcony. When I come back out, the gunner is gone.

"Someone shot our house," Chị Tư says when we all sit down to breakfast.

My ears ring. I can't hear very well. "Six Chicken's father was shooting the betel nut tree," I say.

"It must have been him," Ba says. "No one else is stupid enough to aim at a tree next to someone's balcony." Ba finishes eating and rushes off to talk to Six Chicken's father.

"Stay inside," Má says to the rest of us.

I go upstairs with Chị Tư and Má to look for holes in the tin roof. We find two big tears.

"Well, the holes aren't over any of the beds, and it's not the rainy season," Má says.

Ba comes back, and Má tells him about the holes. He leaves to complain to Six Chicken's father again.

I go up to the balcony and start to make a castle out of my new casings. As I stack them, I look at the bullet hole in the floor that Mr. Three East's man shot when he was watching TV. Every time I sit on the balcony, I look for the hole and for the bullet that's still lodged in the coconut pillar near the top of the roof.

Five Fermented Beancurd looks up at me from his house across the street. "You crazy kid." He chuckles. "That was really loud. You're going to go deaf."

"My ears are still ringing," I say.

He goes inside, and I go back to stacking the casings.

A few minutes later, people run down the alley to the back of our house. One of the younger neighborhood kids, Nhiểu, follows behind, dragging his bad foot. He hops up on the foundation wall of the house next to ours and puts his good foot on the balcony's support beam. He hangs onto the railing and presses his face against the squares of the wire fence that surrounds the bottom half of our balcony. "That's a lot of casings," he says. "Can I play too?"

"No." The balcony is my place. I won't let the other kids in the neighborhood up here.

Nhiều drops to the ground. "All those people ran behind your house. Did someone get a bullet dropped on them back there?"

Cậu Tám Tranh, the nurse, comes out of the gate in front of his house with his medical bag and heads behind our house.

"It was Cẩn." He's a bully and a thief. If someone had a bullet drop on them, I'd want it to be him.

"I'm going to go and see." Nhiều turns to go down the alley on the side of our house.

A few minutes later, Nhiều races back, as fast as he can with his lame foot. "It is Cẩn. How did you know?"

Maybe because I wished it was him. He's so mean even grown-ups hate him, but his parents don't do anything to stop him. When he put little bits of metal razor under his nails and cut my arm up, his mother said he was just playing.

Nhiều keeps talking. "Cẩn was lying in a hammock in front of their house when the bullet dropped on him. He's bleeding. They're taking him to the hospital."

"He's already dead." I don't know why I think this. I just do.

Nhiều runs behind our house again. I go back to adding another level to my castle. Nurse Tranh and another man come out of the alley carrying Cẩn in a hammock. They walk down to the foot ferry dock and get on a boat. Cẩn is already dead. Why are they bothering? The driver starts the motor. The boat goes out a hundred meters and turns around.

Nhiều comes back and squishes his round face into the wire fence around the balcony. "How did you know Cẩn was dead?"

"Because the bullet dropped in his heart."

"That's what Cậu Tám Tranh said. How did you know?"

"Remember how many times Cẩn stole something and said, 'If I'm lying, so help me, let a bullet drop on me?' We all knew he was lying." That's what he said when he stole the watch my uncle gave me.

"So the bullet was looking for him." Nhiều swings his body and drops down. "There's still a lot of shooting. I'm going home. I don't want a bullet to drop on me."

The next day my ears still ring. I go in back of the house and sit in the bellfruit tree picking the flowers and sucking out the nectar. On the other side of the fishpond, Cần's family is having a funeral in front of their house. They wanted a big funeral, but no one has come except the next-door neighbor.

In the evening, Má comes out and talks to Vũ's mother and the family next door. "Cần swore to God he wasn't guilty, but he was," Má says. "Some spirit guided that bullet right into his heart."

"He would have grown up to be a bad man," Vũ's mother says. "Now we don't have to find out."

When no one is around, I climb up on top of the cabinet to check if we have any ammunition left. There are two clips. I'm glad Ba listened to Mr. Three East and didn't fire it all. What good is a gun without bullets?

~

After a week, my ears finally stop ringing. Chị Tư asks me to patch the holes Six Chicken's father shot in our roof with some tar mixed with fiber. Everything needs to be repaired for the New Year. On the first day of *Tết*, I wander behind our house where Anh Chín Phát's family lives. Anh Chín Phát's not there, but his older brother, Cousin Fourth Triều, is home from the front. He sits at a table smoking a cigarette and drinking black coffee, wearing his best pants and a white long-sleeved shirt.

"*Chúc mừng năm mới.*" I fold my arms and give a slight bow. "Live a long time and be happy and healthy."

"The same wishes to you," Cousin Fourth Triều says. Instead of reaching into his shirt pocket for some *lì xì* money, he picks at a tray of *mứt* dried fruit candy. "As a soldier, I don't know how long I'll live. If I have anything, I'm probably going to spend it."

I don't know why he's so pessimistic. There hasn't been any fighting in the news. The North won't be able to organize an attack after all the bombing. Maybe there really will be peace.

I leave to wish our other neighbors. I don't expect any *lì xì* from the people living behind our house, anyway. None of them have any money. The tradition is to wish people well for the New Year, not just get money.

～

Thượng and I go with my cousins to Mỹ Tho to spend our New Year's money. We stand in line at the cinema showing *The Thirteenth Prince.* I reach my hand into my back pocket to pay for my ticket. "All my *lì xì* money is gone." I look around the crowded area. "I've been pick-pocketed." Tears burn in my eyes.

Thượng turns to my cousins. "Take out your *lì xì* money. Let's each give Lượng some." He takes out his money and starts collecting from my cousins.

"No." I shake my head and stop crying. I lost it. This is how life is. I won't let a thief pick my pocket again. I let my brother pay for me so I can go into the film. I sit down in the dark still mad about losing my money. I wished Aunt Curly twice so I had a lot of *lì xì.* The film starts and the Thirteenth Prince and his brothers kill thousands of enemy soldiers invading China. I don't think I'd have the strength to be one of thirteen princes defending my country against thousands of invaders. But that's how many soldiers are coming from the North.

When the Thirteenth Prince is finally captured, the invaders tie him to four horses to be drawn and quartered. He's so strong. Can he hold off the horses? He fights to the end, but even he can't keep the horses from pulling him apart. My problems seem small. When I go to the Army, I'm going to fight like the Thirteenth Prince. I won't be a coward in the end, no matter what they do to me.

Before *Tết* is over, my family and cousins come out to the dock across the street from our house to say goodbye to Cousin Fourth Triều. He walks in his uniform along the planks that run on the side of the stilt houses to catch the foot ferry to Mỹ Tho. "Goodbye," he calls to us. He's on his way back to the front.

"Goodbye," I say along with everyone else. He'll be back, but with the Army you don't know when.

～

On the way home from school, moans and chants come from Bà Ba's house. I follow some other kids up to the open door. A curtain covers the window, but it's still light inside. It's not scary like I thought it would be. I crowd around with neighbor boys and girls. People stand against the back wall. Others chant on their knees in front of an altar. Bà Ba sits on a chair chanting, her head hung down. The color of her robes reminds me of the cubes of pig blood we eat in rice soup.

My friends and I nudge each other and point at the altar statues and the pictures above them. "Which do you think is more scary? The guardian of hell or the god of the underworld?" "Who's that statue of?" None of the figures look kind like the Lady Buddha.

Candles and incense burn on the altar, making it even hotter. "Is a ghost making the candles flicker?" a girl says. I stare at the red face of the guardian of the gates of hell. Will his long black mustache move?

Some kids push past me to leave. Bà Ba calls for the spirit to enter her and speak. She closes her eyes and slowly sways and waves her arms in front of her. Bà Ba gets down on her knees. Her voice goes to a high pitch. It must be the spirit talking. Then her voice gets so low we can't hear. Which voice is supposed to be her and which is the ghost?

"How does she get herself back when the ghost leaves?" Sơn asks.

"Is she still there or not when the ghost comes in?" I whisper to Sơn. "If she's not there, where did she go?"

Bà Ba glances at us as she stands up. She stops chanting and gets some water. Then, she tells Thọ's older brother something. He comes over and pushes us out the door.

We go to the alley and gather around Bà Ba's window to watch. "If you want to see ghosts, you need to watch at night," one of the boys says.

~

After dinner people cluster on the street talking. There's a ceremony at Bà Ba's house, but we're too scared to watch when it's getting close to dark. My friends and I play five-ten or kick the can and then stand around in the street talking about Kung Fu films. A group of veterans leans against a wall. I walk over. I like hearing stories about the front.

A man who's a little taller than me is telling his story again. "I am so chicken," says the tiny man, "I can't even walk out in the dark. When I get scared I freeze—I can't hold a gun—I can't even run away because my legs won't move."

I like the way he can talk about being chicken with no shame. He looks like a kid that didn't grow up. I don't know how he could even carry a gun.

"I failed basic training," the tiny man says, "but they didn't kick me out. They sent me to the front and told me to run at the enemy and shoot. I couldn't. I froze there on the ground."

He freezes his hands like he can't move. Cousin Fourth Triều didn't show any fear about going back to the front. It seems like a job to him.

Everyone laughs. The man unfreezes and starts talking again. "My commanding officer came back and told me to get up and run or he'd shoot me. He went up to the top of a hill and stood waving his pistol for us to come up. It looked like he was going to be shot up there. I froze. My legs wouldn't move." The man tries to pull up his stuck legs. "I couldn't move, so I shot up the hill from where I was."

Cousin Fourth Triều talked like he accepted that he might die when he went back to the front. Everyone has a chance if they fight, though.

"I hit the commanding officer right in the butt. He came back, pulled his pistol out and pressed it into my head. I was so scared, I was leaking, I was shaking, I crapped in my pants. I thought I was dead. But he didn't shoot me. He put me in the brig."

People like him should be cooks or do laundry, not be sent to fight.

"I would have shot you," says an Army veteran.

"I know," the tiny man says. "I don't know why he didn't shoot me."

"You should be dead," the veteran says.

"I should, but I'm too chicken." He looks around. "It's dark now—time to go home." He laughs and acts like he's running home in slow motion.

～

It's a hot, humid day in the beginning of May. My cousin Chị Bảy Ký wails in the backyard. I run out the back door. A cluster of people gather around my cousin's house.

"Where is it? Where is the body?" asks the old man who lives behind us. Chị Bảy Ký sits in the corner sobbing quietly.

Mr. Six West, the medium's helper, points to a canvas bag on the dirt floor tied with parachute cord. A sweet, rotten smell comes off the bag. "That's it. The Army dropped off what's left of him."

"What? That's all there is?" says the old man. "Poor Triều."

It doesn't seem real. How can my cousin be in a bag?

"The soldier who dropped it off said that they don't even know if it's all him," Mr. Six West says. "Multiple shells hit the bunker. The

Army made sure they gave everyone two arms and legs, but they're not sure whose arms or legs."

Chị Bảy Ký sobs. Anh Chín Phát looks at the bag with his brother in it and at the people coming in.

It seems like Cousin Fourth Triều just left. It was only three months ago. At *Tết*, when he said he didn't know how long he had to live, I thought he had at least six months or a year.

People crowd the house. "What happened?"

Chị Bảy Ký sobs loudly while someone explains. Her face is red and puffy from crying.

"Put the body on the altar," Mr. Six West says. People clear one of the altar tables and place the bag on it.

After a while, someone says, "We have to give the body a more restful shape."

Má comes out our back door. Chị Bảy Ký sees her and wails. Má tells her to buy tea and food. She sends Anh Chín Phát to telegraph his other siblings. Má sees me and sends me to buy some incense and paper gold and silver.

I come back with the fake money and incense and place it on the altar in my cousins' house. The bag is gone. I go behind the house looking for it. Two men and a woman crouch by a washing slab that sits halfway outside the house. They take a body bag out of the canvas bag. The body bag is folded over, like there's only half a body, and wrapped in plastic. I remember seeing Mr. Fourth Farmer's shredded body behind our house back in Quới Sơn. What does my cousin's body look like? One of the men sees me. "This isn't something for kids to watch."

I climb into the fishpond stall and hop into a bellfruit tree so I can get a better look. A woman gets a bucket of water from the stream and pours it over a piece of the body on the concrete wash slab. Blood runs off into the fishpond. Part of an arm with the elbow lies in the unwashed pile. Some pieces of flesh look like a leg. There really was a person in the bag. My cousin. The woman turns and looks up at me. "Go away. Be more respectful."

～

The monks calculate that the best time to bury Cousin Fourth Triều is the next afternoon. Inside my cousin's house, two monks sit on the floor facing a table holding a black-stained wood coffin. The lid is on and sealed with wax. My cousin doesn't smell like Grandfather did. But bodies at funerals don't smell as bad as ghost bodies floating down the river. Má says the smell is bad for you. If a person is freshly dead the soul might come and try to take possession of you, so you'd better stay away. Nobody is going to get hold of me. I'll fight them off. I'm not even sure I believe spirits can come back. I haven't seen anything in Bà Ba's séances that makes me think ghosts can grab people in our world.

Cousin Chị Năm Gương arrives from Sài Gòn for her brother's funeral. She stands out with her short haircut and bright clothes and shiny jewelry. She passes out *bánh* and candy, then changes into white funeral clothes and the formal chanting starts.

After we eat the *bánh*, I go outside with the other kids. We climb and hang from the bellfruit trees. The branches are loaded with green fruit. We hunt for ripe ones, the color of human skin. Later, when the body is in the ground, people will stop by to eat chicken stewed in coconut milk, salty pork, and sweet rice, and have tea and cookies. If we set the food out before, ghosts would eat its spirit and it wouldn't be any good. Unwanted ghosts hang around funerals trying to talk to the newly dead.

The men carry the coffin out and lower it in a grave they dug behind the fishpond under a bellfruit tree. An Army captain and four men show up, salute, and fire into the air. Then the men pour fresh concrete over the grave to make the tomb.

My cousins and Thượng and I throw bellfruit at each other. People bring incense and stick it in the dirt around the poured concrete. Anh Chín Phát stands at the side of the grave, throwing paper gold and silver into a fire, so his brother will have money to spend in the afterlife. Another relative burns a set of paper clothes for my cousin to wear. A breeze blows the ashes over to the canal.

Bellfruit drop like rain as I crawl over a branch to dodge the fruit my brother and cousins throw at me. I toss one back at them. It hits a bundle of ripe fruit. The bundle drops on the wet concrete slab.

"Lượng! What are you doing up there?" The grown-ups stare up at me. "Don't you have any respect for the dead?" One of the men picks the bundle of fruit off the grave and tosses it aside. There's a dent in the concrete where each bellfruit dropped. "Your cousin is going to come and visit you tonight because of this."

I climb down the tree and stand next to the grave. "Sorry cousin," I whisper. "A short while ago you were here. Now you're gone."

~

My younger cousins stay overnight with us. Cousin Fourth Triều's youngest brother is more scared that his brother will visit than I am. We sleep together on straw mats on the floor upstairs near the bookcase altar for my grandparents. The oil lamp sitting on the altar casts shadows around the room—my younger cousins say they see ghosts moving. Even though it's hot and stuffy under the tin roof, we pull the blanket over us and hide.

I have nightmares of ghosts chasing me. I wake up sweating. I toss and turn, but the heat of my cousin and brother next to me makes it worse. I don't think Cousin Fourth Triều will hurt me. I didn't mean to be disrespectful. He wasn't that type of person. I was close to him. I give up and throw the blanket off.

By morning, he hasn't come. I knew he wouldn't be upset about something that small.

~

As soon as the lunch bell rings, I rush to the gate of the schoolyard with the other kids. The bigger kids run to the street vendors and call out their orders. I stand back waiting for an opening so I can get close to a vendor's cart. I hope they don't run out of the cheaper food or I won't have enough money for lunch. It clears enough for me to get to the cart with *bánh mì*. I hand the vendor some coins and ask for half a decimeter of a baguette. She slices a piece of baguette open, puts hoisin and pickled daikon inside, closes it back up, and hands it to me.

I sit on the concrete under a tree in the shadiest corner of the playground and take a bite of my bread. The kids in my grade sit scattered around eating bread or sweet potatoes. A few of the students get a bowl of *cháo* or rice noodles every day because their parents don't have as many kids to feed as mine do. But most of us get something cheaper from the vendor like a sweet potato or a taro or cassava root.

Tấn comes up to the tree. I get up to move away. He's a bully, and I don't want to be around him. He grabs the bread out of my hand.

"Give it back," I say. Usually he takes a bite and hands it back.

"It's mine now." He runs off with the whole piece.

"You're stealing from me," I call to his back.

The next day, Tấn finds me before I buy my lunch. He shoves and punches me and grabs the money out of my pocket.

After school, I go to Tấn's house and complain to his mother. The next day, Tấn beats me up and tells me not to go to his house again.

"You better watch your back," I say as he walks away. He won't stop unless I do something.

I complain to Ba, but I know it won't help. The next day, I hide my money in my waistband. Tấn shoves and punches me. He can't find my money, so he leaves. After he's gone, I walk over to the vendors outside the school gate and stand in line to buy a piece of bread. Tấn comes over and grabs the money out of my hand. "Lượng owes me," he says to the kids standing around.

When school gets out, I run home as fast as I can, grab my slingshot, and go up on our balcony. We usually dry mud balls on our tin roof to slingshot, but I find a sharp rock. I step over to the roof of Sơn's house and hide behind the bougainvillea. I haven't played with Sơn since he tried to get me to beg for a raisin. His family doesn't like me on their roof, but the tin is so thick they can't hear me from inside.

I wait for Tấn to pass by on his way home from school. I can't fight him. He's too tough. I saw his father beat him, and there's no way I can take what he can. I won't kill him, just make a hole his head. I'll get in trouble, but no one will pick on me again.

Tấn comes down the street. I pull the rubber bands on my slingshot back and aim right at his head. A soldier in uniform steps forward. The rock hits his shoulder. He jerks away and looks up. I'm so close. How did I miss Tấn and hit him?

I stand up from behind the bougainvillea. "Sorry, sorry. I didn't mean to hit you." I step back over to my balcony. "I live right here." Tấn would tell the man where I live anyway. "I really didn't mean to hit you." I look straight down from the roof at Tấn." I meant to hit him."

"You could have killed him!"

"I was aiming for his head, but I got your shoulder. I'm sorry."

"What! Why were you trying to kill my younger brother?"

He's Tấn's brother? "He beat me up in school for so long. I told him I'd get him back if he kept doing it, but today he took my money again."

The man turns to Tân. "Is this true?"

Tấn doesn't say anything.

The soldier grabs his brother and throws him down. He starts to punch and kick him. Blood comes from Tấn's nose. His face is bruised and cut. Ba whips me with a bamboo cane, but nothing like this.

"I think that's enough," says one of the people on the street.

Tấn's brother moves off of him. He looks up at me. "I think he got what he deserved."

"I just don't want him to take my money again," I say. "That's all."

"I guarantee with his life that it won't happen again." The soldier looks at his brother sitting on the ground. "Don't ever get someone this mad at you again. If I beat you up you'll live, but if someone decides to hit you in the head with a rock you'll die."

Tấn doesn't show up in school for a week. The kids at school say his father tied him up to a post. When Tấn comes back, he seems broken. Did I cause this? I didn't want him punished more than his older brother already did.

∽

School starts to go better. I can finally say all the letters. Mr. Five Fermented Beancurd sees me and asks where Ba is. "You don't have a speech problem anymore," he says when I answer. "You talk better now."

I go around saying all of the words I couldn't say before: *là, lắm, lên.*

Vân gets tired of it. "Stop saying all these *L* words you, you . . . Lượng!"

We run with a bunch of kids up the street to the alley where Dearest and my cousins live. I heard the military police went to look for a *trốn lính* who was hiding. The military police pull him out of the storage shed next to his house. He's shaking. He looks younger than the other neighbors who go off to the war. His mother cries and begs the military police not to punish him. They handcuff him and drag him away. Someone says he was in basic training for a month and snuck home before he had to go to the front. The Army used to have six months of basic training, then three months. Now it's only thirty days.

"When I fight, I'm not going to sit in the fort like Cousin Fourth Triều and wait to get shot at," I tell Vân.

"Sitting in a fort's not a good idea," Vân says, "but you don't have much choice. And you'll die faster outside." Vân thinks he'll probably have to join the Army. Má bought birth certificates for him so he's younger on paper. But papers only work three or four years and then you can't fool anyone unless you buy papers that say you've already served.

"I want to sneak around and ambush the enemy like Lành," I say. "Then they'd be scared." When I'm seventeen, I'm going off to fight no matter what my papers say.

"If someone sees you," Thượng says, "you're going to be dead."

"At least I'll die fighting," I say. "Waiting in a fort until a mortar kills you isn't a good death."

~

A scream comes from our backyard. I run out the back door. An old couple and Mr. Six West, stand in my cousin's house.

Anh Chín Phát sits in the bed holding onto his foot. People put pressure on it. "Have him lie down and elevate his foot," a veteran says.

Mr. Six West grabs a piece of a sheet and starts to wrap it around my cousin's foot. My cousin shakes. Why isn't he screaming? It has to be painful.

"What happened? What happened?" the old woman asks.

"He chopped himself," her husband says. "He's trying to dodge going into the Army."

The old woman takes a look and leaves.

I hadn't thought of Anh Chín Phát going off to the Army like his brother, Fourth Triều. He didn't say anything about it.

A group of veterans and neighbors huddles around him. I stand in the doorway. They put tourniquets under his knee and above his ankle. Anh Chín Phát's eyes are big. He looks like he thinks he's going to die.

"He's in shock," a veteran says. "He won't feel anything for a bit."

"We don't have anything for when he does," Mr. Six West says. "He needs to go to the hospital."

One of the men looks over at me. "Get away."

I walk past them to the back of the house. There's a stump for chopping in the back room. Three toes lie on the dirt floor next to the stump, pale and dead. A thick work knife lies nearby. Someone's tried to clean up, but the dirt near the stump is dark and drops of blood are scattered around. It's strange to see a part of a person detached. I poke a toe with my finger to see what it feels like. The skin is shriveled like a slaughtered pig's and it's cold. How can someone do that to themselves?

What if he missed and took off more than he wanted?

"Get away, kid." An Army soldier on leave who lives up the street picks up the toes. He walks back to the front room and sets them in a bowl on the table.

Mr. Six West comes back with Cậu Tám Tranh, the nurse. Nurse Tranh unwraps the cloth around Anh Chín Phát's foot, puts antiseptic on it, and wraps it in gauze. He gives him a shot. "We need to take him to the hospital."

The soldier on leave puts the toes in a clear plastic bag and hands them to Nurse Tranh. "Maybe they can reattach them."

How? The toes look dead and feel cold.

After my cousin leaves, a crowd forms in our backyard. The soldier on leave says, "He's not going to the hospital. He's going to jail."

~

Anh Chín Phát comes back from the hospital with a cast around his foot and gauze at the end. He hides in his shack behind our house. I thought the military police would take him to jail. I look at his foot when he takes the bandage off. He's missing some toes, but Anh Năm Nổ's foot looks worse. He lost a third of his foot in the Army.

Má says that someone might come and look for my cousin. A neighbor chopped off both trigger fingers and still had to go to the Army. A while later, Anh Chín Phát disappears. Má says he's living and working somewhere else. It took guts to cut off his toes, but he's afraid to die. I check to see if the gun is still above the cabinet. When I get older I'm going to fight. If you fight, you're going to die. But if everyone avoided duty, we'd lose the war.

Blocking Lizards

Light streams through gaps in the wood walls of the book rental store onto shelves full of novels, comics, and adventure series. People read on benches. I pass over the new Spiderman comics to the twenty-four books of the Monkey King series. The Monkey King books don't stack neatly. The pages have tape around the edges to stop the feather-tears on them from spreading. Instead of lying flat, the pages puff out, demanding to be open. The paper cover shows a picture of the Monkey King standing on the cloud he rides through the sky, holding his magic staff. Part of the colorful cover hides behind duct tape wrapping the book's creased spine.

I use the money Ba gives us for lunch to rent the next three books in the series—I don't need to buy lunch out in the countryside. On the way out, I pick an English novel out of a box in the corner—the store gives them away. We hang them on a bar in our fishpond outhouse to use as toilet paper. I search the novel for familiar words. I find the word for few, "*it*," and the word for tingling taste, "*the*."

Reading makes the long boat rides to Cồn Tàu go faster. I envision myself as the Monkey King, flying around whacking people with my stick, disrupting heaven. When I look up, Má has stopped the boat at Six Soybean's house. Quý is there.

"How's the wound?" Má asks. "Is it healing?"

I expected Quý to be limping, but he doesn't seem any different. He just walks more carefully.

"Good. Doing well as you can see," Quý says.

A few days later, my two oldest sisters arrive in Cồn Tàu to study for the entrance test for nursing school. They talk about all the different places that they've been to for boarding school. The world is so much bigger to them. One of them brought home a book with thick glossy pages and color pictures of America. The words are in Vietnamese and English. I don't think I'll see any of the places in the book or even more of Việt Nam. The only way I'll see anything is if I go to the middle of the country to fight on the front. I'll see the country and then come home dead like everyone else.

"What would it be like to be born in a country where you always had enough to eat?" I ask Chị Năm when she comes in to cook lunch.

"It would be like being born in heaven," Chị Năm says.

Quý comes over to visit my older sisters. He brings some *bánh* and tries to talk to them while they read their textbooks.

"What are you studying? What are you learning?" he asks.

I sit outside, straddling the pole bridge and dangling my feet in the stream. I want my sisters to say something clever to send him away. He and the Gecko are the only Việt Cộng I still see around. Lành chased away all the rest.

My sisters answer politely and go back to staring at their books. After a few more tries to get their attention, Quý gets up and leaves. He visits again, but my sisters keep ignoring him and he stops coming. After that, we only see him at Mr. Six Soybean's house. Whenever we see him there, Má asks how his injury is. She wants to remind him Lành is around.

∽

Trực and I wander out in Cồn Tàu fishing. It's just the two of us, since Má doesn't want my brothers in the countryside anymore. We take a small casting net over to the land in the center of the island near the banyan trees. The canals around the small banyan tree have a lot of branches in the water. "There could be a lot of shrimp and fish there," I say.

I throw the net in and pull it up. It's full of fish and shrimp, but it gets tangled on the branches. Trực and I move away from the branches, closer to the edge of the small banyan's canopy. Someone's been trimming back the tree so it doesn't cover the small altar under it.

We move to the strip of land that leads to it. It's a narrow wood shack with a plywood roof.

"Let's leave." Trực crosses the canal to the other strip.

"Let's go by the altar."

I start walking along the strip toward the altar. My skin feels chilled. Can the spirits reach me in the day? I stop three meters from the tattered open door. The floor is clear of leaves and there aren't any leaks in the roof. Someone must take care of it. I want to look inside, but I don't know how close I can get without being disrespectful. Burned incense stuck in a jar full of uncooked rice sits on a table pushed against the back wall. Faded pictures of two men lean against the wall in wooden frames. I look in the corners to see if anything will jump out. I back away.

Trực has already started walking home. I turn and run to catch up to him. "That's not good," he says. "You don't want to disrespect the spirits and disturb them."

"I wasn't disrespectful. I just wanted to see what it looked like."

⁓

"Maybe when the war ends your mother will be returned as a prisoner," I say to Trực when we're out walking. I'm confused about whether the war is ending or not. On TV and the radio people talk about the cease-fire and peace treaty. But the Americans are gone. Can we be two countries, North and South, without their help?

"No," Trực says. "Má is dead."

"Did you get the body back? I saw on TV that some people are missing and some are confirmed dead. And auntie is missing."

He looks at me angrily. "She's dead. She's not coming back."

⁓

Trực and I sit in the boat near Dì Hai Temple's house. We're on the way back to Tân Long, but Má had to stop for a meeting with some Việt Cộng on the other side of the channel. We try to catch shrimp with our hands, but we only bring up mud. I don't have the casting net, so we give up on fishing and throw mud at each other.

Trực scoops his hands deep into the mud. "If you were buried in mud, you couldn't get out," he says.

"I could get out," I say.

"Lie down and try."

The tide is low, so I lie on the muddy river bank and he covers me. It's heavy, but I struggle out.

"Try to get out again," Trực says.

We dig a hole in the bank. I lie in it. "Put your hands down deep so you can't just break through," he says.

I push my hands into the mud, and Trực piles more on top. "Try now."

I can't move. I wrestle against the weight on top of me. I'm completely stuck. I keep struggling, but I can't get out.

Trực gets a strange look in his eyes. "This is how it feels if the tide is coming in and you're trapped. You drown."

He's talking about his mother. How she died tied up to the post with the water rising. I lie there. He stands above me. I can't get out. I'm scared, but I'm not going to show him. I try to walk my fingers up through the mud. "Maybe when the tide goes up I can wiggle myself free," I say.

"No." He turns to leave. "You're stuck."

He goes back to the boat. I lie back and close my eyes. He'll come back and dig me out. I feel the tide coming in. The incoming water will loosen the mud. I wait for a while and try to move my fingers again. Trực comes and stands over me. He starts pulling mud off the middle of my body.

~

I'm out alone in the stream near Dì Hai Temple's hut searching for giant river prawns. They only show up in the winter. I walk close to the bank where Trực buried me. It's cold, but I'm glad I'm out fishing instead of in school. School is better this year, though. I like the fourth grade teacher, Thầy Định, and he likes me too.

Three canoes approach. In the middle canoe a big man with pockmarks and a dark face sits between two guards. Six Gecko.

The tide is going out, so I go downstream. I don't think they see me. The canoes disappear into a side channel. I reach into the mud to check for shrimp. When I turn around, the canoes have come out of the channel. One glides next to me.

"What are you doing here?" a man in the front of the canoe asks.

"Catching shrimp." I unroll my short band to show him the two river prawns I caught. I'm shivering from the cold water.

The Gecko's men paddle next to me. The Gecko leans over. "Who are you?"

"Dì Tám's son."

"What are you doing *here*?" He looks at me as if I'm spying for the Army.

"Catching shrimp."

"Go home."

He slides his canoe into the paddle weeds. The little paddles on top of the stalks waver as the canoe grates along the bank. The men in the other canoes slide into the weeds on either side. When they can't go any farther, the men step out onto the mud and drag their canoes. Two of them push and pull the canoe with the Gecko sitting in it. They disappear into the dark bushes.

I turn around and head home, checking a few underwater branches for prawns on the way. When I tell Má I saw Stone Brave she says, "Remember, the frog dies because of its big mouth."

I don't need to tell anyone. Lành must know the Gecko is here. Why doesn't he get him? Everyone is back to fighting. The war has started again.

～

People come to Bà Ba's house to contact spirits bothering them so they can start the New Year in peace. After dinner, when the sun is setting and it's getting dark, shrieks from a séance come from the medium's house. Shapes of bodies press against a dark curtain pulled across the doorway. Bà Ba moved the curtain so there's no room for us to come in and watch.

I stand in the alley between our lean-to and Bà Ba's house and look through the window. Candlelight bounces off the shiny surfaces of the small mirrors and polished brass dishes on the altar. Red lacquer plaques on the wall above shimmer. A large family gathers around the medium. Bà Ba is dressed in her dried-blood colored robes. She sits in a chair in front of the altar with her head down and a hood covering her face. Mr. Six West sits behind, chanting in the same flowing, reddish-brown clothes.

Bà Ba fingers the Buddhist prayer beads that drape over her neck.

"Spirit, please enter," she says, lifting her face toward the ceiling. The hood on her robe falls off her shaved head. It must be hot and crowded in there.

If the mediums are a gateway to the other side, maybe I can see through a crack in the door they open to the spirit world. The alley is empty besides some banana plants shriveled from the heat. A cool breeze blows behind my neck. Goose bumps rise on my arm. I think about the pregnant woman who was turning into a ghost while asking me for help. When I close my eyes, I see her staring at me.

Thượng and another boy come up. "Have they started?" Thượng asks.

I shake my head. "The spirit hasn't started talking yet." I'm glad they're here. Now we can check each other's back if a spirit comes from behind.

Bà Ba calls out, "You must come to us, spirit. You will gain peace."

We crowd around the window stretched up on our toes. I stare at the altar trying to see the spirit enter. A thick fog of incense pouring out the window makes my eyes water and my nose itch. I fan the smoke away and try to get a better look. At least the smoke keeps the mosquitoes away. The medium rises and a shudder runs through her body. Then she sits silently on the floor and stares straight ahead in a trance as the spirit takes over.

Bà Ba changes her voice and shrieks and moans. People come for two reasons: to talk to a loved one's spirit or to get rid of a ghost that's haunting them. Today it's definitely a ghost.

The medium stands up and dances, talking to each member of the family. We push to see, pressing our faces against the bars covering the open window. "Did you see that?" "What did she say?" "What kind of ghost is that, is it a bad one?" "The last one was so nice."

Bà Ba drops her head and says the ghost has left. She tells the family to pray toward the altar for it to come back and seek peace.

"Did you see the ghost enter the room or anything strange?" I ask.

Thượng shakes his head. "I didn't see anything."

The medium comes toward the window. We step backwards. She slams the shutters.

I turn away from the wood shutter in front of my face. "They'll be even hotter in there now."

There's a tiny crack where the shutters don't meet. The three of us press together to see through it. The medium picks up a big clay jar.

The ghost must be a tough one, one of the generals of the afterworld, if she needs such a large one. Bà Ba motions for the ghost to enter the jar. "This is the only way to advance to a higher spirit level," she says. "We will burn money and incense for you. Your soul will be in a higher form because we will constantly pray to you. If you don't go you will wander forever, a lost soul."

It's hard to see through the crack, but I'm glad I'm outside. The people inside are sweaty, and burnt incense hangs in the air. The ghost seems to be hesitating. "If you continue to harass us," Bà Ba says, "we'll let out a spirit worse than you to torment you and your family." The ghost must believe her threat because she quickly fits a cork on the jar, then covers it with a square of paper with an inscription in traditional Vietnamese characters. She adds two more squares with brush-painted characters to hold the ghost in. Then she places the jar on a shelf in front of the altar with all of the others and tells the family that she'll bury the jars together in a ceremony later on.

The medium walks toward the window. Through the crack in the shutters, we can see the beads of sweat on her face. The shutters snap open. She stares straight into our faces. "You obnoxious children! Go to a different place."

We walk out of the alley into the street. "Anh Bảy," I say to Thượng, "if you were trapping dangerous spirits, wouldn't you put them in a concrete grave like Cousin Fourth Triều's, not bury them in the alley in clay jars that break?"

~

It's a hot day in April. I'll be glad when it's summer and I can go out to the countryside and swim and fish all day. I sit on the foot ferry dock outside of Tây's house. His black dog lies in front. "Mực," I call. The dog's name is ink like his color. I try to pet his head. Mực growls at me. I keep talking to Tây and edge closer. Each time I move, the dog growls. When I get close, Mực gets up and goes inside.

I come over the next day with a piece of a pork bone I saved from dinner. I hold it out and Mực looks at it warily. I leave it. I come over a few days later with another piece of meat. I throw Mực the meat. While he eats it, I pet him. I run my hands along his tail. It has a thumb-size dimple a hand-length from the root. "What happened to Mực's tail?" I ask Tây.

"It got shot. When we were upriver selling salt some Army soldiers tried to shoot Mực and eat him. Mực's a special dog. He got away, but he has a hole in his tail."

I look at the tail again. Wouldn't the bullet have cut it off? How can he wag his tail with a hole in it?

Toward the end of May, everyone in school is doing makeup work, but the teacher tells me that I can be excused because I'm the second best student. I'm not sure how it happened. My teacher understood me and told me I could do well. I tried to get a hundred percent on the first math test and I did. I tried one more time, then another and kept getting perfect scores. I liked school this year, but I like summer more. When Má goes to Cồn Tàu, I ask if I can come along and stay out there myself the whole summer.

"If you're out there alone, you have to be careful," Má says. "Never do any kind of job for the Communists. Once you start small and people know you are a messenger you'll be in trouble."

I nod. "Don't worry, Má. I can handle myself."

She looks at me. "I know you like to play with guns, Lượng. Remember Việt Cộng use guns to try to recruit you. Don't be stupid and fall for that trick."

I've shot enough guns. I don't need to shoot Communist guns. "All I want to do is find fruit bats, catch shrimp and fish, and slingshot birds. That's all. And I can help watch the land and make sure people don't steal fruit."

I bring along extra clothes and a bag of rice. It shouldn't be much different than last summer when I was alone a few times with Thượng. It's too bad he and Vân can't come so it could be the three of us. Má says the Việt Cộng wouldn't bother to recruit my brothers—they'd drag them away. That's what must have happened to my cousin Chị Châu when she went back to visit her family in Giao Long. She was supposed to come back and work, but no one knows what happened to her.

Má, my sister, and Chị Mộng come out to Cồn Tàu to pick fruit every once in a while, but they don't stay overnight with me. They spend most of their time on the land in Giao Long since it needs more work. I try not to go out there. Every time I go to Giao Long, I see blue smoke and hear a grenade going off. When I look into the Death Land, I worry I'll see the woman lying there, her ghost eyes watching me. I'd rather be here by myself.

It's lonely at night, but I have a radio. News about the war and songs about soldiers from the South fighting for freedom fill up the emptiness. I build a huge fire to keep the mosquitoes away. Shadows dance as the flames flicker. I check the walls for movement. Ghosts don't like light. I wonder if any of the spirits from the bodies buried underneath the hut are here watching me. Most of the spirits from the bodies under our hut must have gravitated to the banyan trees because that's where ghosts like to live. But some may have drifted back down. I stay up late to make the night shorter. But I don't care about being alone at night if I can wake up and go fishing.

At the first hint of dawn, I head out to check the fishing poles I placed the evening before. Out of twenty poles I've caught nothing. Maybe there aren't any fish left. I go home and eat some leftover fish from last night's dinner and spend the morning walking between our different plots of land to make sure no one is stealing fruit. The tangerine trees Má planted on the six strips in front of the hut are tall and healthy. It's the first season that they've started to produce fruit. Next year all the hard work and money Má spent on the land will pay off. Then I won't have to listen to my parents argue about how to buy enough rice to feed us all.

Around noon, I decide to empty a pond. I spend hours draining the muddy water with a bucket, but there's nothing at the bottom besides a few shrimp. It's dinner time and I haven't even had lunch. I take my casting net and head over to another canal. After an hour of tossing my net in and out, I catch a few shrimp and some fish.

When I get back to the hut, I feel so tired and hungry I can hardly move. I toss all the fish together into a pan without cleaning them, add some fish sauce and a little bit of sugar, and build a fire to start cooking. The sound of footsteps comes down the path. Bà Năm pokes her head in the door. "What are you having for dinner here all by yourself? Salty tiger?"

"Almost." I was close to cooking fish sauce with a little sugar and chili pepper for dinner. The *cọp cọp* of chopsticks scraping it off the pan is the same as the word for tiger.

She looks into my pot at the leaves and mud mixed in with the fish. "What? You're not cleaning your shrimp or your fish or even washing them off?

"I didn't have time. I'm hungry." I guess I should have at least rinsed them. I twirl my chopsticks in the pot until the antennae of some shrimp wrap around them. Then, I stick them in my mouth.

"Don't be so lazy. People will laugh at you." Bà Năm steps outside to spit out her betel, then steps back in.

"I'll try to do it next time."

"I remember that tough eel you tried to feed me," Bà Năm says. "It was so old it had fins that looked like legs. It was about to turn into a fox and walk away."

"I haven't seen one walk," I say. Bà Năm likes to complain about that eel, but I don't think old eels turn into foxes like people say.

After dinner I tie a knife around my waist and take my stack of fishing poles out past Mr. Six Soybean's house and over to Lành's land. The hut on his land is falling down. Lành's family still comes out to collect fruit, but they don't stay overnight. A shadow flutters on the ground. I look up and see the dark wings of a fruit bat above me. I clutch my knife. It's spooky walking around when it's dusk and ghosts can come out, but I need to put my poles out if I want to eat more than salty tiger tomorrow.

～

The next morning, I bring my catch home and cook it so I have something for lunch and dinner. After I check the land there's not much to do. I walk next door to Mr. Six Soybean's hut. His nephew, Lâm, is visiting from the city. Lâm tells me there's an older girl living by herself over by Bà Năm's. We swim around in the canals and then decide to visit her.

I stick my knife in the dirt by the door of the hut when we get there. A girl sits inside with textbooks spread all around. She says her name is Yến, and she's from Mỹ Tho. Her parents want her to stay out here where it's quiet to study for the test from eleventh to twelfth grade. She failed and gets one more chance. Lâm and I walk around looking for birds to slingshot while she studies.

"I need to go home," I say.

Lâm nods. "I have to get back for dinner."

Yến looks up from the book she's reading. "Don't go yet. It's so scary here at night. It's not like the city. It gets completely dark here, and there are noises everywhere."

"Don't worry," I say. "I'm staying by myself too. If the sound is in the water, it's a mudskipper. If it's on the ground, it's rats running around. If it's in the air it might be an owl, but usually it's fruit bats—

they're the fluttering shadows you see in the moonlight."

Yến shudders. "Why don't you two sleep out on the hammock in front? That way I'll know no ghosts are coming in."

"No. I have to watch my land." Why does she think that we would stay outside and get eaten alive by mosquitoes? Or ghosts? I'm not going to sleep outside. I'm scared enough inside my own hut.

The next time I see Mr. Six Soybean I ask, "Why is that girl out by herself over by Bà Năm's house?"

Mr. Six Soybean shakes his head. "I'm not sure why no one is with her. It's a dangerous situation."

I nod. "It's not safe for a girl."

It's the living ghosts you have to be scared of, not the dead ones. Má told me what happened to Chị Chẳng: my cousin was raped by a Việt Cộng and almost bled to death when she had the baby.

~

When Lâm and I visit Yến, two men in nylon clothes with AK-47s slung over their shoulders talk with her while she tries to study. They're old, over twenty. "Is this flower lost?" one of them says to her. "There's a cluster of canna lilies next door." He's talking about the tall red flowers Bà Năm grows. "But this one is the brightest one."

I don't like all these strangers showing up. Việt Cộng seem to be all over. The news on the radio reports more and more areas are off limits. I tell the misters about Lành and his fort. Maybe that will scare them away.

"We know about the fort," the one who was calling Yến a lost flower says.

He seems like the leader. Why isn't he worried?

"Stay and have some tea," Yến says when Lâm and I want to leave.

"I don't drink tea, I hate tea," I say.

"We'll drink tea with you," the leader says. He turns to us. "You kids can go home."

"I'll get you boys a coconut to drink, then," Yến says. She goes out to the tree in back of her house. Her *áo bà ba* shirt lifts up and shows her waist as she reaches up and cuts off a coconut.

Yến hands Lâm the coconut. He makes a face. "That's a young coconut. It's not ready."

She already cut it down, so I take one of her knives from the wall and start husking it. It's hard because the knife is dull.

The other mister glares at us. "Why are these kids hanging around? Are they your relatives?"

Yến ignores him and puts a few pinches of tea leaves in three cups.

"I'll be an officer by the time we win the war," the leader tells Yến. "I can start a family then."

I hate listening to the Communists talk about what they'll do when they win the war. They'll take our land away, that's what they'll do.

The misters sit down. Yến takes the kettle off the fire and pours water into the cups.

"You pour tea so well," the other man says. "You'd be the ideal wife."

"I'm still young," Yến says.

The coconut is sour, but Lâm and I finish it and start to leave.

Yến gets up from the table. "Wait, I'll get you another."

"Don't waste coconuts," Lâm says.

"Stay with us while we drink tea," Yến says. "It would be rude to go."

Lâm leaves because it's getting dark, and he doesn't want to meet any ghosts along the way home. I have my knife, so I can cut coconut leaves for a torch. I stay around and sharpen Yến's knife with a rough stone. After a while the misters leave. As soon as they're gone Yến says, "I guess I'm fine now. You can go home, Lượng."

I walk home with a coconut leaf torch and my knife. I don't feel lonely until I get home to the dark hut and no one is there.

∾

Over the next two weeks Lâm and I keep visiting Yến. The misters are usually there when we come. On the way over, Lâm and I argue about who Yến likes the best. Lâm says it's him.

"No, it's not. She just wants us around so those misters don't harass her." As soon as I say it, I realize it's true.

Only one mister is there when we get there—the one who seemed like the leader. I guess he won out on who gets to hang around Yến. He narrows his eyes when he sees us. "You kids are becoming water lizards, always blocking people from where they want to go."

People say you have to go around water lizards or you'll have bad luck. The only time I saw one was in a canal by Bà Năm's. It was so big I wanted to eat it. I chased it into the bushes with my knife, but it got away.

The mister stares at us. "You can get hurt if you keep blocking someone. Things will happen to you."

Lâm gets quiet.

"It sounds like you threatened us," I say.

"No, I was giving you advice so you don't do this when you grow up—always interrupting people."

"Well, I'm not scared of you. I'm not scared of anything."

He starts to swear at me. "You're one of these uneducated, unruly boys."

"You're not from Cồn Tàu," I say. "Maybe you should learn how people around here act."

He curses me, then grabs his rifle and leaves.

Where is Lành? Why is he letting all these Việt Cộng stay around here?

The next day, Lâm won't visit Yến with me. I go alone and tell her that she's going to get in trouble if she keeps staying out here by herself. "You should stop offering those mysterious misters tea or anything at all." My sisters ignored Quý and he left. "It's dangerous having them stay with you," I say. "You can get caught in the crossfire. There was an ambush right by Bà Năm's hut. If you don't believe me ask Bà Năm. She'll tell you she wasn't scared of ghosts in her hut before, but she is now."

Yến ignores me.

After a few more times visiting Yến, I tell her that I can't keep coming. It's too dangerous with that mister around. Besides, she's not even that nice to me. "If you want me to stay," I say, "you could tell that mysterious mister I'm your boyfriend. Maybe then he'd leave."

"Absolutely not!"

"Well, the boss of all the mysterious misters out here is Six Stone Brave. Send a message to him if you want his men to stop bothering you."

A while later, the mister comes in the door. He leans in close to Yến as she's cooking rice. She backs away. "So who is Six Stone Brave?"

The mister's face gets flushed. "What? Who told you about him?"

Yến glances over at me.

The mister glares at me. "You? You're the one talking about this?"

Why did she ask him about Stone Brave? She should ask someone trustworthy like Bà Năm or Mr. Six Soybean. Or she could say something like "I was talking to Stone Brave the other day" and scare the mister off. What's wrong with her? "Is that the mysterious mister they call Six Gecko?" I say.

"Never ask for him. Never look for him. And never use that name." He grabs his rifle and storms off.

A few minutes later, I leave. I can't help Yến if she acts like this. She'll get us both in trouble.

Lâm goes back to the city. I stop visiting Yến, so I'm by myself most of the day. A week after the mister stormed off, I walk with my casting net by the stream near Yến's hut. I go inside. Leaves lie on the dirt floor. There's no sign of a fire.

I ask Bà Năm and Mr. Six Soybean if they know where Yến went. They don't. She must have gotten scared and left.

Uninvited Guests

Quý appears out of the bushes carrying his satchel as I gather my
fishing poles to put out for the night. He wears regular clothes,
not nylon like the other Việt Cộng.

"*Chào*, Anh Tám. Have you eaten?" I've already had dinner, but I
offer him the food I saved for breakfast. Quý's not like the Việt Cộng
who were bothering Yến. He treats everyone like a neighbor.

"I've eaten already, but thank you." Quý takes a quick glance
around. "Where is everybody?"

"They went back to town," I say.

Quý asks about everybody in my family. Then he turns and walks
down the path into the bushes. All the Communists have AK-47s, but
I haven't seen Quý with a gun. Maybe he has a rifle that he hides before
he comes.

∽

A few days later, Quý reappears while I'm washing off a basketful of
shrimp in the canal for dinner.

"Is it alright if I join you?" Quý asks, as I take the basket inside.

I nod. He takes a cup of rice out of his satchel and adds it to the
pot. I don't mind Quý eating with me as long as he brings his own rice.
I have plenty of shrimp and vegetables. And we're eating outside. If
Lành attacks he'll have a clear shot at Quý.

Quý looks at the basket of shrimp. "Aren't you going to clean those?"

"I'm too hungry." I drop the shrimp into a pot and start adding fish sauce. Some of the shrimp are so small they're hardly a bite. "This way there's more shrimp in the pot and less work."

I set the salty shrimp and some boiled yam leaves on a small table outside under the overhang and walk around the side of the hut to pick a chili pepper for mixing with my fish sauce. Quý comes and sits on the stool across from me. He keeps his satchel draped over his shoulder. I wonder how much tax money he's been collecting and if he's carrying any right now. If he *is* carrying all that money, he must have a gun hidden in the bushes or his bag.

Quý starts to pick the antennae off a shrimp in his bowl.

"Twirl your chopsticks until the antennae wrap around it and you can pick up a bunch at once." I stick my chopsticks in my mouth and pull the shrimp off. "If you clean the shrimp, you can only pick up one at a time. This way you get a mouthful."

Quý looks at me and shakes his head. He dips some water spinach into a small dish of fish sauce with a chili pepper. "This *nước mắm* tastes pretty bad," he says.

"It's what I eat." In the countryside my family eats the kind of fish sauce we can leave in our hut and no one will steal. "If you want better *nước mắm* bring your own."

Quý shakes his head again. He seems relaxed for someone who's being chased. If Lành attacks Quý here I hope he does a better job than he did when he ambushed him at Bà Năm's.

After we finish eating, Quý adjusts his satchel on his shoulder and gets ready to leave.

"How do you protect yourself?" I ask.

He points to his satchel. "It's not empty."

I knew he had a gun somewhere.

∽

Quý comes by around dinner time again. I've known him so long he seems like an old family friend. I like him, except that he's a Communist. He adds his rice to the pot and then sits and reads while I rinse a bunch of small fish and toss them in a pan.

Quý looks up from his book. "Are you eating them like that?"

"It's too much work to clean all these little fish. Just eat around the guts." I add fish sauce and stir it in with my chopsticks.

"Don't be lazy. You can get sick."

"I'm too hungry. By the time I finished cleaning them it would be time to go to sleep." Má and my sisters can clean fish in a few minutes, but not me.

"You need to plan better. If you make these salty so they keep, you'll have something for tomorrow."

"I just want to eat what I catch, and this is the way I eat it."

When we sit down, Quý pulls a tiny bottle of fancy fish sauce from his satchel. I remember Má complaining how expensive premium fish sauce is. Maybe he skimmed some money off the taxes. I don't think Việt Cộng get paid because they're always hungry and eager to eat our food. I laugh at him. "You eat pretty well for being in the Front."

"Try some," he says. "It's better than your stinky, salty *nước mắm*." He sprinkles a drop on a piece of my fish.

"Too much sugar," I say. The expensive fish sauce Má bought for *Tết* didn't taste sweet like this.

"It's top of the line."

"I only taste sugar." I dip my next bite in my own fish sauce. "You eat yours, and I'll eat mine."

I get up to bring the fish head from the pot over. I take the cheeks out with my chopsticks and eat them first. Those and the eyes are the best parts.

After dinner, we sit on stools around the fire and talk about which neighbor has which kind of boat and where you can find mudfish. I'm not worried about Lành attacking. If he's out there, he'll wait until I go out to the canal to do dishes.

The next day, Má comes with Chị Năm and Chị Mộng to pick guavas and a few bananas and mangoes. Chị Châu isn't with them. Maybe it's true that my cousin got captured by the Việt Cộng. I hope Chị Châu's not going to get herself killed in a firefight— that she's smart enough to find a way to get out. Quý doesn't come to dinner when Má is around, and I don't say anything to Má about him. If I tell Má that he visits, she won't let me stay in Cồn Tàu.

≈

The sound of rain falling on the water coconut leaf roof and the tree leaves blankets the house. I turn the radio on and start to cook sour soup with the snakehead fish I caught. Quý walks up barefooted, carrying his plastic *dép* sandals. I didn't expect him to come in the rain. Army soldiers tell me they get ambushed in the rain because they can't hear anything. Quý looks in the pot. "Ê, you learned how to clean fish."

"I clean it if it's big enough."

An older folk song is playing. "That's a good song," Quý says. He likes the same type of music I like, the older type, not the new music that's fast and noisy.

I turn the radio off after the song ends and set the food on the wooden bed. I sit on the bed, and Quý pulls up a stool. After we eat, Quý lies down in the hammock. It's still raining, so I stand under the overhang and hold the dishes out to clean them off. I should go to the canal to rinse them off so if Lành and his men are watching they can attack while I'm outside. But I stay under the overhang. I don't want to slip and "catch a frog," ending up with my legs splayed out in the mud.

"Is it alright if I stay here tonight?" Quý asks when I step in. "I can sleep in the hammock."

I look to see if he scans around for signs of Lành. My parents say to watch people's eyes. You can tell someone's a thief if their eyes go to your valuables. Quý looks relaxed. He must have scoped out the area before he decided to stay. "Go ahead," I say. It doesn't look like Lành is attacking tonight and it's nice to have company when it starts getting dark.

The rain stops and the mosquitoes come out. I build a fire to keep them away and to roast a yam I dug up earlier. The smoke drifts out the open wall in front of our hut. Since Quý is in the hammock, I sit on a stool. We used to have a lot of places to hang hammocks, but now there's only space for one. Má says she doesn't want uninvited guests. Not after what happened when Lành attacked Quý at Bà Năm's.

I look at Quý in our hammock and imagine Lành crawling out of the stream and throwing a grenade into our hut. I poke my yam into a good place in the fire. "How did you escape from Lành and his men? They were so close to you at Bà Năm's hut."

Quý holds his satchel in front of him on the hammock and thinks for a moment. "I was lying in a hammock just like this. Then *tùm!* A noise came from the pond. The leaves rustled like someone throwing mud. Then *bịt*, one grenade came through the kitchen door, and *bịt*, another came in through the front."

"The Army must have thrown the grenades from the bushes on the other side of the pond, right?" I remember the casings I picked up there.

"Right. The first grenade exploded in the pond and bullets started spraying inside. I was halfway to the back door when something nipped my butt. I thought I was going to crumple down, but my legs kept going, so I figured I wasn't hit that bad."

Quý must be a fast runner if he could get away even after he was shot. "Wouldn't the bullet shatter your leg?"

"The bullet must have ricocheted off the bone. Nothing was there when I checked. You don't feel much at first, but people told me that you have to keep yourself going or you'll start screaming in pain. I ran to the stream and dove in. The water was so muddy, I couldn't even see if I was bleeding or not."

I get up and check the banana bunch I brought in the other day to see if they're ripe. I offer Quý one, but he shakes his head.

"The Army was downstream emptying bullets into the bushes. I held my breath and swam upstream. When I couldn't move anymore, I hid in some bushes. Lành was talking and cursing. Then I heard a burst of fire over by the house and I knew they had killed Bình. Lành is murderous . . . executing an injured person."

"What would you do with an injured Army soldier?"

"I'd let him be and walk away."

"That's not what I heard from the Army . . ."

Quý ignores me. The fire starts going down, so I add some wood. I take the yam out and offer some to Quý, but he doesn't eat after dinner. I'm glad because I don't find many big yams.

I ask Quý how he escaped when Lành attacked him at Mr. Fourth Post's hut. He tells me how he used a hollow stem to breath underwater. Má is right. When Quý gets into the water he's like an otter.

"You have to do it correctly." Quý scans the room with his eyes as if he's looking out for someone. "You don't blow water out when you start out or they'll see it squirting up. You blow it out underwater and cover the end with your finger. And you have to keep low. Sticks don't float upright. But once I made it down to the river, I was free."

"What happened to the other men in your squad?"

"Everyone else died." Quý stares at the wall. "I'm a magnet for death . . . Everyone around me always dies."

Why does he stay in Cồn Tàu? It's only a matter of time before

Lành catches up to him. What I really want to ask Quý, but can't, is how the Communists tricked him into chopping off Lành's father's head. He'd never tell me. Now that he's one of them, if he told me, they'd execute him, too.

Quý pulls a gray sheet out of his satchel and wraps it around himself in the hammock. I can't believe how much he fits in that small bag. He hugs it like it's his baby.

I get up and move our two good knives—the ones Má had made from the shrapnel we found in Giao Long—from the kitchen wall over to the slot in the wall next to the bed. I want them next to me so no one can come by in the night and reach in through the open door and steal them. I crawl under the mosquito net onto the wood bed next to the wall where I stuck the knives and spread out a reed mat. After a while the fire dies down. I don't want to crawl out from under the net to restart it.

"Anh Tám," I say to Quý. "Why don't you sleep under the net with me so I don't have to worry about keeping the fire going all night?" We have two beds, but I don't want to sleep in the back bedroom because it's closed up and too hot. And the mosquito net in there is one Má made from a white parachute she found. It's suffocating.

Quý rolls out of the hammock and moves next to me on the wood bed. He pulls the mosquito net over himself, puts his satchel under his head as a pillow, and wraps his sheet around. For a minute I start to worry that if the Lành's squad attacks, they'll shoot the whole bed up and me with it. Then I think that if Lành is that close he can probably come right up to our bed and just get Quý.

The next time Quý stops by, he doesn't ask if he can stay over. He just climbs in bed under the mosquito net and grabs one of our extra blankets. Then he takes one of our pillows and puts it on top of his satchel and lies down. It's dark, but I can see him reaching his hand into his satchel and putting something between it and the pillow. The soldiers on leave in Tân Long say that the best place to keep a pistol at night is not by your side, but under your head. I want to see what his gun looks like when he puts it back in the morning. I wake up right before the sunrise to check my fishing poles, but Quý is already getting ready to leave.

≈

Bà Năm stops by to check on me every once in a while, and sometimes Má sends a package for me with a neighbor coming down or with the fruit wholesaler. One day, Má sends pork. It tastes delicious after so much fish and shrimp. I'm glad Quý doesn't stop by, so I don't have to share. When Má and my sister come down to collect fruit, I don't tell them that Quý stays with me. I haven't finished all the fishing I want to do, and I don't want Quý to ruin it. Why doesn't Lành come after him? I thought Lành had the Việt Cộng running scared, but now there seem to be more of them around.

Quý comes three or four times a week. I don't get a chance to peek in his satchel. During the day he carries it with him, and at night he sleeps with the strap wrapped around his hand. And he doesn't go swimming. One evening he hangs his bag on the betel nut tree next to the foot bridge so that he can take a shower. I think I might be able to look inside when he washes off, but he stands next to it while he rubs soap on himself and rinses off with a bucket of water from the canal.

～

While we're standing outside by the footbridge waiting for the rice to cook, I ask Quý what an M-16 would do to a tangerine tree. I see scars on coconut and betel nut trees—I want to know which guns make which wounds. "I fired an M-16 before," I say. "It fires pretty well and not much recoil." I only fired it in the river, though, so I didn't see what it could do.

"An M-16's not going to do much," Quý says.

"That's not right," I say. "One of the Army soldiers told me an M-16 makes a pretty big mess when it hits you."

"The M-16 is a toy. An AK is a real gun."

He did get shot with an M-16, and it didn't do as much damage to him as I thought it would. Still, I don't think he's right.

I go to the canal to pick some water spinach. We ate all of the water spinach close to the edge, so I jump in to get some. Quý just stands there. He's an eater, not a picker. I wish he'd help—it's not fun getting wet close to bedtime.

I move the table outside so we can sit in the shade of a jackfruit tree and catch a breeze. I didn't have much luck fishing, only one big prawn and a bunch of little shrimp. I leave the prawn inside in the pot. While Quý and I are eating, I get up and go back to the pot. I put the prawn in my bowl and come back to the table.

"Do you have any more of those?" Quý says.

"Sorry, only one. It was hard work to get." He should help catch them if he wants one.

"That's not a polite way to treat guests."

"Well, guests are supposed to bring gifts. Like pork loin or bacon or something. This guest only brings himself."

"Still you should share. You have no respect for your elders."

"You don't even bother to pick vegetables. Next time I fish you can pick." He can get the water spinach. Or pick yam leaves. I don't like doing that because Má says there are wick snakes in the yam patch— those small snakes will bite you and kill you.

Quý ignores me and starts telling a story about an attack on a fort in An Hóa.

"How many people did you kill?" Does Quý ever shoot at Army soldiers or does he only run? This seems to be the only attack he was in.

"I shot at people, but there were a lot of other people shooting at people."

"Wouldn't you know if you killed someone?"

Quý looks at me. "The soldier I shot at seemed to go down."

That's better than running all the time.

"We only let them go if they beg for mercy," he says.

"Why? So they can come back and get you?"

"No. Once they have their life spared, they're too weak to fight us again. The Army is scared of us. When the Front attacked Lành's fort his men ran away."

I heard the story about Lành's first fort. Lành didn't run away. Quý wasn't even in that attack, so I don't know why he thinks I believe him.

"The tide is going our way." Quý looks at me. "People join us because it's the right thing to do. When we win, everyone will be better off. Even a small effort can help the cause. You want to be on the winning side, don't you?"

He's trying to recruit me? When he's a guest in my house?

"Lượng, I know you like guns..." Quý leans forward. "Do you want to look at my pistol?"

Is he trying to recruit me for real or is he just testing me? Does he really think I'm going to fall for that? "I shot a forty-five before," I say. "One of our neighbors in Tân Long had one. Is your pistol a forty-five?"

"No. It's something a lot lighter. More special."

Why's he talking about his pistol? Má says they use an AK to recruit you. "That forty-five had a lot of recoil. I couldn't hold it down when it fired. I heard that a forty-five will get you dead in one shot."

"Well, this pistol will get you dead in the head, too."

I glance at the satchel on his lap. "I saw your gun. It looked small. What's special about it?"

"All guns are deadly if you know how to use them."

I bet he'll leave me alone if I ask to fire it. All the soldiers in Tân Long say that if you hand someone your pistol when you're on duty you'll get court-martialed. It must be the same for Việt Cộng. "Your gun's loaded, right?"

"Right."

"Can I fire it?" If he lets me fire it, I'll take it to the stream in front of the house to shoot. When it recoils I'll act scared and drop it in the water.

He looks at me. "No."

He probably wasn't going to show me anyway. It's like when someone only has one small bowl of rice and they invite you to eat with them. If you say yes and eat their food, they'll stop asking. He just wanted to see how hungry I am.

Quý keeps staring at me. "Next time I come, I'll bring an AK and we can have some fun shooting."

He really is trying to recruit me. I thought he wouldn't try... I thought he was almost like a friend. I look away from him, toward the three jackfruit hanging from the tree next to us. "No, thanks..."

Quý leans back in the chair. "Big guns are fun to shoot."

I try to think of an excuse. "I like bigger guns. I helped feed the ammunition for a soldier shooting a .50 caliber machine gun during the cease-fire. I only like big guns like that."

Quý looks like he doesn't believe me. "An AK is a big gun," he says.

～

I plan what to do if Quý brings a rifle the next time he comes. I've heard Má and soldiers in Tân Long and everyone else tell me how recruiting works. They'll take you somewhere everyone can see you, like out to the edge of the Mekong and have you shoot at a river patrol boat going by. Then that's it, you'll be labeled a Việt Cộng. There's no way I'm going to get tricked into joining like Quý did. If he asks me to go with him shooting somewhere, I'll tell him I want to carry a loaded gun so I can feel like a real soldier. Before we get too far from my hut, I'll accidentally fire it. When he reaches to take the gun away I'll—I don't want to kill Quý, but if he brings out a rifle that's what I'm going to do. No one will think I did it on purpose.

Two days later, I see Quý approaching from the direction of Mr. Six Soybean's house. He's not carrying a rifle. I'm glad, but why isn't he? Does he have it hidden somewhere nearby, ready to bring out if I ask?

We sit down to eat some sour soup I made with shrimp. I talk about fishing and ask him if he's seen any mudfish around. I want things to go back to the way they were before, so I can stay out in the countryside.

Quý starts talking about the raid on Lành's first fort. "They knew their backup wasn't going to come and help them so they ran away."

"Lành didn't run away." I don't want Quý to think I believe his story. "I heard he and his men were hiding in the bush with fishing line working the guns on the fort."

"They abandoned it . . ."

"It was a trap. Lành rigged the fort with explosives and blew it up when the attackers got inside."

"They left a few booby traps before they ran out of there, that's all."

"But the whole fort blew up and killed most of the attackers." Quý is a coward for not being able to tell what actually happened. Army soldiers tell stories about getting tattered in battle.

"Well our attack shook Lành. He had to bring in reinforcements and build a new fort." Quý eats silently for a while. Then he asks, "Have you changed your mind? We could have some fun shooting together."

"No. I'd rather slingshot birds."

"Think about it. When you get a little older you might decide you want to."

He has to know that he's not going to recruit me. I look straight at him. "When I grow up I'll come looking for you."

Quý doesn't say anything, so I say it again. "I'm going to come looking for you when I grow up."

"You can't say things like that—there'll be big consequences."

I shrug my shoulders. "I'm just a kid . . . I'm only joking."

"Well you still can't say things like that."

"I didn't say anything."

I'm not worried. Quý won't report me. At least I don't think so.

The rest of the night we don't talk about the war. In the dark, Quý breathes next to me with his gun underneath his pillow. I start to think that I said too much. What if Quý thinks I'm going to tell Lành where he's staying? Maybe he and some of his friends will capture me and force me to join. I need to leave.

Unable to Fight

When I wake up, Quý has already left. I hide my favorite knife, the one that Má had made out of an old artillery shell, in the trapdoor in the bedroom floor and put the other two good ones under the eaves. Then I line up the rest of the knives in the wood slot along the kitchen wall so that one faces a different direction. I leave a lid on one of the pots tilted and turn one of the chairs by the table out. I'll know if Quý comes when I'm gone.

I pack up my rice and a small knife and walk to Aunt Curly's hut. She's family since my cousin Chị Bảy Kim married her son. I won't see any Việt Cộng at her house because her son works at Đồng Tâm Naval base. He tells any Communist sympathizers around, "I'm in artillery and your house is only a few clicks away—you don't want a shell to find your house, do you?"

When I get to their hut, Aunt Curly and my cousin are pulling weeds around the tangerine trees. Their *nón lá* shade their faces.

"What's going on, Lượng?" Aunt Curly asks, looking at my rice bag.

"Cô Ba, I don't want to stay alone in my family's hut anymore."

"Ồ. Is that so?" Aunt Curly wipes the sweat from her forehead with her sleeve. "Stay here, then."

She follows me into the house and pushes her *nón lá* off her head. It hangs behind her by the white kerchief chin strap, and her curly hair shows. I put my rice bag behind the shelf of glass jars full of candy and cookies that she sells to make extra money. Underneath she has bottles of soy sauce and fish sauce and in the back corner small sacks of sugar, salt, and a vat of rice—supplies for sale in case one of the farmers here runs out.

I reach into one of the jars and grab a pineapple-flavored candy. "I'm also tired of having Quý hang around." I want Aunt Curly to know a little in case I disappear, but I don't want to tell her enough that she worries and tells Má.

"Be careful around those misters," Aunt Curly says. "You don't want to do anything you can't undo."

"I'm fine. I didn't do anything." I unwrap the candy and put it in my mouth. "He tried recruiting me, but I'm not stupid."

"Ô! Is that true! When your mother comes back, you need to tell her so she can make sure things don't get out of hand."

I nod, but I'm not going to tell Má. I don't want her to make me stay in Tân Long like Chị Tư and my brothers. I want to stay here where I can fish whenever I want.

Chị Bảy Kim comes in. Of my missing aunt's daughters, she's my favorite. Chị Mộng is too loud and Chị Châu just smiles when you ask her something. But Chị Bảy Kim speaks in a soft, beautiful voice. I ask Chị Kim if she's heard any news about her missing sister.

She shakes her head. "I have no idea."

Chị Châu has been gone for so long that I wonder if she's gone from just missing to missing dead like their mother.

The next morning I go to check on my family's land. I scan the trees to make sure no one has picked any ripe tangerines or mangoes. Then I check the house. The knives are lined up straight, the pot lids are on tight, and the chairs are tucked in neatly under the table. Quý. The Việt Cộng aren't supposed to stay in your house when you're not there—that's the rule. I don't like Quý breaking it. I check and make sure the good knives are still where I hid them.

I stay at Aunt Curly's until Má and my sister come back to pick fruit. I don't say anything to Má about Quý trying to recruit me, and he doesn't stop by. When they leave, I go back to Aunt Curly's.

After a few days I get tired of staying with Aunt Curly. I decide I'll go back to my hut the next day. In the morning fat raindrops splash in the canal and make foam on top of the water—bubble rain. The rain doesn't let up until the next afternoon. When I pack up, Aunt Curly says I should stay with her until my family comes back. I don't know when they'll return. There's not much fruit to pick when it rains except bananas and a few jackfruit. The guavas are full of monsoon maggots. I want to get back to fishing, so I leave.

The dark clouds make afternoon feel like night. The rain comes down fine like when you spray water with your mouth—blowing rain. The wind wails and the hut creaks. It feels haunted, but I know now that's not what ghosts sound like. Ghosts sound like the moans of people in pain in the hospital. They look like the eyes of the woman I couldn't help.

I go out in the evening to set my poles. Branches move like someone is hitting them. It's only the rain building up on leaves. I walk toward the banyan trees. I've fished too much by Lành's, so I've started putting my poles over by them. It's almost dry under their canopy. There aren't birds or animals out. Everything is silent and dark in the rain. People say that ghosts show up in blowing rain. I avoid the side of tree the altar is on, but I can see it behind the branches. I still have three poles to place, but it's getting dark, so I head home. A voice calls for me to turn around. It's the wind. I clutch my knife and keep walking. The sound gets more pronounced. I try not to look back. I'm cold from being wet for so long. The sound is coming from the banyan trees. I look over my shoulder. I need to get away. I tell my legs to move, but they're frozen. I take my knife off the strap on my shorts and turn back around.

"I didn't bother you," I call out. "Please let me be." I can't move from the waist down. I take my knife and twist around. I chop the dirt all around me trying to get whatever is holding me. I still can't move. Is it the spirits? Am I losing control over my mind? I put the knife back on the strap on my shorts and use my arms to lift one leg up. Then I lift the other. One leg up and then the other. After three steps I can move. I run.

～

When I get back to my hut, the blowing rain makes it completely dark inside. I shiver while I build a fire. What happened to me? It was still day when I went out by the banyans. The spirits shouldn't have been out yet. I keep the fire burning late into the night—it's comforting to be near light when I look out the open door at the dark everywhere. I lie in bed trying to figure out why my legs froze. I don't fall asleep until two or three in the morning.

I wake up before dawn, but I wait until the sun is high before I check my poles. I bring a big chopping knife along and glance at the banyan trees while I collect the poles. It's still hazy, but the filtered sunlight makes everything bright. I get wet from the leaves, but I don't get a single fish.

A little while after I get back, Má and my sister and cousin arrive on the boat. I tell them how I was paralyzed over by the altar. "The wind called me, and when I turned to look, I couldn't move. Like God planted me there. Did the spirits lock my legs? I didn't have anything to do with the killing, and I didn't bother the dead. Why should the dead bother me?"

"That's their resting place," Má says. "When it's dark and rainy the spirits can manifest in our world during the day. If you're out stomping around during their time, you're not respecting them."

It's hard enough sleeping in this hut and watching out for the supernatural all of the time—I don't want to worry about meeting ghosts during the day, too.

It doesn't take Má and my sister long to pick the few ripe bananas, so they leave that afternoon. As soon as they're gone, I feel ghosts pressing in on me from all sides. I don't want to go out in the blowing rain to put my poles out. Instead, I pick up a jackfruit lying on the ground nearby. Má left it because she can't sell fruit that falls. It's almost half my size. When I carry it in, the prickly skin pokes against my bare chest.

I eat jackfruit for dinner and listen to the radio. It's pitch dark because of the rain. I worry about ghosts coming in, so I move my hand over to the knife next to me. With bubble rain there's a steady noise, but in the blowing rain there's silence until enough water collects on a leaf and it tips it down. Then there's a sudden splash. Or the stream runs so fast that it bends back the leaves of water coconuts, and then the fronds snaps back and forth against each other.

It's still raining the next morning. I stay inside listening to the radio and pulling orange fibers off segments of jackfruit and eating them. I don't want it to go to waste. I collect the seeds on the table to boil or roast later. My stomach starts to hurt. Rain pours all day and into the night. I wake up in pain. I run outside with diarrhea all night. In the morning, I decide I need to find a neighbor and get some medicine. But I've run out of clean shorts, and I can't wash and dry them in the rain. I go to the back bedroom and dig through a pile of old clothes.

The air feels musty—my sisters haven't stayed overnight and used this room for so long—it's probably another place ghosts stay.

Underneath Má and my sister's black pants, I find a pair of shorts that belong to my oldest aunt. Dì Hai doesn't like wearing long pants like all the other women. She's fat and they're too hot. I put on the shorts, yellowed from washing in the alkaline water. I hold them up to my chest, but they still hang down to my knees. As soon as there's a break in the rain, I walk barefoot to Mr. Six Soybean's hut, holding the shorts up in one hand and carrying my sandals in the other.

"Lượng, what's that you're wearing?" Mr. Six Soybean sits inside looking out the open front wall as I balance on the pole bridge leading to his house.

"Dì Hai's shorts," I say. "I'm sick . . ."

"You look pale." Mr. Six Soybean rushes out to give me a hand. "What happened?"

I follow him in and he hands me a rice bowl with sugar water and lime in it. I drink it and hand the bowl back. He empties a package of medicine into the bowl, stirs some water in, and hands it back to me.

Mr. Six Soybean's sixteen-year-old daughter Oanh is in the kitchen with her mother and younger sister cleaning yam vines for lunch. Everything about Oanh makes me wish I were older. I feel embarrassed to be wearing my aunt's shorts.

"The jackfruit near the front door of our house fell down," I say between sips of the medicine. "I only ate jackfruit for two days."

"Stay here," Mr. Six Soybean says. "You can wear a pair of Oanh's pants."

I don't want to wear girl's clothes. "These big shorts are warmer in the rain," I say.

After I drink the medicine, I want to go back, but Mr. Six Soybean insists I stay overnight. I walk home to get my rice and bring back some shorts I washed that are still wet. I can hang them in his kitchen to dry.

The next day, I start to feel better. Mr. Six Soybean tells me to stay and rest, but I need to check on my family's land. He gives me a packet of medicine to take along and tells me to be sure to come back in the evening. I don't tell him that I also want to check if Quý stayed in my hut when I was gone.

When I come back to Mr. Six Soybean's, three mysterious misters are there. They look like they're still teenagers. Việt Cộng seem to be everywhere. Why are so many people joining them? I want to do something to stop them, but I feel paralyzed like I did by the banyan trees.

The new misters strut around showing off their AK-47s, cleaning them and playing with the clips in their hands. They marvel at the size of the bullets as they reload, checking to see if Oanh is watching. Oanh ignores them and helps her mother with the pots on the stove. Mr. Six Soybean comes in from working. He glances between his daughter and the misters as he rolls a cigarette.

"Let me try one of your cigarettes," I say.

Mr. Six Soybean hands me his tobacco pouch. I roll one and light it with his imitation Zippo lighter.

"Aren't you going to try one?" I ask the misters. I know they aren't supposed to smoke.

They shake their heads and shrug their shoulders. "Only if we want to get imprisoned. You shouldn't smoke. You're too young."

"I can smoke if I want to and not smoke if I don't want to." I feel my freedom slipping away with Communists everywhere. How much will things change if they take over? Will they make it so no one can smoke? I roll another cigarette and start coughing.

They laugh.

"I can smoke and cough if I want."

They go back to trying to impress Oanh. I sit on a stool and pull up my aunt's shorts around my shoulders to stay warm. I have to hunch over so they don't fall off. I think about how I can help Mr. Six Soybean's daughter. At least she's not alone like Yến was.

"What great battles have you been in?" I ask one of the misters. "Will you be an officer soon?"

Mr. Six Soybean smiles a little, but his wife looks worried.

"We just joined," one of the younger misters says. "This is an opportunity to achieve. Do something important."

"What are you fighting for?"

Mr. Six Soybean shoots me a warning glance. They can't do anything to me for asking questions.

The mister who seems like the leader answers. "We only take from the wealthy. If you rent land and you work, you won't have to pay money to the rich person sitting at home doing nothing."

"You mean like the Plower owns the Rice Paddy program?" Má got the six strips of land in front of the hut from the program, but she still pays the former owners rent anyway. She says they were chased off by the Việt Cộng, so it should really still be theirs. "It started on the twenty-sixth of March in 1970." I only know the date because it happened on Vân's birthday.

"Are you sure this program happened on that day?" one of the misters asks.

Mr. Six Soybean nods. "That sounds like the day."

"We'll make it more equal than that," the leader says.

"Well, what size are you dividing it into? Uncle Six has over half a hectare. Can he keep all of it? How about my family?"

The leader looks at his two comrades. "I'm not sure."

Mr. Six Soybean glances up at me, then casts his eyes down and does a slow shake of his head. I smile back. I'm not scared of these three new Việt Cộng. I'm scared of losing the war. If we do, we'll lose our land.

When it's time for dinner, the misters use a rice bowl to scoop out their rice and add it to the pot. They don't add enough for a full bowl, even though they eat multiple bowls. One of them tries to add some grain they call *bo bo*, but Mr. Six Soybean's wife stops him and cooks it in a separate pot.

We sit down on the wood floor to eat dinner. I let go of my aunt's shorts so they rest around my waist and cover my ankles. The misters offer me some *bo bo*. It tastes like sawdust.

The leader sits close to Oanh. He wouldn't be so comfortable if he knew Lành's family lived next to Mr. Six Soybean. "Uncle Six, have you seen Lành?" I ask.

"I haven't seen him for a while, but he's around," Mr. Six Soybean says.

What's wrong with Lành that he hasn't cleared out all the Việt Cộng? I start telling how Lành got revenge on the Việt Cộng who attacked him when he visited his family. Mr. Six Soybean shakes his head, but I keep talking. I want to make sure the misters don't come back.

After dinner, the misters sing one of their Communist songs "We All Fight in Our Canoes."

I pretend to sing along. "I hope they all drown and die a miserable death," I sing into Mr. Six Soybean's ear. He laughs.

The misters stay the night, so Mr. Six Soybean puts me in the same bed as his daughters. Oanh says she's the oldest and claims the center. Her little sister falls asleep instantly on the other side. I try to sleep, but Oanh keeps shifting and brushing her body against me. She's doing it on purpose—she must know how it's making me feel. I move as close as I can to the edge of the bed, pressing against the mosquito net so much that the mosquitoes start to bite me.

~

In the middle of the night, the chickens scream. Mr. Six Soybean grabs the night lantern and turns the flame up. Everyone sits up. I wasn't sleeping anyway, so I get up to look around. The leader of the misters asks if we need help. Mr. Six Soybean shakes his head and grabs a long knife from a slot in the kitchen wall. I grab another one and follow him outside. The chickens cluck loudly on a mango tree branch that runs under an eave of the house. Feathers swirl in the drizzling rain. A wide, solid indentation in the mud leads from the tree to the canal. A python trail. I walk to the canal edge and hack a few weeds with my knife, but the snake is already gone.

When I get inside, Oanh has taken up the space on my side of the bed. "That bed has too many mosquitoes coming in," I say, crawling into an empty hammock next to the open wall and wrapping a blanket around all of me except my face. I don't want to sleep next to Mr. Six Soybean's daughter anymore.

When I open my eyes, the sun is already up. The misters are gone. I look over at the bed where the two sisters are. Oanh looks at me in the hammock and covers her mouth with her hand and giggles. She knows she was torturing me.

Mrs. Six Soybean tells Oanh to get up and throw the leftover *bo bo* out to the chickens. The shorts I washed are almost dry, so I take off Dì Hai's shorts and put them on. Then I walk back to my hut. It doesn't look like Quý's been there. It's been a while since I've checked our land, so I walk down the path to my family's converted rice paddy.

On the way back from the rice paddy land, I walk past Mr. Six Soybean's land again, He puts down the pruning shears he has on the end of a long pole. "Be careful. I saw Quý walking toward your hut. Has he been staying with you?"

"Yes."

"Does your mother know?"

"Probably." I haven't told her, but I'm sure he or Aunt Curly will soon.

"Did Quý try to show you his gun or take you out shooting? Anything like that?"

"He wanted me to see his pistol. And he tried to get me to shoot an AK."

"That's not a small thing. Did you tell your mother about it?"

"I'm not stupid. I'm not going to fall for that."

"But if you . . ."

"I know."

"You could never come home."

"I'm not scared. Quý can't impress me with guns or invented stories. I told him to wait until I join the Army. I'll come back and look for him."

Mr. Six Soybean smiles. "Don't tell people that."

Instead of going home, I go to Aunt Curly's house. While I'm taking a pineapple candy out of the jar, Mr. Six Soybean runs up. "There was a gunshot coming from over by your hut."

I stay the night at Aunt Curly's. The next day, I come up to my land from the north so I can see the whole place from a distance. Blood covers the dirt by the side of our hut. The marks look like a tail writhing around—it must have been the snake. I take a knife down from the eaves where I hid it and search through the house checking to see if it's inside. I enter the back bedroom. A pile of moldy reed mats sits folded on the bed. I pull the knife back and flip the top mat open with my hand. First one fold, then the other. Three baby snakes lie in the center, white and powdery as if covered with rice flour. With a few chops, the snakes are in pieces. I go to the kitchen to get a betel nut pod, scoop the minced snakes up, and drop them into the stream. Then I take the moldy mats and burn them so there's no place for snakes to hide.

I go to Aunt Curly's to stay, but come back after dinner. The tide is high—I want to make sure no one is going to load up a boat with fruit from our land and take off.

Quý walks up. "Where have you been?" he asks. "I shot a snake here the other day and couldn't eat all that meat myself."

I glance over at the blood in the dirt. He must have cleaned the snake here before he left. "I was at Cô Ba's house."

Quý grins. "I ate and drank for two days with my friends."

I notice he doesn't tell me who he was staying with. "How did you cook it?"

"We grilled it, fried it, and made a lime leaf and chili stir-fry. It was delicious."

"So where's my share?" Snake would taste good after all that jack-fruit.

"We ate it all. I thought you were gone."

"What? You ate all that meat and didn't save any for me?"

"So are you staying?"

"I was getting my stuff and going over to Cô Ba's house." I can't stand being around Quý knowing his side is winning. I want the war to go on long enough so that I can come back and fight. I'll join the Army as soon as I'm seventeen. Then I'll come back and blow away Quý and all the other Việt Cộng who live out here.

~

I go back to our land when Má and my sister and cousin come out. They weed under the tangerine trees while I look for birds to slingshot. Someone walks noisily on the path. Chị Châu? She's back? She has a backpack on. I'm happy to see her. It's been so long. I thought she wasn't coming back. Where has she been?

"*Chào*, Dì Tám," she says to Má. "I got a ride over with Cô Ba."

"You're a week late," Má says without looking up from the grass roots she's cutting. She turns her head to look up. "Why?"

Chị Châu gives her one of her big smiles and says nothing.

When we go in for dinner, Má tells us that the Việt Cộng forced Chị Châu to join an entertainment group. Chị Châu sits and smiles while Má talks. Má says she got my cousin released because she told the leader that Chị Châu's mother is missing, so she needs to work to help feed her younger brothers and sisters. "You have to be careful because you're attractive to a lot of people's eyes," Má tells Chị Châu.

After dinner Chị Châu does a dance she learned. She moves across the dirt floor with only her feet moving. She keeps the rest of her leg completely still and her knees straight. Chị Châu's shirt stretches in front. I can see why they picked her. She's not missing anything like Chị Năm and Chị Mộng are even though they're older. How can she have that much extra flesh when she eats so little?

"Let's all fight together in our canoes," Chị Châu sings as she dances.

Chị Năm and I sing back at her. "Let's all drown together in our canoes. Then let's all float down the river dead together . . ."

Chị Mộng watches her sister dance and laughs nervously.

A few days later, Chị Châu wears the green nylon pants and shirt the Communists gave her. Má doesn't say anything, but I know she's unhappy. It bothers me that Chị Châu seems proud of the clothes and the dance she learned. Mr. Three East says that we have to all be strong, like South Korea, to have our own country. With so many people joining the Communists how can we hold out?

The next day, Chị Châu's clothes are missing. "I just hung my clothes out over there last night," she asks Má. "Where did they go?"

"Well, did you take them in when the wind blew?" Má says. "They're probably in the canal, go look for them."

I don't need to ask. I know Má made them disappear.

Chapter Twenty-two (Fall 1974–Spring 1975)

Let's All Drown Together

I'm on my knees in front of the class with my arms stretched out and a brick in each hand. I drop my arms a little. *Quực!* Thầy Lộc hits my knuckle with his ruler. I force my arms up.

I thought fifth grade would be a good year for me. It's supposed to be mainly math and all of my classmates come to me when they're stuck. But the math problems Thầy Lộc gives aren't clear. One day our homework was to figure out how long a bicycle rider takes going up and down a hilly road. My answer used different speeds depending on whether the rider was going uphill or downhill. Thầy Lộc gave me a zero. He said the time should be the same as if the road were flat.

"No," I said. "It's a lot faster going downhill than uphill." He tried to convince me, but his reasons didn't make sense. Finally I said, "If you say so, it must be true."

"You disrespect your teacher," he said.

"It's not about respect," I said. "The answer is right or wrong." Now every day I'm on my knees in front of the class with bricks on my hands. He can do this to me, but it doesn't make him right.

I don't know what good I'm doing trapped in school holding bricks up when we're losing the war. As soon as I'm old enough to pass for a soldier I'm going to the middle of Việt Nam to enlist. That's where all the fighting is—on the front. I won't give my real name, so my parents can't stop me. Maybe, once I'm in, I'll tell someone so my family will know if I die. But it will be years before I can enlist. We're losing, and

I'm too young to fight. I feel helpless up here, weighted down with bricks, paralyzed, like when my legs froze under the banyan tree.

At the end of the day, Thầy Lộc lets me take the bricks off. My knees and shoulders ache on the walk home. When I get on top of the bridge where Mr. Three More lives I call, "Mực, Mực, Mực." Mr. Five Salt's black dog rushes toward me. I pet his short, black hair. Mực follows me to the back of my house while I pick bellfruit to eat.

∿

Mực stays inside on the concrete floor of our house napping while I go out to water Chị Tư's flower garden. She put a fence around it because too many people walked by and picked the blossoms. It didn't help, so she gave up. The only plants left are some cooking herbs I'm growing and a seedling that sprouted when someone eating a jackfruit walked by and tossed a seed. I get a can full of water and step over the fence to pour water around the seedling. Jackfruit trees are supposed to grow quickly, but this one is taking a long time.

After I water the garden, I go into the kitchen to help with dinner. Mực follows and sits by the daybed under the stairs watching. I'll feed him some rice after dinner. He doesn't go back home until evening. I reach into the vat to scoop out rice to cook—it worries me how fast it disappears. If the Communists took away Ba's shop or our land, there's nothing I could do to fill the vat up.

Chị Năm squats over the cutting board on the floor. "Did you know that Quý got captured?" she says over the *cụp cụp cụp* of her knife chopping lemongrass.

I look up from the fire I'm building. "Captured? Not killed?" I didn't imagine Quý being taken prisoner. I thought Lành would shoot him.

"That's what I heard."

"Did Lành catch him?"

"No, some other soldiers did." Chị Năm stops chopping. "It's too bad Lành didn't get his hands on him. If anyone deserves it, Quý does for what he did."

"Why wasn't it Lành? What happened?"

"I don't know, but Quý must be in jail now."

I scoop rice into the pot and walk over to the water tank. As soon as I'm sixteen, I'll join the Army and learn how to fight like Lành. Then,

I'll head back to Cồn Tàu. I know where the Việt Cộng hide.

~

On Sunday, people spill out onto the street in front of our house, overflowing from one of the houses built on stilts along the foot ferry dock where someone is having a funeral for a Navy officer. The sound of a large engine comes across the river—a smooth sound, different from the single stroke motor of most boats. I run along the wood planks of the foot ferry dock with Thượng, through the funeral crowd. A patrol boat pulls up between a houseboat and the dock, water blowing behind it and the yellow of South Việt Nam's flag waving.

The tide is low, so the boat doesn't come up to the dock. It still seems huge next to it, running along the entire row of houses. Sailors in blue Navy uniforms tie the boat up and walk up a board leading to the dock. They leave the engine idling and bubbles blowing out the back of the boat. A cluster of kids stands along the board going from the dock to the water, trying to get a closer look.

"How does it work without a propeller?" a group of us shout to a sailor who stayed onboard. We know it's a jet propulsion engine, but it's a mystery how a stream of water can move a boat.

"Hop on. I'll show you." The sailor pulls the rope so the boat drifts over to the board we're standing on. We climb onto the flat edge running around the deck of the boat. I hop down onto the bow of the boat where a tarp covers a gun turret and follow the sailor around the cabin to the back. There's another gun mounted there. The sailor opens a hatch on the deck. Inside tubes wrap around each other looking like intestines in a belly. The idling engine makes a *bờ lụp bờ lụp*. The whole boat vibrates. The sailor explains how some tubes have compressed air and others take the water from underneath the boat. He shows us the large pipe where the water blows out in back.

"But how does it go forward when the water blows out?"

"You have a powerful engine throwing the water back. Come take a look." The sailor leads us into the cabin and lets us look down the stairs at the engine. Then he disappears down the stairs. He must be the mechanic.

We go back to the engine. The mechanic didn't close the hatch, so we stare at the pipes and argue about how it must work. Then, we go to the cabin and poke around. The other kids get bored and leave except for me and another boy.

"Let's look at the guns." I walk onto the bow and pull the gray plastic tarp off. The guns underneath are the same kind that I helped load during the cease-fire, except that there are two of them. I jump down into the gun turret and sit in the chair. The guns refuse to move. I reach down and unlock them.

The other boy comes up to look at the guns moving back and forth. "You better not. You'll get in trouble."

I run my hands over the controls. "These are the handles . . . is this the trigger?"

"You better put it back."

There's a canister of ammunition next to the guns. I pick up a belt. It's heavy. The brass shines in the sun. It looks so pretty in a chain with a dark orange-tipped tracer every ten bullets or so. "I remember that you lift this up . . ." I open a latch and start to load the gun.

"I'm leaving." The boy pulls the rope to bring the boat to the dock and climbs out.

I snap the first gun shut and start loading the other gun. The boat floats away from the dock after the boy climbs out. I like how the turret turns with me as I point the guns straight at the shore and then move them toward the stilts at the end of the dock where Six Chicken's house is. His family rebuilt their house with concrete posts, but left the old coconut trunk posts. In Giao Long, I've seen coconuts along the edge of the river where half the tree is gone because a patrol boat hit it with a bullet with an explosive tip. I want to see what this patrol boat's gun will do to a coconut trunk.

I aim toward Six Chicken's house as low as I can. I'm not sure how the trigger works so I turn the crank around and pull the handle. A burst of bullets comes out. The gun vibrates. It's so loud, I jump back. I'm surprised how much it pushes back even though it's bolted onto the boat. Smoke comes out of the barrel. I try to unload it. The crew runs down the dock toward me. The mechanic rushes out of the cabin. "Get out of there kid, what are you doing?"

I step out of the turret. I'm going to be in the most trouble I've been in in my life. "Sorry, sorry." I point to the pillars under Six Chicken's house. "I only shot the broken posts, not the good ones." The bullets hit near the water so I can't see the holes, but it doesn't look like the posts exploded.

"That's dangerous. You could hurt someone," the mechanic says.

The captain steps on board. "How did that gun get loaded? Did you leave it?"

"That's the radio repairman's son," someone says to the captain.

The captain ignores him and berates the mechanic. I wait for them to do something or tell my parents, but the captain goes back to the funeral with some of his men. This time he leaves two more men behind.

"What is the Navy doing having guns loaded and unlocked next to civilians," one of my neighbors says.

"It wasn't loaded," I say. "I unlocked it and loaded it." The neighbor looks at me and starts complaining about the Navy again.

I don't want the mechanic to get in trouble. I find the head of the family having the funeral. "Tell the captain I loaded the gun. It was locked up. I took it out." He nods at me and goes back to his guests.

I wait around on the dock to see what the boat looks like when it takes off. I want to find out what will happen to all the mud on the bottom of the river when the water jet hits it. After half an hour the sailors leave. The boat backs up quickly, making even more bubbles. As it turns to head back toward Đồng Tâm base, a surge of mud-filled water pushes toward the shore.

I walk around and then go home. I'm sure someone has already told my parents. I worry about what Má and Ba will say. When I walk in the front door, Six Chicken's mother and my parents are standing inside talking.

"There he is!" Six Chickens mother says. "You need to pay for the damage he's done."

"But I only shot the coconut logs," I say. "I didn't shoot any of the concrete posts."

"You could have shot them," Six Chicken's mother says.

"But I didn't. If you swim out there with me I'll show you."

"If something is damaged we'll pay," Má says, "but if there's no damage . . ."

Ba looks at Six Chicken's mother. "When your husband shot our roof there was damage," he says.

Six Chicken's mother walks out muttering. She knows I didn't break anything.

I wait for Ba to punish me. "You could hurt somebody," he says and goes back to work.

A month before *Tết*, the government announces that this year firecrackers aren't allowed. For once I don't care. All I want to do is join the Army and fight. Enemy troops are massing for an advance. The announcers on the radio and TV say we won't be able to stop the North this time because America has cut off supplies. Even the men at tea say it. But America has been with the South for so long—why would it do that? The reason we don't have ammunition must be because corrupt officials are stealing the money. Or maybe America stopped helping because we're not fighting hard enough. I check the gun and ammunition on top of the cabinet. Why did we waste all that ammunition during the cease-fire? When it's my turn, I'll fight hard.

People stop bringing in radios and TVs to be fixed. Ba and the neighborhood men spend more time drinking tea and talking. Mr. Three East and the Army soldiers complain that bullets are being rationed. No one is working, everyone is waiting for the end. Má worries that when the Communists take over we'll lose most or all of our land. If that happens, how will we keep the rice vat filled?

The only one with customers is the medium. With everything so uncertain, people come to clear up their debts and troubles for a better future in the New Year. After school, noises from a séance come from Bà Ba's house. I'm almost sure she can't communicate with ghosts, but I want to be completely sure.

Today, Mr. Six West is supposed to channel the spirit. He used to only light incense and set up the ceremony, but the Bà Ba is getting old. Mr. Six West drops to his knees and rolls his head around, waiting. The spirit is a man, so it's good the medium is having him do it. Once she had to act like the head of a family. It sounded real, but it seemed to exhaust her. She kept sitting down.

Bà Ba calls for the spirit to enter Mr. Six West. He shakes and stops. I stare straight into his eyes. It's disrespectful, but I have to figure out whether he's still there or not. If he's possessed by a spirit, he won't notice.

Mr. Six West shrieks and moans as the ghost begins to talk through him. His whole body quivers. The incense has thinned out. I can see his face clearly now.

"Why are you tormenting me?" the client asks.

I've heard a lot of ghosts answer this question. Most of the time, the spirit wants the client to repay a debt for it. Sometimes it wants revenge.

"You didn't return what I lent you," the ghost says through Mr. Six West.

"I've always given back everything I borrowed," the client insists. I wonder what the ghost will say to this.

The ghost's voice grows sad. "I lent you support and you didn't lend it back to me." The client hangs his head. The mediums must have heard this reply before, just like Ba knows what to say when a customer comes to pick up a radio that he hasn't been able to fix.

"Let go of the secret crime you hold in your heart so we can settle our debt here once and for all," the ghost demands. The family looks terrified. As they each spill out a secret, the ghost uses it against them. Why are people so eager to tell everything about themselves to the medium? The frog dies because of its big mouth.

Mr. Six West makes a slight hand motion behind his back. Bà Ba sways her body and moans as the ghost passes into her. Was he signaling her to take over? He stands up and leaves through the door in the back of the room. After talking in all this smoke, he probably needs a glass of water. When Mr. Six West returns, he bobs his head, rolls his shoulders around, and the ghost passes back to him.

After they trap the ghost, I walk across the alley to the back of my house and sit up in the bellfruit tree. I remember the time Bà Ba looked at her empty glass of water while she was in the middle of channeling a ghost, and Mr. Six West took it and filled it. Like when Ba glances at me and the empty pot of tea and I know to refill it. If Bà Ba were really possessed, she wouldn't be giving Mr. Six West orders. If you pretend to capture ghosts, you can make a lot of money. But if they're not really speaking to spirits, it doesn't seem right for them to take it.

The next day after dinner there's another séance. While Mr. Six West acts like a ghost is coming into him, he slowly brings his head down in a bow and scans the audience for clues. That's a good way for him to check how they're responding. No one looks at your eyes when you're bending down.

A fly buzzes around Mr. Six West and lands on his face. I wonder what he'll do. He's supposed to be possessed. Mr. Six West continues chanting in an unknown language. He slowly pulls one hand behind him and makes a signal. Bà Ba moves in to take her turn and Mr. Six West gets up and pushes the fly away. When he returns a few minutes later, he makes another sign with his hand and takes the ghost back. With all the gesturing back and forth, I know it has to be an act, not a live ghost moving between them.

I don't like Bà Ba, she can get as angry as an evil spirit, but Mr. Six West is so trustworthy in everything. Except this. My parents say that if you cheat, later it will cost you more than you gained. I wonder how much he sold his trust for? Then I remember that when Mr. Six West's son and daughter come into the dock from their farm, they don't have much fruit to unload. He probably can't make a living on his land.

⁓

I finish my homework and head upstairs. Mực stays downstairs. Tây complained to his father that his dog was staying at our house, but I told them it was still their dog, and they said it was alright. It's dark. My brothers must have already gone to bed. The window at the top of the stairs looks directly into a window in Sơn's house. Every time I come up at night, I hope a flicker of light will come from their side, but it's been dark and empty since they moved. No one knows where. His father is American. Maybe they went to America with him.

I glance at the window expecting it to be dark. A pair of glowing eyes stares at me. I scream and dive under the mosquito net in the corner where my brothers are. I didn't know I could scream like that. Whatever it was could come right in. Our upstairs window doesn't have bars on it.

"It was probably a cat," Vân says.

"A cat? No, it was bigger ... it ..." I can't believe I screamed like a girl over a cat. I promise myself that I'll never act scared like that again, no matter what I see. Even if I meet a ghost in the banyan trees.

A few days later, I step out of our upstairs window onto the roof, then over onto Sơn's roof, and close their wood shutters.

⁓

Má sits in the front room talking with the ferryman's wife about all the people they know who died in the war. They list a lot of people I don't know, but every once in a while it's someone I do. Má lists my missing aunt as one of them.

They start talking about people who stepped on grenades. Some are young kids, some are grown-ups. I don't know any of them.

"How about Mrs. Fourth Silk?" I ask. "You didn't count her." I try to not think of her because I know that her eyes will haunt me for not doing anything.

"No. Mrs. Fourth Silk didn't die," Má says. "I visited her in the hospital afterward."

"How could she be alive? She was bleeding so much and all the boats were stuck?"

"Thầy Bi found a boat—I'm not sure how."

The retired teacher must have had a secret radio in that tunnel. Thượng and I heard it when we were there.

"She was so thin when I saw her," Má says. "Less than forty kilos with little black knots covering her body like hundreds of large insect bites."

So many stitches. That must be why no one could stop her bleeding. They couldn't cover a hundred cuts. Maybe she didn't lose as much blood as I thought.

"She told me she had a fight with her husband right before the accident," Má says. "*Hứ.* He's probably the one who planted those grenades in the first place. Cậu Năm Lộc was furious when Fourth Silk's husband came back and took out another rusty grenade on that land. It was on their path to rescue her. If it hadn't been rusted out, that grenade would have killed Cậu Năm or Thầy Bi."

Má looks around at us. "There are two kinds of people: those who accidentally step on grenades and those who go looking for them. Don't be either."

I don't understand why anyone would go looking for a grenade. But I'm glad the eyes I looked into are still alive—that I wasn't looking into the eyes of a ghost.

～

The sounds of a séance come from the window in the alley. Mr. Six West chants in the background on the floor while Bà Ba sits on a chair with the hood of her dried-blood colored robe shading her face. I stand back from the window so she doesn't slam the shutters on me. They can't be catching ghosts because if they were they wouldn't put them in clay pots. But ghosts might be talking through the medium like when Mr. Fourth Post's spirit told Má where his body was. I want to know if spirits really can come into the physical world—if at the banyan tree when my legs froze I was fighting a spirit or my own mind.

Bà Ba's voice goes from high to low and from soft to tough as she searches for the right spirit. Usually families place a picture of the person whose spirit they want to talk to on the altar, but only the god of the underworld and the commander of the gates of hell look over the room. It seems harder for the medium to find the spirit without a picture. The mother looks hopefully at Bà Ba, but her husband and grown daughter squint their eyebrows together and stare hard at the medium's face under her hood.

The man gets up as if he's going to leave. "Please wait," his wife says. "The right one will come."

"There are always ghosts waiting nearby, trying to be heard," Mr. Six West says. He wears a robe, but no hood.

The medium finally finds a voice the mother likes. The father asks the spirit a few questions. He shakes his head at the answers and sits back with his arms crossed. Bà Ba starts to dig, trying to find the words to make the mother happy. The mother looks like she wants to say something to the spirit, but her husband must have told her not to give the medium any information, so she waits for the spirit to tell her what she wants to hear. Each time the medium tries to guess the obstacle holding the ghost back from the afterlife, the father shakes his head and the medium tries again. If Bà Ba can talk to the spirit, shouldn't she be able to tell the family what it wants to hear without hints?

Mr. Six West tells the family he has to get more incense. I bet he wants to get away from the angry stares of this man. Why doesn't Bà Ba tell the father his presence is so powerful that he scared the spirit away? When Ba can't fix a radio, he returns it.

Mr. Six West comes back with another package of incense. He seems surprised the family is still here. He opens the package and pushes another stick into the sand in the brass pot on the altar. Lighting more incense is his answer to any problem. Bà Ba comes out of the trance. "This soul is possessed by another, stronger ghost." A shiver moves up her arms. She shakes. "That's why it lost its history. We'll capture the spirit of your loved one and when the ghost possessing it comes looking for it, we'll trap it and set the spirit free."

"We traveled all the way up here for this?" The man stands up. "I can't waste money. I need it to farm."

That's how I felt when I lost money to the fortune teller on the Coconut Monk's island. I could have used the money for a good meal.

The man steps out onto the street. "I'm from downriver. I can't afford this." Everyone from downriver seems poorer, like my tenth aunt who farms where salt water mixes with the fresh water at high tide. The man walks across the street into Mr. Five Fermented Beancurd's house. "Where can I find the authorities?"

"It looks like this is between you and Bà Ba," Mr. Five Fermented Beancurd says. The medium has a big family and has been in Tân Long longer than almost everyone else. No one wants to make her upset.

The wife and daughter of the man from downriver walk down the dock to their boat. The man steps into our open doorway. Ba comes out of the lean-to where he's working. "I need the police to come and settle this dispute," the man says. "It takes me two months of farming to make this kind of money."

"To get the police, you'll have to go all the way over to Mỹ Tho," Ba says. "But Mr. Three East is the head of the local Civilian Self-Defense. He can handle neighborhood disputes." Ba points the man downstream toward Mr. Three East's house. Mr. Three East would be reasonable. Mr. Six West is usually reasonable, too. People call on Mr. Six West to settle arguments or speak for the neighborhood at events, but today he's hiding inside the medium's house.

The man stands in the street calling for the authorities. His wife gets off the boat and comes down the dock to stand by him. She wants the money back now, too. I can't believe the medium let her customers get mad enough to make a scene.

Bà Ba comes out and calls the couple over. She has a clay pot in one hand. "Here, take it. The spirit of your loved one." She hands the pot to the wife. "If you release the spirit far from here we don't need to catch the ghost enslaving it. Since we only caught one ghost, it's not as much work. Come inside. We can talk."

The man sends his wife to the boat and goes into the medium's house. When he leaves, his jaw is clenched, and he still has heat on his face. If the medium actually freed his family from a ghost, he should be happy.

The next day, I'm back in school with bricks on my hands. I still feel paralyzed and still don't know if spirits can come into this world or not. But I'm almost completely sure that Bà Ba's not talking to them.

Ba and the men at tea discuss how people will stop going to the medium just like they've stopping using the moon calendar for everything except *Tết* and the Moon Festival. That's good. Poor farmers shouldn't waste their money.

∼

There's no séance after school, so I walk around the back of our house trying to see if Mr. Six West is around. I want to let him know that I know. I want him to admit that he's pretending so I can be done watching.

Mr. Six West sees me and calls out from his house behind the medium's shop. "Come inside and have some tea, Lượng."

"Yes, Uncle Six." I hate tea, but now's my chance.

I enter his house and take a seat at his small table. He works the teapot out of the coconut husk that's keeping it warm and pours oolong tea into two cups. Usually, I'm the one taking the tea out and serving Ba's customers. This is the first time I've been served tea as if I were an adult. I take as small a sip as I can and wait for him to talk.

He pulls out a tin and offers me a coconut cookie. "Lượng," he says as I slowly chew on the edge of the bumpy, stick-shaped cookie. "I know you're always watching me when I work. That's alright, but please . . . not all the time."

"You're good. You hardly give a sign. Only when you bowed down. I saw your eyes glance around."

"Yes, I saw you."

I knew he wasn't possessed. I knew he could see me. "I bet when that fly landed on your face you wanted to brush it off."

"Yes, that was bad."

I take a small drink of tea and then another cookie. "You're better than Bà Ba. She covers her face with her hood, so it makes you think she's hiding something. But you don't. If you opened your own shop you'd do better than her. People trust you more."

He holds his cup and looks out the window and back at me. "It's not that simple. When you're the owner, people scrutinize you much more. Besides, it really is easier to do a session with two people."

I finish my second cookie and look at my tea cup. It's a little more than half empty. Empty enough to not be rude, but not enough for him to pour me more. "Now, Lượng," Mr. Six West says, as I excuse myself, "please remember what I asked you. It makes it hard for me to do my job with you staring at me all of the time."

I nod. I found out what I wanted to know. I don't need to watch anymore. Má thinks the spirit by the banyan tree paralyzed my legs to teach me a lesson, but maybe there's another explanation. Maybe my legs got too cold to move from standing in the water fishing.

~

Once *Tết* comes, the medium's house is quiet. Usually, I can buy a few illegal firecrackers from Mr. Three More's wife, who lives on the other side of the medium and whose husband is always away in the Army. This year she doesn't have any to sell. No one else is selling them either. And no one is giving out much *lì xì* money. The only one who gives my brothers and me a normal amount of *lì xì* is Aunt Curly. Everyone seems to be saving since they don't know what will happen when the war ends. Má placed a soursop, a papaya, and a mango on the altar for *Tết*, even though they're expensive this time of year, because the names sound like the words for "wish," "enough," and "spend."

During the holiday, I go out with Má to Cồn Tàu. We pass Lành's fort on our way in. The log dock juts out of the bank, but everything looks overgrown. When we go to wish Ông Bà Năm and Mr. Six Soybean a happy New Year, I ask about Lành. Mr. Six Soybean says it seems like the fort is empty, but no one's checked because no one wants the Việt Cộng to see them near it. I start to realize we won't be able to hold out like South Korea. With all the people in the countryside joining the Việt Cộng we're fighting ourselves.

"Do you know where Quý is?" I ask because people talk about Lành and Quý as if they're brothers. You mention one and the other is right there. No one in Mr. Six Soybean's family knows, so I ask, "Is he still alive?" Because whenever I don't see someone around, I think that person is probably dead.

I stay in Cồn Tàu for a few days, but I don't go out to the banyan trees. There's too much to fight already—I don't want to fight myself again. As I'm swimming in the stream in front of our hut, I see Má getting ready to pick up a huge basket of guavas and take it to our boat. I should help her. Má always works so hard, but lately she keeps asking if all the work she's doing on her land will go to someone else. The basket looks too heavy—I couldn't carry it. As Má heaves the bamboo basket up onto her shoulder and turns to walk toward our boat, her belly sticks out. My family discussed someone being pregnant at dinner, but I didn't think they meant Má. I thought people her age couldn't have more kids. It's not a good time to have a baby when we're losing the war. With ten of us, our rice vat gets empty fast enough already.

Chapter Twenty-three (Spring 1975)

Small Birds in a Flame Tree

My fourth grade teacher talked to Thầy Lộc. Now, I'm only on my knees with bricks on my hands once a week instead of every day. It's like a badge of honor. I can control what I think no matter what they do. I don't think I'm learning anything, though. I wonder if Thầy Lộc is teaching us enough to pass the test fifth graders take to see if they go to middle school or go to work. I might not pass the writing part, but I should do well on the math.

After the *Tết* holiday, Chị Tư takes me on the foot ferry over to Mỹ Tho for the test. "This is important. You need to do your best," my sister tells me as we pass a soccer field and enter a cluster of schools: boys' and girls' high schools, a middle school, and a private Catholic university.

All the fifth graders in the Mỹ Tho area are supposed to take the test here today, but we're early, so there aren't many students around. Chị Tư buys me a snack from a street vendor, triangles of tapioca flour with shrimp cooked in it. It tastes terrible. We walk across to a small deli, and she buys something else. The deli food is bad, too. I'm too nervous to eat, so we end up throwing most of it away. "Just try your best," my sister says. "You're smart, you'll do fine."

"What's the point of taking this test when we're losing the war?" I ask. "No one is going to care afterward."

"It's still the benchmark of intelligence. A high score will help your future."

"I don't know what I'm going to write about." I spent the night worrying about the essay. It won't matter, but I don't want to fail and be embarrassed.

"Write about how you're inspired to be a scientist or an inventor like Marie Curie or Thomas Edison."

I've read all of my sister's biographies of famous people, but I don't want to be like anyone else. I just want to be free. Free from tests and free from Communists.

Chị Tư leaves me at the auditorium and stands outside the fence with the other older siblings and parents. Hundreds of fifth-graders stand waiting to enter classrooms and lecture halls. A row of large flame trees runs along the street—trees with bright red flowers that Phượng, the girl who lives behind us, is named after. Schools usually have a lot of these trees around. It's already late morning and hot, but a few small birds still hop around the branches behind the fern-like leaves. The red flowers are buds. I wish they were open because it would mean summer was here, and I wouldn't be taking a test.

Inside the auditorium, I'm surprised to see the seats and stairs sloping down in front of me. It's the first time I've seen so many students in one room. A few kids from my school sit scattered around, far away from me. I turn over the test. There are so many questions. I keep my head down so I don't get kicked out for looking around. If you fail, you have one chance to retake the test. If you repeat fifth grade. If your parents let you. My parents would, but then everyone would think that I was *đần*.

I do the math and save the essay. When we break for lunch, I find a different deli and buy a sugarcane drink and a *bánh mì* sandwich. The food is better and I can eat. I still don't know what to write for my essay—I'm good at math, not writing. A few birds fly around in the midday heat.

When I get back inside, I write about what I want: freedom. I write how it would feel to be one of the small birds in the flame trees, so common that most people don't even notice. I know what it's like to sit up high in a coconut tree or on the rooftops watching life below you. A bird would see even more. Everything would look different flying over trees and rice paddies—the world below not paying attention to my flight. I'd be free to travel wherever I wanted, free to see more than everyone else. If the Communists take over, I won't be able to roam around freely, but the birds will still be able to.

After the test, I stand on the street looking for my sister and watching the vendors. I know I did well on the math, but I'm not sure about my essay. I start to feel depressed again. What does it matter how I did when I don't know what will happen from day to day?

When we get back to school the next day, everyone talks about how they think they did on the test. We'll have to wait a month to find out. The war may be over before then. My teacher stops putting bricks on my hands and making me kneel in front of the class—I'm more worried about the South losing than doing anything to get in trouble at school.

~

Troops coming down from the North along the Cambodian border force people living there to flee. Some of them come to Tân Long, one more reminder we're losing the war. A widow and her three children anchor their boat at the dock across the street and move into Sơn's old house. They used to import furniture from Cambodia, like Six Chicken's family.

During the night, screams come from their house. I ask the younger son about the cries at night. He tells me that it's a ghost howling. The only ghost in their house is the cat I saw in their window. They don't go upstairs often, but whenever they open the shutters on the window across from ours, I step over and close them.

When the boy asks me over to play, I notice that the refrigerator Sơn's family had is gone. The wet bar looks empty without the clutter of Sơn's father's liquor bottles, and the bar sink doesn't seem to work anymore. This new family must be scared of ghosts because they sleep together in the front room: the two boys on the pool table that Sơn's family left behind, the mother and daughter in a bed next to it. The screams sound like a girl, so I keep asking. Finally the boy tells me that his older sister, Hoàng, has nightmares. What happened to them before they came here?

~

"They're going to take all our freedom away when they win. That's what's going to happen," Cậu Năm Lộc says. He's stopped by to have tea with Ba after ferrying people here from Giao Long.

I wonder what losing freedom will mean. The book *What is Communism?* says Communists can control your thoughts so that you can't even think what you want to. How could anyone control what you think? I can think what I want even if I have to hold up bricks in class. The book says they control you by turning family members against each other, but I don't believe that will happen.

"Everything will go backwards under the Communists," Cậu Năm Lộc, the ferryman, continues. "Decades. Just like China."

How is it possible to go back in time? I read that under Communism things are frozen in time. Not moving forward is bad enough.

"And that's when we're going to starve," the ferryman says, "just like the North."

Some of the men nod and say the people they know in the North are very poor. Others say it's because they're being bombed, and it's hard to know what it will be like in peacetime. I don't know what it's like in the North, but the South has rice paddies, streams loaded with fish, and fruit growing everywhere you look. I know it will be bad, but how could it be as bad as the ferryman says it will be?

~

A few weeks after the test, we're sitting at our desks talking because the teacher hasn't arrived. I walk out to the porch wrapped around our classroom to the back half that sits on stilts over the river. I dangle my legs over the edge, looking for snails or mudskippers in the muddy bank below. Some of the other boys wander around and pee off the porch into the river. After an hour, the school secretary walks past me into the classroom.

"The teacher is not able to come," she says from inside. "You're dismissed."

I can't believe my luck.

Thầy Lộc comes to school the next day. He puts a problem on the board for us to solve, and then spends his time outside talking to the other teachers that made it in. He doesn't show up again for two days. When he comes back he sits at his desk staring while we read silently. "It's not safe for me to leave my house," he finally says. "The war looks like it's taking a path for the worse."

Fewer teachers show up every day. After being absent for several days in a row Thầy Lộc announces, "You should all just try to stay safe.

There's no point in coming to school." Tân Long is fairly safe and Mỹ Tho is supposed to be safe. Even if there's no point in coming to school, why is he so scared?

Only two classes still have teachers. I stop carrying my papers and books to school because we're told to go home every day. One morning, the secretary tells us not to come unless we hear otherwise. When we leave, the attendant chains and padlocks the metal gate.

~

Chị Tư takes me to Mỹ Tho to get my test results. Even with everyone coming to find out how they did on the exam, the cluster of schools seems quieter and emptier than the day I took it. Some of the smaller schools have closed. My brothers still go to school in Mỹ Tho, but they complain that fewer classmates come each day.

Tamarind trees line the street on the side of the girls' high school. People crowd around bulletin boards set up under them. My sister and I head to the pass list first, looking over thousands of names on thirty sheets of paper for *L*.

I search over the heads of people for my name. I don't find it. I scan under all the other letters in case they misplaced it, then go back to *L*. I feel panic and tears start in my eyes. I walk to the smaller fail list. About a third of the students didn't make it. I believe in myself, no matter what any test says. I'll pass someday even if I have to repeat fifth grade.

"Let's check the pass list again," Chị Tư says when we can't find my name on the fail list. I try to blink tears away and scan the pass list again for the letters that make up my name. I still can't find it. My sister goes off to inspect a third list—two sheets of paper framed under a large red sign reading HONORS. I don't know why she's bothering to look there.

"Lượng, come over here," Chị Tư calls.

I walk over, confused.

"Your name is on this list," Chị Tư says. "You did great."

The list is ordered by rank, and my name is close to the top. The tears clear from my eyes. Out of thousands, I'm close to the top? I wanted to prove to everyone that I'm as smart as them, but I didn't expect this. The Communists won't care about our scores, and I can't even brag to my friends since school is out. All that matters is that after all these years of being called *đần*, I proved myself and my family knows it.

～

At the beginning of April, soldiers start to return to Tân Long, getting off the ferry in their uniforms, pretending to be on leave, and then hiding in their houses. They're supposed to fight bravely and die, not run away. They need to hold the line, so when I'm sixteen I can join and fight.

During the hot afternoon, I serve tea and listen to Ba and the neighborhood men. "Did you hear anything?" the men ask each other. "Which provinces have troop movement." They're trying to figure out how fast the country is falling and when it will crumble down to Sài Gòn. The men tell Ba that it must be hard for him having a new baby coming. He nods. At dinner he complains to Má about how tough times are with no one bringing in radios or TVs to be fixed—having a baby will make it harder.

I can't stand waiting to lose, so I go out to Cồn Tàu. The countryside is the emptiest I've seen it. Ông and Bà Năm aren't on their land. Most people have gone to the city where they think it will be safer when the final battle erupts. No one gathers for tea or dinner. People only stop by for a few words and leave. Mr. Six Soybean's family is still around, so I stop over to talk.

"What do you think will happen when it's over?" I ask. I know we'll lose some things like our land and maybe even our house or our TV and radios, but I'm not sure how much.

"I don't know. I hope that people like Stone Brave who come into power won't be unreasonable. If they're local, they should know how things work."

Then Mr. Six Soybean tells me what happened to Yến. She didn't get smart and leave. She was raped by the Việt Cộng hanging around her house and went to Mỹ Tho to have the baby. "Girls shouldn't be alone like that," he says.

The Communists say that they're on the people's side, but they're not. They're taking advantage of them. I shouldn't have left Yến alone, but what could I have done? I want to do more to keep us from losing, but my whole body is stuck, paralyzed, and nothing I do matters.

I leave Mr. Six Soybean's and go out to check our land. The tangerine trees burst with green fruit that won't ripen until fall. Việt Cộng in their nylon clothes march through the main path on their way South. Every time I come out I see a new group—it must be over. I thought the war would go on forever. It's been here since I was born, but it's going to end before I get my chance to fight. If only the South could hold out a little longer we'd have our harvest.

I try to stay in my hut or fish with my casting net far from the main path so I don't run into Việt Cộng squads. But the next time I'm out checking on our land, I run into a group marching through. "Why are you still here? Don't you have somewhere to fight?" I ask.

"We're getting ready," one of the men in nylon says.

"The war will be over by then," I say. They ignore me and walk by. If I saw Lành, I'd tell him where all these Việt Cộng are. The war is being lost in front of my eyes, and I can't do anything.

Chapter Twenty-four

Unconditional Surrender:

April 30, 1975

I put a basket of ripe soursops in my canoe and paddle through the canals to the place where Chị Mộng's in-laws usually tie their boat up to buy fruit. On my way, I pass Mr. Six Soybean's house. No clothes or pots hang outside. He left the countryside over a week ago. I listen for other boats or the rumbling noise from a distant firefight. All I hear is the stroke of the wooden paddle when I hit the side of the canoe to nudge it away from the water coconuts on the bank.

"*Chào*, Cô Tư," I say to Chị Mộng's mother-in-law when I get to the side of their large boat. It would be nice if she had a package for me from my family in Tân Long or bought me some *bánh* like I asked. I hop on her boat and hand her the basket of ripe soursops.

She puts them into a flat bamboo basket so that there's only one layer and hands back my basket and some money. "Sorry, Lượng, I didn't see any good *bánh* today."

That's alright. I can use the money to buy some candy at Aunt Curly's. I can't spend too much, though, because Chị Mộng's in-laws always tell Má what they paid me.

"No package either, but your mother sent a message. She wants me to tell you 'Don't be a lost bird flying away from the flock.'"

I laugh. What a strange message. I guess Má wants me to go home, but Chị Mộng's in-laws are already packing up to head back so I don't have time to go with them. "I understand," I say. "I'll leave with you the next time I have fruit to sell."

Two days later, Chị Mộng's mother-in-law walks all the way to my hut. "Your mother sent another message. You need to go home today. We'll wait for you."

I run out and harvest a soursop I've been watching and a few other pieces of fruit. They need another day to get ripe, but if I don't take them now they'll go bad by the time I get back. I put the fruit in a plastic net bag along with my clothes and the rest of the rice. After I hide the knives and lantern and check that the canoe is tied to a water coconut, I walk through the island to the fruit wholesaler's boat.

The boat turns out of the leafy passages of Cồn Tàu and into the wide open river. It's too stuffy to sit in the covered area with the baskets of soursops, betel nuts, and guavas. I climb up on the roof and sit with Chị Mộng's mother-in-law and her son. After a while I get down and stand in the open back of the boat next to the motor where the husband steers with a pole connected to the rudder. There's nothing to do but look at the brown water curling away from the boat and the trees hiding the edge of the shore next to us. No ghost bodies float in the river. There weren't any on the way down either, and I haven't heard much gunfire. Why have we stopped fighting? The news on the radio is that the Army is fleeing—they must be retreating into position to make their last stand. In history books there's always a heroic battle at the end. No one just gives up. We pass the stream that leads to our old home in Quới Sơn. We already fled once. Where can we go now?

It's evening when we get to the fruit vendor's dock in Tân Long. There are only a few boats tied up. The street is full of people waiting to see what will happen. Small boats travel back and forth across the river.

I find Má in her room. "Good. You're here," she says. "Go upstairs and pack your clothes."

"How are we going to leave?" I ask.

"There's a way." Má has several big travel bags filled and hidden in her bedroom. "Now we're just waiting for your older sisters. I sent a message to Thanh and Lan a week ago. They're still not here. Where are they?" She paces the house searching for things to take, trying to keep the front room looking normal so no one knows we're planning to leave.

I put some shorts and a couple of shirts in a plastic rice bag, but I know we're not going anywhere with my two oldest sisters still at nursing school. And Ba hasn't packed anything.

The next day Mr. Three East mutters to himself as he patrols up and down the street in front of our house. He's the only member of the Civilian Self-Defense still around. Whenever he runs into soldiers he asks, "Are you on break? Why are you home?"

"Our unit disbanded. We didn't have anywhere to go," a soldier answers, "so we put our arms down and came home."

They're running away from the fight.

Ba sees Mr. Three East walking by our house and calls him in for tea. I get the teapot out and set it on the table. "That's it," Mr. Three East says, "they'll surrender soon. Everyone fell out of line. The Army is a snake without a head now. The head was chopped off a while ago." He gulps down his tea and walks back to his house.

Two soldiers stop by the next evening. Má brings them to the dining area in the back of the house. I follow, along with my brothers and the sisters who are home. "Are you coming?" one of the soldiers asks Má.

"I'm waiting for my two oldest daughters," she says.

Ba steps in from the back room of the lean-to.

"It's hard to have everyone together," the soldier says. "Why doesn't your husband stay and wait? We'll send another boat for them."

"What if the carriers aren't there?" Ba asks. "Can we go to Thailand?"

The soldiers shake their heads. "No. There's not enough fuel."

Má tells the men to wait in the front part of the house while she and Ba talk. She chases all of us kids out. I can't hear what Má says, but Ba shouts, "Do you want to kill us all?"

Má comes out alone. "Is there a wave after this one?" she asks the soldiers.

"All the big ones are going in the next twelve hours," one of them says. "All the troop carriers and transports. This is a well-armed convoy and it's being escorted. Only small patrol boats will be left."

"We need more time."

"You have to decide now."

The soldiers leave without an answer. My parents argue for hours. "You don't know where they're going," Ba says. "The Army says the carriers will be there, but other people say you're just going out to drown or get ambushed by the Communists or even shot by the

Americans. If it doesn't work we can't come back. We'll be traitors. Our house will be ransacked the second we close our door to leave."

Aren't the Communists supposed to be worse? After all of Ba's talk about how bad Communism is, why are we staying?

The next day when I wake up, Má is already gone. Chị Tư tells me she went to Mỹ Tho. From our balcony I watch boats of all sizes stream south toward the mouth of the river. They're staggered, three in a row, then two. Large ships, metal freighters, and troop transports in the middle with gunboats rocketing down alongside them, pushing up waves. For the first time, the Mekong looks small.

I walk out to watch the parade of boats from the end of the foot ferry dock. People stand around watching in front of Six Chicken's house. "There goes the whole Navy," someone says.

They're abandoning us.

Soldiers step off small passenger ferry boats onto the dock, saying, "It's over." Everybody expects a final battle at the Army base along National Road 4. But how will it happen with all the soldiers coming home?

A woman selling steamed yams to the people gathered around says, "I have to work . . . Communists or not . . . my family has to eat."

People look around for any anti-Communist posters near their homes and peel them off. Mr. Three East walks by without stopping. He's not wearing his uniform or carrying his gun.

Two men carrying a steel desk get off a small ferry boat. The boat owner says that over in Mỹ Tho people have started looting abandoned offices. Smoke billows out of public buildings from officials burning documents.

Women on a troop transport ship wave at us and point downriver toward the ocean. A soldier comes out and walks among them. The women stop. He leaves. The women start waving again and pointing downriver. Another soldier comes out and gestures them to get below. We should be on one of the transports. Even though we've stopped fighting, we should be with the side that's free. Not stuck back here with the Communists. What is Má doing? Shouldn't she be back by now?

Every once in a while there's a rumble in the distance. Some Army soldiers say it sounds like a B-40 rocket-propelled grenade launcher. Still, it looks like the convoy will make it without being attacked. "What happens when they get to the ocean?" someone asks.

"They'll drown," a couple of people answer at the same time.

"No they won't," says a soldier who came home today. "The carriers are out there. The carriers will pick them up and take them some place."

"What if you manage to get to the carriers, then what will happen to you?" an older man asks.

"They'll probably go to Thailand, create a camp so they can come back and retake Việt Nam," the soldier says. Another soldier nods.

"Come back and fight? With what?" the man says. "Where will they get troops or equipment? No, if you get on one of those boats, it's a one-way ticket."

He's right. I'd like to find out where the one-way ticket goes, though. China has Taiwan and Korea has South Korea. Where will we go? To some tiny island somewhere? Wherever it is will be freedom.

I jump in the river to cool down. Transport ships stop along the way to pick up people who come out to meet them in small ferry boats. Maybe I could hire a ferry to take me out. Then I'd wave at one of the transporters going by to have it stop for me. All I'd have to tell them is that my father is already on a carrier.

A few hours later the boats are gone except for a transporter going full-tilt down the river every once in a while. Má comes back late in the afternoon. "I watched the convoy this morning," I say. "Are we going to be picked up?"

"We're waiting for your sisters," she says. "We'll all go together."

It will be too late. And even if my sisters were here, I don't think Ba would let us leave.

∽

The next morning, I'm out in front of the house waiting for something to happen. The news comes from behind me on an old radio with transistors showing through a missing side panel—one the owner didn't stop by to pick up. My parents listen at the table inside with my older sisters. My brothers and younger sisters sit outside on the steps. I wander in and out. Every once in a while some small-arm fire or grenades go off in the distance. Each time, I hope it's the start of our final fight to push the Communists back.

All at once, people on the street say that it's an unconditional surrender. I run back inside. The voice of the Army general who's been our president for only two days comes over the radio:

The Republic of Việt Nam's policy is the policy of peace and reconciliation, aimed at saving the blood of our people. I ask all the Army to stop firing and stay where you are. I ask our brothers in the Provisional Revolutionary Government to stop firing and stay in place. We wait here to hand over authority to the Provisional Revolutionary Government in order to stop useless bloodshed.

The tape repeats and the unconditional surrender starts again.

I thought we had more time.

Ba walks over to the table with the teapot and turns on a small black and white TV mounted on the wall. The same general is at Independence Hall announcing the surrender. It seems more official on the screen.

On the street people say, "Unconditional? How can that be?" "He was supposed to be negotiating for us ... He must have been working for the North all along."

I come back inside to see what we need to hide. We hid most of the tape players and TVs earlier. Má moves through the house looking for any flags or symbols of South Việt Nam to take down. She finds the flag from the boat and takes it off the pole. Then she gathers up some paper flags on sticks and pulls down posters. She puts the pile of yellow in the kitchen fireplace and lights it. All around us, we smell our neighbors' flags burning, too.

I go around to the back of the house and climb onto the thick tin over the kitchen, the only place on the roof I can stand on now without crushing it. The South Vietnamese flag painted on our rooftop has already faded away. No need to scrape it off. I stop to listen, hoping there's going to be one last fight, but there are only small bursts of gunfire in the distance. A few boats rush downstream. Is it too late for us to go?

I spend the rest of the day waiting for something to happen. In the evening, people stand outside in the street whispering and watching the sun set. As soon as the sun goes down it's completely dark. No one has lights on. For the last three weeks there hasn't been any diesel for the town generators. Someone points overhead to a new formation in the stars—shoots coming off a handle like a broom. I look at stars all the time in the countryside, and I haven't seen a constellation like this before. "It's a sign from the sky that we'll be swept aside," people tell each other. "The Communists will sweep away our wealth, our food, our lives, everything."

I don't need the stars to tell me it's going to be bad.

⁓

The next day, everybody's face has a numb, scared look. The radio stations are down in Sài Gòn and Mỹ Tho. Everything is hushed. Usually with so many people crowded on our small island there's a lot of noise, but even the dogs have stopped barking. I sit on the porch. People in the street say, "I hardly heard gunfire and it was over."

A man walks by in a homemade uniform calling out, "Turn in any weapons you have." As soon as he leaves, people call him an April 30th Communist for converting to the winning side on the day we lost.

I walk a block up the street to a junction with an alley where people are turning their guns in. Another April 30th Communist stands guard in a dark green uniform that looks like it was sewn last night. Some women and a few teenage boys come up with their eyes cast down and set their guns in the pile. One woman carries multiple guns. The new Communist stands there with his cloth hat on, gripping his AK-47 like he's not sure how to use it. There's already a waist-high pile of guns and ammunition lying in the dirt. I had no idea there were so many weapons in our town. I feel my blood heat up. Why are we surrendering so shamefully, laying our guns down at their feet?

When I get home I tell Ba, "If you haven't turned in our gun, I can take it." Maybe I can do something more than just turn it in. Someone should.

"Wait until there aren't any people around," Ba says. "We don't want anyone to report us for having a gun."

When the people in the street thin out, I take our M-2 carbine and the two clips of ammunition down from the top of the glass-door cabinet. As soon as I get a few steps past the house, I slap a clip in. I haven't fired it before, but I know how.

The April 30th Communist standing by the guns doesn't notice me. He keeps looking over his shoulder into the alley. When he turns his head, I go behind a fence on the other side of the street into Mr. Three Belt's shipyard. I'm not sure what I can do. If we have to turn our gun in, I want to do it without anyone seeing which house I came from.

It's dark under the roof covering the shipyard. I brush aside a spider web and glance around to see if the meter-long lizard that lives in the wood pile is poking its head out. Then I get down on my stomach so I can look through a hole near the bottom of the fence and watch the soldier.

The April 30th Communist's knees shake as a woman walks up to him, head down, and puts her family's gun in the pile. He clenches his rifle to his shoulder. His face looks white, like it wouldn't bleed if you cut it, and he keeps looking back at the houses in the alley as if someone is going to attack him. I'm sure he doesn't know I'm here.

I lie with the gun at my side, looking through the hole. Are we all going to stand around and let the Communists take everything away from us? Everything my parents worked so hard for? There's no one else out on the street. It's late morning and hot. I stare at the soldier. Besides being so scared he's probably thirsty. Sweat drips down my face. There's no gunfire, no fighting anywhere. All I can hear is my heartbeat in my chest. What's wrong with us? If one person does something, maybe it will give other people the courage to stand up.

I slide the gun barrel into the bottom of the V-shaped hole. If a shot came, no one would know where it came from. My heart pounds against my ribcage. It feels huge inside my chest. Where's that April 30th Communist's head? I move the gun around until his face is in the sights. He looks straight at me, but he can't see me here in the dark. My hand feels damp against the wood stock of the gun. All I have to do is aim and squeeze the trigger.

My hands start shaking on the gun. What if I pull the trigger and it doesn't fire? How many bullets will it take to kill him? I'll empty the whole magazine. If he's not down, I'll put in the spare clip. If he fires back? He won't make it. I'll run straight to the river behind me, swim out to the deep part, and drop the gun. No one will find it.

Sweat runs down my eyebrows and drips down the side of my cheeks. What if I don't make it to the river? I'd have to kill myself—say goodbye to everything, my family, the land in Côn Tàu. Even if I made it, what if someone found out it was me? My family would be punished. Lying on the dirt, my body feels hot and cold at the same time. My face and tongue tingle. I take a few deep breaths. If I do this, all I'll do is kill him. He's from the South not the North. He's so scared, what's the point? He probably got recruited yesterday. He's just stupid and killing one stupid person won't change anything . . . but it could destroy my family. My knees go weak. I can't feel my tongue, or my eyes. If it was just my life to lose, it would be gone, but I don't want to hurt my family.

The April 30th Communist guarding the pile of guns glances behind at the alley again. I step out into the sunlight, sweaty and dusty. I approach with the gun pointed down and loaded, safety off. If he looks at me like he's conquering us, if he says anything, I'll shoot him. He turns toward me. His knees shake like they're going to shatter and his white knuckles clench his gun. I take the clip out and toss it and the spare into the pile.

I give him a cold stare as I gently lean the gun against the stack of weapons. "Don't you worry that someone's going to blow your head off?"

He looks over his shoulder and back at me. He doesn't answer. He could be dead already. I start walking downstream toward my house. After half a block, I turn back. The April 30th Communist is running toward the town hall, clasping his gun. I killed him without shooting.

A former Army soldier leans against a wall smoking near my house. "Did you see that guard collecting guns?" I say. "He ran away pretty fast."

The ex-soldier ignores me and takes another draw from his cigarette. I walk away. I should have had the guts to pull the trigger.

∽

An hour later, I return to the pile of weapons. It's still there, unguarded. I hunt through it, looking for the big rounds used by single-shot sniper guns. At least I'll collect some bullets I can use for building forts. I think about taking a gun, but too many neighbors are watching. I find a small clip of sniper bullets and head home.

There must be mountains of ammunition over in Mỹ Tho. I have to check it out. I find a ferry going to the Mỹ Tho market. I sit in back by the motor, so I only pay a third of the price. The ferry turns from the main river and heads into the smaller river that divides Mỹ Tho in two. Near the base of a bridge, a standing face boat sits with the flat ramp on its face for loading troops tilted above the shore. The South Vietnamese flag is painted on each side. The captain probably tried to destroy it by ramming it into the bank.

Communist soldiers stand on the bridge looking over the railing. They disappear behind us as the ferry passes underneath to the market on the other side. I get off at the market and walk back toward the standing face boat. Locked iron gates cover the storefronts lining the street. Smoke drifts out of the wide open doors of two administrative offices. Inside mounds of ashes smolder. Scattered paper covers the floor. Only a few large metal desks and file cabinets remain. Kids wander in and out of the buildings looking for anything left.

At the entrance to the bridge, a tank and a personnel carrier stand guard. Two men stick their heads out of the tank and another sits at the gun turret. Nearby is an enormous pile of weapons. Below the bridge, a group of kids and grown-ups scavenge metal chairs, pipes, antennas, and lights from the standing face boat. I go down and climb on the boat. The metal deck lists backward under my feet. Twin machine guns sit on each side of the cabin. I could still do something. The cabin door doesn't have a handle, so I try the door on the other side. It's stuck. I pick up a piece of metal and pry it open. A man follows me inside. I go up to the control panel and push one button, then another. The man glances around for something to take. The radio hisses. I could do something.

"You better get out before you get killed or arrested." The man steps back out.

I lock the doors. On the bridge above, five soldiers stand against the railing. I look around for another exit in case they come after me. There's a hatch in back. This time I could get away. I look through the scope—it's black. I push a couple more buttons. The scope lights up and I can see. I point it down. Below, the tide moves out around the large boats of fruit wholesalers on the side of the river. After I shoot, I could jump out of the back hatch and swim around by the boats like nothing happened. No one knows me here—it's not like the April 30th collecting guns next to our house where the first people they would blame would be the families living nearby. If I do something, then other people might, too.

How do the bullets load? The guns are different than the ones on the Navy boat at the funeral. I drag a chain of bullets from the holding area, push it into a reservoir, and press the load button. The chain snaps in and the guns click. I put my face back into the scope and hold onto the handles. The twin barrels move with me up to the bridge. The soldiers up there look as if they're standing next to me. They wear regular uniforms and hold their guns like seasoned soldiers—not like the April 30th collecting weapons in our neighborhood. If I pull the trigger, they'd be gone. They're looking everywhere but at the guns pointing up at them.

This could make a difference, start something. Sweat spills down my face. I think about the tanks near the bridge. The tank guns can't aim down here and hit me, but some of the soldiers wandering on the street carry B-40 rocket launchers. I'd have to run before they saw me.

How do I aim a gun with two barrels so far apart? I practice sweeping along the top, the crosshairs lining up over the soldiers. It has to be a clean sweep. I just need the guts to pull the trigger. If one person stands up against the Communists, maybe others will. A soldier on the bridge looks down as if he's staring into the scope at me. He moves over to talk to the soldier next to him. They all slowly back away from the railing.

One of the soldiers peeks over the edge. Then, two men jump down the side of the bridge. They'll be here in seconds. Army soldiers say that you need to destroy your equipment, so the enemy can't get it. I grab a fire ax and smash it into the dashboard. I crack the gun scope and handles. Then I crawl out the back hatch and jump onto the shore. I would have done something. There just wasn't enough time.

The soldiers pass by me on the way to the boat. "Who was in there? What's going on over there?"

I'm sweating like crazy. "I don't know."

The soldiers scold the kids playing next to the boat and they scatter. Out of the corner of my eye, I see them approach the cabin, the barrels of their AK-47s leading the way. Relief pours over me. I'm glad I didn't have to make a decision.

There's a pile of ammunition taller than my head near the bridge. I search for something shiny and brass. The soldiers in the tank and on the bridge, the ones I almost shot, look at me but don't say anything. I pull on an ammunition belt. It's stuck. I yank another and it comes up. When I have as much as I can carry, I head toward the ferry dock in Lạc Hồng Garden.

The two teenage sisters of the Eight Talent family have their parent's small boat lined up next to the other ferry boats, waiting to get enough passengers. They live across the canal behind our house. "What are you doing with all that?" one of the Eight Talent girls says. She and her sister sit back by the motor with *nón lá* covering their heads from the sun. "You're going to get in trouble."

"It's just bullets. If you don't have a gun to fire them what does it matter?" I see an even larger mound of ammunition down toward end of the park. "I'll come back."

I drag myself and the chains of bullets over to the other pile. This will be my only chance to get live ammunition. Some might be the type I can empty the gunpowder out of and make rockets with. The Communists won't let us have firecrackers. Two men in a personnel carrier stand guard. They look at me and then at each other. The guns are in a different pile than the bullets—as long as I don't go near them they shouldn't care. I search for something better than what I have. I find a 105 artillery shell. It would make a great post for the fort I made in the alley, but I can barely pick it up. I strap a six-foot chain of 12.5mm bullets over my shoulder and slump toward the Eight Talent sisters' boat with a tank shell in each hand.

The chain is as heavy as I am. I drag it back and exchange it for a long section of M-60s that I wrap around my chest in an *X* like machine gunners do. Two small cans stick out of the mountain of bullets—MK3 concussion grenades. I hook their handles on the back of my shorts and cover them with my shirt. Then I put a tank shell under each arm and cradle some loose belts of ammunition in front of me. I try not to fall down the wide stone steps on the edge of the river leading to the ferry boats.

"Did the soldiers say anything?" one of the Eight Talent girls asks. I make my way over the other boats to hers, trying not to drop anything. "Aren't you going to get in trouble carrying those shells?"

"I took it in front of the soldiers. They didn't care." Their older brother was in the Army—they're probably worried I'm going to get them in trouble.

I sit in back by the Eight Talent sisters and put down the tank shells and loose chains. I wipe the sweat off my forehead. Two older women sit up front with their baskets and shoulder poles for selling on the street. "That ammunition is dangerous, you're going to hurt yourself," one of the old women says. "You should throw it all away."

An ex-Army soldier gets on and the sisters have enough passengers to take off. The motor is noisy so I can't hear the rest of what the women say. "I worked hard to get this," I shout up to them. When the boat is about a hundred meters away from where the Round Fort in Tân Long used to be, I unhook one of the grenades out of the back of my shorts, pull the pin, and hurl it over the side of the boat.

The oldest Eight Talent girl looks at me. "What was that?"

"An MK3, I think."

"What? Are you crazy?" She veers the boat away from where the grenade splashed. I wait. Nothing happens. Maybe it sunk so far down I won't see anything. A low *ục* comes from behind me like someone punching the water. The river churns. The boat seems to rise a little, but there's no large bubble like I thought there would be. And no fish. I thought some fish would get shocked and float up.

I take out the second can, pull the pin, count three seconds to myself, and toss it far behind us. "Don't go so fast," I say to the girl driving. "I didn't see the explosion yet."

"Are you trying to kill us?" the Eight Talent sisters say together.

"It's so far back it will probably sink to the bottom and do nothing. Stop. I want to see if any fish come up."

She looks at me and shakes her head. "No."

Ục. Another explosion punches the water behind us. No fish come up. The ex-Army soldier on the boat says, "Those grenades won't do much. But those tank shells have explosive tips. Don't set them off."

"I know. I won't do anything with them." I'm not sure what he's worried about. They're not activated when they're in the casings.

I step onto the foot ferry dock in front of Six Chicken's house with the chain of bullets crisscrossed over my chest, walking doubled-over with shells under each arm and an armful of bullet chains. People stare at me. "What are you going to do with all of that?"

"Make rockets and build my fort."

I put the shells and bullets in the lean-to and get a bowl of rice. "Where'd you get all that?" Chị Tư asks.

"There're piles of it in Mỹ Tho." I scoop rice into my mouth. "After I finish eating, I'm going to go and get more."

"No," my sister says. "Stay home and play with what you have."

I spend the rest of the day using the vise in the lean-to and a pair of pliers to pull the bullets out of the casings and empty the gunpowder into a tin cup. Ba doesn't like live ammunition in the house. I save two bullets to use as gate posts when I build castles. "That's a lot of brass," Ba says when he comes into the lean-to. "When you're done playing, we can flatten them to make hinges."

By the time I finish, it's night. I can't sleep with the silence. Before, there was always gunfire somewhere, if you listened. I still can't believe it's really over. I lie awake wondering what will happen to our family. I should have done something. It haunts me worse than any ghost.

In the morning, I take my bag of casings to the alley on the side of our house. I line them up along the tops of the old sandbags I made into a fort near the bellfruit tree. As I sit behind the sandbags, neighbors come over and hand me empty 105 artillery shells given to them by relatives in the Army. I've seen the casings in their houses filled with sand with a board on top to make a small table. Now, they're worried about having anything from the old government. I dig the 105s into the dirt at the corners of the sandbags, so that it looks like the Army fort in Mỹ Tho. I want to remind everyone walking by that we shouldn't give up. It's all I have left to remember what we were. A Communist soldier passes by on the street. I aim my fingers and pretend to shoot. Then I crouch down behind the walls.

The Takeover

I n the morning all of the 105 artillery casings have disappeared from my fort. I only have one tank shell left and the bag of small casings I keep inside. I thought people wouldn't take anything that had to do with the Army, that they would honor our past. I feel naive for leaving them out. I wanted my fort to remind people that we used to fight.

Former Army soldiers walk past our house one by one on their way to the town hall. They don't wear uniforms, but I can tell they were soldiers because they look straight ahead and don't talk. The Communists gave them a week to turn themselves in. They say they'll give them a three-day orientation about the new leadership. I think they might not come back. If they're high enough rank, they might even be executed.

Mr. Three East stops by in the afternoon when everyone is inside, hiding from the heat. He stands in the doorway of the lean-to talking to Ba. "All they had to do is burn those files, that's all they had to do," he says. "Now a lot of people won't come home."

Ba sits at his desk listening. Mr. Three East shakes his head. "They turn themselves in and when the Communists ask their name and rank, they all say 'private second class.' The records were supposed to have been destroyed ... But the interviewers hold up a file and say 'according to this you were an officer' ... and the men don't come back."

What about the piles of ashes I saw in the government buildings in Mỹ Tho? If they didn't have time to finish burning the records couldn't they have dumped them into the river? Can't we even do that right?

"Why not turn yourself in at a town north of Mỹ Tho?" Ba asks. "They won't have your records there."

"I don't think I can get away with it . . . If I was returning from the front and no one knew me—but people around here are going crazy. Everyone's asking me, 'Have you registered yet?' They all want points for reporting me."

People are turning on each other so soon? After all the time we've been together? Still, I don't know what Mr. Three East is so worried about. I doubt the Civilian Self-Defense did anything the Communists would care about.

"The American carriers are still out there," Mr. Three East says. "I didn't go because my mother's too sick, but now . . ."

Ba doesn't say anything. Only ex-Army soldiers believe Voice of America's broadcast that there's still an evacuation at sea. My older sisters came home from nursing school, but it's too late. Even if the carriers were still there, if we went down the river now we'd get attacked.

Mr. Three East leaves without sitting down or having tea. I walk up to the town hall to see the men who've turned themselves in. I can report back to Mr. Three East since he can't risk going up there himself. Along the way, an import-export store has a sign on the door that says, CONFISCATED, GOVERNMENT PROPERTY. Three concrete homes across from the market, decorated on the outside with wood and brick and on the inside with marble tiles and fancy furniture, also have signs on them. They're the houses of doctors, lawyers, bankers, and officials in the old government. Our house isn't fancy like those. But there's also a confiscated sign on a large warehouse. If the Communists want an old warehouse, they might decide to take a plain house like ours.

In the town hall courtyard, over a hundred men stand inside a chain-link fence. Instead of the yellow flag with three red stripes of the South, the Communist and Việt Cộng flags fly on the pole above them. I join a group of boys near the fence. Men gather nearby on the other side of the chain-link wall to drink from coconut shell ladles their wives pass through broken links. "Quit talking," the April 30th Communists patrolling outside say. Military police from the North in golden-brown uniforms sit behind tables—everyone has already started calling them Brown Cows. They check in soldiers from the Southern Army.

Some of the penned-up ex-soldiers wear uniforms. I don't know if they're making a statement or if they don't have any other clothes, but that's what I'd do. One of the boys calls out to his brother behind the fence. Another says his uncle is inside. I read about people being sent to the Gulag in Russia. They were either executed right away or died in camps. Dying fighting would be better. If I were one of them, I'd climb over the chain-link fence—it's only two meters high. But the Communists would already have my name.

"Stay back." The April 30ths chase me and the other kids away.

On the way home, a boy my age tells me that he heard there's a regiment of Army Special Forces waiting for the Communists to spread out before they attack. "They're going to come out of a bunker, and there's going to be a fierce fight coming our way."

"I'll tune my elephant ears," I say. "When I hear gunfire, then we'll have something to talk about." If we couldn't win with a whole Army, what can an elite force of 1,000 or even 10,000 do? But I want it to be true. I get my bicycle and pedal down to Mr. Three East's house. I see him through the window talking and drinking. He doesn't come out.

After dinner, I overhear veterans say the first group of men has already been shipped off—anyone who turns himself in now will automatically be taken away, regardless of rank. Women go around wondering if their husbands will come back.

After a few days, some of the men come back—it gives them hope. My missing aunt's husband, Dượng Ba, is one of them. He got a three-day orientation in Mỹ Tho. "You nod and listen and don't say anything," he tells us. "But I'm just an old man."

Most of the men don't return. Someone says that Mr. Three East hasn't turned himself in yet—that he's holed up in his house. The next morning, I bicycle down to check. "He went to turn himself in today," one of his neighbors tells me. "We won't see him again for a long time."

~

My family sits around the kitchen table going through a pile of books and cassette tapes, deciding which ones to turn in. "Is this good?" "This looks beat up." "Which books aren't worth reading?"

What is Communism? goes in the stack. Everyone says we have to turn in the American novels—it's too bad because the pages are just the right size to rip off for toilet paper. We put my older sisters' school books, the Buddhist books, and the book with glossy pictures of America in the bottom of the clothes hamper upstairs and cover them with blankets. Chị Tư hides her biography of Thomas Edison and *How to Meet Friends and Influence People.* All of our favorite music goes in a deep corner in the lean-to.

Má tells us there's talk about shops and houses being emptied in Mỹ Tho and families being herded onto trucks. "Those Brown Cows could knock on our door in the middle of the night and herd us into the corner, even in Tân Long. It happened to the family downstream that won the lottery. The Communists seized the fancy house they built and the family had to go back and live in their hut in the countryside." She laughs. "It could be us, but there wouldn't be much to take." Then she gets serious again. "If they come, don't do anything. If they say 'get out of the house,' don't or you won't be seen again."

Má tells us each to take a couple books or tapes and walk separately to turn them in so it looks like we're throwing away more. "Try to do it when other people are around so they see you."

I take a few cassette tapes and drop them in a mound in the street in front of the alley between our house and the medium's house. There must be larger piles in Mỹ Tho, but I don't want to go over and look. It's more dangerous to be around material from the old government than guns. Both sides had guns, but the Communists say the books and music are diseased and will infect you. At night I lie upstairs on the mat between my brothers. I stretch my elephant ears hoping to hear the sound of fighting, but day after day is silence.

~

A man hurries by our house going downstream. A few minutes later more people run down. They stop at our house and look around. "Did a man go by? He's a former officer. He's not from around here."

He was wearing civilian clothes, so I don't know how they know he was an officer. He must have tried to turn himself in and gotten nervous. The deadline is over.

Má comes out of the house. "Just leave him alone. Not long ago, wasn't he serving the country?"

Ba follows her out. "Let him be," he says. "People are in enough trouble already."

Soldiers from the town hall come down. "Did you see a man go by here?"

My parents shake their heads and go inside.

"Who?" Mr. Three The, the medium's son, says.

The widow Chị Ba Dung stands inside the door of her hut next to the foot ferry dock. "I don't know," she says when the soldiers question her.

My friend Vũ's parents also say they don't know.

Some people downstream wave the soldiers toward them. "He went into the sawmill," a man tells them. Right away I can see who is still on our side and who isn't.

The soldiers head downriver. I run down with some other kids. I step inside the fence around the sawmill with them and head toward the plum trees at the far end. I want to find the man. I can help him escape. We're right on the river. He could jump in the water and hide behind the coconut trunk pillars the freighters tie up to. All he'd have to do is hang on until the tide goes south, then drift down into the countryside. If I were him, I could get away.

"Come back, it's dangerous," someone calls after us. "Stand back. There could be a gunfight."

Soldiers chase me out to the street with the other kids. A few minutes later they come out with the man between them. His hands are tied. He doesn't have a gun.

That night, I lie awake for hours. When I fall asleep, I dream about sneaking down to the river and helping the man escape.

⁓

I'm sitting on the front steps of our house stacking my small casings into a miniature version of the old fort in Mỹ Tho. Mr. Tư Hạnh walks toward me with a notebook and pen in his hand. What's he doing here?

Mr. Tư Hạnh steps into the front room, looks toward the lean-to, and clears his throat. He reminds me of a teacher with his clean pants and long-sleeve shirt. He used to be a clerk in Mỹ Tho before the take-over and his wife sells baskets, *nón lá*, some food, MSG, and spices in the front of their house.

Ba comes out of the lean-to in a T-shirt and shorts. "*Chào, Cậu Tư.*" He shakes Mr. Tư Hạnh's hand. "What brings you here?"

They sit down together at the table. I get out the tea, then go back to the castle I'm building on the front step—I don't want anyone to steal the casings I have left. I move over to the corner of the door to listen. I've only seen Mr. Tư Hạnh come down to tea with Ba twice before. But, no one comes for tea anymore—everyone is too scared to be seen talking.

"I'm compiling a list of the activities of the families in the neighborhood." Mr. Tư Hạnh opens up a notebook and takes a pen out of his shirt pocket.

Already? Just the other day, someone brought over a Communist booklet written in the overly-flowery way Northerners speak. It explained how we're going to have neighborhood groups to ensure everyone is attached to the skin and blood of the Communist being—so the Party grows. It listed committees we should form and explains how we need to watch out for any rogue cells that will harm the body of the Party.

"I fix radios," Ba says. "But you know that."

"How about your oldest son? What has he been doing?"

I wait for Ba to kick Mr. Tư Hạnh out, but he answers, "Vân is a ninth grader in school."

"And your older daughters? I haven't seen them around. Have they joined any committees yet?"

"They're back in nursing school."

Mr. Tư Hạnh writes something in his book. "According to my recollection, you had a nephew in the Army?"

He knows my cousin died in the war. He just wants to remind us what side we were on.

"That's right." Ba points toward Cousin Fourth Triều's concrete grave in the backyard. "You're welcome to go back and interview him."

Mr. Tư Hạnh frowns and looks down at his notebook. "What about your nephew's younger brother? The one who chopped his toes off. What was the result of that?"

"He's around somewhere. He doesn't live with us. If you can find him, you can ask him yourself." Ba walks back to his desk.

Mr. Tư Hạnh calls into the lean-to after him. "So can you tell me who else you know who was in the Army?"

Ba comes back out of the lean-to, his jeweler loupe in one eye. "Do you have some sort of paper from a higher authority you can show me?"

"It's for the list I'm compiling. I need to know everyone's background so I can report it to the authorities."

Traitor. I wish Ba would kick him out. Ba walks back into the lean-to and picks up a circuit board from his scrap pile to start testing.

Mr. Tư Hạnh stands, looking in the doorway of the lean-to. "I have more people I need to interview . . . I'll come back later."

He walks down the steps past me. I stand up and watch him go over to Cậu Tám Tranh's house, open the gate and disappear inside the front door. Nurse Tranh had a son in the Army. He won't be happy to see an April 30th Communist. A minute later, Mr. Tư Hạnh comes out with Nurse Tranh's small dog chasing after him.

He walks into the alley between our house and Sơn's old house, back toward the huts where some old Army veterans live. They're usually drunk, but they've been quiet since the surrender. It's too bad Crazy Two A got into a fight and died a few months ago. I would have liked to see Mr. Tư Hạnh interview him.

Mr. Tư Hạnh and his wife walk around the neighborhood bent over their notebooks recording who's going where and doing what. Everyone looks the other way when they come up. He's tall and thin and his wife is short and broad. I thought his wife was friendly because she had a smile on her wide face whenever I went to their store to buy rock candy or packaged *bánh*. Now I know her smile was fake. I'll never buy anything from them again. Then Mr. Six Silk, the tailor who sewed us clothes that didn't fit for *Tết* one year, and his family start to run around looking for things to report, too. "Keep an eye out for anything that deviates or is counter-productive from the guidelines and funnel this information to your group leader," the Communist booklet says.

～

The Communists announce they're showing a film at the market in Tân Long. My parents aren't sure whether it's mandatory or not. According to the booklet, "Not attending meetings is disagreeing and actively undermining the efforts of the Party." Everyone in my family goes except me and my two littlest sisters. I want to see what's going on, but I'm supposed to watch them and the house.

After half an hour, Má comes home. She says it's too hard for her to stand and watch with her pregnant belly. I run down to the market. There's a projector and cheap, blaring speakers setup in the clearing where they used to have shows. I find my brothers and stand next to them. On a large screen, drawings of red blood cells flow through blood vessels to deliver oxygen. Pictures of white blood cells fight against bacteria and viruses. It's the first time I've seen drawings that move. Kids run back and forth and people chatter. "Is that real?" "That's a lot of drawing to make a film—how can they do that?" "Where's your brother?" "Who's watching the house?"

Young, Hằng, and Sang in 1975.

The drawings are mixed in with real pictures of sick people and cells under a microscope. A narrator explains how the immune system works. The pictures are as good as the Chinese films the cinema shows. The drawings stop. A man in a white lab coat looks out at us from the screen. "Communist society is much more advanced than the capitalistic world." He speaks in a Northern accent. "We are seeing the advent of countries like Hungary and East Germany and the many things they've discovered..." The man points a stick at a picture of the cells. "This bacterium is like the Army and this virus is the nasty American Imperialists. The white blood cells are the super warriors of the North and the red are the Northern infantry who came into the body of Việt Nam to wipe out the disease of the Americans and the puppet Army."

I want him to stop talking so I can see more of the drawing film and cells fighting. I want to learn something, not listen to propaganda.

∽

In the morning, people on the street whisper to each other that the Brown Cows came in the night and took Mr. Three More. I rarely saw him before the surrender. I only knew that he was in the Army and always gone. After the surrender, he registered himself as a private first class and came home after a short reeducation class.

"The Communists found out he worked for the CIA," one neighbor says. "There was some paperwork somewhere. They stormed into his house, tied him up, and tossed him in a boat."

I walk past the medium's empty house to the concrete bridge next to Mr. Three More's. His house sits on stilts in the canal the bridge runs over. I've spent a lot of time there playing with his son. I call into the house. It's dark and all the windows are closed, but I know someone's in there. I call again. Mr. Three More's wife opens the door a crack.

"Are you well?" I ask. "Can I buy you something from the market?"

"I can't talk." She closes the door.

Why doesn't she trust me? Can't anyone trust anyone else now?

～

The next time Chị Năm goes down to our farm to pick fruit, I go along. I want to go out to the countryside where I can swim and fish and be freer. As soon as I get to Cồn Tàu, I stop by Mr. Six Soybean's house to hear the news. His house is filled with his children and his mother, Ba Bảy, who helps cut the grass on our land.

"How much land do you think they'll let us keep?" I ask. The rumor is that we can keep a tenth of a hectare. I don't know how you could put a hut on that and still have room to farm.

"Your family has ten children," Mr. Six Soybean says. "If you divide your land between you, the government won't take any away."

His mother sits in a corner chewing betel. She smiles and nods. He has all his family staying with him to justify having so much land.

"I don't think that's how it works," I say. "The government will tell us, 'your family has two hectares and that family that helped the liberation doesn't have any land so you're going to share.'"

Mr. Six Soybean's wife looks over at me from the kitchen where she's washing dishes. "Be careful who you say this to. Don't be so gloomy."

"How are all the neighbors doing?" I ask. "There are a lot of new people out here." Ông and Bà Năm have their grandchildren staying with them and other people seem to have family or friends staying at their house or setting up their own huts. Everybody is either occupying their land so it won't be taken away or, if they don't have land, staying on their relative's land so they won't be sent to the New Economic Zones.

Mr. Six Soybean goes through what's happening to all the neighbors. "Lành's back in the area," he says. "He flew a helicopter to Thailand, dropped his men off, and flew back to Sài Gòn."

"What? Lành escaped and came back?"

"He was called to shore up another area toward the end of the war. When the surrender came, he and his team left in a big helicopter for Thailand."

I knew Lành wasn't in Cồn Tàu when the war was ending. If he had been here, he wouldn't have let Việt Cộng walk all over the island.

"Who flew him back?"

"He flew himself back."

"Really?" When did Lành learn to fly a helicopter? There aren't even any helicopter pilots in Tân Long. "I would have stayed in Thailand and been free. Did he come back to fight?"

"No. He came back on the third of May and turned in himself and the helicopter."

"How could he fly back with all the Communists pointing guns at him? Wouldn't they shoot him down?"

"I don't know. But the government rewarded him. They said that he's repented because he brought in equipment to help the cause."

Rewarded by the Communists? Lành? He's a good leader if he got his men out, but aren't you a traitor if you turn a helicopter over to the enemy? "Why would he come back if he wasn't going to fight?"

"I don't know," Mr. Six Soybean says. "It must have been something important."

It must be his mother. Má is the only reason I'd stay.

I ask about Quý. Mr. Six Soybean and his family don't know anything about him. No one's seen him for a long time. If he's alive, he must be doing well for all his hard work and contributions to the Communists.

~

In the afternoon, one of Chị Năm's friends comes over to visit us at our hut. "Someone spotted the entrance to an underground bunker in Mỹ Tho," she tells my sister. "There's a special division hiding, ready to fight."

"If we know about the entrance they can't be hiding," I say. "They're either captured or dead."

Chị Năm's friend turns to me. "Maybe they've started fighting already."

"I didn't hear any fighting," I say. "That sounds like wishful thinking." We gave up without a fight. The Communists captured everything intact. Even Lành helped them get a helicopter.

"Go over and look yourself," my sister's friend says. "It's by the ferry dock in Lạc Hồng Garden, across the street near the radio tower."

"No one will be there. I saw the whole Navy go out. I saw soldiers fleeing from the front to Tân Long. Then I saw them get rounded up. It was an unconditional surrender."

That afternoon I hitch a ride back to Tân Long. Even though I know the bunker is a rumor I have to check.

The next morning I walk to the town hall to take a ferry over to Mỹ Tho. On the way to the ferry, I pass the lot where Mr. Three More's house used to be—his wife moved away and had it dismantled. While the ferry driver waits for more passengers, he tells a man on the boat that he's been seeing freighters and trucks of supplies going North. "What's that mean?" the passenger asks.

Má says it means all our rice is getting sent to the North. When she went to visit my tenth aunt downriver in Bình Đại, she saw piles of unhusked rice sitting in the market ready to be loaded on a freighter and shipped North. She said it was seed rice the government confiscated from farmers.

"Unless they replace what they're taking there's going to be a problem," the driver says.

I ask the ferry driver if he knows about a bunker in Mỹ Tho.

"I thought that rumor died a while ago," he says.

I wander around Mỹ Tho near Lạc Hồng Garden looking at buildings and trees for fresh nicks from bullets. Anything so I don't feel so ashamed we gave up without a fight. A few street vendors walk around. No cars go by. I ask a cyclo if he saw anything. He shakes his head. It's dead like the late afternoon, even though it's the morning—as if someone took a brush of silence and repainted the town.

I walk across the street to the radio tower and check for signs someone tried to blow it up or for damage from a fight. The ham radio tower is lying down, but the radio station tower and TV antenna look intact. So do all the station buildings. I know someone sabotaged the radio station because it's only static now, but why didn't they use a phosphorus grenade to knock the antennae down, too? Why make everything easy for the Communists?

I buy a sugarcane drink from one of the street vendors and walk up to some people in the park sitting on a bench facing the river. "It's a little quiet around here," I say. "Is there a reason?"

The people on the bench look at me, but don't respond. I wander over to a man in his late thirties wearing a tattered Army uniform. "Look how empty the river is," he says.

"I guess all the Navy ships went south," I say.

He lets out an enormous sigh like he should have been on one of them. Coming over here was a waste of a ferry fee. I knew the bunker was a rumor. There's not going to be a last stand.

~

When I get back down to the countryside, I stop by Mr. Six Soybean's house. He tells me someone saw Quý tied up to a flagpole in the market on the Bến Tre side of the river.

"That must be a mistake, it couldn't be Quý. Why would anyone do that to him?" People are getting silly with all these rumors.

"That's what people told me," Mr. Six Soybean says. "We'll have to wait to hear more."

After a few days, I go back to Tân Long. I ask Má if the rumor about Quý is true. "Fort Hag is the one who had tied Quý up to the flagpole," she says. "That's what the Giao Hòa ferryman told me."

"Is she the lady leader that gave Chị Năm and me a hard time when we were walking around?" The one who spoke out against Má at a meeting and almost got Má's head chopped off? The one who testified against Mr. Fourth Post?

"That woman is an evil witch," Má says. "Only she would subject someone to this. After all that time Quý served the Communists. It's not right."

"What did Quý do?" It's not fair, but it's funny.

"When the Army caught him spying, they put him on the front carrying ammunition for a machine gunner."

Quý on the front? I thought he would be a prisoner. Did the Army run out of men to send?

"Quý thought he'd be a hero when he came back, but Fort Hag said he was a traitor. She had him get on his knees and tied him to the flagpole in the center of town. For three days. She was upset when Stone

Brave told her to let him go. It's not right."

Can they really do this to their own people?

~

The Mỹ Tho radio station comes back online in time for the Communists to announce fireworks to celebrate their victory. I stand with my family in the dark near the town hall waiting for fireworks to shoot over the river from Lạc Hồng Garden. This time Chị Tư stayed behind to watch the house—she doesn't like to go out in the night because she gets cold. I've only seen fireworks in pictures or on TV. After weeks of silence, explosions fill the air again. *Ầm! Ầm!* Flower firecrackers blooming in the sky. They go on and on as if they're coming down on us. Maybe if the Communists can afford all these fireworks they can bring some wealth or food to the South. Maybe it won't be so bad.

For All Your Hard Work and

Contributions

I follow my sister to the town hall. Chị Tư carries our *"Hộ Khẩu"* paperwork, a small booklet with a faded cover and cheap paper that says how many mouths our family has to feed. A long line winds out of the town hall and wraps around the shaded side of the building. People walk out with toilet paper, but Chị Tư and I hope there'll be canned meat or rice to buy.

I wander to the front to see if the line is moving. Someone asks an official, "Where can I buy fuel for my boat?"

"You can achieve a lot with your two hands," the official responds.

He sounds like the officials on TV telling us "there is glory in physical labor." Everywhere on the river people stand up and lean on long oars because they can't find fuel. Má has to go to the black market in Mỹ Tho to sell fruit and buy diesel. "Don't wear out your clothes and be careful not to break any dishes," Má says. "Everything is going to be harder to come by." Street vendors have started to disappear and everyday there are fewer items in the market. Imports stopped after the takeover, but where did all the food go? Did the fish stop swimming in the river? Did rice and fruit stop growing?

I go home to help watch the house. Chị Tư returns with a little sugar, a tube of toothpaste, and nine rolls of toilet paper, one for each member of our family living at home. She says that was all there was to buy. She didn't know if it was a crime not to buy our weekly share.

Some people try to impress their block captain by holding up the toilet paper they bought as they walk home and saying loudly, "Newspapers are bad for you. This is the way developed countries do it." But on the other side of the canal behind our house, the mother of the Eight Talent girls yells at her oldest daughter, "You spent our food money on this? This isn't something we can eat."

∾

The toe strap for my *dép* sandal breaks. There used to be piles of plastic replacement straps at the market, but no one is selling them now. Neighbor boys start wearing tire sandals, like we saw Northern soldiers wearing on TV. We call them *dép râu* because the black inner tube straps look like a moustache. They seem like a good idea. They're tough because they're tires. Everybody is buying moustache sandals or making them for themselves. My brothers and I each buy a pair.

The sandals curve against my feet trying to go back to the shape of a tire. My feet blister. Maybe the Northern soldiers used bigger tires so they curved less. I file the inside to make them flatter. Moustache sandals are too hot and heavy to wear in the street, so the next time I go to Côn Tàu I take them along to try in the countryside. With each step, I struggle to pull my feet out of the mud. I guess moustache sandals are only good in the rocks and mountains in the North. I throw them in the corner of the hut. It's easier to walk barefoot.

I go to Mr. Six Soybean's house for news. He says Lành and Quý are both in Côn Tàu. I wonder what will happen when they meet now that Lành is a hero for the Communists and Quý is an enemy to both sides.

Mr. Six Soybean worries that he doesn't have enough land to feed his family. The Communists want everyone out of the cities and into the countryside. If you don't have land you go to a New Economic Zone. Everyone whispers that the New Economic Zone means either the jungle in the mountains or a leach-infested wasteland.

The next day, when I come back from swimming, Chị Năm and Chị Châu are standing inside talking. "If we divide our land in Côn Tàu, we have four pieces," Chị Năm says. "I wonder which piece we're going to sell?"

"What?"

"Má says we're selling the land—you need to keep it a secret."

How can we sell the land? I feel like the land is part of me.

On the boat ride back we decide that if Má does sell any land, she

284 • *For All Your Hard Work and Contributions*

shouldn't sell the six strips in front of the hut or the converted rice paddy land. She should sell the land in Giao Long. That land doesn't grow anything.

"I'll sell whatever I can," Má says when we get home, "before the government takes it away."

"But the government is sending people to the New Economic Zones if they don't have land," I say.

"We're not going to sell everything," Má says. "But since we're not leaving, we have to find a way to make a living. We can sell the land and use the money to get to Mỹ Tho—there are fewer eyes watching in the city."

"How can we even sell land under Communism?" I ask.

"I have to figure that out."

"We should concentrate on holding onto what we have," Ba says. "If we try to sell, we're just going to set our family up for trouble with the government."

"People can't get fertilizer or fuel," Má says. "We'll starve on the small amount of land the government will let us keep."

$\sim$

"Make sure there's no erosion or brown leaves on the trees," Má tells Chị Năm at dinner. "Cut out the dead branches and make it tidy. You can pick the inside fruit, but leave some of the ripe fruit on the outside to show."

"You sold the land?" I say.

"A Chinese man, the pharmacist near the market, is buying the three strips across from the converted rice paddy land. He didn't even squabble about price."

I didn't know the pharmacist was Chinese. "Why does he want to buy *that* land?" I say. I'm glad it's not my favorite six strips where our hut in Cồn Tàu is. The strips he's buying are the ones next to the land the Communists executed Lành's father on. There's no fruit there except for a few tangerines.

"This way he doesn't have to go to the New Economic Zone," Má says.

"I have serious doubts the sale will go through," Ba says.

"We'll see. The buyers are willing to sign as partners so that I can sell all four pieces at once."

We're selling all the land in Côn Tàu? What is Má doing?

"We need to watch out that we're not put on trial for this," Ba says. "We don't want to be sitting in court for undermining the government's program for collectivization."

∼

Má's seventh sister, Dì Bảy, stops by. She was as thin as a reed before, but now the wind can blow her around.

"The officials put stakes in my land," Dì Bảy says. "They're claiming over half of it for themselves." Dì Bảy stands next to Má, towering over her. "I won't accept it. I've told everyone I sharpened my sickle and long knife. I'll hack up anyone who dares to come on my land."

Would my aunt actually hurt someone?

"Make sure you let everyone around you know about this," Má says. "It makes it harder for the government to make you disappear."

"They're not going to put a bag over my head," Dì Bảy says. "I yell at everyone who comes along the road, 'My seedlings are getting taller and I can't replant them because the government won't let me have my land.' I told those village officials that if I go to another meeting I want it out in the open. I know how it was before."

She means like what happened to my missing aunt.

Dì Bảy continues, "The village officials told me, 'No one is going to kill you, they just want to take your land,' and I said, 'You'll have to kill me to take my land.'"

∼

"It was a huge auditorium," Má says when she gets back from going with Dì Bảy to meet the province officials. "Dì Bảy brought her children with her and told the officials, 'With a fifth of a hectare I can't feed my four children, so how does this work? My neighbors are keeping more land. I thought you were making everybody equal. This isn't what Communism is about.'"

Má laughs. "I didn't expect her to speak her mind like that."

I can't believe that my aunt can say that much when everyone else is scared of being dragged away at night. If your husband was burnt by the Army and carried on a pole through town, I guess you can say whatever you want to the Communists.

"'But this land is not really yours,' the official told her. 'It was part of the Plower owns the Rice Paddy program.'

"'Yes. I thank Thiệu Văn Nguyễn for that,' Dì Bảy said. 'I thought that the liberation won and kicked Thiệu out. And now they're trying to take my land? If Thiệu comes back I'll give him the land. Is the old regime back?'

"Those officials didn't know what to say," Má says. "They left to talk among themselves and came back with their final blow. 'Well, regardless of everything,' they said, 'you owe 200,000 đồng to the bank.'

"Dì Bảy glared at them and said, 'I owe nothing. Let me see the paper.'

"They showed her the paperwork and she held it up and said, 'Ổ, this document? This is an *American* bank. Didn't we chase them away? If you ask them to come back I'll pay them. I owe *you* nothing.'"

How did she know to say that? I thought my aunt was just a simple rice farmer.

"Dì Bảy stood up and said, 'Children you get ready to go home and be robbers because we got robbed and that's the only way we can live.' Then she looked at the officials and said, 'Unless you can adopt my children and feed them.'

"The officials talked together and finally said, 'We'll postpone this case and reconvene in the future.' Dì Bảy still can't plant, though. And now she's worried about going missing."

∾

"They're unloading rice like sand at the town hall," someone says on the street. "Looks like it's time to buy your month's supply."

I run up to the docks by the town hall. Out on the river, men with bamboo baskets on their heads walk down a plank between a freighter and a small boat. They dump polished rice into the boat until there's a white mound. Then they ferry it to the dock. They stomp on the rice as they scoop it, like when they unloaded sand to fill in the moat by the old fort. Rice spills over baskets onto the ground.

I walk around the line forming at the town hall. Inside, piles of polished rice sit on the floor. Farther in, another room is filled with more husked rice. Maybe this is why Dì Bảy was complaining that all the husking machines were busy. My aunt said she had to husk her rice by hand by putting it in a bag and pounding it all day. "Why are they husking all the rice?" she wanted to know. "How are they going to store it without it getting wormy or eaten by rats?" The Communists must have new technology on the freighter to keep it from spoiling. Otherwise why would they husk so much rice and leave it sitting?

I walk by the open wood panel doors of the rice dealer's concrete house. We used to point to one of the bins full of different types of rice lined up against the back wall, but all the bins are gone. The husband and his wife sit at a table in the corner of their long narrow front room. "We're buying rice from the freighter," I say to the husband. "How's this going to affect you?"

The two older sons sit on a bench and the daughter sweeps the floor. The husband smiles. "Buy all you can, if you have money."

Why doesn't he care that the government price is a third of his?

When I get home Má looks at the rice Chị Tư bought. "This rice is too good," Má points out the clear grains, longer and fuller than normal. "This is seed quality rice—if you eat your seed you'll starve"

The rice smells good and tastes great. Only farmers would notice and worry.

I stop by the rice dealer family again.

"Come on in and have some tea, Lượng," the husband says.

"I don't like tea," I say, "but I'll drink it." I sit down and they hand me a cup.

He points to the bare wall where the rice bins used to be. "My supply line is gone. Soon they'll be no supply at all."

So that's why he doesn't care. He can't get any rice to sell anymore. "Where did the Communists get all the rice?" I ask.

"They confiscated it from the big resellers' warehouses. All the rice has been husked," the rice dealer says. "It's all going to rot. Rice is going to be hard to find and some people won't find it."

I think of my cousins.

"Don't go saying this around, now. You could get in trouble, but watch and see."

We buy all the rice we're allowed with our *Hộ Khẩu* book. Má tells our cousins and neighbors who don't have money that she'll give them a few kilos of rice if they use their *Hộ Khẩu* book to buy for us.

Má puts a lid on the giant clay vat holding our rice to keep it dry in the humid monsoon season, but the rice on the freighter and in the town hall is out in the open. The rice on the bottom of the freighter is wormy before the workers finish unloading it. They start unloading the rice on the top of a second freighter. Soon all the rice in the town hall is rotting and no one will buy it.

People say a third of the rice on the second freighter was dumped overboard. A man says he was hired to take the rotting piles of rice in the town hall to be ground into flour and mixed with banana trunks to feed pigs. I walk up to the rice dealer to see if they know if another shipment is coming. I stick my head in the one open slat of the wood panels covering the door. The rice dealer doesn't invite me in.

∾

Dì Bảy stops by our house to borrow some rice. "There's no rice to buy anywhere." She can shop at special government stores because of her family's status as martyr to the cause. "There's only toilet paper and soap, but I don't have money for that. What's wrong with banana leaves—they're free."

She eats lunch with us, siting with her foot on her chair and her knee bent up. Her light gray pant legs show graduated stains from farming in the hard water in her rice paddy. "I told the village officials I want a paper that says no one is going to take my land away. Can you believe they told me not to make it difficult for *them*? I said, 'I have a dead husband and this is what I get? You're going to starve us.'"

Dì Bảy bends her face down and wipes her mouth with her pant leg. "They finally gave me a paper that said 'In consideration of your contribution and counting the number of children you have you should be able to keep half a hectare.' I tore out the stakes in my land and planted that day. But it's too late. I'm going to be short."

It took my aunt so much trouble to keep half a hectare of land. I don't see how we'll be able to keep our two hectares in Cồn Tàu. And we can't sell it either. The collective there is trying to block Má. Now she has to go to a meeting with the officials.

After we eat, Má dips a bowl into the clay vat and shows Dì Bảy the clear, long grains of rice. Má and my aunt look alike, squatting over the rice vat, both with their hair tied back in a tight low knot. "This is seed rice," Dì Bảy says. "If there's no seed left, what are we going to plant? I'm going home and asking the officials if any of them are crazy."

How Far Do You Follow the Wind?

A skinny fifty-year old man in a plain uniform with officer insignia on his shoulders comes to the door. He wears a pistol in a holster. Two bodyguards stand behind him in uniforms that look crisper and newer. He seems half-drunk. Why is someone high-up in the Communists visiting us?

Má greets him and calls him Uncle Three Wish. He's one of the Việt Minh nationalists who fought the French and went North in 1954. It's good to know someone high-up. Then, the government can't make our family disappear. "Your mother must be happy to see you after all this time," Má says.

"Do you know what I got the first time I saw my old mother after twenty years of fighting to liberate the South?" Uncle Three Wish says. "I got a slap in the face. A slap in the face. And she's right ... I thought that I was going to be the pride of the family—"

I'm glad he got slapped for helping the Communists.

"Well, now that you're governor of Thạnh Phú," Má says, "maybe you can do something for your family."

Since he knows he made a mistake, he'll be willing to do whatever he can to help. Maybe he can help Má sell our land.

"I put my whole life in and all I did was damage all the people that I care for," Uncle Three Wish says. "My whole life—"

"My niece and nephew will be waiting to see you." Má says. She waves toward our backyard where Anh Chín Phát and my other cousins live. They're closer relatives to him. He stopped to see Má first because their mother died, so she represents them.

Uncle Three Wish comes back to say goodbye after visiting my cousins in back. "Everyone should slap me for being stupid." He talks louder and seems drunker. How did he get more to drink? My cousins don't have anything. Before the takeover they had barely enough to eat. Now they can't even put a piece of fruit on the altar for their mother.

"The first thing... when I got back and saw all my siblings and my nephews, they all wanted to bury me in spit. And then my mother slapped me on the face and said she had hoped that I was dead." His bodyguards stand behind him saying nothing. He moves out onto the street. "I made a mistake... They misled us Southern patriots."

Some of the neighbors come out to listen. One of the bodyguards puts his arm around Uncle Three Wish and tells him to quiet down. Má's uncle sidesteps away from the guard's arm. "I don't want to say this in the house. I say this on the street where everyone can hear."

He staggers and walks across the street toward the widow's hut near the foot ferry dock. "They told us the South went backward after I left in '54. That it went to the cave ages and you were all starving and enslaved by the American Imperialists... We worked hard because it's our homeland. Now people are suffering."

His pistol swings on his side. The neighborhood team leader, a woman who lives south of us, comes out and looks at him with her arms crossed. Mr. Tư Hạnh stands on the other side of the street writing in his notebook. When Uncle Three Wish sees them he starts to swear like Crazy Two A, yelling at anyone in the neighborhood and cursing the Communists. People start to go inside.

The mayor of Tân Long and his security officer come down. Uncle Three Wish's bodyguards glare at them. "Salute me and go to a different place," Uncle Three Wish says to the mayor. "I have things to say and unless you did something to contribute to this tragedy get out."

"It seems like you're tired," the mayor says. "You should rest."

Uncle Three Wish stares at him. "Did you do anything that helped cause this hardship for the people?"

"We all worked together as comrades to help the liberation."

"So do you have anything to say to a high-ranking official?" He scowls at the mayor, then turns his back and puts his hand on his pistol.

The mayor glances at the bodyguards. One of them moves his eyes to Uncle Three Wish's pistol and then back to the mayor. The mayor turns and walks back to the town hall.

Má comes out of the house. "Have some tea. My daughters are making a meal for you. It's a long way to get here and you should rest and have dinner." It's the middle of the afternoon—everyone has eaten lunch, and it's not time for dinner.

"We have some things to do," a bodyguard says. He turns to Uncle Three Wish. "Remember we need to be back in Mỹ Tho?"

"That's right. We need to go now," Uncle Three Wish says.

"Please come and visit again," Má says.

He walks toward the town hall swearing. I follow. The air is heavy with everyone informing on everyone and here he is walking around cursing the Communists in the middle of the street. I'm glad someone can stand up to them. I pass the hole in the fence where I pointed our gun at the April 30th Communist. Every time I walk by it, I wish that I had stood up too.

$$\sim$$

A man pulls a spool of wire along the street up toward our house. He sets the ladder against the betel nut tree next to the empty lot where the medium's house was. I step around the *bạc hà* and bananas that the medium's son, Mr. Three The, planted in the dirt lot and look up. He's nailing the wire to the top of the tree.

"What are you doing?" one of my neighbors asks.

"Putting up speakers." He moves the ladder and leans it against the betel nut tree in our yard and strings the wire across the alley between the two trees.

"What for?" the neighbor asks.

He runs the wire over from the tree and attaches it along the front of our balcony with bent nails. "It's my job to put up the line, that's all."

He moves his ladder to the roof of Sơn's old house and attaches the wire there. Then he moves down the street toward the sawmill. What is the government going to do with this?

A loud *rẹc rẹc rẹc* interrupts dinner. Everyone runs outside. "This is a communication test from your civic leader of Tân Long."

Má looks up at the speaker attached to the betel nut tree in our yard. "They had to put it right next to us."

There's another speaker on a post, farther down toward the sawmill. So this is how the town hall is going to communicate with everyone.

At five o'clock in the morning the speaker starts:

*Get going, going and exercise. Move. Keep going, going, going.
Get out of the house. Stretch! Physical activity will make you
strong to build our nation.*

I didn't know they were going to use the speakers to wake us up
this early. Thượng and Vân stay in bed. I can't sleep well anyway, so I
go out and sit on the porch to see who comes out. I'm not sure if this
is mandatory or not.

Outlines of neighbors exercising appear in the dark. A song comes
on about how great the Communists are, how great Uncle Hồ is, and
how great life will be. Ba's already up, so he starts stretching to show
that our family is participating. A lot of people have come outside, but
not everyone. I stretch on the porch and swat mosquitoes. Another
song, 'We Fought and Won' comes on. Má sticks her head out. "What
is this?" she says under her breath. "In the morning?" She goes back in.

The program goes on for an hour and a half with more songs and
a story of the morals of Uncle Hồ and how we should look at making
his teachings part of our everyday life and practicing every moment to
be like him.

The speakers come on again before dinner. Some of the program
is new, but most of it repeats. Every morning and every evening, the
speakers blare. Má calls it kneading your skull. The Communists don't
just want to take over our country—they want to crawl under our skin
into our blood and take over our body.

~

Ba joins the neighborhood watch—everyone is supposed to participate
in a committee. When they meet at our house, I have to serve tea. It's
mainly our old neighbors. Besides Mr. Tư Hạnh, it's hard to tell who
really supports the Communists and who is only here because they
have to be.

Ba tells me not to lie under the table and listen to their meetings. I
don't want to stay around anyway. The meetings are usually in the night,
when the mosquitoes are biting. And it's not the kind of talk Ba used to
have at afternoon tea where people could say what they felt and argue
about it. Everyone has to agree with each other and try to prove who's

the most loyal to the Party. "Is anyone in the neighborhood currently working against the Party?" they ask. "That family there, the father is a drunk," someone says, or "That family was caught speaking cynically, showing a lack of moral support for what the Party is trying to do." Another family's kids don't behave and say the right things. They keep track of points for who's done what and who's reported who.

～

After a while, fewer people come out in the morning when the speakers come on. It's not good to exercise and get hungry when there's not enough food. Still, we have to listen to the skull kneading. I have to do something. I wait until the hot afternoon when no one was else is out. I stick Ba's pliers in the elastic band of my shorts and find a rope to loop around my feet. No one should care that I'm climbing the betel nut tree—I do it all the time.

I hug the tree and press the rope loop between my feet into the trunk. When I get up to the speaker, I take the pliers out. I thought I'd pinch the wire with the pliers to give it a head start shorting, but the bent-over nail holding the wire is rough. I loosen the nail so the wire can sway back and forth against it. When the wire rubs against it in an afternoon thunderstorm, it should short by itself.

The next time there's a thunderstorm, I stand under our balcony and watch the wire swing. The speaker next to us comes on in the evening with a loud *RẸC RẸC*. The sawmill speaker downstream stops working.

Chị Tư and Ba say, "It looks like that speaker is blown."

We can barely hear over the noise. "Do we have to live with this?" Má says.

The *RẸC, RẸC, RẸC* goes on for over an hour. I've made it worse.

～

The man who put the wire up comes back with the ladder. He cuts out the piece of wire frayed by the nail and splices in a new piece. The sawmill speaker starts to work, but the betel nut tree speaker next to us still squawks.

I need to break it completely. They're probably using old military speakers and don't have a replacement. I remember getting shocked and flying backward when I tried to hand Ba a capacitor he removed from a TV. That would short the wire. I find an old capacitor in Ba's workshop. When we run our generator to watch the news, I ask Ba if I can charge it.

I don't want to get shocked, so I pick an afternoon when it's not rainy and take a wire cutter up where the speaker wire runs along our balcony. I pinch cut the wire coating, then I place the prongs of the capacitor over the cuts. It snaps. The speakers squeal like pigs before they're slaughtered.

I hurry back inside. People come out on the street. "What happened?" They look up at the speakers. I should have done it in the rain or when they were broadcasting. Then, people would think there was a reason for the speakers to short. What if the man who put the wires up comes out to look at it and can tell what happened? When everyone goes back inside, I creep out to inspect the wire along the balcony. The brown plastic covering is wrinkled from heat distortion where I shorted it. But the cuts I made in the wire are so small I wouldn't know where they were if I hadn't made them.

When the evening announcements come on, the sound drifts to us from speakers upstream and across the river. "Looks like the speaker died," I say to a neighbor.

"That speaker has been sick for a while," he says. "Hopefully they don't replace it."

The man with the ladder comes back. I worry he'll find out it's me. He checks areas where the wire bends or sags, but he doesn't look along our balcony where the wire is taut and all the nails are tight. I don't think he'll find where I shorted the wire. We're a long way from the town hall, and there are so many places the connection could go bad.

∾

A woman screams. I run outside.

"I'm not going to leave," the widow who lives in Sơn's old house yells at two Brown Cows with AK-47s standing inside her front door. I don't know how the widow's family has managed to stay here for so long. "I'm a merchant, not a farmer. Don't send me out to the New Economic Zone."

The Communists want everyone in the countryside. Most people who fled to Tân Long at the end of the war are already back on their land or in New Economic Zones.

"We'll come back for you," one of the Brown Cows says. "You're not supposed to be here." The Brown Cows leave and everyone goes back inside.

The next day, there's more screaming. By the time my brother and I run out of our house, all we can see is the naked backside of the widow chasing four Brown Cows down the street. Everyone comes out to watch. The Brown Cows walk backwards, looking in the air and to the side, trying not to see her nakedness as she charges at them, the meat on her backside flapping around. I laugh with all the neighbors at the Brown Cows running away. I can't believe they're scared just because she took off her clothes.

Hoàng comes running out of the house with a blanket, her face red. She moves her hands around frantically trying to cover her mother with the blanket and get her inside.

A neighborhood woman says, "She's so bushy she's probably scaring all the neighborhood boys."

"No she's not," the other boys and I yell back.

The widow comes out with clothes on. "Don't come back," she yells down the street at the Brown Cows. She turns to the people watching. "I'm going to say one of them was touching me if they try to drag me away."

"I heard they come late at night and grab you before you can scream," one of the neighbor women says. "But those young men don't seem to know what to do."

When Ba and the neighborhood watch meet at our house, they discuss suggestions to send to town hall about the widow. Mr. Tư Hạnh wants the widow arrested because she's making an example of being disobedient. The woman who's the head of the watch wants the widow sent to a reeducation camp. "The government should leave her alone," Ba says. "People will find the right place for themselves."

The widow's son tells me that he and Hoàng have been sleeping out on the boat while his mother and older brother sleep in the house. That way if the Brown Cows come in the night someone in their family will be able to scream.

Ba warns the widow that people are trying to decide what to do with her. "Don't send us to the New Economic Zone," she says. "My husband and I sold furniture. I don't know anything about farming."

∾

"Watch everything you do," Ba says one morning after a late night meeting with the neighborhood watch. They don't meet at our house because Má said it's too hard getting my younger sisters to sleep with them in the front room talking until ten or eleven o'clock at night. Ba tells us that reports are coming in about the smallest details: Someone claims their neighbor has an Army surplus chair. Someone's neighbor seems suspicious, always watching him. The neighbor counter-reports that his neighbor seems suspicious because he's always spying on him. Someone spotted a man carrying an American novel to the fishpond outhouse.

Ba sees Mr. Six West in front of our house. "I haven't seen much spiritual work. How is it going for you?"

"The Communists have chased all the ghosts away," Mr. Six West says. Everyone keeps their altar out of sight because dealings with spirits are illegal. Ours is upstairs where no one can see it.

Mr. Six West sees me playing in our backyard and calls me over. With all of our next-door neighbors reporting on everything it seems like we can only trust Mr. Six West and Nurse Tranh now. I stick my head in his door. "Lượng, come in and have some tea."

"No thanks, I don't like tea." His house is empty. I don't want him to think he has to keep bribing me with cookies.

"Did you tell anyone about our conversation?"

"No. That's between me and you." I told Má and Ba that he and the medium were fakes but not anyone else. I'm not going to report anyone. He should know me better.

"Good," he says.

The ferryman comes to visit. "Looks like things are changing with all this reporting," Cậu Năm Lộc says to Má. His eyes move toward the door after Ba walks out. "It's difficult to trust people with so many eyes and ears around."

Are people worried about Ba reporting them? Doesn't he know that Ba goes to the meetings just for show?

"When the wind blows you bend with it," Má says.

"You can only bend so far before you break," the ferryman says.

∾

Right before the new baby is due, Má tells us at dinner she was at a meeting to sell the land. The meeting was in Long Phụng, the town where Quý was tied up. "Fort Hag was livid I was doing this right under her jurisdiction," Má says, "but Six Stone Brave is the provincial governor of Gò Công now. He told Fort Hag that the decision doesn't belong to her, it belongs to a good resolution."

I didn't know the Gecko would have the power to overrule everyone. He's higher up than I thought. I finally realize Stone Brave was the reason Má was able to take the Death Land sign off our land in Giáo Long when the neighbors couldn't.

"Stone Brave asked me, 'You turned this rice paddy land into strips for fruit trees and did all the hard work on your land through the war in all that danger. Now that the land is safe and free, why do you want to sell it?'

"I told him, 'I was younger then, my health is failing now.'

"He looked at the crowd and said, 'In life, you depend on your family if you can, but sometimes you have to depend on your possessions.' Then he turned to me and said, 'In this case, you need to sell the land so that you can live off of it, since you can't take care of it any longer.'

"Now we just need to wait for the buyers to raise the money to pay," Má says.

Má is working on buying a beauty shop in Mỹ Tho. Mrs. Seven Dancer, who lives behind the thief family, asks Má, "How can farmers run a beauty shop?"

I know Má can run a shop. The real question is, why would anyone want to have their hair shampooed or curled when they don't have enough to eat?

~

My new baby brother comes into the house in Má's arms bundled in a white knit cap and white kimono shirt.

"Look at him. He's like a prince," the Chinese doctor's wife says, pointing out his fair, smooth skin that doesn't have a single mark or blemish. He looks like he's from another world with his glowing skin and perfectly-formed little face.

My aunts cover him with kisses, exclaiming over his full eyebrows, round, bright eyes, and downy, black hair. I let him grip my finger and touch my face. He doesn't seem to belong to our family that can barely feed the kids it has or this country where everything is going backward.

"He'll bring luck to your family," Aunt Curly says when she comes up from the countryside. My parents name him Chu Ngân, the crystal sound of a bell in a temple, but I like their second choice, Tự Hưng, self-made man. I call him that instead.

The neighbors and my brothers and sisters kiss him so much that I wonder how he can put up with all the viruses. Ba seems uninterested. He's not around much anyway. My parents say you have to bend with the wind, but I don't like that Ba spends all his time at Communist meetings.

My oldest aunt, Dì Hai, stays with us to help. She cooks pig heart in ginger for Má to eat. Even under the Communists, Dì Hai manages to be plump. Maybe it's because everything she cooks is a little better than everyone else's cooking. Even when there's nothing to cook but fish sauce, she can make salty tiger taste like a meal. Má lies in bed and talks to her sister. I hear the name of my favorite uncle and sit down the hall on the stairs to listen.

"After April 30th," Má says, "the Communists put Chú Thạch's family under house arrest. When I went up to Vũng Tàu to visit, he had nothing left in his house or yard. The government had taken a truck and loaded everything up."

How will Chú Tư make a living if they took away all of the surplus he was selling? He can't buy fuel for his transportation business.

"Is he still a believer now?" Dì Hai asks.

"He's still singing and chanting the praises of Communism." Má gives a little laugh "He says it's part of the process and things will get better. Is he that blind? The government was trying to take away more than his possessions . . . But his wife is raving mad they'd treat their supporters this way."

"It serves him right," Dì Hai says.

At least my aunt woke up. I wonder if my favorite uncle still believes or if he doesn't have a choice. Uncle Three Wish admits he made a mistake. Why won't Chú Tư?

When I go upstairs to bed, I overhear Ba say to Má, "You get what you ask for, you get what you work for—now he might lose everything."

But I'm losing everything, too. The land in Cồn Tàu means the world to me and as soon as the buyers pay for it, it will be gone.

∽

Má sends me to Cồn Tàu to watch the land, since she needs to rest and take care of Chu Ngân. When I come back, my new brother seems different, colder, like there's something wrong with him. But how can I think something bad about my baby brother?

Má lays Chu Ngân on a spare bed pushed against the coolness of the cement water tank that forms part of the back wall of the lean-to. In the middle of the afternoon, the baby seems too quiet. I go into the lean-to to check on him. My brother lies asleep face up on a cream blanket with good luck pictures of dragons and goldfish, his lips moving in his sleep and his chest rising up and down. I sneak around trying not to wake him up, but he opens his eyes and turns toward me. It's as if someone who has died is looking back at me. As if his life is already missing.

"Ồ, there you are little brother." I smile so I don't scare him and put my hand on his cheeks to feel his temperature. He seems cold. I adjust his blankets. He gives me a little smile, then turns his head straight up. Like a ghost looking at me, but at the same time telling me it's alright.

I need to do something to protect him. I find Má in her room. "Má, that lean-to bed is too cold for the baby because of the water tank."

Má says he's fine, but I keep complaining he's too cold. After a couple of days Má moves Chu Ngân back to the daybed under the stairs by the kitchen. I expect to feel his warmth returned, but he's even colder, like he's being stolen from me. I try to fight the feeling, shake it off. I don't want to scare myself with spirits that aren't there. My sisters cuddle the baby, and Vân squeezes his cheeks and kisses him on the daybed. Even my little sister Young plays with him. Chu Ngân doesn't look at them the same way he looked at me—like a ghost. I sit at the kitchen table and try to figure out why I feel so worried. Vân calls me over. "Come on and play with him."

I don't want Chu Ngân to give me the look he gave me in the lean-to, so I stay back and peek at him.

When Vân and my sisters leave, I stand close to the daybed watching the baby. He looks at me and it's the same look, as if I'm seeing his future and he knows it. He gives me a soft smile, and I come over and give him a kiss. I shouldn't think this way. I might bring bad luck.

Four days later, Chu Ngân gets a fever. This is it. "We need to take him to the hospital," I tell Má. "He's very sick."

"It's nothing to worry about," Má says. "He only has a little temperature." I can't tell her about my feelings. What would she think of me? I pace the house. The fever goes higher and the hot and cold medicine doesn't take it down. The baby won't drink much. Má starts to worry, but she still thinks it's not that bad. "Lượng, what's wrong with you?" she says when I'm not hungry for dinner.

After dinner, Nurse Tranh comes over with his bag. He listens to the baby's lungs with the stethoscope and takes his temperature. "It's probably hemorrhaging fever." Last winter it was going around Tân Long, and everyone said that this year it would be bad. Nurse Tranh packs up his bag. "This is definitely a case where the baby needs to go to the hospital. He might even need to stay in a cold room. There's a shortage of medicine, though. You'll have to pay a lot."

"Go get your father," Má tells me.

Ba has been at Communist meetings since eleven o'clock this morning. I don't know where they're meeting, so I walk around the neighborhood looking for lights. As I come up to the shipyard, I search for the hole in the fence. The one I hid behind with the gun. In the evening light it's only a dark spot near the bottom. I should have done something.

Several lanterns glow from Mr. Three Belt's house inside the shipyard. I walk past his gate to a gap in the fence that looks directly into the open door of his front room. Mr. Three Belt sits at the head of a long table with Ba, Mr. Tư Hạnh, some other men, and a couple of women.

Mr. Three Belt's booming voice asks about sanitation and literacy programs, food supplies, and the harvest. Someone told me he became the group leader because he's the only one with a big table and lots of chairs for meetings. Mr. Tư Hạnh wanted the job, but no one voted for him.

The members go around the table, taking turns talking. They all seem so serious. I worry Ba won't be able to leave. Mosquitoes bite me while I wait in the shadows. As the minutes go by, I put my face farther through the gap in the fence. Some of the members notice me spying on them. Ba sits toward the end of the table close to the door. I try to catch his eye after he's done speaking. He must know it's me, but he doesn't look my way. They've gone around the table. The meeting should be done. Instead, Mr. Three Belt calls for more tea.

From the head of the table, Mr. Three Belt looks straight at me out the open front door. I'm still afraid of him. When my friends and I tried to collect his worker's discarded cigarette packages to use as trading cards, he'd yell at us.

"There's a kid waiting out there," Mr. Three Belt says. "Whose is he?"

"He's mine," Ba says.

"What does he want?"

"It looks like you have a family issue," Mr. Tư Hạnh says. "You should take care of it and let us continue the meeting."

Ba gets up. I walk around the fence to meet him. "Chu Ngân is really sick. Má wants you home so you can help."

"I'll be home when we're finished. Go home."

After a half an hour, Ba hasn't come back. Chị Tư asks Má if she's going to take the baby to the hospital. "Your father asked me not to make a decision without him. Everything is expensive now. Doctors won't help you unless you pay them under the table and buy the medicine on the black market."

Má sends me to try to get my father again. I go back and stand in the gap in the fence and wait for him to notice me. Mr. Three Belt looks out from the head of the table at me, but he doesn't say anything.

One of the women talks about the virtue of the collective and how every thought is supposed to be lined up with the *Đảng*—the Communist Party and the three old men on top. Before the takeover, Má used to yell "*các đảng*" at us when she was mad. She meant a bunch of living dead. That's still what I think when I hear "*Đảng*."

Mr. Three Belt glances at me a few times and then leans forward and says something to Ba. I come up to the porch and stand to the side of the door. "Go ahead and leave," Mr. Three Belt says to my father.

Ba comes to the door. "What is it?"

"Má wants you to take Chu Ngân to the hospital right away."

"I told you before, I'll be home when we finish. Don't be a pest or you'll be punished."

"We can adjourn now," one of the members says.

I run back. Nurse Tranh is checking the baby. "He needs to get to the hospital soon," he says.

When the nurse leaves. I check my brother's forehead. It's even hotter. I walk right back and stand in the front door of Mr. Three Belt's house. They're all still there. Mr. Three Belt looks directly at me and stands up, the big belt buckle on his pants showing below his potbelly. His belly isn't as big as it used to be. He walks to the door. "What's wrong?"

"My brother is ill. We need to take him to the hospital."

Ba glares at me. Mr. Three Belt turns around to face the table. "The meeting is adjourned. Now." Everyone stands up and shake hands. Mr. Tư Hạnh tries to stay and talk, but Mr. Three Belt pushes him out.

I wait down the street for Ba. When he comes out of the gate, I move down a little bit trying to stay out of his view. He cuts into the alley by Mr. Tư Hạnh's house. He's not coming home? I follow him in the shadows onto a footbridge of broken, mismatched boards over a canal. He walks toward the house of a young widow, the one everyone says is pretty, and goes in the door. The rumor is true. I stand there crying. My brother will die if we don't get him to the hospital. I finally make myself walk home in the dark. I wipe my eyes before I come in the house, but they're still watery.

"Why isn't your father home yet?" Má asks.

"I don't know. The meeting is over." I glance up at clock above the hallway entrance. It's ten o'clock.

"Go look for him."

I run back into the alley. A lantern flickers in the upper window of the widow's house. I could walk to her door and knock and beg him to go home, but it won't do any good. I go home and tell Má that he's not at Mr. Three Belt's house or Mr. Tư Hạnh's. It's not good for Má to know. She knows about others, but not this one. I kiss and hug my brother goodbye. His skin burns. His face is still so perfect. I go to the kitchen where no one will see me and breathe in and out trying to clear my face.

Má tells me and my brothers to go to bed. I keep coming downstairs to check on the baby and see if Ba is home. He comes in after the grandfather clock chimes midnight and yells at Má for not taking care of the baby. She starts crying.

I drift in and out of sleep. At five o'clock, my parents and Chị Tư say they're going to wake up a neighbor to ferry them to the hospital. I go down and lock the door behind them.

The boat comes back to the dock twenty minutes after eight. Ba and Má cry while they're getting off. My brothers and sisters rush out, but I stay at the door. I don't want to see my father's face. The old couple who lives in back of our house comes around to the front door and asks me what's going on. "My young brother died," I say.

Má has the baby in her arms and tears coming down her face when she steps in. She tells us to remove all of the baby things that were on the daybed except for a pillow, mat, and blanket.

"What happened?" Nurse Tranh asks Chị Tư. My sister tells us that blood started to ooze out of my brother's nose and pores. When they got to the hospital the doctor said, "Why did you bring me a dead body?"

I lean over the wood planks of the bed and reach across toward my brother. His warmth lingers on his cheeks and forehead. He feels more real to me than before. "I'm sorry little brother. I tried."

Ba comes up to me. "I came home," he says. "I came home and it was too late to do anything."

"I didn't hear you because I was asleep." I walk away.

Mr. Three Belt comes to visit. "I'm sorry," he says to Má, his face flushed. "If I had known the baby was that sick I would have ended the meeting sooner." When he leaves, he stomps down the porch stairs.

A few hours later, Mr. Three Belt comes back. One of his workers follows, carrying a plain-wood coffin on his shoulder. Mr. Three Belt tries not to look at my father. Ba goes into the lean-to. Mr. Three Belt says something to Má in a low voice and gives her the coffin and a bundle of money.

Má shakes her head. "Thank you, but I don't dare to accept your generosity. The baby was too young."

Mr. Three Belt forces her to take it.

Má arranges Chu Nhân's body in the coffin with all of his baby clothes. I no longer see my brother. I touch his hand. He's cold. He knew he was dying. My older sisters get out some cookies and make tea to serve to visitors. Ba rolls the clay vat full of rice we bought when the freighter came to the lean-to so that people won't see it when they come in. It's not good to show you have so much rice when everyone else is complaining they're hungry.

"How could such a healthy looking boy die?" Everyone asks. "Why didn't you bring him to the hospital last night?"

"It's all these meetings," Má says. "They steal too much precious time. Everyone has to be there."

Mr. Three Belt finds me in the kitchen. Heat comes off of his face. "I'm sorry," he says in a voice too low to sound like him. "If I had known the severity, I would have ended the meeting sooner. You were waiting a long time."

I feel awkward having an adult apologize. "It might not have made a difference."

"Your father didn't come home."

"I know. I followed him." I don't know how Mr. Three Belt found out, but it makes it easier knowing he bears the secret with me.

Mr. Tư Hạnh walks into the kitchen, and Mr. Three Belt turns and walks out the door to the back without meeting his eyes. I follow Mr. Three Belt outside where some neighbors are digging a hole next to the concrete tomb covering the grave of my cousin. I stand next to the patch of herbs Ba used to heal me when I was sick and the Western doctor couldn't help. Má and Chị Tư stand by the grave. Ba is inside. Mr. Three Belt paces around muttering to himself as if he were responsible. Like he knew better.

It starts to rain and water fills the hole while the men dig. Someone brings the coffin out and sits it on the edge of the grave. Rain pounds on our tin roof, running into the concrete water tank that makes part of the back wall. We wait for the rain to let up, but it keeps pouring. As the men lower the coffin into the grave, the sky opens up. People scatter inside while the men hurry to put dirt on top.

When it's my turn to put dirt in the grave, it's so full of muddy water that I can't see the coffin lying in it. I'm sorry, I tell my brother in my mind. For the short amount of time you were here, you were a brother to me. I can't feel my tears in the rain. It's only four in the afternoon, but the sky is dark and I'm cold. I look up and everyone has gone.

When I come in a woman says, "When it rains on a coffin it's the same as fortune going into your family."

I don't believe it.

Ba talks to a few men in the lean-to by his desk. "Well, the boy had this hemorrhaging fever and we tried to take him in to the hospital, but he didn't make it because there's no treatment for it."

I don't want to listen to Ba make excuses, so I go to the kitchen. Around the dining table, Má tells people the baby only got sick last night. "At the crack of dawn we took him to the hospital and they said that when this hits they die."

Mr. Three Belt's voice booms in the front room announcing he's quitting as group leader. "These meetings just waste time. Time that could have been used to save this boy's life."

Only Mr. Three Belt thinks he could have done something.

≈

The next day, a boy comes up to me when I'm walking around. "I saw your father go into that house," he says and points to the alley.

"Stop making things up." Later, another kid says he saw my father go in into the widow's house. "I know. I was watching," I say. "She's pretty isn't she?"

A woman who lives in the alley near the widow stops me on the street. "Do you know about your father and that lady?"

"I knew a long time ago."

"Does your mother know?"

I nod. I don't know if she does, but I figure it's the only way to shut people up.

When I get home, Mr. Three Belt is telling Má that he's quit as the group leader. "None of that talk does anyone any good," he says.

"You don't have to quit," Má says. "Maybe you can do something in your position."

"I did nothing but waste time and lose trust," he says.

No one replaces Mr. Three Belt, but Ba seems to go to more meetings and be in charge of a larger team. My parents fight at night. "How far do you follow the wind?" Má asks.

"You have to show your participation," Ba says.

I know what my parents say about surviving, but Ba is bending more than the wind is pushing.

The Quiet Way Out

"**I** thought that you'd get privileges if you made reports," the old widow who lives behind us says to the mother of the Eight Talent family. They talk across the canal while I sit hidden up in the bell-fruit tree looking for some late season fruit. "But what can you get? There's nothing to buy at the government store . . ."

"How do they even know you made a report?" Mrs. Eight Talent asks.

At first Ba took notes when neighbors came to our house with reports. Now he listens but doesn't write anything down. People's eyes stop tracking everyone as they walk around. Mr. Six Tailor stopped competing with Mr. Tư Hạnh to report everyone's offenses. Then Mr. Six Tailor swallowed poison. His neighbor said he took the quiet way out. Only Mr. Tư Hạnh still goes around reporting. All we're going to do under Communism is starve—why does he want people to hate him? When he walks by, people say, "I'm busy. Can you write your report somewhere else?" or "I hope you report on everyone else as well."

I wander around looking for something to do. A lot of people stare blank. When I walk by or stand near them, I get a strange feeling, like they aren't there. They don't seem all the way alive. Everyone whispers. People used to talk, laugh, or argue. Even kids are quiet—probably because they're hungry. No one scolds and the dogs don't bark. The oppressive heat was here before, but the river was full of the *rồ rồ rồ* of boat motors, and people were full of life because it was fruit season and fruit was coming in. Now the river is silent.

A man's voice shouting in the street stands out against the quiet. I walk in the back door and through the house to the front door. Uncle Three Wish stands in the street cursing the Communists, the same two bodyguards with him. Two Brown Cows stay off to the side holding their AK-47s.

The Brown Cows warn all the neighbors back. Mr. Tư Hạnh stands far up the street with his notebook.

"Get that drunk out of here or we'll have to arrest him," one of the Brown Cows yells at the bodyguards.

Uncle Three Wish reaches for his pistol. "Who dares to issue an order to arrest me?" His bodyguard puts his hand on his and stops him from getting it out.

"I order you to leave," Uncle Three Wish shouts at the Brown Cows. "If you don't obey, I'll shoot you."

"It's peace time. You can't do that," a Brown Cow says.

The bodyguard keeps his hand over Uncle Three Wish's. "Come on, we have to go."

Má comes out. "Just make sure you'll be there when I visit," she says.

Uncle Three Wish lowers his voice when he speaks to her. Then he turns toward the rest of the neighborhood. "They put me in a totally symbolic position." He turns to curse the Brown Cows. "I have no more power than a guard dog . . . Everywhere I look my neighbors and their children, they're all hungry and I can't do anything to help. I'm sorry I worked so hard to bring terrible things to all the people of the South."

The bodyguard shouts to a Brown Cow, "We're going to leave and you're going to leave, too."

Uncle Three Wish starts walking toward the market with the Brown Cows in front of him, cursing louder than the last time he left. His hand is on his gun. His bodyguards walk close by to keep him from pulling it out. The streets are clear. It seems like it's only a matter of time before he shoots someone. He's wasting his chance to help anyone by being drunk all the time. Can anyone stand up to the Communists?

~

Má says that when the Communists tried to tear off the roof of the Buddhist Temple in Mỹ Tho the workers coughed up blood and one of them fell down and died.

"If Buddha had any power then wouldn't he stop them before they took down the roof?" I ask.

"The Greater One will push down those with no respect for the spirits or the gods," Má says.

I want to see if Buddha really did stand up to the Communists, if anything can stop them. I saw the Tân Long temple after it was destroyed. All the wood pillars and rafters were gone and only the foundation was left. Nothing happened to the workers. But if Buddha is going to resist, he wouldn't let them destroy the enormous statue of him in the Mỹ Tho temple.

I take a passenger ferry over. It's early afternoon when I get to the temple, and no one is around in the heat. The massive structure with the two-story high wood door is gone. All that's left is a huge pile of smashed concrete. I don't see any remnants of the gold Buddha that stood three stories or any sign of the rainbow halo of electric lights. I knew that statue didn't have any power, but I hoped something could stop the Communists from destroying everything. Buddhism has been part of us for so long—I don't want it to be taken away when it means so much to Má.

I go back and tell Má the temple is gone. She looks like she wants to check for herself. "If they destroy a sacred place, they'll be punished." She shakes her head. "They can't get away with it. They don't know what higher beings will do."

I don't think anything can stop the Communists, natural or supernatural. China, Russia, and North Việt Nam don't believe in religion and nothing has happened to bring them down.

∾

Mr. Tư Hạnh's daughter comes to visit my parents carrying something wrapped in paper. Everyone says she should have gotten married—she's in her late twenties. She tells Má and Ba that her parents are working hard, but don't bring home food. I saw them come back from their land with only one basket of fruit. Her parents work hard reporting on everyone, not farming. And no one will buy from their store anymore. I don't think Mr. Tư Hạnh's daughter agrees with what her parents are doing. It's too bad she can't convince them to do something to survive.

She unwraps the package partway to show a pair of brass candlesticks. "These have been passed down through our family for a long time, but now the altar for our ancestor isn't in use. I wonder if your family has a need for nice candlesticks?"

Why would you sell items from your family altar? It's like selling your ancestor's bones. Who else would want them?

"Thank you. These are very nice, but we don't have a need," Má says.

"Ô, it won't be expensive." She unwraps the candlesticks more to show the details on them.

"We're not making any money, and we have no need. You should look for someone who has the money and the need."

Mr. Tư Hạnh's daughter holds the candlesticks out toward Má. "It's really hard to find and we really need to—"

"Hopefully you can find a buyer," Má says and turns away.

The daughter rewraps the candlesticks and walks out the door.

"What is she thinking?" Má says. "That we're going to buy something from her so her parents can report us for having extra money? If they're hungry enough they can eat those candlesticks."

~

I hope the Communists won't get organized enough to send us to school. It's September already. I try to stay out in the countryside as much as I can. On the boat ride down to Cồn Tàu, I help Chị Năm and Chị Châu pull worms out of the rice we brought for the trip and throw them overboard. Now that we're closer to the bottom of our vat, the rice is full of them. Every day before dinner in Tân Long, my brothers and sisters sit at the kitchen table picking worms out of our rice. They're hard to find since they're white and the length of a grain of rice. It takes an hour to go through the rice one grain at a time so that we have enough for dinner. When I put the rice in the pot, more worms float up, and I pick them out. After the rice is cooked, we pick out worms we missed.

My sister and cousin go back to the city after spending the day picking fruit, but I stay out in the countryside. Mr. Six Soybean says he's having a gathering at his house the next day. He invited Lành and Quý, but he doesn't know if Quý will come—he's not accepting invitations. "I want them to have a chance to talk to each other," Mr. Six Soybean says. "To make peace with the past. But first they have to meet."

"I hope they do a lot of talking. I'd like to hear it." I want to see how they face each other now that they can't shoot anymore. I have a lot of questions. Lành must have flown the helicopter back, otherwise the Communists would have made him disappear. But Fort Hag couldn't really have tied Quý to a flagpole . . .

The next afternoon, I walk over to Mr. Six Soybean's house. I look around, but I don't see Lành or Quý. Mr. Six Soybean and three men sit on the floor in a circle smoking and drinking tea and flicking ashes into a flat can in the center. Mr. Six Soybean's children sit in the corner. I don't want to sit with the kids, so I pull a stool to the edge of the circle of men and wait.

Mr. Six Soybean sits like a farmer with one leg bent up and his arm resting on it. He nods toward me and then to the person sitting cross-legged on the wood floor next to him. "Lành, this is Dì Tám's son."

This spiritless person is Lành? My image of him at the fort standing tall with his pistol drops away.

Lành looks at me and asks about my parents. His crooked teeth show. He looks old. "How is Thanh?"

"Good," I say.

He asks about each of my four oldest sisters by name. I'm surprised he remembers.

"How are the tangerine trees over by the canals with milfoil?" I ask. "I used to fish there." I haven't been near his land since we sold the converted rice paddy land.

"Some good, some not so good." He looks away and pulls hard on his cigarette, then stares into the rising smoke. He still smokes like a military man, but his shoulders droop. He must know he made a mistake coming back. After he finishes his cigarette, he flicks it over his shoulder out the open wall of the house into the canal. Only when Mr. Six Soybean brings more tea, does he look up and give a slight smile.

I move over to the open side of the house and look out toward the canal where the python slid away the night I stayed here. I wonder if Quý will come.

The men start to talk about fertilizer and if it's possible to get a good price for their fruit. Mr. Six Soybean sighs. "No one wants fruit anymore, just rice."

Two men emerge through the leaves onto the path toward the house.

Mr. Six Soybean looks up through the open wall. "There's Quý."

Is he sure? Neither of the men look like Quý.

When the men turn to cross the footbridge, I see the outline of their faces. I recognize Quý's profile. He looks so dark, and his face is gaunt, dried up.

They walk in. The other man greets Mr. Six Soybean like a cousin, bending down to shake his hand. Mr. Six Soybean must have sent him to bring Quý.

Quý says *chào* to Mr. Six Soybean, then turns to Mrs. Six Soybean in the kitchen and says the same to her. Mrs. Six Soybean says *chào* back and stares. Quý turns back toward the circle. Lành casts his eye up at him. Quý gives a quick nod of his head and sits down in an open place in the circle.

I turn to Quý. "Anh Tám."

Quý glances over at me. He's missing the tooth next to his front teeth and maybe more inside. "Lượng. How are your mother and sisters?"

"They're well. I haven't seen you for so long." How did he manage to age that much in a year?

"Yes."

"Did you come down here to stay?"

"Yes."

"How's the farm doing?"

Quý lights a cigarette and blows it in front of him. I don't remember him smoking before. He's so broken. It must be true that he was tied to a flagpole. The men drink tea and smoke. I glance between Lành and Quý. Lành lets his smoke rise, but Quý keeps his around him like a screen. I expected more than them sitting and staring at the air in front of them.

Mr. Soybean talks about how hard it is to buy fuel for his boat. He complains about all the new people being forced to move to the countryside. I like the countryside, but I'm glad Má is poking the government's eyes buying a shop in the city when everyone else is being pushed out.

I go over to where Mrs. Six Soybean washes something in the kitchen. "Are people catching any shrimp?" I ask. "The other day when I fished along the way from my house to yours I only caught two."

She lifts a piece of clothing out of a plastic tub of water and scrubs it between her hands. "There are more people out here now. Even little shrimp get caught and eaten."

I leave and come back when the gathering is over. "Quý sure got a lot for all his hard work and contributions," I say to Mr. Six Soybean.

"What we have are two smoking, staring men," Mr. Six Soybean says. "I told them they need to take care of themselves. They're both drinking whenever they can get any liquor."

"I didn't think it would end like this. I thought one of them would come out on top. I wanted it to be Lành, but I'm glad it's not Quý."

Mr. Six Soybean sighs. "They're competing for who goes to the grave first now. And Quý's winning."

~

When I get back to our house in Tân Long all our rice is wormy. Everyone is talking about how people in the North eat a grain that's nutritious, high-yield, and can grow in the New Economic Zones. Not *bo bo*. I remember trying it at Mr. Six Soybean's house when the three misters staying there brought some. It's tough and dry, like chewing sawdust. But everyone is required to buy *bo bo* at the government store. Then Ba comes home from a meeting and says that everyone also has to buy a hundred kilos of sweet potatoes.

"Don't buy it," Má says. "Buy rice. Let other people buy it."

I like sweet potatoes for a snack, but not for every meal.

"We have to buy it or we'll look bad," Ba says.

So we mix sweet potatoes with *bo bo* when we cook it. Sawdust with mud.

"What can we do so we don't have to eat this?" Má asks Ba at the table.

"I think this is a new way of going back in time," Ba says.

"Let's not fall too far back," Má says. "We need to figure something out."

Má goes down to the old rice dealer and says we want to buy so many liters of rice. She hands him some money. Soon someone comes to our house with a small sack of rice.

~

At the end of September, the Communists announce that they're changing the currency. Má runs around like it's a family emergency. Each new dollar is supposed to be worth one American dollar. People who exchange their money walk home complaining loudly that when they got there, the government only gave them thirty dollars worth and took the rest. Má runs into the bedroom and comes back to the kitchen. She has us call our cousins to come over and pulls them into the kitchen to talk. Ba stands back in the corner. "The rule is each person can exchange only a small amount." She counts out the bills. "If you exchange this for us, we'll give you thirty percent."

When my parents aren't looking I go into their room. Piled in the corner behind where they hang their clothes are two pillowcases filled with money. How did we get this much? Why didn't we exchange it for gold or something useful? There's been a rumor about a currency change for a while.

When I come back to the kitchen, a neighbor is looking skeptically at Ba in the corner. "Where did you get all this money?"

"We got it from selling the land."

All the money from the third piece of land? Those six strips bursting with tangerines? I thought everyone bought and sold land in gold?

Má gives Chị Tư some money and tells her to take it to someone to exchange. She calls people over to our house to see if anyone will help. Some of our neighbors exchange it, but most refuse. Má even has the employees of the beauty shop she bought exchange money for her.

The day after the currency change, Má empties the leftover bills in the kitchen fireplace and lights a fire. "Extra money is trouble," she says.

All that money, all that hard work on the land. Burned.

◈

Má sends my sister and cousin down to Cồn Tàu to hand over the last piece of land. Mrs. Fourth Real who's buying the last four strips of land and the hut finally collected enough gold to pay. Má won't accept the new money for anything. Ba sets the price of fixing radios in rice.

We tie up the boat at Bà Năm's house. I walk ahead with my slingshot. I hope Má knows what she's doing selling the last piece of land in Cồn Tàu. Even though the beauty shop in Mỹ Tho has space for living above it, the officials won't accept our residency there. Ba worries that if we all move there, we won't be able to buy anything from the government stores with our *Hộ Khẩu* book. "As if I really wanted to buy more toilet paper from the government," Má says.

When I start to cross over the low bridge, Mrs. Fourth Real comes out of the hut. It doesn't seem like the hut I stayed in all those summers anymore. "Ê! Don't stomp on the bank." Her voice sounds like rattling metal. "Can't you see the path's been blocked?"

"We're just picking up the last of our things," Chị Năm says.

Mrs. Fourth Real hands my sister a small hand basket. "I have everything here."

My sister bends the water coconuts down over the stream to walk across.

"It's going to erode if you trample it like that."

Chị Năm looks back. "We did this before. I don't know why it should change."

Mrs. Fourth Real watches us leave like she's watching a store, making sure we don't take anything. Mr. Six Soybean didn't mind if we ate his tangerines, even though he acted like each piece of fruit had a name. I don't belong here anymore. Cồn Tàu's not the same place. When we cross over to Mrs. Ten Sea's land, we reach out and grab a tangerine from one of her trees. Mrs. Fourth Real doesn't know about being a farmer and sharing fruit with each other.

Chị Năm says we should stop to say goodbye to Bà Năm and Ông Năm. They aren't in their hut, so I slingshot small guavas at water coconuts while we wait for them to come back. I pick an orange for the boat trip back. This is it. I don't think I'll walk on this land again.

～

It's a humid, overcast evening. Inside our house in Tân Long, it's suffocating. After dinner people come out of the alleys with chairs and stools to sit near the foot ferry dock and talk and smoke. Ever since the takeover, people usually hide in their houses, but today it seems like the whole neighborhood is outside.

The widow Chị Ba Dung's hut sits right next to the dock. Half of the houses on the ferry dock have been pulled off, leaving only rotted posts behind. The widow's new husband smokes on a plastic stool outside her house. He doesn't come out often, but today he sits around seeing past everything, talking about life and philosophy. I sit on a cheap plastic chair next to him. I joke with an old man and another boy sitting with us, but the widow Chị Dung's new husband stares through us at something we can't see. He talks so softly that only the three of us sitting nearby can hear. His bad luck started after the boat he rented to start a transportation business sank. He and his wife are in debt.

Our house is just across the street, so I hear Chị Dung yell at him that he's good for nothing, worse than nothing, and with his lack of skills he'd be better off dead. Everyone knows she's having an affair with my old fourth grade teacher. My favorite teacher. He shouldn't do that to someone's wife.

Chị Dung sits behind us in the light from a tin can full of oil and a wick. Their house is smaller than our hut in Cồn Tàu was, just a front room for Chị Dung's sewing machine and a bedroom under a low roof. With the front and back door open, sitting in their house is like being outside.

Chị Dung's new husband stares past us at the street. "The only thing I can do now is pedal a cyclo," he says. "But I couldn't even get enough customers to pay the rent for the cyclo. There's no future."

Pedaling people around on a cyclo would be the worst job you could do. But ex-Army soldiers can't get any other jobs.

Some high-flying birds circling above make a loud noise. "Vultures," someone says. "Watch the direction they exit the circle—it will point in the direction of death."

I thought owls meant death. If owls tell that death is coming soon, what do vultures tell? That death is even sooner? Did someone make this up?

The widow's new husband doesn't notice the vultures. He looks straight through everyone as he talks. "How did it come to this? I went to school. I was in the Army. And now I'm nothing. What do you do when you're a failure and you have nowhere to turn?" He looks more gone to the world than Lành and Quý did staring into their smoke.

I look around at the neighbors gathered on the street having their own conversations. Everyone else is in just as bad shape. We all have a hungry belly. Do something about it.

The vultures spread their circle out, then unwind and fly off southeast toward the sawmill. "Someone downstream will have bad luck," a few people say.

How can birds that fly so far up predict something down here?

～

About two in the morning we hear screaming. Everyone comes out in the street. It's too dark to see. Someone says "suicide." I know who it must be. I sat next to him. He was saying goodbye.

Across the street people crowd inside the widow Chị Dung's house. I stick my head through the propped up window, but can't see much in the light of their tin can lantern. "Hold him," Nurse Tranh says. The widow's husband thrashes. "We found a bottle of poison. Get him to a boat so we can take him to the hospital."

Two men come out of the widow's house holding the arms of her new husband over their shoulders, dragging him to the dock. Nurse Tranh walks beside them. "Whose boat has fuel?" he asks.

Liquid gurgles from Chị Dung's husband's mouth. His face looks dark and puffy. It takes guts to have poison tear through you. I wouldn't do that.

"Take him back to the house. He's dead," the nurse says.

Má says she'd spit on our graves if we killed ourselves after all the effort she's put into keeping us alive. But the way he talked about having no future . . . That's one way to solve the problem, but I don't like that you don't solve it for anyone else.

Small Acts of Defiance

I start to forget about losing the land in Cồn Tàu and worry about school starting. The Communists are sending all the sixth graders to a school we haven't heard of. At six in the morning on the first day, I walk to the elementary school up the street. A teacher and a few parents tell me and fifty other sixth graders they'll take us to a middle school south of Mỹ Tho.

We get on foot ferries and go across to the city. Then we walk through Mỹ Tho until we get to a dirt road that takes us deep into the countryside. Hours later, we finally get to a red dirt schoolyard. There's a flagpole in front of a large wood and concrete one-story building with a tin roof. It looks like a warehouse. We scoop water out of the rain barrel with our hands and try to avoid the mosquito larvae. The principal comes out of the building. "I can't teach with students coming in almost two hours late. Where do you live?"

"Tân Long," one of the parents says.

She shakes her head. "I don't know where that is."

The next day, only half of the kids go. I pedal my bicycle with my friends. We get there forty-five minutes late. The kids walking come an hour after us. The day after that, my fourth grade teacher stands in the road catching kids about to take the ferry over to school. "You don't have to go to school over there," he says. "We're having sixth graders stay in Tân Long now." He's the principal of the elementary school here now.

"They don't teach English in Tân Long," I say. "They only teach French."

"Why do you want to learn English?" he asks.

Learning English feels like I'm choosing freedom, but I just say, "It's the most widely used language in the world." Even if they offered English in Tân Long, I wouldn't stay. It depresses me to be here.

I pedal my bicycle with some kids who live upstream and didn't get the message from the principal. The rocks in the dirt road poke holes in our tires so we end-up pushing our bicycles and walking together.

The next day I pedal my bicycle to the faraway school alone. I like going to a school far away, where no one knows me. I can wander and no one will report back.

After another week of school, the principal of the faraway school calls me in. "You're late again," she says.

"But I leave right when the sun comes up," I say. "It's just that I got a flat tire on the way because of the road.

"You don't belong in this area."

"I want to study English and this school teaches it."

She tells me that I can try to go to the school my brother Vân goes to in north Mỹ Tho. They have English there.

~

The school Vân goes to isn't as far away. My brother walks with a friend, and I walk by myself. It takes an hour each way. When I get home, Mực jumps up and wags his tail.

"You'd better hold onto Mực when the new mayor walks by," Ba calls from the lean-to. I knew the North was taking over when the new mayor came. All the people in charge now are from the North. "Today, Mực ran out of our house and started growling at him."

Mực looks up at me, his brown eyes shining out of his pure black face, and wags his tail.

"I went over to Mr. Five Salt's house to warn him to watch his dog," Ba says. Mực is officially Mr. Salt's dog, but unofficially he's mine. "Mr. Five Salt told me Mực doesn't like guns."

Before the takeover, Mr. Three East carried a gun and Mực didn't growl at him. And all the Army soldiers on leave had guns. "It's because he's a Communist with a gun and the dog can smell it," Má says when she hears.

I make sure Mực doesn't go out in the morning and afternoon when the mayor walks by on his way to the town hall. All I need to do to keep Mực by my side is put my hand on the soft, short hair on his head.

A few days later, while I'm in the front room, Mực bolts out the door. I run after him. Mực points his snout right next to the mayor's holster and growls. A guard carrying an AK-47 tries to pull Mực away, but the dog shakes loose and snaps at the mayor's hand as he tries to grab the gun on his hip. "This dog is always trying to attack me!" the mayor says.

I call Mực and put my hand between the dog's nose and the holster. I push Mực's muzzle to the side.

"I'm going to kill this dog," the mayor from the North yells toward our house.

I get Mực to sit down next to me.

Ba comes out. "Sorry, the dog just hates guns."

"This dog is anti-Communist," the mayor says.

"The dog doesn't know politics—the dog just doesn't like guns. Maybe you could try to hide yours?"

After the mayor leaves, Mr. Five Fermented Beancurd steps into the street. "He's going to shoot that dog one of these days," he says to the widow Chị Dung.

He can't shoot Mực. If he did, people here would turn against him.

The next time the mayor walks by his gun peeks out of a shoulder holster. There's no guard with him. I guess he figured out he didn't need one in a small town like Tân Long. I keep my hand on Mực so he doesn't start growling. I don't think the shoulder holster is going to fool my dog. Mực knows Communists shouldn't have guns.

∼

"Help! Grab the dog."

Mực stands in front of the mayor on the street. I run as fast as I can toward them. The mayor tries to dodge him, but Mực keeps moving in front. "I'm going to shoot this dog. I'm going to shoot."

Mực stands on four legs with his nose pointed up at the shoulder holster. The mayor tries to reach for his gun. Mực growls.

"Mực come here," I call from up the street. Mực turns and runs to me.

"This dog deserves to be shot," the mayor says. "It's against the regime."

Ba comes to the door. "This dog doesn't like guns and you have a gun."

"That dog is working for the enemy. I bet it belonged to the puppet Army."

"Do you really need a pistol here in Tân Long?" Ba says. "Why don't you try to go without a gun? If the dog still bothers you, then we can talk."

The next time the Northern mayor walks by, I'm sitting on the steps on our porch with Mực in front of me. I don't see his gun on his hip or in a shoulder holster. He keeps looking back at me and the dog as he walks toward the town hall. Mực ignores him, but I'm ready to grab him if he starts growling.

After a couple days, it seems like the mayor has stopped carrying a gun. I stop holding Mực. One day the mayor stops by our house. Mực lies on the concrete floor in the front room. "See," Ba says coming out of the lean-to. "The dog just didn't like your gun. Why don't you come in and have some tea?"

The mayor looks at Mực and then me before he steps in. I call Mực over. The mayor stands still as Mực sniffs him. Mực wags his tail. The mayor reaches out and pets him. Mực wags his tail again, and the mayor smiles.

"Look at his tail." Ba grabs Mực's long, black tail at the base and points to the dimpled scar where the bullet went through. "That's why he doesn't like guns. The dog used to live up in the mountains with Mr. Five Salt's family. Some Army soldiers tried to shoot him and eat him, but he ran away."

Mực's tail escapes Ba's hand and starts moving back and forth again. I always wonder how Mực's tail can still wag after being shot all the way through.

"I can see this dog is smart," the mayor says as he pets Mực.

I don't want him to think he can conceal his pistol. "Mực can smell guns, too," I say.

"Smart dog," the mayor says, still smiling.

I nod. If the North is taking over, at least Mực got one of them to get rid of his gun.

⁓

An ex-soldier gives me a floppy hat made out of tigerstripe camouflage cloth—the kind worn only by the American Green Berets or the South Vietnamese Special Forces. I hide it in my satchel. On the way home from school, I wait until I'm past the busy market near the reservoir before I take the tigerstripe hat out of my satchel. I tighten the cord under my chin and put my head down, trying not to make eye contact with any Brown Cows. I don't want them to stop me and take my hat away. I take the hat off before I reach the street that goes by the governor's mansion and the barracks where the North Vietnamese officers live.

The next day, on the way home, I wear the hat a little longer. I'll see what I can get away with before some official takes it away. No one is outside the barracks and the governor's mansion. I keep the hat on and walk along the abandoned tennis courts next to the mansion. Across the street, workers push a gurney with a body covered with a sheet to the morgue behind the hospital. I keep hoping they'll throw a body out and I'll see it. They don't notice me or my hat.

In front of the tennis courts, a heap of used casts and a pile of cloth overflows from the hospital's huge garbage bin. I hold my breath as long as possible to see what else is in the bin—a piece of leg cut right above the knee sticks out—it must be full of amputated limbs. Goats graze near the tennis courts and eat from the trash. Next to the bins, people sit outside in a café. They don't pay any attention to me. There's a sign for goat curry special—I'm not going to eat there.

I start putting the hat on as soon as I get off the ferry in Mỹ Tho. People turn to look. "Ê! Where did you get the hat?" a cyclo calls out. "Is that your father's or your brother's?" "Can I give you a ride?" another cyclo asks. They're all ex-Army.

Soon I'm wearing the hat all the way to and from school, only taking it off at the school gate and before I get on the ferry to go home. I walk head down along the white wrought iron fence in the back of the governor's mansion. When I look up, two workers in Communist uniforms wave me over. They're using poles to pick tamarind and have a small pile of ripe pods in the lawn.

"Do you want any tamarinds," one of them asks.

"Sure." I stick my hand through the rails in iron fence.

"Give me your hat."

I hesitate. He smiles. It's such an open smile that I give him the hat. He looks at the hat and me. I smile back. "I like my hat."

He walks over to the pile of tamarinds. "Do you go to school near here?" he asks while he squats down and fills the hat. He has a Southern accent.

"Yes, but I live in Tân Long." I'll give my friend Kiệt's name, if he asks.

He introduces himself, but doesn't ask my name. He passes the hat full of tamarinds over the top of the fence to me. "Anytime you walk by and need more, just call out my name."

I carry the tamarinds in my hat and eat them on the way to the ferry.

"Do you know what that hat is?" the ferry driver says.

"Yes."

"Those Brown Cows could arrest you," a passenger says. "You should get another hat."

"Well if the Brown Cows trade me their hat for mine, maybe," I say. If the workers at the governor's mansion don't care, why would the Brown Cows?

I eat tamarind from the hat when I get off in Tân Long. No Brown Cows stand around the town hall. I pass Mr. Tư Hạnh's open front door. He's not there. His store shelves are empty. I can look in one end of his house and see the other end. Even his bed is gone. When people have nothing, it's easy to see.

The next day I wear my hat through the school gate. It's early and not that many students have come in. "That's the hat of the old Army," a boy standing in the schoolyard says. "The principal might expel you."

I ignore him and keep my hat on. I'll make the principal take the hat away from me. The principal stares as I walk by her office. I sit down in the back of my classroom. The teacher walks up to my desk. "These are the symbols of the puppet government," she says.

"It's just a hat." I shrug and tuck it into my satchel. The teacher goes back to her desk. I can't believe everyone lets me wear an Army hat. Even the Brown Cows along the way only look at me in a strange way.

The next day, I wear the hat all the way back to Tân Long. When I walk past Mr. Tư Hạnh's house, he comes out and follows me. I keep walking to where Three More's house used to be. I turn around to face Mr. Tư Hạnh. "*Chào, Ông*," I say and nod my head. I give him a smile and tighten the cord of my hat.

Mr. Tư Hạnh glares at me. "Where did you find that hat?"

"One of the soldiers who turned himself in for reeducation gave it to me. I've been wearing all over Mỹ Tho."

"Did any of the police think this is a sign of rebellion?"

"I walked pass the governor's mansion. They just waved to me."

Mr. Tư Hạnh looks at me. "Did they talk to you?"

"They gave me a lot of tamarind."

"They have tamarind there?"

"That's what all the trees are in back."

"I don't believe . . . You shouldn't . . ."

I don't hear the rest because I stroll away.

A new boy shows up in school. He talks like he's from the North and wears a long-sleeve shirt and pants with a belt. How is he going to survive in the South with those hot clothes?

On the way home, I walk face down with my hat on, thinking. When I look up, I see the new boy walking on the other side of the street. We approach Reservoir Market where cyclos sit on the side of the street their feet up waiting for customers, ready to yell at kids walking by. Even Vân is scared to pass by the cyclos, but the other side is filthy from spoiled food from the market and sellers yell and fight with each other. I choose the side of the street with the cyclos—they don't give me any problems now because of my hat.

"Your mother! North kid," one of the cyclos yells. The new boy is walking on the other side of the street, next to the market, as far away from the cyclos as he can. "Go back to the North," another cyclo calls. The boy speeds up and looks down at his feet. They shouldn't pick on kids. I got picked on for not talking correctly—I know how it feels.

When I start walking home the next day, I see the new boy again. His name is Hà. There's going to be a lot of people from the North, I might as well get to know them. If he walks with me, the cyclos will leave him alone.

"Do you walk this way?" I don't have my hat on yet.

"Yes."

"You just got transferred in, right?"

"Yes, from the North."

I have three pens in my T-shirt pocket: black, blue, and red. Hà has those as well as magenta and green. He's good at drawing like my brother Thượng.

After a little ways I pull my hat out of my satchel and put it on. "It's hot."

Hà looks at me.

"Special Forces."

"Are you going to get in trouble?"

"It's a gift. I like my hat, so I'm going to wear it. So far no one has bothered me."

The smell from open sewers on the sides of the road signals we're close to Reservoir Market. We start walking toward the cyclos lined up across the street from the market.

"This side." Hà pulls me over to the other side of the street. It's full of water the fish sellers have dumped.

"No, you have to walk on the correct side." I steer him away from the dirty water, next to the cyclos lined up on the other side.

"Your mother! April 30th." A cyclo calls at us. Another cyclo looks at him and then me. I adjust my hat and look down at my feet. The cyclo gives me a smile and starts talking to the man who insulted us.

Hà relaxes. Maybe I can teach him how to dress so he doesn't stand out so much. When we get away from Reservoir Market, I ask, "Aren't those moustache sandals kind of tough on your feet?"

"No. Tire sandals are great. They're broken in so they're soft." He stops and takes them off to let me try them. "They're sturdy, too."

His sandals are thin and comfortable, not thick and curved like the ones I had. "They're a good idea—it's tough to kill a tire." I put my *dép* sandals back on. "But look around, how many people do you see wearing moustache sandals?" No one wears them anymore.

"I don't think anyone notices."

"If it's not this cyclo, another cyclo is going to tease you and beat you up."

Hà looks down and doesn't say anything. We're close to the barracks next to the governor's mansion. "I take it you live in that compound over there?"

Hà nods. It's surrounded by a wrought-iron fence. I'd like to see what they're doing in there.

I walk home from school with Hà every day. After a couple weeks he asks me if I'll walk with him in the morning, too. The cyclos are worse then.

The next morning, I wait outside the wrought-iron gate for Hà. People inside the compound look at me. "Are you waiting for someone?" a man calls over the fence.

"A friend, to walk to school."

Hà comes out of one of the long, rectangular houses behind the iron fence and walks to the gate. He has new plastic sandals. Not *dép* sandals, like mine, but the more formal kind with lots of straps. At least he won't stand out as being from the North now.

When we get to school, Hà tries to get me to sit up toward the front of the classroom with him. I stay in the back. I don't feel like we're learning anything. We have three hours of political teaching every day and once a week we have a labor day where we have to clean the school. Only Ba is learning because he takes classes on reading and writing in Vietnamese. I didn't know he only knew how to read Chinese. I guess that's one thing the Communists are doing right.

The next day, when I meet Hà at the gate, he says, "People say it's really bad to have friends that are former government Army."

"We're not," I say. Someone in the compound must have said something to him. At least he doesn't say puppet Army. "My father is a team leader in the neighborhood and I have an uncle who's the governor of Thạnh Phú." I heard that Uncle Three Wish shot an officer from the North and got transferred, but I don't tell Hà that. Transferred usually means something bad.

Hà looks at me like he doesn't believe anything I say. "Maybe you shouldn't wear that hat."

"I like my hat. If you don't want to be friends with me because of it that's your choice."

"But other people see the hat and—"

"What if it has memories that are important to you? Do you give it up? All those men were sent to reeducation—they're not coming back."

Hà looks down. "I don't know much about that . . ."

He stops asking about my hat. I walk him from the gate of the barracks to school every day. He talks about his mother and father. His father works at a desk.

"I'll take you to the beauty shop we own one day," I say.

"If you live in Mỹ Tho, then why do you walk this way—it's so much longer."

"I stay in our other house in Tân Long." I don't care if he believes we own a shop or not. "How come you don't have a bicycle?"

"My family doesn't have much. Everyone's very poor in the North. We came here for a better life."

"Well, things aren't going that well. The country's sliding backward. It's tough to buy fuel and lots of other things."

"There's so much more here than we had in the North. What was it like before?"

"This is just a remnant of what it was."

It's a long walk. I complain about all the propaganda in school. "It's hard to learn anything with all the political teaching. I'm too scared of saying anything and making a mistake."

"It's worse in the North," Hà says. "I feel more free here."

When we get to the compound gate, I say, "How about if I come inside and get you in the morning? My ferry gets here at different times, so I have to wait here for you until you peek your head out." I also want a chance to see inside the compound.

The next morning, Hà's father comes to the gate to let me in. I follow him between long, rectangular wood barracks. Laundry hangs behind the houses so that it's hidden from the street. Officers and their families stare at me walking in with my hat.

"Come in," Hà's mother says when I come to the door. "I heard a lot about you from Hà."

I'm surprised she asks me in. I thought they'd be afraid to be seen with me. Hà's parents ask about my family. I tell them about our shop and that I don't like the city, so I stay in our house in Tân Long. The barracks they live in is small and plain. There's a simple chair and table, a kitchen, and a front room with a desk. The bedroom in the back is hidden by a wall. Everything is well-organized and put-away.

His parents must be scholars because they seem so open. I ask his father what he does. He says he's an officer from the North. "A lot of people complain about your hat," he says.

"It's Special Forces or Green Beret, something like that," I say. "People keep saying things about my hat, but it's just my hat."

He and his wife laugh. "Well, some people don't get over the old things." They don't talk like other Communists. At least some of the people from the North who are taking over are like them.

"Stop by in the afternoon," Hà's father says. "I'll be at work, but Hà's mother will be around."

The next morning a man stops me from entering the compound gate. "You can wait on the street."

After a while, Hà comes out. "They're concerned about something," he mumbles.

"What?"

"I don't know."

The next day I wait outside the gate, but Hà doesn't come out. I finally have to leave so I won't be late. When I get to school, Hà is already there. I try to walk home with him, but he waves me off. "There's trouble. People don't want me to walk home with you," he says.

I walk ahead of him. I turn and take a path through a rough neighborhood instead of my usual way home.

I wait outside the gate again the next day. I want to know what's going on and at least have a proper goodbye. Someone inside the compound calls out, "Sorry for your waiting, but that family was transferred."

Transferred? The Communists would transfer someone over this?

I don't see Hà at school. On the way home, I walk by the gate and look in to see if he's still around. An office worker in the administration building looks out an open window at me like he's about to come out and chase me away. I leave.

I look for Hà on the street when I walk to school. Every once in a while, I walk by and look into the compound. I don't ever see him. It must be true that they were transferred.

Shoulder Pole Seizures

On the first day of *Tết*, Má stays home. She says she feels tired. My sisters are working, though, because beauty shops have to stay open during the holiday. A lot of beauty shops have gone out of business, but ours is on the corner of a busy street market. I can't believe people spend money on their hair when there's barely enough to eat.

Má watches Six Chicken and me perform a dragon dance in the evening in front of our house. I'm the dragon and he's the dragon tamer. I put a basket on my head and then drape a white sheet over me and tuck it into the basket to make a dragon head. Six Chicken hits a big can and I buck my head up and down to the beat as I follow him. The Communists have outlawed firecrackers, but we wouldn't have money for them anyway. We can barely feed our family after a judge labeled Má a "rich capitalist living on the blood of the people." One of the girls in the beauty shop demanded a raise and Má said, "We should wait until we have more customers." The girl's Northern boyfriend stormed into the shop and yelled at Má that he'd sue her for everything she had. Má had to pay her a whole year's salary. Now Má works even harder.

On the third day of *Tết*, Má gets a fever and goes to bed early. In the morning, she sits hunched over the table eating plain rice and salty fish with us. We've already run out of Ba's favorite dish, pork belly and boiled eggs stewed in coconut juice, because we could only make a small pot. Má's jaw starts to spasm and tighten. "Take me to the hospital." She can barely open her mouth. "Get Cậu Tám Tranh to help."

Nurse Tranh comes in and takes a quick look. "It's shoulder pole seizures. Get her to the hospital."

Shoulder pole seizures? That means death. Má can't be dying.

My sisters start packing Má's clothes. "You can get those later," Nurse Tranh says. "Just go."

Ba takes Má to the hospital in Mỹ Tho with my older sisters who are home from nursing school for *Tết*. My sisters come back and tell us the hospital has run out of the medicine they need to treat Má. She's having seizures and passing in and out of consciousness. The next day I hear that Má's at the main hospital in Sài Gòn, but they don't have medicine either. In the afternoon, my sisters come home and tell us that Má is in a coma in one of the special cold rooms in a small hospital called Restaurant Market Hospital. One of the doctors at the main hospital whispered to them that if we took her there, we could buy medicine on the black market. "This hospital is good," my sister says. "All the well-known doctors went there after the government took their jobs away at the big hospitals and gave them to jungle doctors."

"We could go bankrupt," Ba says. "Why is it so expensive?"

"She has a cold room just for her and there's all the black market medicine to buy."

"What are these medicines? How long will it be?" Ba asks. "We can't afford to have her stay for more than seven days."

I look up shoulder pole seizures in one of Chị Hai and Chị Ba's nursing books:

Tetanus causes severe muscle contractions especially in the jaw and neck that can interfere with swallowing and breathing. In cases where the disease is fatal, death usually occurs in ten days.

It sounds like the disease punishes your body, making it spasm and arch. I hope we can get the medicine Má needs. As long as Má doesn't die right away, she should wake up and be cured. Má's strong. She has to get better.

~

A week after Má goes to the hospital, I hear a commotion in the back of our house. I rush outside. A man crawls out of the ditch over where the old widow lived. He's covered with mud and yelling for help. Someone brings a rag and wraps it around his leg. When Nurse Tranh gets there, the man unwraps the bloody rag. He's still bleeding and a splint of wood is stuck in his foot.

"Are these other cuts from metal?" Nurse Tranh asks.

"There's a lot of nails and cans down there," the man says. After the old widow died, her children hired him to pull up the stilts the house was built on so they could divide them. "My feet are too tough for the cans to cut, but the nails got me."

"You could get shoulder pole seizures," the nurse says. "Do you have money? You should go to the hospital now."

"No. I barely have enough to eat."

"Well, if you get it you'll probably die."

"I'm strong. If I get it, I'm going to beat it."

Later, I see the man trying to finish pulling up the posts even though he has a fever. "I can't afford to miss a day's work," he says.

One afternoon, when I get home from school, I hear people talking about the man. "That house behind you is cursed," a neighbor says. "First the old widow living there drowned and now the worker pulling up the posts has shoulder pole seizures."

"Is he dead yet?" I ask.

"No, he's tied up and fighting it," the neighbor says.

I walk down to where the man lives. His house is just a roof with a bed in the corner. He's too poor to have a door, so anyone can look in. The man stands inside with his arms stretched up and tied between two poles. He's wearing only shorts, and he's full of muscles. His young kids play in the dirt in the backyard. People stand back as if he's contagious. His muscles tense and his back arches like a bamboo shoulder pole with baskets on each end. He fights against it. The weight of his body keeps him down so he doesn't curl up. There's phlegm in his mouth. He closes his eyes, then opens them and spits. His muscles stand out like he's displaying them—long and ropy, not bulked up like the bodybuilders that worked out at my cousin's exercise room in Sài Gòn. The seizure ends and the man hangs his head down.

"He's not going to make it like this," a neighbor says.

"Ô, he was worse before," someone else says. "When they first tied him up, you could see the house shake. We worried his arms were going to break."

"Maybe he's just too weak now," another person says, "He hasn't eaten for two days."

The sick man's wife stands on a stool and twists a banana leaf into a funnel. She pours some water in her husband's closed mouth. It runs down his neck and shorts.

Má's not strong like this man, but she's in a hospital getting medicine. She must be going to make it. It's been over ten days.

∼

I hear that the man who was tied to the poles is sitting up by himself in bed. Shoulder pole seizures isn't the death sentence everyone says it is. Má's symptoms started before his. I haven't visited her in the hospital yet. I want to see if she's better, too.

I ride the bus to Sài Gòn with Vân and Chị Tư. We hire a cyclo at the bus stop to take us to the hospital. The cyclo driver drops us off at the edge of a street market filled with vendors. A string of restaurants and cafés lines one side of the street. On the other side stand the buildings that make up Restaurant Market Hospital. The hospital is smaller than the one in Mỹ Tho.

We walk into a courtyard between the buildings of the hospital and then turn and walk up a few steps into an open hallway with a linoleum floor. It smells of disinfectant. Glass windows looking into cold rooms line the hallway. Má lies in a big room all by herself with a white sheet over her. The room is yellowish and looks old and dirty. She has something in her mouth. A nurse comes into the room from a door on the other side. She turns on a monitor and uses a machine to suck the phlegm out of Má's throat. The nurse watches the monitor for a few seconds, then turns it off and leaves. We lean against the glass window.

A saltwater infusion drips silently into Má's arm. Every few seconds another drip comes from the bag. Bubbles curve down around the plastic tubing. Má seems farther away than someone sleeping. I wonder what she's dreaming.

A hospital orderly wheels a woman on a gurney past us and down the steps.

"Do you think they're taking that woman to the morgue?" Vân asks.

"I don't think she's dead," Chị Tư says.

"She looks dead," Vân says.

"They cover dead people up with a sheet," I say. I look over at Má.

Another drip comes from the bag. She doesn't shift or make noise. You're going to wake up and be fine, I tell her in my head.

"Maybe they put the sheet on when they get to the morgue," Vân says.

Má's head arches straight back. Her body bends. She doesn't fight like the man tied to the poles. Mucus and saliva drip from her mouth and nose. Her chest hardly rises under the sheet. I worry she's going to stop breathing. But she's been here for two weeks. It must be alright.

Another patient rolls by in a gurney being pushed in the same direction. "Where do you think they're taking them if it's not the morgue?" Vân asks.

"I don't know, maybe it is the morgue," I say.

Saliva builds up in Má's mouth and mucus piles around her nose as if it's trying to suffocate her. She lies absolutely still, no sigh, no movement to wipe it away. Won't she choke? I look around for the nurse. Why isn't someone coming to clean it up? Now I know why the man in our neighborhood with shoulder-pole seizures wanted to be tied standing-up—so he wouldn't choke to death. Saliva dribbles from Má's mouth. The nurse finally comes in and sucks it all away.

A body covered by a white sheet disappears around the corner. "That person's dead for certain," Chị Tư says. "The morgue must be that way."

Vân and I leave to buy some sticky rice outside in the market. We find the cafeteria and buy ice water in a plastic bag with a straw. The door leads out to a courtyard between the two hospital buildings with a concrete path and benches under large, old trees.

We sit down to eat on a bench facing a building where mental patients live behind bars like monkeys at the zoo. The patients in the cage have their hair and clothes messed up and make noises. "It's like they're in jail," I say to Vân.

Even so, it's more alive here than watching Má through the glass window of the cold room. Two more gurneys head toward the morgue. How many people die here every day? Maybe Má won't make it. She looked so far away lying there. How do we know that she's not gone already? I concentrate, trying to see if I can reach Má's mind with my thoughts.

Two men sit inside the cage playing chess and talking about politics. They seem normal, not like the other patients making strange noises. One of the men playing chess asks one of the crazy patients something. The crazy man responds normally and then goes back to making noises. A guard walks by the courtyard. One of the crazy men reaches into his pants and tosses poop at him. He misses and all the patients in the cage start laughing.

Vân and I approach the bars. A man steps up and looks at Vân. "Those teeth of yours are like a military fence," he says. "If a B-40 launched at it, it'd slingshot backward."

Vân's face gets red. I laugh. Má still calls Vân eagle beak when she yells at him because of his overbite. The patient keeps telling us jokes. He's funny, but after a while all his jokes are the same. We walk back to the cold rooms.

"Say goodbye to Má," Chị Tư says. "We don't know if we'll see her again."

"No," I say. I will the words to Má—you're strong. I know you'll wake up and be better. "I'll see you at home," I say aloud to her. I walk out to the street before I hear any goodbyes.

When I get home, I feel Má's presence stronger than before. For once in my life I can sleep at night. The man who was tied up with shoulder pole seizures has started to walk around the neighborhood slowly, in pain, asking for work. He can't get any more work dismantling the hut behind us because everyone says it's cursed. "It's good you're young and strong," people say when they see him moving around.

Má's not muscle-bound, but she's strong. She can lift huge baskets of fruit on the farm. And her will is strong. A few days later, Chị Tư asks if I want to visit Má again. "No," I say. "She'll be home soon."

～

After forty-five days Má comes in the door leaning against Chị Tư. My aunts and older sisters follow her in. Her skin stretches over her bones. I didn't know someone could get that thin. Her face has sucked in her eyes, and she has patches of missing hair. If didn't know it was Má, I wouldn't recognize her. My younger sisters run away and cry.

Tears start in Má's eyes. I knew Má would come home, but I didn't think she'd look like this.

I run after my little sisters. "Go to Má."

Hằng runs away. Má comes toward Young. Young cries and backs away.

"This is Má," Chị Tư calls after her.

Má stays back and cries. She looks so frail. Her arms hang as if she can't control them.

Nurse Tranh comes over and cleans the sores on Má's back with alcohol. Dì Mười helps him. "How could it be that she was in a hospital with an open sore and ants eating her flesh?" my aunt says.

I've heard of rats running in hospital hallways, but cold rooms are supposed to be sealed tight. What if the ants were eating bodies in the morgue before they bit her?

"It was so peaceful," Má says about the dream she had in her coma. "I was on a boat with my parents, floating on a river covered with lotus flowers. It was so beautiful that I wanted to stay, but my father told me I had to go back—that I had children waiting for me to take care of. It was so hard to leave and wake up."

Was she living another life when she was in the coma? She wasn't dead, but she wasn't here. She must have been somewhere. "Má, were you always with your parents while you slept?"

"I was there the whole time," she says.

If you can hold a thought for a month and a half, your mind is in another life.

Má's oldest sister, Dì Hai, stays to cook for us. While I light the fire she says, "If it were up to your father, your mother would be dead. After seven days, he came to the hospital and told us he was taking her home. Dì Mười and I told him to sell whatever he has to sell, borrow whatever he has to borrow, our sister will stay here until she gets better."

I'm glad my aunts made the decision, but I'm not mad at Ba. He didn't want to bankrupt our family since he didn't know if Má would live.

Má asks to lean on her sister's shoulders and walk around. She can't raise her arms above her stomach. She practices lifting her arms every day and has us rub her muscles. Ba tells her she is going to be a cripple and that she should quit trying and rest. Her sisters tell her that she should regain her strength before attempting to walk. "No," Má says. "If I rest now, the disability will be permanent."

More aunts come to visit. Every day, they have to get a stamp from Mr. Tư Hạnh approving their stay with us. He reports all visitors to the town hall. After a week, my aunts come back upset. Mr. Tư Hạnh won't approve them to stay longer.

Má grumbles about the rules. "Let me go up and persuade him." She gets her two canes.

"Focus on recuperating," Dì Bảy says, "I'll go up and talk to him."

Dì Bảy got her rice paddy back from the Communists—she can handle Mr. Tư Hạnh.

Mr. Tư Hạnh comes back with my aunt. He ignores me. I still wear my hat when I walk past his house, but he doesn't do anything since the workers at the governor's mansion and the people at the town hall didn't.

Ba and Dì Hai come out to talk to him. "*Chào,* Thiếm Tám," he calls down the hallway where Má sits at the dining table. "Are you well?"

Má clenches her face. Her eyes look huge and white as she stares at him. "I need a lot of peace and rest."

Dì Bảy stands tall over Mr. Tư Hạnh in the front room. She smiles at him. "It costs *me* money to be here and visit. *I'm* the one who has to get back to my farm and plant. It doesn't cost the government anything." Even with her smile, Dì Bảy looks like she's going to start sharpening her sickle.

"We have to help our sister recuperate," Dì Hai says moving into a chair. Sitting down she looks even fatter. "Do you want more of my sisters to come, then?"

"Well," Mr. Tư Hạnh says, moving away from Dì Bảy, "As long as you don't have any one person's name down for longer than a week."

"My wife's sisters all look alike," Ba says. "Sometimes I can't keep track of them." Besides my oldest aunt, Dì Hai, who's fat, I have a hard time keeping my aunts straight, too. Their names make a poem: Thành, Phải, Vui, Chơi, Mừng, Rở, Nở, Nhụy, and Tuyết. Becoming, Right, Happy, Play, Cheerful, Ecstatic, Opening, Flower, Snow. Má is Rở. Ecstatic. She's also Dì Tám, number eight in the family like me.

"They have a lot of resemblance." Mr. Tư Hạnh stands up to leave. "Well, just make sure that there's not a name on the paper for more than the allowed number of days."

My aunts come in and out of the house to visit, swapping names and papers so that my oldest aunt can stay longer and help.

∾

Má spends all her time in the back of the house exercising. She looks skull-like and irritated. Thượng helps Má the most. He's constantly massaging and exercising her arms and having her lean against him to practice walking and moving her arms around.

Má plays badminton with whoever will play with her. We use a string as the net and draw lines in the dirt for the court. Má tells me to go ahead and smack the birdie when I play with her, but when she reaches out to hit it back, she crumples in pain. I worry she might break a bone when she falls down. After a week I get used to it.

Neighbors stand around and watch. Má can barely hold the racket. The old women tell Má that she should be thankful she's alive and accept being a cripple.

At dinner, Ba tells Má the neighbors are complaining about her acting crazy in the backyard, stretching and playing games with kids. "You should exercise out of sight so there's less talk."

"It looks silly, but I have to do it," Má says. "I'm not going to be disabled." My sisters in nursing school and the ex-Army soldiers say she has to exercise to recover.

While I'm playing badminton with Má and my little sisters, Mr. Tư Hạnh comes down the alley into our backyard.

"Thiếm Tám," Mr. Tư Hạnh says, "you should know that people have warned me that you're being disruptive and acting funny like a crazy person."

Má sneers at him and goes back to playing with us.

He stands near the kitchen door. The steam and smell of fresh cooked rice come out. I wish I could tell him to leave. Mr. Tư Hạnh speaks up. "The government could take you away to protect the people."

Má laughs her irritated laugh and doesn't look at him.

Ba comes out the back door. Mr. Tư Hạnh looks in at my sister cooking as he glances to greet him. If Ba offers him anything to eat, I'll be so upset I'll hit something.

"I think I heard your wife calling," Ba says.

"It's nothing," Mr. Tư Hạnh says.

"Well, you should check," Ba says.

Mr. Tư Hạnh has no choice but to leave.

Chapter Thirty-one (Spring–Summer 1976)

It Only Takes a Day to Get Hungry

"The parents can't help," a woman says to Má in our front room. "They're very poor. The baby will die if people don't help."

The woman has come by several times before, but Má has always been out. Thượng helps her get around.

"That girl shouldn't have had a baby." Má says. She tells us it's a time for death, not birth. There aren't many babies around.

"Yes. Well, I'm not related to them," the woman says. "All we can do is try to help so they're not hungry."

I like that the woman's trying to help, that people have stopped being too scared someone's going to report them to do anything.

"The mother is so young that even if she worked she could barely feed herself," Má says. "No one is making it. How can a baby make it?"

"Think it over," the woman says as she turns to leave. "You'd be creating goodwill."

"I saw the baby," I say. "Her parent's built a shack for her in front of their house." When I went by the girl lay curled up with the baby naked and gray beside her, his breath throbbing, murmuring in pain. If Má saw those bulging eyes staring out of its bony body, she'd give something.

"Did they build the shack over the fishpond?" Má asks.

"A little. It's mainly between their house and the road."

Má looks incredulous. "They don't have any land."

She'll have to see it. Then she'll help.

When everyone is inside avoiding the afternoon sun, Má heads downstream toward the girl's shack. I follow at a distance. Má crouches down to enter the low door. It's too hot for the girl to put even a sheet over it. After a few minutes, Má comes out. I start walking back to the house ahead of her.

Má catches up to me. "That baby isn't going to live for long," she says. "The girl just lies there hoping someone will take care of them."

"Did you give something?" I ask.

"Not enough to raise the baby. She has to find a way to feed it. Their family can't afford another mouth."

By the way Má is talking, she gave funeral money. That would be enough to feed them for a week.

The woman collecting money for the girl comes by our house again. She says that the girl's aunt tried to get the boyfriend's family to help, but his family is so poor they had to move to the New Economic Zone.

"The girl's parents need to take care of the baby so she can work." Má's voice starts rising as she talks. "She's young, she's able to work." If the girl asked Má for work, she'd find some for her. Má moves her arms up and down as she talks. "If they don't help her work, they need to help that baby die." Her voice cracks. "It can't suffer like that. They're displaying starvation in front of everybody."

The woman leaves. Má already gave a lot. She can't keep doing it. If the people know you have extra they'll report you. On the street, people talk about wanting to help. "But who has extra?" They laugh cynically. "Only capitalists have extra."

∽

Mr. Tư Hạnh comes into our front room. "I've been taking inventory," he says.

Inventory? I come out from the kitchen to listen.

Mr. Tư Hạnh stands talking with my parents. "You have two banana flowers."

"What bananas?" Má says.

"There are two flowers on the plants behind your house by the fishpond."

Má turns to me. "Are there two?"

"I think so."

Mr. Tư Hạnh writes something on a piece of paper and hands it to Ba.

"These bananas belong to the government now. We'll come back to collect them when they're ripe and give you government credit."

"But they're just small," Má says. "A lot of people steal things back there."

With the thief family living right next to those bananas there's no way they're going to last.

"Make sure you watch them so they get nice and big," Mr. Tư Hạnh says. "The government depends on you so we can export them to Russia."

"How are we going watch these bananas?" Má says. "We don't live back there."

"I put a tag on them. Together the community will help watch everything that's supposed to be delivered to the government."

"You can't hold it against me if people steal it."

"We'll have an investigation if it's missing. If anything happens to the bananas you'll be responsible."

After Mr. Tư Hạnh leaves, I go out and look at the banana plants. Mr. Tư Hạnh has tied a clear plastic bag to each flower with a note in it. I can only make out the top of the note without untying the bag. It says: GOVERNMENT PROPERTY.

∼

I walk downstream to slingshot the birds that come for the small, blue berries on one of Mr. Seven Coal's trees. The girl holds her baby near the door. It's too hot inside. The baby's arms hang like sticks. Only his hands, skinnier than anything I've seen, move a little. He looks longer than before. I don't know if he's grown or if the girl is holding him stretched out. He wheezes unevenly, his breath barely there. He reminds me of my baby brother. I couldn't do anything to help him either.

Whenever I'm downstream around dinner time, I hear the baby crying. He cries louder then. He must smell all the food cooking. I stop going near the girl's hut, so I don't have to hear her baby cry.

One of the neighbor kids says, "Let's go see the starving baby."

"Leave them alone if you're not going to help," I say.

When I go to the kitchen to cook rice for dinner, I look at the two bowls we have for the dog, one for scraps and one for rice and meat. The baby and mother could live on what Mực eats. I stop adding extra rice to the pot—I'll only give Mực the scraps and bones we can't eat. If a baby is dying, a dog should die first.

When Chị Tư cooks rice, she hands me some to feed Mực.

"Don't do that," I say. "People are starving. The baby is dying, I can't feed Mực." Our family doesn't have that much anyway. My parents always find rice to feed us, but it's barely enough. I thought we had so many farms in the South, streams full of fish, trees with fruit, that we couldn't be hungry. I didn't think the Communists could do this to us.

"Mực has been a good dog," Chị Tư says. "He's your dog."

"But so many people are hungry. Our cousins don't have enough to eat."

"We can't help everyone. We have to take care of our family, and the dog is part of the family."

Mực greets me with his tail wagging. I want to hide. Sometimes I feed Mực the yams I get for a snack. But how can I feed a dog rice when a baby is starving? Ba tells me it's alright to feed Mực a little. I offer my dog a bowl of rice and fish sauce. I'm stealing life from people who could use it.

～

I go out to some land on the backside of the island with Thượng and some older boys. We throw mud at each other in the stream near the land Sơn's family came back and tried to buy. When the tide comes up, we get out on Sơn's land. People say it's not really their property. The owners moved after Sơn's family paid them for the land, but the government says the sale isn't allowed. Sơn's mother had a hut built on it anyway. They're trying to hide in the back of the island because the government labeled them traitors for having an American father.

We play in their canal throwing mud around. Above us bellfruit and plum trees dangle green fruit. We throw mud to knock it down. Sơn comes out of the hut. "You can't come here and play. You'll erode the bank."

"It's not your land," we all say.

"We live here. It's our land, we bought it."

"But the government says it's not yours."

Sơn goes inside. His sister Simone comes out and talks to us. "It isn't anyone's land," we say, "so we can be here." We play for another hour and then get hungry and leave. The next day we play again. We come back a few more times, even in the rain.

Then Má finds out. "That's Sơn's mother's land. You don't just trample on it when they don't want you to."

"What did the government decide?" my brother and I ask.

"Sơn's family bought it fairly. The government just wants to prevent the sale like they did for our land." Má shakes her head. "Those strips of land. There's nothing over there. They just want to live. Why won't people let them be?"

∼

The rainy season starts early, and I'm soaked when I get to school. Parts of the rim begin falling off my hat and the sun has faded the color. "You don't have a hat," my classmates say. "Why do you keep wearing that rag on your head?"

I get sick from sitting in class wet and stay home the next day. I hear voices I don't recognize coming in from our backyard. I stick my head out the back door. Two men wearing uniforms walk away with the bananas from behind our house.

I run in to tell Ba. "The government just collected the bananas."

"But I was just out there using the fishpond and those bananas are still very young." He walks out to look. "There're gone," he says when he comes back. He goes to find Mr. Tư Hạnh.

Later, Mr. Tư Hạnh comes over with a voucher for the bananas. Má looks at the voucher after he leaves. "This is only a tenth of what you'd get in the black market, and you can only use it in government stores. All they sell there is *bo bo*."

I stay home from school again the next day. When Ba isn't around, Má finds me. "We don't want something that we're responsible for that we don't get anything out of." She looks at me. "We shouldn't have any more bananas."

I nod.

I get a knife and go out in the rain. With the knife, I dig into the dirt under each banana plant and come up into the stalk and hollow it out. After a few days the tops of the plants start to turn yellow.

∼

The top of my hat comes off so my head sticks out. When I try to sew it back on, the cloth tears. All that's left is the shape of a hat and a strap that can barely hang on. I have to throw it away. I look all over for another hat. I even ask the ferry drivers, but I can't find one.

I need something else to remind me of freedom. After school, I stand around my backyard with some younger neighbor kids. "Wait here," I tell Nhiều and Trắng. I leave them in the backyard and go upstairs and find the picture book of America in our hamper. I walk downstairs with the book open. I don't want Nhiều and Trắng to see the cover and know that it's about America.

"Look," I say. I flip the page to a picture with snow.

"Pretty," Nhiều says. "The paper is so thick and glossy."

The bright pages remind me of our old schoolbooks. Now we only get gray recycled paper, and it keeps getting darker and darker. I turn to a picture of a boy walking in an orchard with a narrow stream running by and salmon jumping.

"Look at the colors," Trắng says. "Those apples are so red."

"This picture has to be fake," I say. "See how clear the stream is. What would the fish eat?" Fish need to be in muddy water where there are creatures for them to eat.

I go inside and hide the book. I can't bring it out all the time. I need something else to remind me there's freedom somewhere else. I remember a few lines from "Hận Đồ Bàn," the song that honors the Hmong Hill people who fought with the CIA against the North. The words go through my head as I hum it walking around:

> *Wild jungle!*
> *Buries so much hatred between enemies*
> *Thousand winds murmur,*
> *10,000 echoes through blind night.*
> *Heron calls mist!*
> *Reminds us the many times we overthrew . . .*

I like how each line builds on the next. The souls buried under the jungle whispering, until their echo leaks out. A heron sensing the murmur of the buried souls in the mist and calling out in sorrow to remind us of the many times through history we overthrew the enemy.

"Do you know what that song is?" Mr. Three The says when I walk on the street past his house.

"I'm just humming the tune. It's up to you to put the words in."

"Still, you could get yourself in trouble."

I hum "Hận Đồ Bàn" all over Tân Long.

∼

When school ends, I go out to Giao Long with Má to take over watching the land from my step-grandmother. Má makes sure there's always someone on our land, so the government doesn't divide it up and give it away. We sold our boat, so Má and I ride down to Giao Long with the retired teacher who has land next to ours. People in the countryside are even hungrier. There's more work to do and less food. But I feel better in the open. And I won't have to avoid Mực or the starving baby.

Scrawny chickens wander around as we walk up to the hut. A long, light-colored pig sleeps under the overhang in front by the woodpile on the side of the house. I look around for my favorite hen among the chickens wandering around, even though I know it died. My step-grandmother comes out to greet us.

"It's too bad the hen is gone," I say. "That hen was so good at raising chicks and taking care of them." We lent the hen to Great-Aunt Six when she was sick, so she'd have an egg to eat every day.

Step-grandmother nods and spits some betel out. "That hen was too old to lay eggs much anymore. It was tough to eat."

That hen was round and heavy, like a walking coconut. "I bet it was tough. It was old and smart. It escaped when some Army soldiers shot at it with an M-16. Great-Aunt Six ran out there and yelled at them for trying to eat her chicken."

"I heard that story," step-grandmother says.

"Some Việt Cộng tried to catch it, too, but it made the loudest noise running away, so Great Aunt Six heard and came out and yelled at them."

Step-grandmother smiles. Her few remaining teeth are stained reddish-brown from betel. "That hen was a smart one."

Inside the hut, there's a cage filled with tiny rabbits. "What are these for?" I ask.

"We're raising them to sell or eat," Má says.

I walk over with Má to greet the neighbors. We used to have to go the long way round by the ferryman's house if we wanted to go to the market. Now the Death Land sign and grenades are gone, so we can walk along the stream past the teacher's house toward a new neighbor. I look over into the land on the other side of where the Death Land sign used to be. I can still see the blue smoke, hear the grenade. I think I see a leg waving in the grass. The woman's eyes beg me to help, and I can't do anything.

"Chào, Dì Tám," the new neighbor says as we start to cross two bamboo poles tied together to get to his house. I only know that he was a Việt Cộng soldier.

Má calls him Dũng and asks about his family. Dũng sits under the overhang of the front door of a wood house on two small strips of land surrounded by water. Kids with tattered clothes full of holes run around.

Dũng asks softly and politely about Ba and my sisters. He seems to know everyone in our family. His wife comes out and points toward him. "All these years Anh put effort into fighting," she says, "while other people built their families—all we ended up with is a piece of land only big enough to get down and squat on."

After the war, Dũng moved his family's house to this small piece of land. A tenth of a hectare. That's what the Communists give contributors.

"Things are difficult," Má says. "Hopefully it will get better." Má knows who owned the land before. She's not happy it was taken away. The other half of the land has a foundation on it waiting for another contributor's family.

"My husband should do something to provide for the family," Dũng's wife says. "This little bit of land isn't going to do it. Our kids are hungry."

Dũng looks off in the distance. How can his pride take it?

"How old are your kids?" Má asks. She nods toward me. "This is Lượng. He's the youngest boy."

Dũng's wife looks at me. "What grade are you in?"

"I'm done with sixth."

"He's going to spend the summer here," Má says.

"If you need anything let us know," Dũng's wife says.

Dũng walks with us to the bridge, staring at the ground. "Only my wife can criticize me," he says. "And she's right."

"Make sure the government takes care of you," Má says.

"Yes." He doesn't look up.

I follow Má along the stream toward the market. "Dũng's family used to own a lot of land on the other side of Cậu Năm," Má says. "More than a hectare. He sold it so he could keep doing Communist work."

"Now I guess he only has enough dirt to eat," I say.

"He shouldn't have sold his ancestor's land. It was disrespectful. Now he has to scrape dirt with his teeth." She laughs. "But the government probably didn't give him enough dirt to eat." We walk a little farther. "You should know that Dũng was an assassin for the Communists."

"How many people did he kill?" He doesn't have a cold look like Crazy Two A or other soldiers. Even Mr. Three East looked more like a warrior than Dũng.

"A lot of people," Má says. "His wife helped scout for him."

"What rank is he if he did so much? Shouldn't he be an officer?"

"The government didn't think he was fit after the war. He's like a hunting dog that's been discarded."

"If you had rank, wouldn't you still have it after the war? Who else got discarded?"

"The others kept their land. If they didn't die in the war, they went back to farming."

Má stops by a small store near the stream and buys some incense and a tin of biscuits. When we get to the intersection of a dirt road, Má turns toward Great-Aunt Five's house.

Old trees with owls living in them shade Great-Aunt's house. Má sticks her head into the door and calls a greeting. Pictures of ancestors, Buddha, and warrior protectors line tables against every wall. Great-Aunt has lit so much incense that smoke hangs in the room. "Are you healthy?" Má asks as Great-Aunt comes out.

Má puts the biscuits on the main altar and hands me some incense. I place incense in front of the ancestors and Buddha. I ignore the other figures. I don't know them and some look as scary as the devil. Even Má had nightmares when we slept overnight here with the altar pressing around us.

"What news is there in the village?" Má asks Great-Aunt when we're done praying. "I heard there's been a lot of commotion."

I stand next to Má looking at the ground. Great-Aunt complains if you don't stand respectfully.

"Anytime there's commotion it's Dũng," Great-Aunt Five says. She has a scowl etched on her face.

"Dũng was quiet when we stopped by," Má says, "But his wife sure talked a lot."

"Dũng's only quiet at home," Great-Aunt Five says. "He gets drunk in town and staggers around saying 'I need someone to kill. I need someone to kill.' He gives the town hall headaches. They have to put him in jail to sober him up. Then they send him home with rice and yams."

"I guess he's more scared of his kids' hunger than getting in trouble with the authorities," Má says.

"The authorities make sure everyone knows that only Dũng can get away with this."

Má tells me to go out back and cut the fallen coconut fronds into sections for cooking and stack them. I'm glad to get away from the smoke and Great-Aunt's glare.

Before Má leaves she says, "Don't get Dũng mad or get in trouble with him. He's drawn a lot of blood and taken a lot of lives. Now he has a small amount of land and can't provide for his family. Be polite but don't get close."

I don't plan to get close to him. People like him are the reason we're stuck with Communism. Everyone had to deal with the Communists in order to farm their land, but he killed people for them.

～

I help my step-grandmother by gathering wood, cooking rice, and washing dishes. I collect yam leaves to feed the rabbits. Step-grandmother takes care of the pig. She talks to it while it roots around, ột ột ột, in its pen on the side of the house. When she cleans out its pen, she tells the pig where to go and it moves over. She flicks it back with her hands when she puts its food in. It waits for her while she moves the tray.

Má leaves the same amount of rice with me to eat as if I were in Tân Long, but I swim and do more here, so I get hungrier. The only extra things to eat I have are coconuts and a few guavas. Not much grows out here. I wish we could have sold this land, instead of the land in Cồn Tàu.

Whenever I walk by Dũng's house, I hear his kids cry of hunger. Everyday his wife yells at him louder and more foul-sounding than a fish seller. "After all the work you did, we don't even have bananas to eat. Go find some food. The kids are hungry." She points around at the dead leaves strewn on their land. "Catch some fish. Look for a fallen coconut. Anything."

Dũng just sits and smokes in the front of their house. If his wife yells too much, he walks away. Couldn't he plant vegetables they could sell? The soil isn't fertile here like in Côn Tàu, and their house already takes up a lot of their land. But if Má had that land she'd grow something.

∼

One day, when it's too rainy to go out, step-grandmother asks, "Do you want to try some betel?"

"Alright." She's asked before, but I always said no.

She puts a nut, leaf, and white paste from a seashell together. I stick it in my mouth. It burns my nose and my tongue. I chew for fifteen minutes to show her I can. Maybe then she'll stop bothering me. When I spit it out on the mud bank of the canal, it's turned a bright red, not the dark color she spits.

"Open your mouth," she says. I open it. "That's the most beautiful color. Chew some more."

I put the new wad of betel she hands me in my mouth. I spit a lot to keep from taking it into my body. Má says it's bad for you. It's probably bad for my teeth, too. My spit is the same beautiful, bright red.

"The color is so perfect. It must agree with your body," step-grandmother says.

"No." I spit the whole wad out. "I don't know how to eat it."

"It's supposed to be good for you and protect your teeth."

Step-grandmother has more teeth left than most people, but I don't like it. "I won't chew betel anymore. It's disgusting spitting everywhere."

"You have such a beautiful color. I wish I had it."

Through the rain, we hear Dũng cursing on his way home. "The *Đảng* mistreated me," he says. "I helped them get power, but they forgot about me. I did all this work for the *Đảng* and what do I get? I get cursed at by my wife and see my kids go hungry."

Where does he get the money to drink when his family is hungry? "How do so many people with no money end up drunk?" I ask step-grandmother.

"I don't know much about him," she says. Step-grandmother isn't local, so people don't talk to her much.

When Dũng's wife sees him staggering home, she starts yelling. I can hear her even though they're on the other side of the teacher's land. I feel sorry for his wife and kids—he deserves it.

⁓

A new house made of water coconut leaves goes up on the land between Dũng and the teacher. It's on the other half of the land the government took away to reward contributors. It looks worse than Dũng's wood house, more like a long hut. Tall grass surrounds it and some small, unhealthy banana plants grow wild. Everyone wonders who's going to live there.

Lately, I've seen more people walking around that I don't know. Some are returning to their land, but others are new. There's not much land for them to live on. "Giao Long is probably better than the New Economic Zone," Má said when she came to visit and saw all the new people. "But they'll still probably have to eat dirt."

In the late morning I visit Trực. "Some more people moved into the house in the coconut grove," Trực says. When he walks back to my house with me, we pass through the coconut grove. Two teenage girls sit on the front of a new house pulled together from a mix of plywood, coconut tree boards, and canvas. The roof, front and door are made of woven water coconut leaves.

The girls point at us and laugh. "Ê, country boys." One looks like she must be seventeen. Her younger sister must be at least two years older than me, maybe fifteen.

"I go to school in Mỹ Tho," I say.

"You country boys don't fool me," the older one says.

I laugh back. "I guess not." Trực has a shirt on, but I'm walking around with my beat-up shorts and nothing else.

We see the girls again in the evening. They're dressed up in bright clothes and act like they're in the city strolling around the coconut grove path. "What do you do for fun in the country in the evening?" they ask. "It's so dark here at night. No streetlights or anything like the city."

"Well as you can see the mosquitoes have started to come out," I say. "We go inside."

"It's so boring here. No one knows anything." They throw their hips and shoulders out and give us a look.

Trực looks down. I smile. "But there's fish to catch, birds to slingshot, and streams to swim in."

"You country boys don't know what evening life is."

"Maybe you can teach us," I say.

They shake their heads as we walk away.

Their family won't make it out here. Not unless they decide to eat coconut leaves and coconut everything. Nothing grows in a coconut grove.

~

The new contributor's family moves in between Dũng and the teacher. The father starts clearing the grass. He says he works in Bến Tre. His wife smiles and greets Dũng's wife and the other neighbors when she goes out to their washboard over the stream. Dũng's wife ignores her. They have a boy a couple of years younger than me and another smaller child. I can tell from their faces and accent they're from the North.

Soon after they move in, my step-grandmother has to leave to help her daughter. Má sends word for me to go with her. Trực will watch the pig. It's the only animal left. The rabbits got a disease, and we already sent the chickens to my family to eat. I pack rice, fish sauce, and a shirt in my step-grandmother's bag.

We walk along a gravel road toward Quới Sơn. A canal ten or more meters across runs next to the road. Algae and water hyacinth clog it. I've heard about these canals. Everyone sixteen and above had to help dig them. Even my skinny sister Chị Tư had to help dig a canal south of Mỹ Tho. She got yelled at because she only managed to shovel one square meter of the nine marked off. The next time Chị Tư was called to dig, Má paid a man to say he was her.

Step-grandmother stops at a log bridge built like a ladder that leads to a hut sticking out on stilts over the canal. "This is it," she says.

The water coconut leaf walls of the hut are tattered from the wind. I bend down to enter. I have to hunch around inside, but step-grandmother can almost stand straight. She introduces me to her daughter, another woman, a boy about nine, and an older girl. Her daughter was evicted so they live over the canal illegally.

They have one bed and no altar. No pots or hats hang on the walls. Step-grandmother said they take care of a water buffalo. I hope I can ride it. I go outside and look around the neighboring rice fields for the buffalo. All my life I've seen pictures and heard songs about sitting on the back of a water buffalo.

Step-grandmother starts building a fire for dinner. I take a rice bowl and scoop some of the rice I brought into their bent-up pan. My rice sits whiter and cleaner on theirs until they swirl it together. All they're cooking is rice. Aren't they going to pick some vegetables or catch some fish?

I go out to the canal. If I do a little work, I can usually eat. The water is reddish-brown from the iron. I see a salamander, but nothing else. All the water spinach on the edge of the canal has been picked. I walk to a rice paddy. By this time of year the rice stalks should be full of green kernels, but there are only a few. I look for fish or apple snails. They used to be everywhere. I don't see any crabs burrowed into the mud. What do they eat?

I bend my head and come back inside. "There's nothing to catch."

"All this *phèn* water kills the fish," my step-grandmother says.

"Maybe there's water spinach or something?"

"We ate it all."

We sit down around a straw mat on low stools to a meal of rice and fish sauce. They hand me a pair of crooked, mismatched chopsticks carved from bamboo. The boy eats out of a coconut shell because I'm using his bowl.

They divide the rice so everyone has a bowl. There's hardly any left. I added enough rice to make two and a half bowls, but they must not have added much. I'll just be a little hungry. I'm not going to be here that long.

"The government wanted that canal," step-grandmother says. "Now we're starving."

"The canal was supposed to bring in water from the river to dilute the *phèn*," her daughter says, "but it's so long, it doesn't flush out. The same water moves back and forth. When it rains it overflows and poisons the land."

Everything they own—clothes, knives, hoes, fingers, and feet—is stained yellow or dark brown from the *phèn*.

"Hopefully, the canal will get clogged up, and we'll go back to the old ways," the other woman says.

Small pebbles in the rice makes it hard to chew. That's why my family brings rice from the city.

They go to bed early because they don't have lanterns. I'm hot—I'm not used to the open fields—so I wander along the canal looking for snakehead fish. There's more starlight here, without all the trees hiding the sky. When I finally stop sweating, I try to sleep in the hammock. I keep sinking into a big hole they've tried to cover with a mat. I move to a straw mat on the floor. Bed bugs bite. Salamanders and minnows surface in the canal beneath me. I hardly sleep.

The next morning, my step-grandmother says I should help her grandson with the water buffalo. "Go to the tree across the road and he'll meet you there. He went to get it from the owner."

I thought they owned the buffalo. Then they could at least rent it out.

The boy leads the buffalo by a ring in its nose. "Why don't you ride?" I ask. People say you can write poetry on the back of water buffalos.

"The buffalo hates riders. I got thrown off a couple of times."

I feel small next to the buffalo. If it stomped on me, it would squish my guts. And it has horns. Still, so many songs describe how peaceful and carefree it is to ride a buffalo out in the open field feeling the breeze on your face. "Can you show me how?"

The boy looks at the buffalo. "You can try. The buffalo is in a good mood."

He climbs up and sits on it to show me. Then he gets down and helps me up. The wide back stretches my legs. Its skin feels smooth, but the flies can't seem to bite through it. I look down to see if the buffalo's still happy. Its eyelids are full of bugs. The horns curve up at me. "Tell me when I need to get off."

The boy leads the buffalo along a strip of land between the road and a dike blocking the stagnant canal water from the farms. The buffalo's bony hump hits me. It tries to pull over toward the fresh grass on the other side of a small canal. The boy pulls it back.

"Let's go on the other side." I'm hot, thirsty, and hungry. Riding the buffalo isn't anything like the songs. "It's cooler in the shade and there's some grass for the buffalo to eat."

The boy chases away flies from the buffalo with a small branch. "I have to stay here. If someone sees us over there, I'll get in trouble." The buffalo snorts. "You'd better get off now."

I scramble down.

The boy seems fine, but I'm dying of thirst. I cross over to some sheltered land and look around for a young coconut to drink. The boy ties the water buffalo under a thorny tree and hunches down so no one will see us. I find some green guavas. They're sappy and dry.

I lie in the shade of some coconut trees while the water buffalo stands nearby. Its mouth goes back and forth, back and forth. I thought buffalos would have a good life. This one seems too hot and only has dried grass and twigs to eat. A water buffalo fly snatches a chunk out of my arm. I didn't know these flies could take a piece out of you. I try to wave them away. "Out here everything is slowed down except the flies," I say.

We start walking again. Some banana plants with brown leaves and a few small, flat bananas grow on the strip we're on. I reach for a green banana. I'm hungry from only eating rice and fish sauce for dinner and breakfast.

"Don't," the boy says. "The people who own the land won't let me bring the buffalo here if any fruit is missing."

I should be as tough as the boy, but I can't take it. I go back to the hut. The rainwater vat is empty. I use a coconut shell on a stick to scoop the canal water for washing that's in another vat. "Scoop it gently so the sediment doesn't come up," my step-grandmother calls from inside.

The water tastes like metal and decomposed mud. I thought people in Giao Long were poor, but they're poorer here. The New Economic Zone must be worse, but I don't know how. I find my step-grandmother and tell her I'm leaving. I don't want to stay another night.

~

I get back to my land in the late afternoon. The next day, my step-grandmother's daughter comes to check on me and gather some things her mother left behind in our hut. I put some rice in a bag. "Here's grandmother's rice," I say. I have extra since she was supposed to stay with me.

Trực has to watch his brother's land, so he can't stay with me. Even having someone small around, like my step-grandmother, made the noises in the night less scary. The pig must miss her too because it refuses to eat. After a couple days, it gets hungry and eats again, but it lies around. I walk over to get to know the family from the North that moved in between Dũng and the teacher. Má says Northern Communists shouldn't be down in the South. But she didn't tell me not to play with the boy.

The boy tells me his father is an officer with people reporting to him. Everyday his father goes to work in Bến Tre. In the evening, the boy runs over the stream along the path past Dũng's house to meet his father. "Bố! Bố! What did you bring?" he says.

I remember how Ba used to bring something home for us when he went to the city on his moped.

The officer brings home a steering wheel from a military vehicle for the boy to play with and some plastic buckets. Their house is empty, so I guess they're filling it up. Some days the officer brings home chunks of roast pig. The smell drifts over, and I wish I had some. One day, he even brings a little toy car. Dũng's wife stands by the pole bridge muttering. As soon as the officer appears through the trees, she stares at him the whole time he walks home. She stands outside cursing after he goes into the house. Then she turns to yell at her kids.

I go over to visit the boy. The steering wheel and red toy car lie in front of the house. Inside, the boy tosses flat, square batteries onto the floor like they're cards.

"Where did you get those?" He has a stack of them. The Americans must have left them behind. Each square is 1.5 volts like the big batteries the radio uses.

"From Bố's work."

"Can I have some?" If I connect them with a wire I could listen to the radio for a long time. Nothing we can buy now lasts: batteries play the radio for fifteen minutes before dying, *dép* sandals last two days before the toe-strap breaks, bicycle tires go three kilometers and get flat.

"They're special. They're for communication machines. You don't know how to use them."

"I'll make you a slingshot if you give me some."

I make him a slingshot and teach him to use it. His father brings a stack of batteries home for me.

When I go back to Tân Long for supplies, Ba seems happy to get the batteries. I stay in the house until it's time to take the boat back to avoid running into my dog. Mực wanders around, his black coat no longer smooth. Chị Tư tells me Mực doesn't come by that often when I'm not around, but she still gives him scraps. She's probably feeding him too, but a big dog can't live on a bowl of rice a day.

I put a set of batteries and the older of our two shortwave radios in a cloth bag and take it down to the countryside with me. I wait until ten o'clock at night when everyone else should be asleep, to bring the radio out. I turn the knob to find Voice of America. The radio whistles as the station drops in and out and a woman's voice speaking Vietnamese comes into the hut. She talks about the news of the rest of the world openly—her words don't seem constrained like those of the announcers here. I can't believe there's so much freedom somewhere else. I don't know how many of us escaped in 1975, but whenever I hear the announcer's voice, I know that one of us is free, and she's lending me her eyes to see the world. I hold onto that.

～

I go over to see how the officer's son is doing with his slingshot. He's stopped running to greet his father. All the toys are inside. While I show him how to aim at a leaf on a tree, he tells me he's worried about Dũng's wife yelling every day.

"Stay away from Cậu Dũng," I say as we walk to the boy's house.

The boy's father hears us. "My wife says it's strange, the way Anh Dũng's wife stares at her when she goes out to the washboard."

"Sometimes Anh Dũng's wife points at us," his wife says.

"It's Anh Dũng you should be scared of," I say.

She looks at me. "No one tells me anything about him."

No one talks to them because they're outsiders. I don't really like outsiders, but I feel bad for the boy. It's not his fault. His family needs to know. "Dũng's got a bunch of kids and no land to live on," I say. "I heard some people hired him, but he worked a little and got drunk . . . The work he knows how to do isn't fit for peace time."

The wife stares off, her face partly blank.

"I don't see him working the land," the officer says.

"It takes a while for things to grow," I say. "He's been a local here all his life, and he sacrificed a lot. Now his kids are hungry. He's very angry, stay away from him."

The officer glances at his wife standing stiffly at the window. "The authorities will keep order," he says.

The wife lets a long breath out.

"Go into town a day you're not working," I say. "You'll see who keeps who in order."

"I'm surprised he's not locked up," the officer says.

When I go to visit Chị Ba Chẳng, she tells me that the officer went to town to complain about Dũng. "The officials said they would investigate."

"The officer's family is scared," I say. "His wife has stopped coming outside. Either Dũng or the officer will have to go. But the officer's from out of town . . ."

"These out-of-towners shouldn't move next to Dũng like that," my cousin says.

I don't think the government can make a local person like Dũng disappear without protests. I want to see how far he can push the government. If people still have power.

Chị Ba Chẳng starts cooking rice for dinner. "Cook a little extra rice for me," I say.

"I don't have any."

"I'll pay you back more than you cook." Before, she'd invite me to eat with her.

"Sorry." She shakes her head. "I just don't have any."

I look at her kids. They're all skin and bones.

On the way home from my cousin's, I walk through the coconut grove. The father of the girls from Mỹ Tho stands guarding the bellfruit and mango trees he planted along the path under the canopy of coconuts. People pull the leaves off of everything within arm's reach when they walk through. Chị Ba Chẳng told him that he has to clear the coconuts first. Then, the roots have to die and he has to turn the soil. He said, no, if he put good soil around it should grow.

The girls see us and laugh. "Ê, country boys."

"What do we country boys know that you don't know?" I ask. "Maybe there's fish down in your canal you can catch?"

"Our father is trying to catch them," one of the girls says.

"First you have to make sure you have fish in there. If you want fish, throw in half coconut shells and build a house for them. If you want shrimp, toss in twigs and branches. They need some place to live and something to eat."

"How do we catch them?"

"There's lots of ways to catch fish," I say. "You can place poles at night. If its shrimp, you can scoop it up with a basket. If you know you have fish you can build a barrier and drain the canal."

"Tell us how to make a barrier."

I tell them how to get big branches and set them at an angle and then build the mud up. "But city girls couldn't do this," I tease. "Only country people can."

The next time Trực and I pass by, the girls are standing in the canal building a barrier. It's falling in on them. They didn't use any strong branches. "Take some coconut debris and toss it on," I say.

We go away and come back. They've started bailing water out of the canal. Their clothes are wet and their breasts show through. If their parents weren't right inside the house, I'd volunteer to help.

"Where did the fish all go?" the oldest one asks.

"Did you test with a pole to see if there were any in there?"

"No."

"Did you test with a basket for shrimp? You always test first." I remember when I spent all afternoon draining the fishpond in Cồn Tàu and didn't have anything to eat afterward.

"You didn't tell me any of this before."

The girls get muddier and their clothes cling to them. Trực turns red and leaves.

"Did you put branches in to give the shrimp a place to live?" They're doing everything wrong.

"No. Our Ba didn't want us to step on them and get hurt."

"Fish hide in the mud or run into the coconut roots," I say.

"Come down and help us."

"I'm not about to get muddy and have gnats bite me." I can't be that close to these girls like this.

They get a little stick and poke the coconut roots.

"Try using your leg."

"What if something is in there?"

The older girl tells her sister to go through all the mud. The younger one looks like she's about to cry. I leave before their father comes out and realizes they won't have anything for dinner. If my cousin has farmed here her whole life and she's starving, how can city people survive out here?

〜

The officer's son tells me that Dũng came over and took the banana bunch on the plant next to their washboard. "Cậu Dũng's wife stood next to the canal and told him, 'Do you see that bunch of bananas? Go over there, cut it down and bring it back.'"

That banana bunch was one of the healthiest around. The plant must have gotten something extra being by the washboard.

"We were right there in the house," the boy says. "We saw it from the window. Cậu Dũng cursed and grabbed a big knife. We couldn't see him when he went into the canal, but we heard two chops and saw him carry it into his house."

"Really?" Dũng could get himself in trouble for stealing.

I walk up with the boy to look. Dũng used one chop to crumble the plant so he could reach the bunch, then another to hack the bunch off. Like a farmer would.

"It's not a big loss," I say. The old plant will get replaced by the baby plants.

"Mẹ is so scared she hasn't slept for a lot of nights," the boy says. "Someone told me Cậu Dũng used to kill people in the night. Is that true?"

"I heard the same thing." I shrug. "He was a local Communist. I guess that was his job before."

❧

Dũng's kids try to get across the slippery bamboo pole bridge to their house in the rain. The older ones get across, but the youngest boy is stuck on my side of the stream. I go over and help him back to the house.

"Those kids should know better than to go out like this," Dũng's wife says when I bring her son back. She turns to shout at the older kids. "You're wet and muddy! What are you trying to do? Drown your younger brother?"

The kids go inside. Dũng's wife nods her head toward the officer's house. "Did you know them before?"

"No. I know the man works as an officer over in Bến Tre. I just play with the son." I look toward the canal. "He told me someone took their bananas."

"They eat full and enough."

"I don't know. Maybe."

"I can smell it." She motions her head toward the officer's house. "Those Northerners come and take what should be ours."

When Dũng gets home he sits on the dirt step of his house chopping wood with a big knife and looking over at the family from the North. The smell of their cooking wafts through the air. He stops chopping and stares.

◈

"Things are getting dangerous," I say the next time I see the boy. "You should help take care of your mother and make sure neither of you are alone."

"Cậu Dũng sits staring and muttering," the boy says. He probably sees Dũng staring at their hut through the slivers in the weave of the water coconut leaf walls. "Mẹ won't go outside to cook until Bố gets home."

"If you give me your rice, I'll cook it for you, and you can come over and get it."

"Come home with me," the boy says.

I shake my head. "I can still swim with you, but I can't go over to your house."

I leave and go back to my hut. Something's going to happen.

The boy comes over and asks me to slingshot birds with him. He doesn't ask me to cook their rice. I play with him a little but mainly stay in my hut or on the backside of our land.

When I walk by the boy's house, his mother sits inside by herself. "Make sure that you're not alone," I say. "Don't make any eye contact with Anh Dũng. It's getting dangerous. You can feel it, you can see it."

Later, Dũng's wife sees me placing my fishing poles in the canal. "Where are your cousin and the other boy?"

"I don't know. I don't play much with that boy."

◈

I wake up and the boy and his family are gone. The house is empty except for some wash pans, buckets, and rags. I didn't have a chance to say goodbye. Some men come and start disassembling the house. Dũng sits on the end of his log bridge watching them and smoking.

"Where are they moving the house to?" I ask.

"I don't know."

I look around. His wife is gone. "Your wife is really mean to you," I say.

"She has all the right, and I don't. Before we had enough to live, now we don't have enough to eat. It's my fault."

I remember what I heard Cậu Năm Lộc, the ferryman, tell Má. "All those Communists' regret won't fix it. We lost a lot of lives and everyone's still in poverty. Then the government tells us to go home and eat dirt."

Dũng blows smoke out in front of him. "No one will hire me because they're scared of me ... They should be."

I look toward the officer's empty house. "That family was scared." They're probably happy to be somewhere else.

"Those people didn't fight for years like me. Then they want to take the land that belongs to the locals here."

I nod toward a pole bridge going across to the officer's land from the main path. "You should pull the bridge. They're not coming back." It *is* Dũng's fault and people like him, but outsiders shouldn't have it better than the locals. "They aren't farmers. We are."

"He came home with a toy for his son one day," Dũng says. "My kids didn't have anything to eat—and he was bringing home a toy. I almost killed him for that toy. I almost killed them all. The only thing that stopped me was the thought of my kids."

"The government should take care of you more." I point toward the officer's house. "Are you going to plant yams around the foundation?"

He takes a draw from his cigarette. "I have to wait for the soil to soften."

I Can't Feed Rice to a Dog

I go back to Tân Long in the fall. Everyone around seems hungry. I try to avoid my dog. The baby must be already dead. I'm glad when school starts, and I can leave Tân Long for the day. The school for seventh grade is the one Thượng goes to. It's close to our beauty shop and only a ferry ride and short walk from Tân Long. I don't have to make the long trip to Vân's school anymore.

The principal of my new school tells us all to meet for a parade in Mỹ Tho. We're told to wear our best clothes and look cheerful. We're supposed to show everyone in the world how happy we are to be liberated. The next day, I have to leave before the sun comes up to check in for the parade. Each school assembles along the parade route. From six in the morning until noon I stand in a line with my classmates smiling. We're part of the decorations.

There's no food or water or bathrooms. My friends and I make a circle for each other to pee in, but the girls don't have any place to go. A band and soldiers march by us toward a platform with officials on it. Tractors roll past us with wheels taller than we are. A banner proclaims they'll transform farming. Flatbed trucks follow carrying more tractors. I look around trying to figure out how I can skip the next parade without anyone noticing.

After school, I climb the bellfruit tree in the alley. I can tell by amount of steam coming out of our neighbor's pots how much rice they're cooking. It's not much. People cook a lot of watery rice soup and it smells different. Even the thief family is hungry—usually they manage to steal things.

At dinner, I sit on the front door step with a bowl of rice. Neighbors stand around watching me eat. It's the worst feeling in the world. What I have isn't enough, but they have nothing. I wouldn't sit around and watch someone eat. It doesn't help.

One day after school, I see Mực eating poop by the widow's house. I run out and call him. He follows me inside. I look for something he can eat. There's nothing.

$$\sim$$

Má tells me that she wants me to stay in Mỹ Tho above the beauty shop. She wants me to be less country. Everyone says it will be good for me. I only agree so I don't have to see Mực hungry.

The city is a different world. I watch money exchange hands in the beauty shop and I can't believe people spend that much washing and cutting their hair. No one goes to my cousin Hai Thăng's barbershop in Tân Long, but city women come to our beauty shop each week to get their hair set in curls. Poor farmers come to get their hair shampooed after selling their goods in the market right in front of our shop door. If I lived with Mực here, where everyone isn't so hungry, I could feed a dog.

Thượng takes me to a place where we can rent a ping pong table and tries to teach me to play. Afterwards, we cross the street to the line of tractors that have been parked on the side since the parade. A sign on the tractors says: STAY OFF OR YOU WILL BE ARRESTED BY THE GOVERNMENT POLICE. We climb around on them anyway.

I get sick and lose a lot of weight. The only reason I can stand being in the city is that our family is defying the government by being here when everyone is being pushed to the countryside. Ba comes over and sees how sick I am. He tells me how much Mực misses me, and that I should come back to Tân Long. The next day after school, I pack a bag of clothes and my school books. I get off the ferry by the town hall and start walking home, talking to people I haven't seen for a month. Before I cross the bridge where Mr. Three More used to live, Mực comes running and jumps up and licks my face. I wrap my arms around him. He jumps up, scratching me and whistling the whole way back to my house. I can't believe I mean that much to the dog and the dog means the same to me.

Tây comes up from where he was playing in the field where the old fort was. "Mực never jumps, he never whistles," he says.

Mr. Five Salt comes down from the dock. "That's right. That dog is so happy to see you."

That evening, I give Mực part of my rice and fish sauce. The dog wags its tail and looks up at me while eating.

The next afternoon, no one is around but me and Mực. I pet him. His hair feels scraggly, no longer smooth. His ribs stick out. I go through his fur trying to catch fleas. "I'm sorry I can't feed you," I say.

That night I feed Mực again. I start to eat one less bowl of rice each night and give the extra to my dog. A few times, I even give Mực a piece of pork. Every day before dinner, I go to the land where the old fort was and find two or three green bananas to eat so I can stop myself from eating and save rice for Mực. I told Ba and Chị Tư I wasn't going to feed him, but now I'm doing it in secret. It's my food, though. It's not hurting anyone else. Still, I feel like I'm stealing from my family. They wouldn't cook as much if I took less.

∼

I have a toothache again. I don't know where you are supposed to go to get your teeth fixed now. After the Communists took over, they closed the free clinic in Mỹ Tho. I wander around trying to find a place. On the way to school I walk by street vendors with signs that say they can pull out the worm that's eating your teeth. Má said she had it done, and they gave her a worm from her mouth. It must have been a trick, though, because when Má got all her teeth pulled out at the clinic she didn't bring back any worms. Teeth decay because you don't take care of them, not from worms eating them. I try to brush mine with toothpaste on my finger at night.

I've seen a fancy dental clinic next to the market by the Vĩnh Lợi Cinema. The sign says it's for Communist officials and their families only. Ba's involved with all the Communist meetings, maybe I can go there. After school, I walk to the clinic. I pass the street where the tractors from the parade are parked. They sit along the edge of the road unused. The entrance to the clinic is a small door next to the cinema. The vacant reception area has three padded cloth chairs and paintings on the wall. It's cleaner than any doctor's office I went to with Má. I'm sure they can do a good job here.

"I need my tooth fixed," I say.

Three dentists and their assistances step toward the reception area and look at me. I only need one dentist. The receptionist looks at me from behind her desk. "Who are you?"

"My father is the mayor of Tân Long." Ba being on the neighborhood watch must count for something.

She points me toward the first of three empty dental chairs. "We'll take care of that for you."

I lay back in a cream chair. Three doctors lean over me as they inject numbing medicine. The tooth that needs to be taken out is buried beneath my gums. They start to dig gently. "Go ahead and dig harder," I say. "I've had worse." I worry they're going to find out I'm not the mayor's son before they finish.

The three dentists give me another numbing injection. I feel them digging, digging into the bone. There are no windows, so I can't tell where the sun is. Hours seem to be passing. No other patients come in. Up front, the office manager says, "Look up and see who this patient is for the service record."

I hope they finish soon. The second round of numbing medicine is wearing off. "We should give him another injection," a doctor says.

"We've gone past the allotment," another doctors says.

They're cleaning up. It's almost done. The receptionist comes up and whispers something to a doctor. Do they know? If they're professional, they should finish the job anyway. They start to shove my mouth and body around roughly. They know. Gauze square after gauze square comes out with blood. "Bite on this," one of the doctors says.

I bite.

"Now get out."

"Thank you very—"

They motion for me to leave. When I stand up, my face feels like it was pushed with a boat pole. I sit back down. "I don't think I can stand. Can I sit here a minute?"

"Get out."

I stand up. Things look blurry. I lean against the wall and make my way to the door. The gauze overflows with blood. I spit the blood out, twist the gauze, and put it back in. I need to sit down. Everything is out of focus. I don't want to go far from the clinic in case something happens. If I start to bleed or faint, they'd have to help me. I feel my way along the brick wall until I get to the steps of the Vĩnh Lợi Cinema. I sit on the top step and rest my head against the outside wall. It's clean and dry from an earlier rain. The few vendors left in the market look at me spitting blood out. I press my finger over the soaking gauze to try to stop the bleeding. The receptionist from the clinic comes out and peeks around the corner at me. My eyes close, and I drift off.

After a few minutes, I open my eyes and watch the people come and go into the cinema. I don't think I can stand up. The receptionist comes out again. This dental clinic must be a showcase and not meant for real work. When I can stand up without being dizzy, I walk to the ferry to Tân Long.

〜

Mr. Five Salt says he's going to move his family down river closer to the sea where he collects salt. "The government won't allow people to live where they don't work, so we have to move." He asks me to keep Mực.

"No," I say, "You take Mực." I want to keep Mực, but it won't look good for us to feed a dog rice. We already eat rice not banana trunks mixed with *bo bo* like most people.

Mr. Five Salt comes over and asks Ba to keep Mực. "You have more resources to take care of a dog."

"Let Lượng decide," Ba says.

"I can't," I say. Ba complained to Má that he didn't want to feed an extra mouth when my baby brother was born. How can he be willing to feed a dog? Mực eats more than a baby.

"They'll take Mực down to the countryside," Chị Tư says, "and eat him or sell him." Mực hangs around her desk when I'm at school. She's been feeding the dog, too.

"It could be. But I still can't."

I tell Tây and Mr. Five Salt that I can't keep Mực.

"You only wanted Mực when he was young and healthy," Tây says. "Now that he's getting old, you don't want to take care of him."

"No. I'm going to be sad to see Mực go. But if there's extra food, people need to be fed. We're watching kids die. Nhiều goes around begging for food. Trắng used to be a little plump, but now he's not. Look at you. You were skinny before, now you're skin and bones."

Tây doesn't talk to me for the rest of the day. The next day he comes up to me and says, "Mực's my dog and I won't let anything happen to him. We'll starve together."

I'll keep feeding Mực my rice until they leave. I've learned to lie around and do nothing after dinner and go to bed early. Some nights, I'm so hungry I put a pillow under my belly and lie with my face in it trying to kill the feeling. I'll only have to eat less until Mr. Five Salt's family leaves.

One of the neighborhood watch leaders talks to the sawmill owner about the missing bananas since they own the land the abandoned fort is on. It's not just me. A lot of neighbor kids steal them, too. The owners hide in the banana plants and chase us when we come. Then, they start to harvest the bananas when they're too green for even me to eat. I take Mực to the backside of the island to look for food. I don't think people like Mr. Tư Hạnh go out here and tally plants. They just harass people about the things in front of their face.

Mực starts regaining strength. I teach him how to catch and eat shrimp. It seems like it makes me more hungry finding them, and Mực's constantly cold because he doesn't have enough fat. I try to get him to eat bananas, but he won't eat green ones, and we rarely find ripe ones.

When I come back from school one day, Mực is gone. I thought Tây's family would be here longer. I gave away half of myself.

A few weeks later, I dream Mực is in pain. I'm there, but I can't cradle him, I can only watch and walk around him. He's my old Mực, with the smooth black coat, before he got sick and unhealthy. Mực's muscles convulse under his ribs. He looks straight at me while shaking and heaving. I don't know what to do. I want Mực to fight this. After hours of pain, Mực rolls over, still looking at me. I can't get close. Mực's breath gets shorter and the convulsions stop. Mực's body twitches a little, then stops breathing. I reach out to touch his black fur. I wake up. I close my eyes and try to go back to the dream, but I can't.

I go out and sit on the front steps. Mực's dead. He was fighting hard, but now he's dead. I lean back and count mosquitoes. People walk by in the dark on their way to the market. After a while, Chị Tư starts cooking breakfast. I go in and help her. "It's just a dream," she says when I tell her Mực died last night.

At breakfast, I force Má and Ba and my sisters to hear about my dog's suffering. I won't let them talk about anything else.

"It's just a dream," Ba says. "Forget it and go to school."

"It's not a dream. Mực is dead."

Two weeks later, when I come home, Mr. Five Salt's son Tây is talking with Chị Tư. I didn't expect to see them this soon. They live so far away.

Chị Tư turns to me. "Lượng told me about his dream two weeks ago, right when you said Mực died. He can tell you."

"What did you dream?" Tây asks. "Your sister says you know how Mực died."

I knew Mực died that night. As I tell him my dream, Mrs. Five Salt comes in. "Did you see anyone with the dog?" she asks.

"No. Just Mực on the dirt floor."

"How could you see it so clearly?" Tây asks. "It's almost as if you were me watching Mực die."

"I don't know. After Mực died, my dream ended."

"You and the dog are linked," Mrs. Five Salt says. "Tây was with Mực the whole night. His older brother got exhausted. We knew it was poison, but we didn't know what to do. We have nothing. We just tried to give the dog some water."

"I was sad I couldn't do anything to help," I say.

"Life is really hard down there. People poison dogs to eat. Mực managed to make it home."

"How can you eat something with poison in it?" I ask. "Won't it poison you?"

"Drain the blood and throw the guts away," Tây says.

"We buried Mực in the morning," Mrs. Five Salt says.

After they leave, Chị Tư says, "Mực came and got you that night. That dog was special."

∾

It's close to the New Year. Má sits in the kitchen with us talking about which families are eating *bo bo* and which have to mix bitter old banana tree trunks with rice to stretch it—even pigs don't like to eat that. Má knows what everybody eats. So do I.

"If everyone weren't so hungry," I say, "I could have kept my dog." Now that Má is well, it's getting better for us, but it's worse for everyone else.

"People are hungry," Má says. "We don't have extra and we don't know what tomorrow will be like."

"Mực was a good dog for our family." Chị Tư looks at me. "A good watchdog."

"We need to take care of people," I say. "That baby died of starvation last summer. If we can't take care of a baby, how can we take care of a dog?"

"The baby died a few days ago, not last summer," Má says.

"How?" I ask. "Last summer it was hardly breathing, skin and bones."

"Neighbors kept giving a little bit when they could. People gave the water from cooking rice for the baby to drink. Finally, on a cold night the baby died." Má shakes her head. "That was too much suffering for too long."

Trying Our Luck in Sài Gòn

The sun hasn't come up when Thượng, Trực, and I say goodbye and head out the door of my family's beauty shop. "Listen to Thượng," Má says. "He's in charge. Don't get lost. Sài Gòn is busier during *Tết*."

Trực's older sister calls after him, "Be careful not to lose your *lì xì* money and listen to your older cousin."

We walk quickly to the bus stop on the edge of Mỹ Tho. This is the first time we've gone by ourselves and everyone says Sài Gòn is the best place to eat *Tết*.

It's still dark when we crowd onto the bus. I search for a spot close to the window—I hate being cramped up. There's space on the wood bench between an older man with glasses and a girl in a blue *áo dài*. I try to sit next to the girl, but Thượng beats me. I end up squashed between him on one side and Trực on the other.

The bus gets onto National Road 4 as the sun rises over the rice paddies on the side of the road. Below us, bicyclists with wooden crates tied on the back, duffle bags, and chickens in cages pedal to the market. The bus speeds by them. I wonder how fast it goes.

Thượng tries to lean into the girl on the side of him more than me. We're all so hot and sweaty—she can't like that.

The bus stops in a small town. Vendors hurry to the side and sell sugarcane drinks through the window. I'm thirsty but I don't want to have to pee. It's seventy-two kilometers to Sài Gòn, but it takes about an hour and a half to get there with all of the stops along the way.

A woman comes on the bus holding sticks with spears of mangoes soaked in saccharine on them. Another woman sells *bánh cam* and *bánh tiêu* pastries. I'm starting to get hungry, but we need to save our money for the zoo.

"What animals or rides in the zoo do you know about?" Trực asks.

"Canoe racing," I say.

"Big slides, flying elephant swings, and . . ." Thượng looks at the girl in the blue *áo dài* next to him, "a Ferris wheel. The perfect place to get a view of the city with a pretty girl."

〰

The Sài Gòn bus station swarms with men in long-sleeve silk shirts and women in short skirts. We stand out with our white, short-sleeve shirts and denim-colored bellbottoms—yesterday's style, like everything else in Mỹ Tho. Our belts, the cardboard ones kids get that crack where you bend them, make our clothes look even cheaper. I'm worried that we'll make an easy target for pickpockets. I touch the *lì xì* wadded in my front pocket—no one is going to get my money again.

A man walks by in a red silk shirt and white bellbottoms that look like sailor pants. "Nice shirt," Thượng says. Only Thượng blends in a bit—his hair is like the city men, longer and pushed behind his ears like a girl's, not crab-cut tight and close like Trực's and mine.

"Too hot," I tell Thượng. It's bad enough Má made me wear long pants today. I wouldn't want to wear a long-sleeve shirt as well.

The man in the red shirt greets a woman in a tight minidress. Thượng checks her up and down and adds, "I like what he's got there even more."

She's not that special. I think of Phượng, the girl who lives behind us. She's so pretty in a quiet kind of way.

A cyclo grabs us and tries to pull us to his cart. Thượng haggles for him to take us to the city center. We hop in the cart in front as the cyclo climbs onto the bicycle seat in back and starts pedaling. The wide streets seem vacant with so few people out walking, and the restaurants are mainly empty. There are less people than when I came to see Má in the hospital. The Communists keep sending everyone out to the countryside to farm.

After only a few blocks, the cyclo drops us off in front of Bến Thành Market. We could have saved money by walking.

Street vendors sell fruit, steamed soup, and fried bananas on the side of the market. Only a few vendors sell flowers—under Communism you aren't supposed to have luxuries. No one wants to decorate when they're hungry, anyway. "Let's get some *phở*." I head toward a vendor on the sidewalk.

Thượng spots people squatting around dice games along both sides of a small side street. "I'm going to play gourd crab," he says. "Look how much that man is winning over there. I'm going to bet on his money, and I'll have enough for a silk shirt or two."

"I'm hungry." I smell bananas frying in an open pan. "Let's grab something to eat while we walk to the zoo."

"Just a couple games, then we'll go." Thượng puts his hand in his front pocket and heads toward the gourd crab dealers.

I don't want to spend my time in Sài Gòn gambling—it's like burning money on the altar. We came to see the zoo. But Thượng is the oldest, so we follow him over to a group of people squatting around a large mat with a gourd, crab, shrimp, fish, deer, and rooster printed on it.

Thượng crouches down and places a handful of his money on the crab, alongside the money from the man who's been winning. Six choices to bet on and a one-sixth chance on three dice to win: Not good enough odds for me. The dealer puts the dice on a plate, covers it with a bowl and shakes. He lifts the bowl and reveals a gourd and two deer. Thượng doesn't turn around to look at us. He's lost enough money to buy us all a great lunch.

The man who had been winning places his money on the deer. Thượng follows. The dealer shakes the dice in the bowl and lifts it up: three crabs. Another few bets and Thượng's lost about half of his *lì xì*.

"We have to go, we're going to lose all our money," Trực says.

Thượng stares at the pictures of the six items on the mat as if he's trying to will it to tell which character to choose. He sees someone winning at another dealer's mat so he goes over to place a bet on their money.

"This doesn't look good," I say to Trực.

Trực nods.

"If he loses all his money, I can probably get us into the zoo. We'll be short though."

Trực looks at my brother. "I can hardly wait to get going."

Thượng stands up from the game and walks over to us. "Anh Trực,

I need to see your money. I need to recover mine." Thượng holds out his hand.

Trực looks down at his feet. He should outrank us both since his mother is older than ours, but Trực's sister works in our shop and Thượng is older and in charge of this trip.

"I know I'm going to get it back," Thượng says. "I've figured out how to win. I have a system now."

Trực digs into his front pocket and slowly brings out a wad of bills. Thượng grabs it out of his hand and heads back to the game.

"How do we get into the zoo or even get back home if he loses my money, too?" Trực asks.

"I have enough for bus tickets back," I say. "I'll make sure we get home." Trực stares back down at his sandals. He looks so out of place here. I must look the same way.

Thượng squats around the mat with the other gamblers. From the back, his long hair makes him look almost like a city boy. He places small bets on multiple animals. So that's his strategy. He'll just lose more slowly. I have to get away before he asks for my money. I wander over to watch a card game a few steps away. I wish the police would show up to close down the games. I'm sure we could outrun them. Then, we could go to the zoo.

Thượng comes up me. "Where's the money?" he asks.

I reach into my pocket and separate the bills with my fingers. I look my brother in the eye. "We have no way to get home if you lose this money." I give Thượng the same amount Trực did, leaving some in my pocket. It's not enough for us to get home, though.

Thượng takes the money. "Is this all you have?"

"I'm younger—I didn't get as much as you."

He starts to play conservatively, making small bets. I feel sick watching him gamble my money away.

Down the street, a dealer sits by a gourd crab game with no players. I walk up to his game and watch his hands as he holds the dice. The dealer moves his empty hand into his money pouch and when it comes out he switches the dice he's been rolling. He's practicing using loaded dice. I look at the new dice and see a corner of the paper by the rooster torn the slightest bit on each one. This set will favor the shrimp on the other side.

I wink at the dealer and he winks back. "Nice move," I say. But even without loaded dice the dealer always wins.

"Nobody's playing, though," he answers.

"I'll play for you and get people to your game. Let me win enough to get people excited. When enough players start making bets with me, I'll lose and split the take forty-sixty with you."

The dealer glances at me and then looks back at his hands.

"Agreed," he says. "Here's how it works. I'll signal with my hand one through six to tell you what I'll roll next. One the shrimp, two the crab . . ." I squat down next to the mat, nodding as he continues.

The dealer pulls out a new set of dice. "Come place your bets, double or triple your money in one roll," he shouts to people on the street, waving his hand over his board with three fingers slightly extended.

I place a few of my bills on the third character on the mat, the fish. If I lose it, I'll grab the dice and yell that the dealer cheated me. The dice roll and three fish come up. "I win!" I shout and gather my money in my fist.

"A triple win for the play on the fish," the dealer says.

A couple people come up and squat around the mat to watch me play. They're well-dressed. City people seem to have more money.

The dealer doesn't signal, so I keep all my money on the fish. I feel numb and tingling waiting for people to bet. This time it's two fish and a deer. The loaded dice aren't perfect, but I've doubled my money.

"I can't believe it. I win again!" I stare at the money and run my hands over it.

"Another win for lucky fish," shouts the dealer.

"He's on a winning streak," someone behind me says.

I keep my money on the fish. A man and his wife put theirs down with me. A single man also places a bet on the fish. The dice roll three fish again. I have enough to get us all bus tickets home now. I put most of my winnings in my pocket. How do I get out of this? Any minute the Brown Cows will come and break up the gambling

"Who's going to be the lucky winner this time," the dealer calls out to the players. He urges them to place their bets with four fingers sweeping over the mat. I place my money on the rooster. How does he switch the dice so fast? Each time he rolls, I worry I'll get caught cheating. I'll just say I'm lucky.

"Why are you moving away from your lucky fish?" the woman asks me. Her husband stays on the fish. Some new players bet on it, too.

The dice come up as two roosters.

"He's got a talent," the woman tells her husband, "bet where he does."

"Yes, he's on a roll," another man says.

The dealer signals six. The deer. I have to lose now so that the house wins. That's the money we're going to split. I put a small bet on the shrimp and put the rest in my pocket. The dealer sees me. I need to find a way to leave. Four other players put big bets along with mine. I glance around for Brown Cows. I wish he'd hurry up and roll. Two deer and a gourd come up.

"What happened to your luck?" the woman asks.

The losing players swear. Most walk away. They were going to lose it anyway—the house always wins in these games.

I stick out my hand to the dealer. I want to get paid before the Brown Cows show up and close him down. He holds up an open palm signaling me to wait.

I start betting and winning again. What if the dealer is waiting for the Brown Cows to come so he can run away without giving me my cut? I need one more big win before I take off. The dealer sweeps his hand across the table with two fingers extended: the crab. I'm supposed to stay on the deer and lose. I place my bet on it. The other players follow my luck and place their money with mine. Right before the dealer lifts the bowl, I switch to the crab. He glares at me, but it's too late. Two crabs come up. The dealer grudgingly pulls the money out of the pouch around his waist and places it in my pile. I put the money in my pocket. He signals four.

I salute the dealer and walk away. Someone calls "Police! Brown Cows!" and the street becomes a mess of dealers collecting their games and gamblers running to get out of sight.

I run out of the street with a crowd of people and break off into a smaller alley. Once I'm in the clear, I walk around other side streets looking back until the Brown Cows leave and the dealers start setting up their games again. I spread my winnings between my pockets so no one will notice a lump and head toward Bến Thành Market looking for my brother and cousin. I see them standing on the sidewalk in front of the market and under the clock tower. It's almost noon.

"Where were you?" Trực asks.

"Looking at one of the games over there."

Thượng backs up a little and pretends to be looking at leather belts hanging from a street vendor's cart. I don't have to ask if he lost the money I gave him.

Trực comes closer and leans his head toward me. "When I was looking for you, a man came up and asked me if I knew someone who was dressed like me."

It must have been the dealer looking for me. He probably thinks I was the one who yelled "Police." If Trực weren't taller and skinnier, we could pass for twins. "What did you say?" I put my hand around the bills in my pocket.

"I told him I didn't know."

"Good. He was probably with the secret police."

Trực's eyes get big—then he goes back to looking at his feet. "How are we going to get home?"

"Let's walk to the zoo," I say. "Maybe we'll find a way to get in anyway." I don't want to stand around waiting for an angry gourd crab dealer to find me.

Thượng acts like he can't hear. I turn toward him. "Thầy Bảy, come on. Let's try to see if we can still get into the zoo."

We make our way through the throngs of people walking around the park in the city square. I stare at the shady trees inside the entrance to the zoo. We haven't eaten since five o'clock in the morning, but the sun is making me more thirsty than hungry.

I tell Thượng to go along one side of the wall to see if he can find another way in, and Trực to go along the other. When they come back, they shake their heads.

Two large families try to organize to show their tickets to the man at the gate. "I bet we can get in with them," I say.

The three of us meld together with the families as the ticket taker waves them through. We step under a canopy formed by trees lining a winding path. Near the gate, a woman with a vending cart puts a stick of sugarcane, a kumquat, and a slice of orange through a press. How am I'm going to get us fed and home without letting Thượng know I have money? We walk toward the monkeys and tropical birds, stopping on the way to watch a lion sleeping in the shade of his den. Then, we head toward the river at the back of the zoo where the canoe races are.

"Let's stop and get a drink." Thượng walks toward a concrete drinking fountain. He presses the button, but nothing comes out.

Trực stares at water twirling in a grassy area. "Maybe we could get a drink out of the sprinkler."

I walk over to the sprinkler. Brownish water comes out. "I don't think it's drinkable. It looks like it's coming straight from the river."

I motion for Trực and Thượng to sit on a bench under a tree. "Maybe I'll be able to find something to drink. Wait here."

I head toward the sugarcane drink cart I saw on the way in and order two. The liquid from the sugarcane and citrus fruit run down from a press into a plastic bag. The vendor adds a bit of crushed ice and a straw and ties the bag up with a rubber band. I'm so thirsty I can't resist drinking it at once. I order a third.

Meat skewers rest on another cart. The sweet smell of sauce and meat makes my stomach feel empty. A vendor with a cart selling sticky rice parks around the corner. Sticky rice could fill us up a bit and it looks the same whether it's new or someone has eaten half of it and left it. The vendor scoops a lump of sweet rice dyed bright orange into a piece of newspaper and hands it to me. I walk back, taking a long drink from each sugarcane drink to make them look as if someone bought it and couldn't finish.

"Ê! Give me one of those," Thượng calls out.

"I want one too," says Trực.

Thượng takes a sip and then asks, "What do you have there? Give me some of that, too." I unwrap the newspaper and tear off a piece from the orange clump of sticky rice.

"Where'd you get this?" Thượng asks.

I point in the opposite direction of the vendors I bought the food and drinks from. "I found it lying around, over there. Someone must have ordered too many." A lot of people overspend on New Year's.

I tear off a few more pieces to share and the rice disappears. The sticky rice leaves my mouth dry. I loosen the rubber band around the straw on my drink and open the plastic bag to retrieve the small pieces of ice leftover. It would have been better not to eat anything.

"Let's go and see if there's more." Thượng gets off the bench and heads over to where I pointed.

Trực gets up and follows. He finds another sugarcane drink sitting on a bench where someone left it, but there's barely a sip left. In the center of a mass of marigolds and daisies, a stone fountain spouts waters into the air. I step through the flowers and peer into it, but the water in the fountain base looks murky and green algae clings to the inside wall. "Let's walk over to the river," I say.

On the river we see kids lined up to race canoes. The kids splash as they try to beat each other paddling around a small island. That could be us. A half-full bag of sugarcane drink lies in the path in front of us, maybe dropped by a young kid with a stomach ache. I kick it. The bag rolls over and liquid spills out.

Trực shouts at me. "We could have had that." He looks around to see if there's any discarded food nearby.

We walk next to the river on a wooden walkway. The walkway spans over pens of small deer lying down on the dirt in the shade of trees. The deer don't bother to look up at us.

It's getting toward evening. The only place we can go is to our cousin Chị Năm Gương's house. "She lives in District 1 around Lê Lợi and Freedom," Thượng says.

We walk out of the zoo toward the port on the Sài Gòn River and then back to the city center. I've only been to Chị Năm Gương's house once, a few years ago. We wander until we find Lê Lợi and walk along it until it intersects with Freedom Street. The Communists renamed Freedom Street, just like they renamed a lot of places. No one likes it. The street names used to be kings, warriors, and generals from our history. Now they're named after people I've never heard of before. Was some suicide bomber as important as a general who fought the Mongolians? We still use the old names.

A few blocks into Freedom Street, Thượng says, "This is it."

He walks around the corner of a brick building to a restaurant entrance. A waiter steps out from amidst the empty tables to intercept us. Thượng walks past the waiter toward a staircase in back. Trực and I follow him up the stairs. He knocks on the door at the top.

We wait. He knocks again. A door inside creaks. Chị Năm Gương opens the door, and a big smile breaks over her broad face. "*Ê! Chúc mừng năm mới.* I'm surprised to see you."

"*Chào*, Chị Năm, *chúc mừng năm mới!*" We wish her a happy New Year together. Maybe she'll give us *lì xì* money, and we can use that to get home.

"Come in. Come in." She leads us into her apartment on the right. In front of us is the reception area of the exercise room she owns. I glance over my shoulder at the deserted training area. Dim lights show a few mats set out and some equipment. Free weights, benches, and weight machines lay undusted in a makeshift storage area. The last time I was here, the room was filled with huge men in shorts and tank tops. The trainer, who was spotting customers struggling to lift weights, was the largest of them all. Now, no one comes to an exercise room: if you want to work out, you can work out in the field farming.

"What are you doing by yourself in Sài Gòn?" Chị Năm Gương asks. She starts filling glasses with water from her kitchen faucet.

"We went to the zoo," I say, taking one of the glasses. I glance at my cousin's plain clothes. She's always been the city relative, well-dressed in expensive clothes even when she came to the countryside.

"I bet you're hungry. Come. Sit down and eat." She puts a rice bowl filled a third of the way up in front of each of us and sets out small dishes of water spinach and fish sautéed in fish sauce. While we eat, she asks about the health of her ten siblings down in the countryside. It's been a long time since she's been down to visit, and she wants to know what each relative has been doing.

I look for more rice, but the pot is empty. I walk away from the table and bring back a plastic container with New Year's *mứt* candy, and we start to eat the dried pineapple and coconut and the red, toasted watermelon seeds.

"Still hungry?" My cousin starts cooking another pot of rice. Her small rice cooker can barely cook enough rice to feed one of us. I go into the bathroom while I wait for the rice to finish. The bathroom has a porcelain toilet with a seat. I don't know anyone else who has one. The toilet doesn't gleam white anymore. It's caked with dirt, and the front of the seat is broken off.

The rice cooker switch clicks off. We eat it quickly and Chị Năm Gương cooks a third pot. She sets it out and starts cooking another. She keeps cooking rice and feeding us until we finally slow down.

"You can sleep on the mats in the training room," she says. "I'll get you some blankets and pillows."

Chị Năm Gương comes back from her bedroom with her hands full of bedding. I wait to see if she'll pass *lì xì* envelopes out, but she just hands us a blanket and pillow. "Can you lend us some money for the bus ticket back tomorrow? We're completely broke." I laugh to try to make it seem lighter.

"Aren't we all," she says, her smile fading. "I'm sorry I don't have any extra money. You'll have to stay here until your mother sends you some."

We go into the training room to sleep. Thượng lies down in his clothes on a mat. I walk over to the window overlooking the street and motion Trực to follow me. Down below us mopeds and pedestrians pass back and forth on Freedom Street. Streetlights glimmer and street vendors start to put away their wares. "Anh Trực," I whisper, "don't ask how, but I've got money for us to go home. Be careful not to say anything to Thượng."

I'm the first to wake up. I put my clothes back on and go in to say good morning to Chị Năm Gương. She has a baguette from the restaurant downstairs for our breakfast. She's surprised when I tell her we're leaving. "Thầy Bảy," I say, walking over to my brother sleeping on the mat. "Get up. It looks like we've found some money to go home."

"How?"

"I picked it off the street when the Brown Cows came. Someone dropped it. I didn't tell you before because I didn't want to get in trouble with the police."

"Do you have more?"

"If I had more I would have bought food at the zoo."

~

After Trực and I tell Má and his sister that Thượng lost all of our *lì xì* gambling, they give us some more money. They have a little extra since the beauty shop is busy with customers during the New Year. I tell Má that there are still some things in Sài Gòn that Trực and I want to see— she lets us go without Thượng.

We don't waste money on a cyclo and walk straight to an upscale, air-conditioned restaurant in the city center. The restaurant is right on Lê Lợi Street. "Are you sure we should eat here?" Trực asks. "It looks expensive."

"I'll pay." We don't have restaurants this big in Mỹ Tho—I want to try it out. We sit toward the middle, but we can still see across all the empty tables to the street. Only two other tables in the back are occupied, and the people there are sitting back and smoking.

A woman in her early twenties comes in wearing a mini skirt and makeup. "Where are you from?" she asks pulling up a chair. Trực blushes.

"From Mỹ Tho," I say, "and my cousin is from farther out in the countryside. We're going to the zoo."

"Are you looking for an extra good time?" she bends one of her legs up. She's not wearing anything underneath her skirt.

Trực's face turns redder, and his hands shake. I see prostitutes with customers behind *nón lá* in the cinema all the time, but he probably hasn't seen a girl naked before.

"I think we'll stick with going to the zoo." I've heard stories of men getting robbed by prostitutes and having nothing left but their underwear. I turn to talk to Trực. "So what do you want to do at the zoo first?" The woman doesn't leave, and Trực doesn't answer me. "Should we go on the canoe racing first?" I ask. "Or do you want to go on the Ferris wheel?"

The restaurant owner comes up behind the woman and motions with his head for her to leave. She leaves and hangs outside the door on the street.

"How much is this?" I ask the owner, pointing to an item on the menu.

"How about this?" I ask. We decide on two bowls of egg noodles with quail eggs and shrimp and dessert drinks with coconut milk and red kidney beans.

The prostitute stands in the shade on the sidewalk a building down from the restaurant. She spots us when we leave, but Trực and I walk the opposite direction and cross the street. It's a short walk to the zoo when you aren't hungry and thirsty.

I pay for our tickets at the gate, and we go straight to the rides. A lot of the rides are closed, but we go on all of the open ones. Our last ride is the canoe race. Trực and I paddle together and loop around first. After the canoe race, we stand and look over the river behind the zoo, watching the water hyacinths float down and the fisherman on the edge. Trực asks, "The secret police were looking for you, we're eating out at this fancy restaurant, and we have all the money to go to the zoo, what aren't you telling me?"

I don't answer. I don't want Trực to think I picked somebody's pocket, but if my parents found out I was gambling they wouldn't trust me to go to Sài Gòn alone again. He doesn't press. Sometimes it's better not to say anything. Sometimes it's better not to know.

We turn back toward the zoo and get ready to leave. I complain to Trực that so many rides have closed since I was here with Má in 1973. And the ones that are open aren't lit up like before. Even though it's getting run down, the zoo is beautiful with pathways through green lawns and flowers blooming. I try to imprint the scene in my mind. Sài Gòn is dying. If it's dead, there's nothing left in this country.

Red Scarf Girls

On the way out of the school gates, I look back and see Thượng pull a red scarf out of his pocket and tie it around his neck. Then he walks with a Red Scarf group over to the groundskeeper's shed to get tools to clean up the school. I know my brother well enough to know this has to be about a girl, not joining the Communists. It still makes me mad—he's always trying to get out of work at home.

I don't get a chance to talk to Thượng about the scarf. I go home to Tân Long, and he stays above the beauty shop in Mỹ Tho. The next day, I catch him after school. "Do you learn anything going to those meetings?"

"There are these two girls . . ." Two? I thought it would only be one. "One of them is pretty, but the other. You have to see her. She's the most beautiful girl I've seen. She won't talk to me at school, but this way I can get close." Thượng tilts his head toward the schoolyard. "Do you see the girl over there?"

"Which one?"

"The one in the white shirt and blue skirt. She's so gentle and refined. Look how nice her clothes are."

She's staring at the schoolyard with an empty look. She doesn't seem that pretty to me.

"Funny," my brother says. "Today, she dropped her notebook, and she was all red-faced trying to pick it up."

What he likes is her short skirt.

"Come to the meeting with me. Maybe you can encourage her to go out with me."

"I'm not joining and becoming one of Uncle Hồ's nephews."

"Don't worry about that. It's not like you become one of them or anything. You go and meet girls. The girl over there with the long hair." He nods his head toward a pretty girl in my grade that I've seen with him before. She's smiling and talking with a friend. "She already likes me. Maybe you can see if she likes you, too."

She's prettier than this new girl. Maybe, besides meeting girls, I can also find out what they do in these Red Scarf groups.

I find Tuyên, the leader of the Red Scarf group for my grade. He's helping the teacher clean up. He always has his red scarf around his neck, not like my brother who takes it off unless he's going to a meeting. Tuyên looks at me in disbelief. "If you really want to join, come to an orientation after school tomorrow."

I tell my friends I'm going to go to a Red Scarf meeting.

"I don't think that you're the type who would join these things," Mến says. His father died in reeducation camp. He already has a red scarf. He's always trying too hard to fit in.

"Why don't you join the group, too?" I say to Nhả. "I heard they do fun things. And there are a lot more girls than boys . . ."

Nhả shakes his head. "I don't believe it."

The next day after school, two other boys from my grade listen with me as Tuyên opens the rule booklet and reads what it means to be good Nieces and Nephews of Uncle Hồ.

On our day off, I grab a notebook and walk to the school with Thượng. A block from the gate, he ties his red scarf around his neck and fluffs it out. "It looks sophisticated, doesn't it?"

"I'd rather be dead than wear that." I wish I had my Special Forces hat back.

When we enter the schoolyard, I walk over to the beginner's group with about ten seventh graders. Thượng goes to the middle group. There's another group for advanced students.

"Lượng, you're here?" Tuyên, the class leader, says. The two boys from orientation didn't come, but my friend Mến is there.

I lean against my knees, squatting above the dirt yard in a circle with the other members. There's no dust on the ground. Someone got here early and swept the dirt.

Tuyên introduces me and has the other kids in the circle say their names. I take out my notebook and write them all down. I try to look over to Thượng's group to see the two girls. They're both in my grade, but they're in the middle group with my brother.

Tuyên goes around the circle asking for confessions of wrong thinking or reports on family members not following the Communist way. Some of the kids like Mến don't say much. "My relatives' talk isn't aligned with Communist goals," one student says.

"Yes, your family's head and brain is of the Americans and their puppets." Tuyên writes something in his notebook. Then he looks at me. "Lượng, do you have anything to contribute to the meeting?"

"I'm new. I don't know enough." This is wrong, giving away family secrets. They're training little spies and enforcers.

"Hopefully you will learn and help us make the cause great by cleansing society."

The groups break up to do their good deeds. Thượng comes up to me while my group sweeps and picks up trash in the auditorium. "Do you see her?"

I look around. "Which one is she?"

"That one over there with her hair to her shoulders . . ."

"Which?"

"In the white shirt and pants."

I don't see what's special about her except her white clothes. Not many people can afford to keep clothes white.

At the end of the meeting, Tuyên hands me a gray handkerchief with a red band sewn on one edge. "This is the first step to becoming a member. You have to earn your red scarf by doing good deeds and writing a report that's signed by your leader and approved by their leader."

I nod. I won't get that far. I fold the gray scarf and stick it into my shirt pocket. "Can I switch to the group my brother is in?"

"That group is for more advanced students, what would your reason be?"

"I have a lot of questions. I think they require advanced answers . . . How long have you been doing this?"

"Two years."

"Well, I'm going to be on the fast path. Can you tell me about the levels and how to get extra credit? Why are there so many layers if we're all supposed to be equal—"

"It would be better if you went to the other group."

When we get up to clean the school, Mến comes up to me. "You're going to get yourself in trouble," he says.

~

I walk with Thượng to the next meeting. He takes his scarf out and ties it around his neck when we get close to the school gate. "Try to be friendly and say something nice about me if you can." He looks over at me. "You should put your scarf on."

"I'll wear it when I get to the meeting." I take the gray handkerchief out of my notebook and stick it in the waistband of my shorts.

"You should do it now. You're supposed to be wearing it all of the time."

"I'm not a member yet."

I squat in the circle next to Thượng. The leader of his group looks at the scarf shoved halfway into my shorts. "That's very disrespectful."

"Where do I put it? I don't have a pocket?"

"Fold it neatly when you're not wearing it, don't wrinkle it."

"That's why I put it here." I touch the scarf draping over my shorts.

"You have to wear your scarf if you want to be here."

"Right." I pull it from my waistband and tie it around my neck. If it were red, I wouldn't wear it. But if they make me wear this scarf, it means I'm supposed to be learning what they stand for—I'm going to ask them questions.

I squat next to my brother in the circle, boys on one side, girls on the other. The group leader starts off the confessions with a story about a long-running disagreement between his family and the neighbors. He makes it sounds like his family is trying to put up with the bad actions of the neighbors, but can't anymore. I see what he's doing, using the same story every time for his confession.

The leader points to the girl Thượng likes. "In the old days," Hoàng Trang says, "my family was wasteful in daily living. We threw away clothes that weren't old."

When it's her turn, the pretty girl says, "My family used to waste food that was still edible."

They shouldn't say anything about their families. Even if it was before the war ended.

The leader calls on my brother. "Well, some thoughts are not productive," Thượng says. "Being greedy is not helpful. Taking from people . . ." He's good at saying a lot of nothing.

Then it's my turn. "My confession is that I have questions," I say.

"This new member was moved from the first group." The group leader nods toward me. "I understand you have questions?"

"Well, you're reporting on us, and someone above you is reporting on you. Where does all this information go? Who reports on the people on the top?"

The team leader asks if the group has any answers for me. Hoàng Trang raises her hand. "If you work hard you can earn your scarf and stripes and get recognized by the upper leadership. Then you can grow."

"That's not what I'm asking. You don't know anything. You're just saying what they told you."

Her face gets red and her eyes angry. Thượng stares at me. I don't care that my brother likes her. She's spouting this stupid propaganda.

I turn to the group leader. "We'll work on an answer for you after we finish our duty," he says.

We leave our notebooks in our place in the circle and walk back toward the three-hole outhouse. Thượng follows Hoàng Trang over to where the shovels are. The pretty girl who likes him gives him a nasty look. She looks scary. I don't like any of these girls. They're all too city for me, not like Phượng, the girl behind our house. Phượng is prettier, too, but what I like about her the most is that she's nice. I grab a broom and try to sweep the hallway instead of cleaning the outhouse.

The group leader comes up to me. "You need to help."

"I have a gagging problem. Tell me something else to do."

"Keep sweeping."

As I sweep, I watch my brother move shovels from one group to another, pretending to work. The group leader won't assign him to work with Hoàng Trang, so he tries to catch her eye whenever he walks over to her team with equipment.

After two hours, everyone comes back to the circle again. I squat in the same place as before. The girl who likes my brother glares at him when he sits next to Hoàng Trang. Hoàng Trang's white clothes are dusty and wrinkled, but my brother's are clean. At least I worked hard sweeping.

"I have another question," I say.

The group leader nods at me.

"Communism promises everyone a full belly, but people are starving." I think of my rice farmer aunt and my relatives in Giao Long.

They're pushing all the people out to the countryside to share the same amount of food. "The collective assigns twenty people to a plot of land that two people can farm. This is our second year and it feels very difficult. How does this work in a perfect setting? What—"

Thượng interrupts. "He's asking how the collective divides up all of the food that they produce."

The group leader stands up and steps into the middle of the circle. He looks straight down at me. I look straight back at him. "I just want to see the whole picture of how this system will work," I say. "I do trust the upper leadership, but I want to know what path we're on."

Right now we're on the path to starvation. And the New Economic Zones are worse. In Tân Long, we see people who've walked for days to get back from them because they don't have money for the bus. They come back to ask their relatives for food. They look so hungry and their skin is sunbaked and stained from the iron in the *phèn* water out there. They put seeds down, but nothing grew.

"We have other issues to address," the group leader says.

"We're all supposed to be equal, but I have no access to any of the information funneling up. If I need to talk to Uncle Hồ, I should be able to." He's dead, but someone needs to take responsibility for the situation we're in. Everyone is following without thinking.

The leader dismisses us. The other kids head home. Thượng stays behind trying to console Hoàng Trang.

I walk over to the leader, "So you don't really know? This is a very simple question." There are people like Mr. Tư Hạnh and then he reports to someone and there are a least five layers above him. Where does all this information go? Who gets the end reports?

"That's not our mission."

"I thought we were supposed to learn. I need to understand if I'm going to join."

"You need to go to the group with an older leader. He can answer your questions."

That evening, my brother comes to the Tân Long house and finds me. "I can't believe you insulted Hoàng Trang like that."

"Like what? All she did was repeat what was kneaded into her skull."

"But you don't go into a meeting and the first thing you do is tell everyone that they're stupid."

"I had questions and the leader didn't answer them. Hoàng Trang tried to jump in. The students who were smarter didn't say anything . . . How close are you to her anyway? If she snapped at me it's like her snapping at you."

"You're the obnoxious one, not me. I thought you could be a help, but you're ruining it. I had to stay and tell Hoàng Trang that's just the way you are. I can't believe it."

"Well, I made you look good. Besides she wasn't as pretty as you said."

"You have no eye for beauty. You need to say something nice to her. If you make trouble like that, they won't let me stay in the group."

"I'm in the advanced group now. I just want to ask the top person my question next time."

"That's not a good idea. They might write it down and follow you."

"I'm not asking anything illegal. I just want to show that they don't know anything. Once I'm done, you won't be able to offer me anything to go back."

～

The next meeting, the leader of the advanced group and the girl who's the vice-leader try to address my questions. They don't do any better. When it's time for good deeds, the leader hands me a booklet about the *Đảng* and how the Politburo works. "Read this while we work."

He walks over to talk to the leader of Thượng's group. I watch them while I glance through the booklet. All the diagrams show power flowing to the top.

The advanced group leader comes back and tells me that I'm back in the middle group. When they're done working, I sit down next to Thượng. "*Anh Bảy*, I'm back in your group . . ."

He looks puzzled.

"I'll say something nice to your girlfriend."

"You better say something so she's not mad at me anymore."

I hand the booklet back to the leader of the Thượng's group. "The *Đảng* is treated as if it's a worship word in this book," I say. "You fear your superior, getting your points taken away, being punished. That's not equal, that's terrifying."

"You're just looking to argue, not to learn anything."

"If you don't know the answer, it's a secret—if it's a secret then we're not equal."

"As a guest on our team you haven't grasped the concepts. You need more basic training."

"All I did was ask questions."

"I think you should study some of this political information first." He tells me to go back to the beginner's group. I wander around for a while and find Tuyên after the other members of his group have gone home.

"I got put back on your team. I have a basic question about the leadership structure for you to answer."

"Yes."

"It took you two years to get one step up the ladder. If there are fifty steps, you won't ever make it to the top. How does anyone get there?"

"You work hard in these meetings and the leadership will recognize you."

"No. You have to be the son or the daughter of those people up there and start on step forty-nine. Otherwise you'll never get to the top. That's not equal."

"Maybe you're not ready to be the nephew of Uncle Hồ," he says.

"I'm not, but you are."

I leave to look for Thượng's girl. She's getting ready to leave. "Hoàng Trang?"

She looks like she doesn't know whether she should come over or not.

"I won't be back." I don't think she even remembers my name. "Look. I had a lot of questions and none of the leaders answered them. I think I insulted your team leader more than you."

"So you won't return to the meetings?"

"None of the leaders can answer my questions." I give her a full smile. "My brother told me that you're really beautiful . . ."

She gives me a smile back. She does look pretty when she smiles.

". . . I think so too," I say.

My brother is outside the gate waiting. "So what did you tell her? What did you say? I saw her smiling a little."

"I was nice." As we walk around the corner, I take off my scarf and wipe my sweat with it. Then I shove it into a wad into my shorts pocket. I'll give it back to Tuyên tomorrow.

Chapter Thirty-five (Summer 1977)

The Poor Have More to Lose

We have a few days off, and Trực comes up to visit. I complain that we don't learn anything in school because of all the propaganda. "Education will give me the best chance to have enough to eat," he says.

"That's the only way," I say. His family wants him to quit school and help work their land, but if he does he'll just be a slave for his brother.

We look for something to do. The place for renting ping pong tables is closed now because a local official disapproved of it. We decide that Sài Gòn is pretty close—we can bike there. I've bicycled to visit my aunts in Bến Tre, and I went thirty kilometers to Gồ Công farther down the delta to see what it was like. Seventy-two kilometers shouldn't be that far.

I tell Má that we are going to try to bike as far as we can on National Road 4. We take the best bicycle, the one with the aluminum frame that Ba repaired with a black market Michelin tire in front. I start out pedaling with Trực sitting behind me on the metal rack in back. Then we switch off and Trực pedals. Thanks to the Americans the road is wide and smooth and even has a shoulder. There are hardly any sounds from motors. People use ox carts or huff and puff peddling a three-wheel bicycle with a flat tire full of yams to take to the market. The few motor vehicles that pass us belch and smell bad because the gasoline gets mixed with diesel.

Ahead a mass of birds sweep back and forth across the road, eating rice in one field, then the next. A passing bus drives straight into the flock and scares it off into the field. We ride into a cluster of dead birds. In front of us, a bird flops on broken wings as it tries to rise off the asphalt.

Trực puts on the brake. We set our feet on the pavement. "Look at all these birds," Trực says. Rice farmers catch them and bring them to the market in cages. They'll butcher and fry the one you point to.

"We could have them for lunch." I bend over to pick up a small gray bird by the tip of its wings. They taste crunchy fried. We could have as many as we want here without paying.

Ahead of us are more injured and dead birds. I pick up another, and Trực starts pedaling. "How are we going to cook it?" I ask. "We don't even have a knife or a match."

"I don't know," Trực says.

I throw the birds on the side of the road.

I'm thirsty, and I'm sure Trực must be too. I look for a stream. The rice paddies are filled with stagnant, dirty water and the farmers' huts are too far back into the tree line to stop by and ask for a drink.

"Let's go home," Trực says.

"No. We're going to make it," I say. "We're almost halfway there."

I pedal faster. My knees start to hurt. They've never ached like this before. We wobble around on the shoulder as I try to keep going. I make it to Bến Lức, about halfway. We cross a river, but it looks too dirty to drink from. We enter the market and buy a sandwich to share and two pennywort drinks from a street vendor.

"Anh Trực," I say, "You're going to have to pedal back home—I can't keep going, my knees hurt too much."

On the way back to Mỹ Tho, Trực does most of the pedaling. I sit behind watching the tires. If the tire blew out, we'd have to walk for hours before we got home. We'd have to carry the bike, too.

It's dark when we finally get back to the beauty shop in Mỹ Tho. "Look at that bicycle tire!" Má says. "It was new when you left and look how worn and old it is now. It could have blown at any time."

"We're so tired and hungry, Má," I say. "Can we have some money for a rice plate?" Má hands me some money, and we go out to a street vendor serving after dinner snacks.

We stand under a street light eating. I know Trực is thinking that he'd never go again, but when I go again, I won't take just one bike for two people . . . and I'll find a way to bring some water.

❧

When school gets out, Má tells me to take over watching our land in Giao Long. I pack my clothes and slingshot in an empty rice bag. Má gives me a bamboo basket full of chicks to raise. I set the basket next to me on the ferry. The chicks are so small. They *chiếp chiếp chiếp* the whole way down to the countryside.

I let the chicks out on the side of the house and throw some unhusked rice on the ground for them. They can't go far surrounded by canals. I'm glad to be back in the countryside. There aren't as many eyes and ears to report what I do.

I take my slingshot and walk around to see what's new. Behind the hut, the tops of the sugarcane plants curve under their weight above me. The last time I was here, they were only small pieces of cane cut up and stuck into the ground. Má tried tangerines, guavas, okra, and corn. Sugarcane seems to be the only crop that will grow. I cut a piece to eat—it's still watery and bland.

Trực comes to stay with me. One of my cousins is usually staying with us—we have enough rice and their families don't. We watch the chickens wander around scratching and pecking the ground. They aren't laying eggs yet, but they're getting bigger.

"It's been a long time since I've had any fat," Trực says.

We're supposed to raise the chickens, not eat them, but I guess it won't matter if we have fourteen instead of fifteen. I point to a cluster of coconuts hanging from a tree in front of the house. "If you get me a coconut, I'll kill one of the chickens." I'll tell Má that one of them got sick.

I inspect the flock. My family will notice if the biggest hen goes missing. I throw some unhusked rice down. When they rush to eat, I grab the second largest hen.

I fold the hen's wings behind it and put my foot on its back. *Bịt.* A coconut drops. *Tũm.* Another splashes in the canal. "We only need one," I say without looking up from the chicken.

Trực comes down and starts husking both coconuts. He wants to take the extra one home—they don't have a coconut tree on their land.

I pluck the chicken's neck clean and slit its throat. Blood runs into a bowl. While we wait for water to boil to loosen the feathers, Trực and I walk around to the side of the house and pick some cumin leaves and thin, scraggly chilies. Soon the smell of chicken stewing in coconut milk rises around us. I take the blood, organs, and feet and start to make rice soup. In another pot, I sauté some of the meat with fish sauce so it will keep until breakfast. We cook extra rice and eat until our belly is full—we don't want anything to spoil. It's not often we get this much food.

A few days later, Vân shows up with a bag of clothes and supplies in one hand and his guitar in a case in the other. "I got sent to this sad place," he says. I'm not surprised. The last time I went home to get supplies, Ba complained that Vân sat on the balcony playing music instead of filling up the water vat.

I help Vân carry the supplies across the coconut log bridge that leads to the front door. I wish the door faced land, but Má wanted the house facing south for luck even if it meant the door opened up into a canal. Vân and I unpack the supplies. The fish sauce goes near the stove. The rice sits on the wood top of the old rabbit cage. I reach up and put the fresh eggs, sugar, and MSG in a basket hanging from the ceiling where the rats can't get them.

Across the stream, Dũng's wife screams at him. "Get out there and do something. Don't just sit around. The kids are hungry." Dũng started to farm the land he scared the Northern officer away from, but whenever I walk by, his kids still cry from hunger. Even his chickens are scrawny and have to roam a long way to find worms.

"His wife sounds scary mean," Vân says.

"He deserves it," I say. The town hall gives him some scraps to keep him from making trouble. Still, I try not to catch his eye when I walk past.

After dinner, Vân sits on a stool in the doorway and plays a love song on his guitar. He probably misses being in the city and having girls come over and admire him. The two teenage girls from Mỹ Tho that the Communists forced to live out here have already crept back, unregistered, to the city. Their family couldn't survive on the small piece of land in the coconut grove.

Besides Vân's guitar playing, there's no other sound except for birds, the rustle of the wind through the trees, and a neighbor's voice every once in a while. The ferryman's nine-year-old son, Thiệu, hears the guitar and comes over. By the time his older brother yells across the stream for him to come home, he's squeaked news about everybody in the neighborhood. We'll have to be careful what we say around him. He'll tell anyone everything he knows.

~

"Lượng, Vân, what do you dream about?" Thiệu asks one day when it's rainy and we're stuck inside our hut. Before my brother came, I only saw Thiệu when I was wandering around our land in back. He'd ask for a piece of sugarcane and sometimes I'd break one off and toss it over the stream to him. Now, as soon as it's two or three o'clock and he's done with his chores, Thiệu's over asking, "Lượng, Vân, what you doing? Can you play? Can you talk?" When we get ready for dinner, he asks, "How are you going to cook that? Can I have some?" We share boiled green bananas or yams with him, but we only give him a bowl of rice if we've filled up on cassava roots.

I glare at him. "Call my brother Anh Sáu." Thiệu always forgets to use proper rank when he talks to us.

"Wouldn't it feel like heaven if we could have some roast pig with crunchy skin." Vân's voice sounds soft and dreamy. He picks up his harmonica and starts to play something. He's just learning, so he's not that good.

"I'd like that," my cousin says. "I'd also like some *bún* or *phở*."

It's been a while since Trực and I ate the chicken. "I'd like some chicken *cháo*," I say. I can hear the chickens making noise in their throats, huddling to keep dry in the guava tree branches and under the eaves of the house in the woodpile. We'll bring them in before we go to sleep. If we leave them out in the rain, they'll get sick.

"I like all of that," Thiệu says. "How about some *bánh* to eat right now?"

No one dreams about shrimp or fish. That's what we usually catch and eat.

"Wouldn't it be great to live in a foreign country," Vân says, "and be able to get all the food you want?"

We haven't heard much news from other countries. My brother brought the shortwave radio with him, but it uses batteries too quickly. Once they're gone, we won't be able to listen at all. I've lost interest, though. We're trapped here and the rest of the world seems to matter less and less. I feel desperate. Everything keeps getting worse.

"Thiệu come home." Thiệu's older sister, Nguyên, stands out in the rain in a clear raincoat with the hood pulled up. "Thiệu are you in there? I know you're in there."

Thiệu listens to Vân playing the guitar and doesn't answer. Nguyên looks into the open door from the other side of the coconut log bridge. "Thiệu come home before Anh Hai comes over and gets us both."

"We're not going to peck or bite you," I say. "Come over and get him." I don't like all the yelling.

Nguyên walks across the bridge and stands at the door.

"Come in until the rain stops," I say. "Thiệu doesn't have a raincoat."

Nguyên steps in and pulls her hood off. She stares at Vân playing the guitar. "It's raining hard," I say. "Stay for a while." Nguyên stands watching my brother as if nothing else exists.

The next day, when I walk through our land with a big knife trimming overhanging branches, Nguyên stands on her side of the stream listening to Vân play. Soon she's crossing the stream, pulling up a wood stool in our hut, taking a look at his music book, asking him if he can play a song she knows. She always brings Thiệu—it wouldn't be proper for a girl to stay alone in a boy's hut—but she stays so late that I have to walk her and Thiệu to the stream with a light. I chop down some water coconut fronds and lay them in the stream to make a bridge so they can get home without going the long way around. I don't want them to get in trouble.

⁓

Thiệu comes over in the afternoon before his sister and squeaks about traveling singers who have stopped in town and will be putting on a show every night. I sit on the frame of the front door, and Vân sits in a chair we've dragged outside.

Vân turns to me. "We're going."

"Go yourself," I say. I used to like shows, but now they're put on by the People's Entertainers or Red Scarf groups. Even if you tune out the propaganda, the musicians aren't professionals like the old traveling performers.

"It's a waste of money," Trực says. "I'd only go if it was free."

Phèn, a cousin my age who's been staying with us for a week, nods.

"I'm not walking into town in the dark by myself," Vân says.

"I don't like shows," I say.

"I went out catching giant river prawns at night with you," Vân says.

He thought he helped? "If you and Trực hadn't dropped all three lanterns in the water, I would have caught a lot more." How could they even think the huge river prawn I caught was a ghost that would disappear?

"It's going to be fun," Vân says. "We can get some food and maybe meet some girls. It's boring out here. Let's go."

"Alright." I really don't want to spend the money, and we'll have to pay for my cousins, since they're staying with us. "But you have to go out catching river prawns with me again."

～

Thiệu comes over to walk to the show with us. We call the chickens, and they run inside and hide under the bed in the front room. They treat the house like their nest, waiting until we let them outside in the morning to poop.

I worry about how to lock up the house. The front door locks from inside and the back door doesn't have a lock. Trực helps me dig a stick into the dirt floor to jam the back door. After everyone leaves the house, I latch the front door from inside with a piece of rope. Then I jump onto the bedpost, step onto a high windowsill, and climb out a gap below the tin roof. I drop to the ground, and we head out. Thiệu's older brother calls from the other side of the stream, and he runs home. Thiệu said he was coming to the show. Maybe he doesn't have any money.

I shoot my slingshot into the trees as we walk along raised strips of land running along the canals, crossing pole bridges along the way. Trực carries our coconut leaf torches and stashes them in trees along the path for the walk home. We talk about whether there will be food for sale at the show and if we'll meet some girls. We each have in mind the perfect girl: our own version of Hằng Nga, the moon fairy with her fair skin.

In the town center, three or four hundred people, some of them dressed up, stand outside a fenced-off area where the show will be. I don't see this many people together out in the countryside anymore. How did they all get money to pay for a show? Aren't they all hungry? It's hard to see in the dusk, but we search for someone we know. None of my other cousins are here—they're all too poor to spend money on a show. We walk over to the food vendors squatting on the ground outside the fenced area. They're selling boiled bananas, yams, and corn—nothing good like *bánh* or *chè*. We add up the price of a ticket for all of us. We only have enough left over to split some pieces of boiled corn on the cob on sticks.

A little more than half the people have money to go inside the fenced-off area for the show. I stand squished next to Trực. A generator powers lights as performers come out on a temporary wood stage. The singers are good, but the songs hit the same two Communist-approved notes: victory and build. A man or woman comes home heroic from fighting the puppets and the Imperialists. Workers sing how pure and good it is to build this great country under the guidance of Uncle Hồ.

The performers wear soldier uniforms and farmer clothing. There are no bright satin costumes anymore. When they're doing a skit, I start humming a pre-1975 Army song. Trực looks around to see if anyone is listening. He always worries when I hum Army songs. "This is boring," I say. "We could have bought food."

Trực ignores me, but on the way home, away from everyone, he says, "If one of us hadn't gone into the show, we could have bought food instead."

I carry the torch waving it side-to-side to get the embers on the dry leaves to glow. When it's close to burning down, we collect one of the torches we hid along the way.

Trực reaches the house first, climbs up the windowsill, and disappears into the gap between the wall and the roof. Something bangs and clatters. "You tricked me!" Trực calls from inside.

We cross over the log bridge and crowd around the front of the house. "Open the door. Open the door. Are you alright?"

"That pot wasn't here! You put it here."

"What are you talking about? Just open the door."

Trực runs out the door at us. "Lượng. Why did you put a pot on the bed post?

Torchlight shines on a pot lying on its side near the bed and spilled water on the dirt floor. "I didn't put it there."

"I got hurt," Trực says.

Pots filled with water run along the bed and the railing. The bag of rice we had on top of the rabbit cage is gone.

"Someone broke in," Vân says.

We crowd around the torch peering out at the dark corners in the room. What if the thief leaps out?

Vân and I look at each other. "We have to check the bedroom." I blow the embers on the torch to light the wick in a can full of diesel and put it next to us on the rabbit cage. Vân lights another can and heads toward the bedroom.

Trực and Phèn stay in the corner with the light. I take the torch and follow Vân to the back of the house. The back door is pushed in. I stick the torch in the clay stove on the floor and grab the knife I hid under some kitchen things. Vân comes out of the bedroom.

"Did you look under the bed?" I ask.

He shakes his head. We go back in together. There are two of us and I have a knife. No one is there. I feel numb. I want to check the trapdoor under the bed to see if our radio and money are there, but I need to wait until my cousins aren't looking.

We start cleaning up the pots of water. "I hurt my leg tripping on one of these pots," Trực says. He has welts on the front of his shin and a cut behind.

After we stack the pots, we put the lights on the table and sit facing each other on the beds in the front room.

"It's quiet." Vân points below the bed Phèn and I are sitting on. "I don't hear the chickens."

I pick up a diesel can lamp and crouch down to look. "I can't believe it. The chickens are gone." I raised them from tiny chicks. My blood boils. I'm not scared anymore.

"Are you sure you put the chickens in?" Vân asks.

"Yes." It's the rainy season, we always bring them in.

I go out the back door with Vân and Trực to check. Phèn stays inside—he's scared of everything. Maybe the chickens are roosting outside in the guava tree. If we just lost the rice, we could buy some more without having to tell Má. I hold the lamp up to the tree. It's empty.

"I'll kill the thief if I catch him." My brother curses in a rough voice.

We head in opposite directions looking for the thief. If I find him, I'll kill him too.

My feet sink into the fresh mud my cousin's husband spread on our land when he cleared the canals. We usually have it done before the rainy season, so it dries faster, but he was too busy with other jobs so we had to wait.

"I found footprints," I whisper to Vân. I stand near the concrete slab we use as a washboard that sits on two concrete beams over the canal in back, shining my light on prints made by large bare feet. They're easy to see in the fresh mud. They lead to and from the back door.

"It's so dark out here," Trực says. He stands around with Vân while I follow the prints toward the ferryman's house, trying not to step too near them and mess them up. How could the thief carry all those chickens? Maybe he's coming back for the rest. I listen for clucking. There's nothing.

Vân stands on the raised dirt foundation of the house. "Where'd he go?" he calls.

"He went to the canal and crossed," I say. "I couldn't find anything."

We wash our feet and come inside. I check the rest of the knives to make sure the thief didn't steal one. My brother goes into the bedroom. "Is anything missing?" I ask when he comes out.

"No, but you should check yourself."

We sit on the wood beds again. Trực inhales over his teeth as he puts peroxide on the cut on his shin. Besides the rice and chickens, the only thing missing is a cloth bag.

"Do you think he'll come back?" Vân asks.

"He won't," Trực says without looking up from the bruise on his leg he's inspecting. "He's eating the chickens."

"We need to set a trap in case he does," Vân says.

I remember people saying that thieves come back when you get new supplies. "We could get some more rice and chickens."

Trực ties an old piece of cloth I gave him around his cuts, but a nasty bruise still shows. "He only came because he knew everyone was at the show," Trực says." It's too dangerous for him to come back."

"How did he know we were going?" Vân says.

"Why did Thiệu leave?" I say. "He agreed to go with us before."

"Thiệu probably told everyone we were going," Vân says. "He talks too much."

"Thiệu saw how I climbed out of the house. He must have told the thief. That's why the thief put the pots of water on the bedposts—to warn him if we came back."

"We'll tell Thiệu we're going to the show again," Vân says. "Then we'll hide outside and wait for the thief."

"That's a bad idea." Trực shakes his head. "A bad idea. Dangerous, too."

We stay up going over our plan, watching black pieces of soot, the fruits of the diesel lamps, grow out of the wicks. Smoke drifts out through the gap between the roof and walls. None of us sleep well. The thief could still be around, waiting to cut our throats. But I'm too mad to be scared.

$$\sim$$

In the morning, I feel exhausted. I miss the rustling and clucking the chickens usually make under the bed. I go outside hoping they'll be there, but the guava tree is still empty in the morning sun. I find the footprints and measure them against mine. It's definitely a man's foot. We'll catch him. I go inside and close the door to the back bedroom. I pull on a fishing line to open a trapdoor hidden under the bed. Everything is there like Vân said. I take some money for the ferry, drop the wood trapdoor back, and recover it in dirt. Vân doesn't want to get yelled at for losing the rice and chickens, so I head home alone for new supplies. We need bait to catch the thief.

When the ferry gets to Tân Long, Ba isn't around. He's always at one of the Communist meetings. I find Má in the kitchen. I'm glad she's here. Usually she's at the beauty shop. If I had to go there I'd miss the ferry and have to take the hot, crowded bus back to Giao Long. "We need more rice and *nước mắm*," I say.

Má looks at me funny. "I thought you had enough."

"Our cousins stopped by and joined us eating... And, can we have more chicks? A little bigger this time?" The last ones took so long before they got big enough to run around themselves.

"Have you been eating them?"

"No." I shake my head. "We went to a show. Someone broke in and stole everything."

"What? You all went? You're supposed to watch things. You don't just leave the house at night with no one there."

"I know—it was a mistake."

Má gives me money for supplies, but not more chicks. I look around the house to see what else I can take. We need more bait. All I can find is an extra blanket. In the market I buy rice, fish sauce, a little 100 gram bag of sugar, a small bag of peppercorns, and ten grams of MSG. When I get back to Giao Long, I carry the supplies from the ferry through the whole neighborhood. I want to make sure that everyone knows we have more rice.

In the afternoon Thiệu comes to listen to Vân play his guitar. I tell him we're going to the show again. Thiệu says he's going with his sister. I take a knife and hide it along the road so I'll have a weapon if the thief comes. That night, my cousins, Vân, and I head out together with the retired teacher's son and some other neighbors. Partway there, the teacher's son excuses himself and heads back on some errand. After he leaves, my cousins and I drop away from the crowd saying that we need to stop at Trực's house. Vân stays with the group to make it look like we're all going to the show. He'll hurry back before it gets dark.

I break away from my cousins to collect the knife I hid. As I come out of the brush, I see the teacher's son. What's he doing here? He doesn't see me. I step to the side of the road until he passes. When I get back to the house, Trực and Phèn are already there. "You wait in the front," I say. "The thief will probably come in the back door like last time so it's safer there."

I hide in the sugarcane so I can see the back door and both sides of the house. It starts getting hard to see. Vân stumbles back. "I was afraid I was going to get lost in the dark," he says.

"You wait on the side of the house near the back door," I say. Vân's the biggest, so he can leap out and fight the thief.

We sit in the moonlight and wait. The sugarcane leaves sway. Every shadow seems like it could be the thief. Or a ghost. But I'm not scared with everyone around. I watch mosquitoes bite my arm. The thief might be nearby so I can't slap them. I put my hand on them and squeeze.

"Are you still there?" Phèn says. Why is he scared? Trực is in front with him. "Sáu Vân, are you still there?"

"I'm right here," Vân says. The silence must be working on Phèn's mind.

"Don't talk so much," Trực whispers.

I quietly scratch the bites on my arms and legs. Maybe the thief hasn't come yet. Maybe he didn't hear all the noise.

"Lượng," Phèn calls. "Are you there?"

Please calm down and be quiet.

"Are you there?" Phèn yells louder.

He's going to give us away.

"I'm right here," Trực says.

"I thought you tricked me and left," Phèn says.

"The mosquitoes are killing me," Trực says. "I don't think the thief is coming back with all the noise."

It's hopeless. "Let's just go to bed," I say.

We clean our feet on the washboard and go inside.

∼

The next day, I try to convince Vân to wait outside for the thief again. He shakes his head. "The performers have left, besides, what are we going to do with Trực and Phèn while we're out there?" Phèn's too scared, and Trực won't go out again with all the mosquitoes.

Thiệu comes over, and we tell him about the theft. We decided he isn't working with the thief. He just talks too much. Later, Nguyên calls across the stream as my brother plays the guitar. "Thiệu said a thief came. What did he take? You still have the guitar."

"He stole the chickens," I say.

Nguyên looks shocked. "All of them?" Stealing something alive seems worse than taking rice. Everyone in the countryside has chickens running around, and no one steals them.

In the evening, Nguyên comes over with Thiệu to listen to Vân playing. We hear their older brother call. Vân stops playing. "Nguyên, go home or you'll get in trouble."

Nguyên ignores her brother's calls and asks Vân about his music. Her older brother comes in and drags her and Thiệu home. They scream and cry across the stream. I can't stand listening. The next day, they're too scared to come over to our land. Nguyên is covered up, but I see bruises from a bamboo cane all over Thiệu's bare arms and legs.

A few days later, Thượng comes down and tells Vân he needs to go back to Tân Long. Nguyên and Thiệu's father, the ferryman, complained to my parents that his son and daughter were always coming over to our house. I wish he had come to talk to us instead. Nguyên didn't deserve a beating. Vân feels bad for her, but he's happy to go home. He says the countryside is too dark, too full of gnats and mosquitoes, and too lonely.

My cousins leave too. I don't mind. With them around I can't catch the thief. After two nights alone, I see Thiệu across the stream. His bruises have healed, but he's still too scared to cross over to our land. I tell him I'm going to visit Trực and stay over for a while. He'll squeak the news to everyone. Before I leave I make a hiding spot in the sugarcane. I line it with the brown leaves Má had us pull off the lower parts of the canes. I hide a knife underneath.

I bring rice to Trực's house and cook there. Every time I visit I remember how their house was before. They've reoriented it four or five times since their mother went missing to avoid more bad fortune.

This time it must have worked because I haven't felt any ghosts and neither have they. Still, whenever I stay overnight, the altar for my missing aunt is right there next to the bed. I wonder if her spirit is active because of how she died.

At twilight, I tell Trực I forgot something and need to go home for the night. I sneak back to my hiding spot and wait with my knife stuck into the dirt next to me. The sugarcane rises two meters above, hiding me in more darkness than the night. A constant misty rain keeps the ground damp. Even though I put leaves down, I end up squatting. The sugarcane moves with everything—bugs, mice, with the slightest breeze the whole field of green sways. My heart thumps. I keep turning around, worrying someone is sneaking up on me. I have our best knife with me, the one Má had the blacksmith make out of an old artillery shell riveted to a guava wood handle. The thief won't have a knife because he needs to carry things. I've used this knife to chop down a mango tree. If he fights back, I'll charge him and chop him up.

After a couple of hours the mosquitoes stop biting so much. By midnight I'm wet, hungry, and itchy from bug bites. I sneak to the back of my land, then pretend I'm coming home from my cousin's house.

The next day, I get some branches to sit on and some fruit and hide in the sugarcane before the sun sets. The mosquitoes bite as soon as dusk falls. Then, it starts to rain. I'm hungry and wet. I go back inside. I need to figure out a way to be more comfortable.

In the morning, I use a strip of coconut leaf to tie two guava branches into an X. I make another X and then put a branch across them to make a stool. It's about to rain, so I leave the stool in my hiding spot covered with a piece of plastic. After dinner, I put a bowl of rice and fish sauce and a bunch of green bananas under the plastic for later. I don't think the thief will come until everyone is asleep, and the mosquitoes are worse in the early evening, so I stay inside listening to the radio and reading, like I normally do. When I think everyone else is asleep, I blow out all the lights and sneak out the back door using a string to pull it shut.

I sit on my stool and eat all the rice and bananas. I go over everything that could happen if I meet the thief. The sugarcane is black at night, but outside of the field I see silhouettes and shadows in the moonlight. I start to get comfortable and sleepy. I'll go inside after another hour. I'll try one more night after this. If he doesn't come, I'll be done.

A shadow near the back door moves. My heart pounds. It becomes a man. I run toward him. The thief hesitates on the sticky mud. I slow down to line my steps up on one of the concrete beams holding the washboard over the canal. When I get to the other side, my feet sink into the mud. I pull my feet out, and chase after the thief. He's too far ahead. I won't catch up. I aim at his neck and throw my knife. As soon as the knife leaves my hands, I hope it will miss. It hits a branch and falls on the ground behind him. He runs off.

I find the knife, wash my feet, and go back inside. Lying in the bedroom under the mosquito net I finally understand the story Má told us about the Chinese doctor. When we lived near him in Quới Sơn, he had a small window he left open to pass medicine to patients who came in the night. One night he heard something. When he came out of the bedroom, he saw a hand reaching into his house through the window, trying to grab something. The doctor picked up a knife and brought it down on the hand. "You missed," the thief called as he ran off. In the morning, the doctor saw blood near the window. He followed a trail of blood to a house and found a man inside with his hand dangling from his arm. The doctor took him to the hospital, but they had to amputate the thief's hand. I always thought the doctor did the right thing defending his house. I didn't understand why he gave the man money and felt responsible, why he and Má say that you can take so much more away from someone than they took from you.

I feel a terrible sense that things could have turned out worse. I was aiming for his neck. I could have killed him. I go out and pee in the canal. Did I check the knife for blood? No. It missed. It hit a guava branch. Usually when I can't sleep, I sit on the door ledge and look into the darkness with a light behind me and a knife beside me. Sometimes I even build a little fire. But I don't want to be seen tonight. I sleep away from the gaps in the wood wall where a blade could reach in. I have all of our knives in the bedroom with me so the thief can't come back and use one against me. I don't want to catch the thief anymore—chickens aren't worth a life. But if he attacks me, I'll fight. I can reach a knife from any direction.

∾

A few days afterward, Trực tells me his older sister wants to talk to me. I walk over to Chị Ba Chẳng's house. Her floor feels damp on my bare feet from the leaks in her water coconut leaf roof. I don't know how she survives. Her family only eats a little rice and water spinach or yam leaves fried in fish sauce. Before the Communists took over she didn't have enough. Now she has half of that.

"Lượng." Chị Ba Chẳng sees me come in.

She has a big frame, but she's bony. How much less can she eat and still live? Everyone is getting poorer. Soon no one will have money to go to our beauty shop. Our land doesn't grow much. How long will it be until my family doesn't have enough to eat?

"A neighbor told me she saw Anh Tư Quân selling some chickens in the market." She pauses to look at me. "He doesn't own any chickens."

"He did? Are you sure?" Anh Tư Quân lives in a hut one house over. They were displaced after April 30th. His family doesn't own any land, so they built a hut in the canopy of a coconut grove with the owner's permission.

"That's what I heard. Anh Tư Quân tried to sell chickens. When people in the market asked him how he had chickens to sell, he left right away."

"I'll check it out." What will he do when he sees me? Will he deny it? I'll just warn him. I tried to take his life. I don't want to take anything else away from him.

The land around Anh Tư Quân's hut is filled with coconut tree roots—nothing can grow there. He probably came here instead of going to a New Economic Zone.

I stick my head into the open door of their coconut leaf hut. A mother sits on a low two-legged stool, stirring a pot of watery rice and sweet potatoes over a small clay stove on the ground. A boy about ten stands nearby. Two scrawny children lie on the dirt floor in tattered clothes staring at the pot. The youngest seems about three and is small and dirty, like the baby that lay dying in Tân Long. They don't have any rice left. Anh Tư Quân must be too scared to try to sell another chicken. That's why he came back.

The mother looks up and goes pale. Her hand clenches the wooden spoon she's stirring with. She stops feeding the fire.

A coarse sack cut open to use as a blanket hangs from the wall. An extra pan leans against another wall. There's no bed unless they have one in the back room. They don't have a table, just a few pieces of wood with two short legs for sitting and eating on the floor. There's nothing else: no tools or hats and clothes, no framed pictures or a clock. I stay in the doorway. "I just stopped by for a visit."

The mother and the older boy stare motionless at me. They're not used to stealing like the family that lives behind us in Tân Long.

The smell of cooked chicken comes from behind the closed door of the back room. "That salty chicken smells good." I nod toward the back. "Things are pretty hard now. It's hard to get enough to eat."

A couple of chickens make breathing noises behind the door. They must have eaten most of them. A person moves around. "Ồ, hopefully I didn't wake up your husband from a nap? I'd like to meet him and talk."

Anh Tư Quân comes out. He must have heard me. He stands next to where his wife squats on the floor by the stove. He's wearing a dirty white short-sleeve button shirt and shorts. He looks down at his wife. She looks back up at him.

"Take them away," the mother says to the older son.

The older boy is pale and his ribs and collarbone poke out along with his jaw and cheekbones. He still manages to grab his siblings' arms and drag them out.

"I'm hungry. Where are we going?" the younger kids cry. The older boy picks up a stick and hits them while he pulls them out. It's hard to watch.

I turn sideways in the doorway to let them by. "Don't hit the younger ones too much," I say. They're starving, but I don't think they get beaten. They don't have any bruises.

"We'll get you when we're ready," the mother calls after them. Her voice trembles.

I only take one step inside—I don't want to be trapped. "I'm Lượng."

Behind me, the younger kids stand out at the edge of the canal crying. "Go farther away," their mother calls. She forces her hand to pick up a piece of wood and feed the fire.

I tell them my family's been here for generations and list all my cousins in the area including Chị Ba Chẳng, who lives one house over. "How did you end up down here? What were you doing before?"

Anh Tư Quân says he does labor, but doesn't tell me where they're from. "No one hires me." He looks down. "It's horrible. The family is hungry...What can I do?"

"You have to get a reputation for doing good work. If people know you do good work, they'll pay." The kids outside have stopped complaining about being hungry. "My cousin's husband has a damaged foot, but people still hire him." He's busy because people know he'll get work done.

"It's so hard."

"If you're not here it will be a lot harder."

He looks at me.

"I saw you," I say.

"I didn't know where you came from. You just appeared."

"I had to run across the washboard. That's why you had time to get away."

"I saw a big knife and tried to run as fast as I could. I was so scared—"

"You might not be here." I'm glad he ran so fast. What will people do to them if he keeps stealing? What will happen to those kids without a father?

The wife looks up at me. "Please, we're so desperate and hungry."

I can't take the chickens back. I'd have to carry them and then everyone would know he was the thief. What would happen to his kids then?

"From now on, you'll do honest work?" I smile. "I live nearby, if you have anything you want to talk about." If someone is looking for a worker I can tell him.

"Thank you, thank you," Anh Tư Quân says. "I swear—"

"The people you care about are your family and children." I start to walk out. "Enjoy the chickens, don't sell them."

He stares at me.

His wife stands up. "Thank you."

The man steps out the door and starts thanking me again. I feel uncomfortable. I wave and yell for the kids to come back. I thought it wouldn't matter to the poor if the Communists took over, that they had nothing for them to take. I didn't know the poor had more to lose.

～

When I see Chị Ba Chẳng she asks, "Did you catch the thief? I told you who tried to sell chickens."

"We have an agreement," I say.

The next time I stop over she asks, "Why didn't you do anything?"

Every time I see her, she asks. She wants the thief arrested so she doesn't have to worry about watching her chickens.

Finally, I say, "I took care of it. We're not going to talk about it anymore." Má will understand. She's the one who tells the story about the Chinese doctor.

When it's time to go back home for school, I stop by Anh Tư Quân's house and drop off the two liters of rice I have left. I give the kids a handful of the cookies I had as a treat. Before they can make me uncomfortable, I leave.

When I get back to Tân Long I find Má in the kitchen. She looks at my empty hands. "Where are all of the supplies?"

"Trực helped me eat them."

"Chẳng told me about Tư Quân trying to sell chickens he didn't own."

"I went and talked to him. I told him to work instead of stealing."

"Did you do anything else?"

I shake my head. "No. They were hungry."

Planning Revenge

There's a new principal at my school. She's from the North. She holds an introduction in the courtyard and talks authoritatively, but in a suspiciously sweet voice. A few days later she holds another assembly.

"Now that the liberation has come from all of your hard work, you can contribute because you are no longer under the suppression of the Imperialists or the puppets . . ." This time her voice is loud and sharp. It's like snake venom going through your skin.

She keeps us out in the burning sun and doesn't let us get our lunch. "Take a moment of silence to remember all the people that sacrificed themselves for you to be here and to think on what you can do to be good to Uncle Hồ."

She has us salute. She goes on through lunch and the class after. I used to dislike saying the pledge of allegiance under the South, but now I wish I could do that again. At least that was about loyalty to our country, not obedience to the godlike leaders of the *Đảng*.

$\sim$

The next time the principal talks to us, it's rainy, so we go to a big, warehouse building on the school grounds. There's no room to sit down, so we crowd together standing. I'm hungry, but I'm used to being hungry. What I hate is being too hot, pressed against the sweating bodies of my classmates. At least in political science class I can sit in my chair and draw funny pictures while they talk.

The noise of everyone breathing makes it hard to hear, but the principal uses a microphone. "Communism is the most perfect system of government in the world." Her voice blares down from speakers in the rafters. "I will instruct you on how to be a good student for Uncle Hồ and tell you what you need to do to ensure the greatness of our society. I will make sure that you are worthy. Students who don't do these good things will be disciplined . . ."

I take a yam out of my pocket to eat. I know we won't have time for lunch.

A few days later the principal calls another gathering. We all run to pee before we go into the warehouse—her lectures cling and stretch like leeches.

The principal stands at the podium with a scowl on her face. "Be a good obedient follower . . ."

I'm stewing in the heat. My head hurts and my ears itch. It's like being eaten alive by ants. I feel a pressure in my soul. I want to kill her so she'll stop talking. I look down at my foot and notice the blue-gray cable. It must be from the microphone to the amplifier. I can't believe the wire is by me. Why did they run it down the middle so that everyone is standing on it? I stoop down and pretend to scratch. I bend the wire and use my fingernails to scrape off the plastic.

The boys in the group of friends I'm standing with look down. "What are you doing, Lượng?"

I stand up. "Stand closer to me." My heart pounds against my ribcage. I bend down and flip the plastic covering off the wire. "I'll silence her."

"What? What?"

"Watch, so no one sees."

I cross the wires and put my foot over it while I stand up. I put my toe down on the wire. Nothing happens.

"The virtues of Communism are—"

I put all my weight on the wire. The microphone starts to make a funny noise like it's being choked, then it goes silent. "I can't hear," students in the back whisper. The principal raises her voice as loud as she can.

I lift up my toe. Her voice is deafening. She lowers it. "Oh, it's working again."

"You did that?" my friends say.

"The wire at our feet, that's the microphone wire."

"Hồ Chí Minh is the shining path of your life. Everything in your life must emulate him."

"Watch. When I say, '*Im*,' she'll be silent."

"Communism is the best invention of humanity—"

"*Im*." I press my toe down. After a minute I turn it back on. I make it random. When my sister and father fix electronics, sporadic problems drive them the craziest. My toe slips off. My heart races as I bend down and cross the wires again. No one looks at me. No one knows besides my friends.

"Are you still doing that?" they ask when the microphone goes off again.

I lift my toe to let the microphone go on again. I only hear her voice. She's turned off the microphone and is saying we're dismissed. Students stream out. I bend over to straighten out the wire and pull the coating back over it.

❧

Young and Hằng come home singing Red Scarf songs. "We're going to join," Young tells everyone. Hằng follows her as she sings through the house.

"This is the way that they get you," I tell my sisters. "Then they'll have you reporting on all your friends and family."

"We don't do any reporting," Young says. "We just go and learn songs and dances."

A few days later, they walk back home with their friends. I'm in the house when they wave goodbye and come into the front room. My sisters have red scarves around their necks.

"You're wearing a symbol I disapprove of," I say. "It represents that you're going to become an informer, telling your team leader what's going on in the family. That won't happen."

Young says, "They make you feel like you're part of the team, that you're participating."

I come down on her head with my knuckle.

"*Ui!* That hurts."

I look at them. "Our family will not allow this. You think they'll give you some sort of credit, but they're getting you to trust the Communist system over your family or neighborhood. If I see you wear this traitorous symbol, it means you're going to betray our secrets . . . I'll kill you. Look at Ba. He participates, but he's not going to tell what's going on in the family."

Young looks at me defiantly. "We'd never."

I look them in the eye. They're too young to know better. "While I'm living you're not going to do this. I'll protect the family. Go back and turn the scarves in."

The next day, I don't see the scarves. A few weeks later, Young comes home and tells us that she announced to everyone in fifth grade that she wants to learn English so she can go to America someday. "Good," I say, "but how will that ever happen?"

~

When I enter the warehouse at school for the next meeting, I don't see the wire on the floor. I find it running along the bottom wall. I tell my friends, "Let's go over by the wall so we can hear better."

Mến glances at the wire on the wall and stands away from us. The other four come with me. Behind us, I see gray tape on the wire where I broke it last time. Phục looks at me, and I nod. He's a little taller than me so he can cover me up.

The principal asks us if we can sit down on our feet so she can see everyone. She stands on a platform next to a podium. I'm happy to bend down—I'll be able to use my hand to control the wire. I take a rock I brought out of my pocket and slice the wire in two places. An offset splice—Ba does this all the time. I fold the wire and touch the two exposed pieces together.

This time when the microphone goes off, the principal tries not to yell. I can only hear part of what she's saying. The students behind me probably can't hear at all. "The microphone was working before. And it's not working now," she says.

I let go of the wire and the sound comes on.

"This is suspicious." The principal's words come through the speakers.

My friends nudge me. They want me to stop, but electronics malfunction regardless of threats. I let the microphone go silent again.

A teacher starts walking along the wire. As soon as they go a few steps, I let go of the wire and it straightens out.

"Keep checking while I talk," the principal says. Everyone's eyes follow the teacher checking the wire instead of looking at the principal. As soon as the teacher gets to the end of the room, I short the wire again.

I glance at my friends. If you cut their faces, they wouldn't bleed, especially Mến.

The principal starts talking in high-pitched shrieks. "There's something going on." She calls for the next gathering to be out in the courtyard.

"The principal will start to interrogate people now," I tell my friends as we walk to class. "We're all in it together, so no one say a thing or we'll all go down together."

"We're in trouble," Mến says.

A lot of my friends probably realize now that I really was the one who brought in the itchy cat's eye leaves last year.

The next day, I bring a small screwdriver and piece of wire and a wire stripper to school in my shorts pocket. When I had to take a turn staying overnight and watching the school, I saw where the wires ran. There's a junction where they're partly exposed in the back corner of the building the administrative office is in.

After school, I tell Phục to come with me. We pretend we're going to pee over in the corner of the building. Phục stands lookout, while I walk over to the pile of leaves near the wall around the corner. There's a vocational school on the other side of a wire fence, but no one is outside. I stand in the leaves and dig into the flaking cement with the screwdriver, behind where the wire comes out. I keep looking behind at the wire fence between us and the vocational school, worried someone over there might see me. If someone from our school comes around the corner, I'm ready to throw the evidence over the fence.

I reach the wire in the termite-eaten wood, scrape the covering off the cable, and take out a thin piece of wire I brought from home. I hook the wire so it rests loosely on top of the exposed cable—when the electrical current is strong enough, it will cross the wires.

～

It's sunny the next time the principal has us gather in the courtyard. We stand in puddles from the morning rain in front of the steps leading to the administrative building. The Red Scarf groups stand at attention in front, while the principal paces back and forth along the steps. Mến has his red scarf on, but he can't be in front—his family's not upstanding. Once everyone is silent, the principal goes to the microphone. "There's a saboteur in our school," she says in a low voice. "We'll investigate to find out who is responsible and punish—"

The speaker goes off. It worked better than I thought. She's so angry, she trembles. She sends the ninth grade Red Scarf group to look for students who've strayed away, since there aren't any wires in the courtyard. She tells the teachers to take roll call.

My friends look at me. "I'm here with you," I say. "There's something wrong with her. Maybe the ancestors or higher spirits are stopping her from blabbering nonsense."

Phục looks at me and smiles.

The teachers and Red Scarf members walk around. There's a big RẸC, and the principal's voice comes back.

"We will get the secret police to investigate this sabotage. This is working against the People and the *Đảng*. We have to root out the saboteur!" She paces while a teacher traces the microphone line back into her office in the building. They replace the wire. She talks some more. RẸC. The speaker stops. She drinks water and yells until she can't yell anymore. "I want every class to look into what members could be involved."

"Does anyone know anything about this?" my chemistry teacher asks. Our class stands in a group around her.

"We're all here," I say.

"Yeah, she has a problem over there," Mến says.

"It must be a malfunction," Nhả says.

My friends seem relieved that it looks like I couldn't have done this.

"Well, the principal believes someone knows what they're doing," the teacher says. "The sabotage of the microphone wire was quite sophisticated."

They must have found the cuts in the wire from my offset splice in the warehouse. As long as my friends are quiet, though, there's no way they can get me. The kids at school know about our beauty shop, but none of them live in Tân Long and know my father fixes electronics.

After school, I tell Phục to go behind the building again. I reach into the hole in the wall and take out the piece of wire. I fold it up and toss it in the dirt near the fence.

The next day, the principal calls us out again. The speaker should work, but the principal doesn't seem to want to try.

"How dare someone do this," the principal shouts. "The police are sending investigators down."

The next day during class, voices come over the speaker as someone tests them. My friends glance over at me. I stare forward. So does Phục. Later, we see a man walking around the building looking for evidence. Our chemistry teacher says, "The principal is very preoccupied with this."

One at a time, I ask my friends, everyone except Phục, to come out under the tamarind tree. "I didn't do this last thing, but we have to hang together. Don't chicken out now. They're going to investigate."

"How did I end up in this?" Mến says. "I didn't want to be."

"I was in the courtyard," I say. "I didn't do it. But if you open your mouth . . . if they don't kill me, I'm going to come back and get you."

Dũng leaves school. He's a farmer's son and his family is starving. Everyone knows he hates the Communists because of it. Kids start to say that it was him, but Phục and I defend him. Dũng got blamed for the cat's eye with me even though he didn't do it—I'm not going to let him get in trouble for this.

Then Phục tells me that his father wants to see me after school.

I'm dead. I bicycle to his house after school.

Phục's father has me sit down at the table with him. He speaks softly. "I was in the Army. I spent a year and a half in reeducation camps. I'm blacklisted. I don't want to be redlisted. Our family already has enough trouble. Please let my son go."

"I understand."

"Be careful."

I find Phục and tell him to avoid me. He misses school for a few days after that. The investigators must be going through the list of kids with ex-Army parents. Tuyên must have mentioned who it could be. If Dũng's family goes missing, I could be next. I have to plan what to do. I bicycle to his house to check if they're gone. I can see his family inside, so I leave and go home. The police probably just gave them a hard time—they're always giving ex-Army families a hard time.

The investigation team leaves the school, but the principal says she's determined to solve the crime. Red Scarf members stop students in the hallway to ask which class was sitting over the wire in the warehouse. No one remembers.

The principal calls another meeting in the courtyard. They've pulled a new wire for the speakers. "The saboteur should come forward and admit the crime." She doesn't talk in a sharp voice anymore. She tries to talk nicely. "Sooner or later we will catch the person responsible. We will continue to look into it."

∼

I need to do something more. I can't accept this and live with it. I make plans for loading up the capacitor and blowing the speakers or bringing in a whole bag of cat's eye and walking by the principal's office and letting the itchy leaves fly in.

My grades start to go down because I don't pay attention in school. Phục gives me the answers for homework and tests. All of my other friends avoid me. During one test, Phục nudges me and uncovers his paper. I shake my head. After class I tell him that I appreciate his friendship, but I don't need his help.

Chị Năm (Thơm).

A few days later, Chị Năm says, "Your chemistry teacher came by the shop and told me that you're failing. What's going on? You had A's before."

I didn't think my teacher even noticed me. "The principal is a Northern Communist. I don't want to learn any more propaganda. Why didn't she get bombed to death before? Why did she have to come here?"

Chị Tư finds out my grades are failing and talks to me while she fixes radios at her desk. "You have to try to learn what they teach," she says. "Ignore the propaganda."

"I can't ignore it," I say. "They weave it into everything, then test us on it."

"You have to try to beat them at their own game," Chị Tư says. "Isn't there a lot of repetition so it becomes like a rehearsal?"

"I hate it so much, I can't memorize it. It used to be that way, but in eighth grade it changed. They don't look at how good you are, they try to pick up if you're a non-believer."

"You still have to try. Other kids try. Your brothers are doing fine."

I shake my head. "I'm not going to learn anymore."

I go out to water the jackfruit tree in Chị Tư's flower garden. It's about my height now, but people walking by yank on it with their itchy fingers. The main branch was torn by someone. It looks tattered. It matches this whole place and Communism: it won't ever produce any fruit, it's just waiting to die.

When Má comes to Tân Long she finds out about my failing grades. "Don't do anything foolish. Maybe we'll figure out something for you to do."

Maybe I'll get caught, but I have to do something. I'm not going to sit in the sun and listen to propaganda. I'd rather be the ghost of my country than a king for somebody else.

Half-Legal Boats

Má hasn't been acting normally the last few days. She's been washing clothes and cooking good food for dinner and breakfast. Last night she made the salty pork that Ba likes. And she's been standing and talking politely to Ba instead of asking him to do something as she rushes off somewhere. This morning she seems to be waiting for Ba to be free. I tell my parents I don't have school because it's a labor day, but the school doesn't have any cleaning for us to do. If something is going to happen, I want to be here.

When Ba goes out to a meeting, Má stays home washing clothes instead of leaving for work at the beauty shop. Ba comes home for lunch, then goes to the lean-to. He sits facing the backside of his desk, the only place on it clean enough to write a report. After Má washes the dishes, she comes up to him. "When I went to Sài Gòn," she says, "I heard that Chinese were buying boats in Vũng Tàu and leaving. I went up to check. People are leaving everywhere."

Is that what Má has been doing on her trips? Everyone says Chinese are unwanted because of the conflict in Cambodia. Could we really leave because Ba is Chinese?

Ba takes off his reading glasses. "That doesn't sound believable. I should have heard something."

"You should be able to talk to people and find out," Má says.

In the afternoon, Ba goes to check with some distant Chinese relatives, the owners of a fabric store in Mỹ Tho. I believe Má—I just hope Ba lets us go. "There seems to be a program," he says when he returns, "but no one is sure about the details."

"In Vũng Tàu, people were paying the government eight sticks of gold to leave half-legally," Má says.

Half-legal? What does that mean?

Ba walks back to his desk. "Well, we don't know what could happen to us if we make it known we want to leave."

He has to let us go this time. We can't stay trapped here.

"The police were watching people get on boats," Má says.

"It's too early here." Ba starts working on his report again.

I wait until Má goes back to the kitchen. "Má, staying in school could be trouble. All this propaganda. I'm going to explode." No matter how many speakers I dismantle, nothing is going to change.

"You have to try—"

"I can't stand the Communists any longer. Remember all the boats leaving in 1975? We weren't on them . . ."

Má nods. "We have to take this opportunity."

"What about Chị Hai and Chị Ba?" My older sisters work in Cần Thơ as nurses now.

Chị Ba (Lan) and Chị Hai (Thanh) in their nursing uniforms.

"We'll get your sisters to go this time. We'll get the whole family to go."

~

I start to hide from school whenever I can. During the day, I walk up and down Tân Long stopping around the dry docks to see if anyone is fixing up a boat for an ocean trip. Soon, Mr. Three Belt's shipyard is busy again and so are all of the other dry docks in Tân Long. People all over Mỹ Tho start to talk about leaving half-legally.

"Why half-legal?" I ask Má. The term bothers me.

"Half-legal means it's not an official program," she says. "The government is accommodating the Chinese people's desire to leave."

"If it's not legal, won't the illegal part get us in trouble?"

"We don't know how long this opportunity will be here. The government might round up the Chinese who stay."

We should leave soon. Since the program's not fully legal, the government could change its mind at any time and arrest our family.

At home, I listen to Má trying to convince Ba. She makes his favorite foods and asks neighbors if any of their relatives have a twenty meter or larger fishing boat to sell. She puts an offer on a boat named the *Pearl Orchid*, but people from Sài Gòn come down and bid it up. Prices for ocean-going fishing boats go from 200 sticks of gold to over 1000. No one can believe it when a rotting fishing boat tied up close to the town hall, one with barnacles on it and water worms eating the wood, sells for 300 sticks of gold.

Why is Ba worrying when people all around us are buying up boats? Every hour he doesn't agree presses on me, trapping me here. "What if Ba blocks us from leaving?" I ask Má.

"If your father doesn't change his mind," Má says, "we'll at least send your older brothers—I don't want them sent to fight in Cambodia."

"Doesn't Ba have to sign them up?"

"If you're a descendant you can sign up."

I don't think of myself as Chinese, but if it means I can leave ... If Ba won't sign us up, then I'll find a way to go myself. I walk around the shipyards watching the boat building. These Sài Gòn people don't know much about working on boats. I'll help them and earn my passage. If I stay here, I'm just going to get expelled ... or worse. It would be better for my family if I wasn't around.

Lượng and his siblings in 1978. Back row: Hằng, Lượng, Chị Năm (Thơm), Thượng, Vân, and Young. Front Row: Sang, Chị Ba (Lan), Chị Hai (Thanh), Chị Tư (Huệ).

Ba sits down to dinner. "I went to sign our family up to leave. Now we have to figure out a way for us all to be able to go."

He's going to find a way to make it happen?

"When I went, I learned there's a lot happening I didn't know." He looks at Má. "Help me not to look like a fool. What didn't you tell me?"

Má laughs nervously. "When I came home from Vũng Tàu, I thought people here would be leaving too. I walked all along the river looking for people building boats, for some activity—but there wasn't anything. I couldn't sleep for three days. I didn't know who to ask without getting arrested. When the chief of police came into the shop to get a pedicure, I thought I could ask him."

Ba moves his eyebrows together as he scoops rice into his mouth with chopsticks. Má gives a small laugh. "When Châu worked on his feet, I saw that his calves were swollen. I said, 'Go upstairs afterwards, I have some rub that will help.' After I put it on I said, 'Let me offer you something to eat while the ointment works.' Then I went out to the street and bought a large bowl of *cháo* with a lot of meat.

"When he started to eat, I said, 'I have a question for you. Can you promise me that you won't make a crime out of it?' He looked up from the bowl of *cháo* and asked, 'What is it?' 'First promise you won't put me in jail,' I said.

"He said, 'Alright,' so I said, 'I went to Vũng Tàu and saw that Chinese people can sign up to leave half-legally in boats. My husband is Chinese. Can we sign up?'"

All this time Ba's been afraid of showing we want to leave and Má already asked the chief of police? We have to count on Má if we're going to get anything done.

"He looked hard at me." Má laughs. "I thought I made a mistake. Then he said, 'I don't know. Give me two days.' When he came back, he told me he had gone to Vũng Tàu with the governor to check out the program. He said, 'The answer to your question is yes.'"

Ba sets his bowl down. "The problem is money. The price for a space on a boat went up to ten sticks. If we sold everything, we could get fifty at most."

Ten sticks each? How many people can afford that?

"The only way for the whole family to leave is to get a boat and sell spaces on it," Má says.

"Boat prices have gone up too much," Ba says. "We can't get one now."

If Ba hadn't waited so long, we could have gotten one before everyone else—Má was the first one in Mỹ Tho to find out about the program.

"Ask the Chinese store owners if they want to be partners," Má says. "If we charge ten sticks of gold and pay the government six sticks, we'll make a profit."

"I'll help with the boat, Má," I say. "I'm done with school."

"When we get a boat, we'll need to make it ocean worthy," Má says. "You can watch the workers."

"I'll help with whatever I can." We have to leave this time.

∽

I stop going to school the next day. Má can't find any boats for sale nearby, so she says she's taking a bus upriver to where Six Chicken's family moved. Not Six Chicken's boat. It seemed thin-skinned when we played five-ten on it and tall and unstable when we dove off the top. We'd hold our breath and try to swim underneath it in the muddy water, guiding our hands along the curve of its belly, hoping we'd come up for air before we got stuck. With a belly like that, it will flip over in the waves.

"Do you have a partner yet?" Má asks Ba when she gets back. Six Chicken's family won't sell, but a neighbor of theirs with an identical boat will.

Ba shakes his head. "It's difficult. If someone has money, they can just buy a space on a boat."

"This boat can fit 360 people," Má says. "Tell the Chinese shop owners that they can bring all of their extended family and make money as well."

Ten days later, we're partners with the Chinese man who owns the Vĩnh Sương Hardware store, and a tall, unstable boat, exactly like Six Chicken's, pulls into the dock. How are we going to make that boat go on the ocean? It's a river boat, so it has a number, not a name like an ocean boat. Ba goes to register boat 014 in Mỹ Tho with the half-legal program.

∼

Cậu Năm Lộc steps through the open door panels into the front room. He doesn't run a ferry anymore—fuel is too expensive—he only farms.

Ba smiles. "Come in. Have some tea."

I move from the railing in front of our house to sit on the groove where the door panels slide open.

The ferryman stands near Chị Tư's desk. "Thank you, but I'm just stopping by." He hasn't had tea with Ba since Ba started going to all the Communist meetings. "I heard about a program. Is it true? You're really leaving?"

"Well, my wife started this whole thing. I didn't know anything." Ba's anxious that people might think he was lying to them, planning to leave the whole time he was going to Communist meetings. Integrity will get you more customers, he always says. "But it's a lucky opportunity, this conflict with China. Otherwise there's not much choice."

The ferryman looks at him. "So . . . you're not continuing your participation?"

I want to know the answer, too. Where does Ba stand on these meetings?

"Well, I don't have to bend with the wind anymore," Ba says.

The ferryman stares at him. "It looks like you bent with the wind, but the wind changed."

"Times were very hard. You have to work with the system."

"It's difficult for everyone," the ferryman says. "You didn't need to bend so far."

It wasn't just me that thinks my father abandoned us by going to all these meetings.

"How's working and living going for you?" Ba asks, changing the tune.

"There's no fertilizer," Cậu Năm Lộc says. It's the same complaint everyone has.

~

I wait until the school day is almost over before I go to Mỹ Tho to tell my friends I'm leaving. Outside the gate, the flame trees along the street are about to bloom. It seems hopeful. When the bell rings, I wander around the courtyard, taking in everything for the last time. I walk around to the side of the school, behind the main building. The open sewer that the overflowing three-stall toilets empty into is black—it hasn't rained. The school seems so small and dirty now. Students stream out of classrooms carrying their notebooks while Red Scarf groups walk around busy with some activity. I feel sorry for them staying back here. Life will be hard.

My friends come out of the classroom in a group. Phục walks past me. We nod to each other, but I don't go over. I'll honor his father telling me to stay away.

Nhả and Mến walk out together. Mến has his red scarf on.

"My family is going to leave Việt Nam," I say.

"You can't just leave," Nhả says.

A girl wheels her bicycle past us. Mến glances around. "Be careful what you say," he says. "You'll get yourself in trouble."

"I'm going to tell the teacher," I say. Nhả and Mến follow me back to the two-story building they just came out of. They stay behind with some of my other friends while I walk up to the second level to talk to the chemistry teacher.

The teacher looks up from the stack of papers on her desk. "I haven't seen you for a while." She glances over at Tuyên, the Red Scarf leader, cleaning the blackboard and goes back to sorting her papers.

I wait in the back studying the periodic table on the wall. Tuyên hurries through his cleaning. When he steps out, I walk up to the desk. "I'm leaving."

"Lượng, you don't know what you're saying." She picks up a pile of papers and puts it in a box.

"We already signed up. I'm helping build the boat."

She glances toward the open door. "Don't say things that aren't true. It could be bad for you."

"I'm not coming back to school."

"Don't talk anymore." She starts organizing another stack of papers.

I walk down the open stairs. Tuyên is waiting at the bottom. "I don't know what you're talking about," he says. "This sounds strange."

"My family's building a boat and leaving this country." I step past him and walk over to where my friends wait on the concrete area under a tree. There are only a few students scattered around the courtyard.

"I told the teacher goodbye," I tell my friends. Tuyên stands at the bottom of the stairs watching.

"Where will you go?" Mến asks.

"We'll go to Singapore or Indonesia." Ba wants to go to Singapore first because the people there are mainly Chinese. Everyone says they'll welcome us.

"How big is your boat?" another friend asks. "What will you have on it?"

"It's twenty meters—"

"Lượng." My chemistry teacher walks over to us carrying the box of papers. "How is your family's beauty shop doing?"

She's trying to change the tune, worried about what I'm saying. "It doesn't matter much, we're leaving soon—sometime after we finish the boat."

"Tell her about how people sign up," Nhả says.

The teacher looks over at Tuyên standing by the stairs. "You don't know what you're saying. All this nonsense could be misinterpreted."

"I don't think Lượng is joking," Mến says. "Tell her that your whole family is going."

"If you're Chinese you can sign up with the government and pay money to leave," I say. "It's been going on in Vũng Tàu for months. If you walk down to the river you'll see a lot of activity."

She looks around the courtyard. "If this program is for Chinese people how would your family go?"

"My father is Chinese." No one would think that there was anything Chinese about me. "That's why I have this last name. But I don't speak Chinese—"

"He's actually leaving," one of the boys says.

"They have to pay ten sticks of gold per person for twelve people," another friend says.

The teacher glances over at Tuyên again. "How can anyone get that much money?"

I wave to Tuyên to come over. "I don't know. We're building a boat and people can buy a space on it, but they have to pay the government first."

"I still don't think you know what you're talking about." She watches Tuyên walk away. "I better go now."

My friends and I walk to the gate. I look back and see Tuyên going toward the principal's office. I wave. "Farewell," I shout across the courtyard. "I won't see you again."

Later, I find Phượng, the girl I like, in back of the house. Maybe we could find a way for her to go with us. I glance at her face. She's pretty even with the scar she has on her cheek from falling down as a kid. "Have you ever dreamed of going somewhere?"

"Absolutely not," she says. "But my cousin would."

"The question's not for your cousin." I ask her another time, but she says the same thing.

≈

Ba and our partner spend the week meeting with boat builders, discussing how to make the boat ocean worthy. The most well-known boat architect in Tân Long goes out to the sawmill where we have the boat dry docked. "It's not strong enough," he says. He refuses to work on it.

The second best architect says that he can transform our river boat into an ocean boat by creating a new skeleton on the outside. We'll need to buy a long solid tree and bolt it to the round bottom to make it more V-shaped—this will be the new spine of the boat. Then, we'll add two ribs that come from the spine and wrap around the belly to strengthen the sides. To keep the boat from rolling over in the waves, we'll need to add fins. "Then, we'll have to strengthen the nose," the architect says. The front of ocean boats are pointed, so they cut through the waves. Our river boat's round nose would get hit straight on.

"Why not build a new nose?" Ba says. "If we're going to get people to sign up for spaces, we have to make it look like an ocean boat."

My parents put me in charge of paying the workers and checking on the construction. One night at dinner, my sister says that my chemistry teacher came by the beauty shop to ask if I really am leaving. Why didn't she believe me when I told her? "I told her you were helping the family with the boat," Chị Năm says. At least my teacher cares about what happens to me.

I start to sleep on the boat to make sure that the wood and tools don't disappear. Inside there's a small vase filled with uncooked rice and burnt incense sticks. An orange rests against it. I push another stick of incense into the rice in the vase and light it. I'm not sure what spirits we're offering this to. It must be what you do on a boat. I put my straw mat and pillow on the smooth wood floor in front of the engine in back and wrap myself in a blanket.

In the morning, I go home for breakfast and then come back to watch the construction. One of the workers says, "Someone told me your boat is haunted."

The other workers stop sawing and pounding.

"Who told you?" I ask.

"Well, I heard that the lady owner died in childbirth. Have you seen anything?"

"I'll let you know." I haven't seen any ghosts, but now I will.

At dinner, I ask Má if the story is true.

"Ô, that was long ago," she says. "I've made an offering to the spirit. We'll need to have another offering before the boat launches."

So that's who the orange and the vase with incense are for.

A few days later, a neighbor tells me, "Did you know that a baby got stuck coming out of the mother and they both died on your boat." Everyone knows when someone dies like that the spirits will be active.

"I thought that was a long time ago."

"It happened not long ago. The spirits are probably around."

I didn't want to know. I don't think there really is a ghost, but when

I'm all alone that night, I light the incense and call out, "Spirit, spirit. If you want something, ask. I'm here respectfully, please don't scare me."

~

I walk with Ba past the sawmill and through the Chinese plum trees to the house of a family that owns an engine. The three-cylinder Yamaha engine on Six Chicken's boat isn't enough to get our boat through the ocean. Ba says not to tell the man who owns the engine that we need it to power a boat. He's worried he'll raise the price.

When we get down to the river, Fourth Mechanic greets us from the door of a house on stilts. I haven't seen him around since April 30th. He leads us through the back to a front room with glass windows overlooking the river. Most houses just have wood shutters. His family was well-off before.

A pile of junk covered with a thick-gray cloth takes up the center of the front room. Fourth Mechanic and Ba sit in chairs pushed against the wall. His wife starts boiling water for tea.

"So, we're looking for an engine," Ba says. I stand near a window propped open to let in a breeze and look out across the river to the south part of Mỹ Tho. "How many cylinders is the engine you have?"

"For a boat, right?" Fourth Mechanic says.

"Well ... yes."

Fourth Mechanic takes the tarp off the pile in the center of the room. An engine with a big side air intake is underneath. I walk over from the window. It's rusted.

"So, this is it?" Ba asks.

"Well, someone stole the fuel distributor, but it's a good engine. Everything else is new."

I bend down to take a closer look. None of the parts look worn—it just hasn't been used for a long time.

"I was supposed to take it out of a dump truck and put it into a freighter. After April 30th, I kept it. It's worth ten sticks."

"Is it actually going to run?" Ba says.

"If you want to see it run it will cost a lot more."

Ba gets Vũ's father to come and look at the engine. He says it looks new, but he hasn't seen a truck engine on a boat before. Fourth Mechanic says the price now is twenty-five sticks. Money is more important to him than his word, but I guess he has to get what he can if he's staying here. We put a deposit on the truck engine and hope no one out bids us before we get the rest from selling spaces on our boat.

~

The new, pointed nose of the boat makes it look more like an ocean boat. I climb inside the boat to see how the workers attached it. Nails from the new nose stick into the boat, tearing up the wood. They used regular fishing boat nails, not the shorter ones for thinner wood. How could they do this? We could have gotten the right size nails from our partner's hardware store.

I go back home to find Ba. "You have to come down to the sawmill and see the damage to the boat."

When we get there, I have Ba come inside the boat. I point to the splintered wood and the nails sticking out. "Look. The nails they used tore up the wood. They've made the boat weaker."

"Why don't you help make it stronger?" Ba says. "Bend the nails back nicely."

I pick up a hammer and turn toward the workers. "If you hear banging, it's me. I'm going to bend every single nail over so it doesn't come out."

The oldest son of the owner of the boat next to ours watches me walking around with the hammer checking everywhere. He glares at me as he takes his sandals off. Then he turns and carries his sandals up the ladder to his boat. He thinks I stole his expensive sandals when he left them at the bottom of the ladder. I told him my family owned the boat next to him, and I'd ask around for him. But he didn't believe me. Since I'm always around, he thinks I'm a worker's son. Those Sài Gòn Chinese always take their shoes off before they get in their boat. We take our shoes off in the sleeping area at home and in the boat, but we always bring them inside—if you leave them out they'll grow wings.

Nhiễu walks toward the sawmill, his toes brushing the ground as he pulls his bad foot along. Trắng comes behind him. I told Trắng that if he even takes a loose nail from here, I'll make mush out of his insides. I know he took the sandals. I tried to pay him to give them back, but he wouldn't admit he stole them.

"Come here," I say. "Help hold the boards on the outside while I pound from the inside." Nhiễu and Trắng hang around the sawmill with me all day, but as soon as it starts getting dark they're gone. I didn't tell them the story about the lady who died on our boat, but someone must have.

When I finish bending the nails back, I look over at the boat owned by the Sài Gòn Chinese. The wood on their boat is twice as thick, the kind meant for the sea. It would be nice to have a real ocean boat like that.

~

As soon as the new nose is on the boat, my parents and the partner try to find passengers. We need money to finish fixing the boat and to pay for the engine. Ba only lets potential customers look at the boat from the steps of our house where its new nose rises over the fence of the sawmill across the street. No one is allowed to tour it until it looks more like an ocean boat. One family insists. "The workers are superstitious," Má says. "If someone accidently walks over a beam while they're building it, they think that beam will break." I haven't heard anyone say that before.

Ba goes with our partner to Mỹ Tho to collect deposits from passengers. When he comes home, he sits at the table in the kitchen and pulls out over thirty sticks of gold from his satchel, each the size of a New Year's red envelope and wrapped in paper stamped with Chinese characters. He and Má unwrap each one and hold it up to check the Chinese words stamped on each side of the rectangle. I reach over and pick one up. It feels heavy. My parents stop talking every day about how we're going to eat.

We can finally pay for the truck engine. When Fourth Mechanic comes to collect the money, he says that he has another offer from the owner of a boat anchored next to the rotting boat near the town hall. "If you want it you have to pay fifty sticks," he says.

"Your engine doesn't even work," Ba says. If Fourth Mechanic had a real offer he wouldn't be here. "I'll give twenty-seven sticks instead of twenty-five. Any more than that and I'll buy a truck and take the engine out."

Ba goes to the lean-to, and comes back with the gold. Fourth Mechanic puts the twenty-seven sticks in his front shirt pocket.

Má looks at him. "You broke your promise."

Fourth Mechanic looks down and mutters. "You have the engine, you can go somewhere. I have money now, but I'll just eat it and have nothing."

~

I stand on the long, wood fins bolted onto the sides of the boat to keep it from rolling in the ocean. The panels move. I find the boat architect. "The fins are going to tear off in the ocean," I say.

"I know," he says, "but fixing it will add a lot to the cost."

"But if it tears a hole in the boat we'll drown." Even the workers have been complaining that the fins are flimsy.

"True, but it will cost."

Ba is the one who set the limit on cost. I ask him to come down to the sawmill and show him how the fins move up and down. He tells the architect that he'll pay to reinforce them. After they add more wood and bolts, I can't move the fins.

The last change that needs to be made to the boat is to add-on to the round back to make it look square like a fishing boat. The architect says we can put the bathroom there—a room with a door and two holes in the floor that empty over the water.

It's hard to get wood now that everyone is building boats. When we cut down the big mango tree in our fishpond, the neighbors come out to watch. "You're using mango wood on a boat?" they say. "That wood is too soft. It's not good for anything."

"Well, I'm using it above the water," Ba says. "It's just a platform in back. If it comes off it doesn't matter that much."

While we're adding on to the back of the boat, I see the son of the Sài Gòn Chinese boat owner sitting next to a pile of shoes at the bottom of the boat ladder left by passengers touring his boat. I laugh. "You're stuck watching sandals."

He swears at me. "You have the most ridiculous boat. It won't even survive when you launch. It's going to break apart."

I don't care. I have a chance just like he does.

~

I pedal my bicycle to the school to see my classmates and the chemistry teacher one last time before school gets out. It's hot, so I wait in the shade of a tamarind tree. The flame trees along the street are in full bloom now that it's close to summer. If I ever come back to Việt Nam, the trees will still be here, but this crumbly school will be gone.

I see the girl my brother used to be crazy for leaving as I walk in the gate. He never got Hoàng Trang to like him. Now he's after the best-looking girl in high school.

"I'm leaving Việt Nam," I say.

Hoàng Trang gives me a friendly smile. "I heard. Have a safe journey."

"I just hate Communists. I'm going to America." I don't know where we're going, but I want to poke the government in the eye, saying that it's their enemy. Even my sister Young tells everyone that's where we're going.

"When are you going to leave?"

"September or October."

"Don't forget me."

I look for Phục, but I don't see him around. He probably quit school. I heard him say that the government wanted to ship his family to the New Economic Zone, since his father doesn't work in the city.

Tuyên, the Red Scarf group leader, comes up. "*Ê mầy*, Lượng. I haven't seen you for a long time."

"I'm building a boat and leaving. I'm looking for freedom."

"How is that?"

"We're going to pay the government money and leave. You can stay here and have all these Red Scarf meetings yourself."

Tuyên takes my insult and smiles. "Where are you going?"

"We're going to Singapore or Indonesia, and then we'll go to some other country that's free."

"What country would that be?"

"It doesn't matter as long as it's free." I don't say America this time. I want him to know that anywhere is better than here.

My chemistry teacher walks down the stairs into the courtyard. I head in her direction at an angle so we'll end up meeting away from everyone. "I came to say goodbye," I say when we meet. "I'm leaving the country and going to a foreign one. But a lot of people die, I might not make it."

She nods. By now, everyone's heard stories of half-legal and illegal boats sinking.

"I wouldn't stay in school anyway. I can't stand all the propaganda, I'm glad I have the choice or I'd go mad."

"I understand." She looks at me seriously. "I hope you have a safe journey. Think of us sometime."

My friends see us and come over. "Remember us all."

"Send a letter," my teacher says. "If you have anything extra, send something. You know how hard life is here."

"Stop by the beauty shop," I say. "I'll tell my sister to give you a haircut." When I leave, I just want to forget.

～

Má, Ba, and the neighbors stand around the sawmill watching as workers take the blocks off the boat. With the new nose and square back, the outline of our boat starts to look like a fishing boat. The neighbors say it has a chicken head and duck butt, trying to be something it's not. The boat is supposed to roll down the dry dock stern first into the water. It just sits there. The workers attach a cable to the back of the boat and get another boat to pull it off. *Rầm.* A cable snaps. I look for a hole in the boat. A single board on the mango wood outhouse in back is all that's broken.

The tide will only be high enough to get the boat into the river today and tomorrow. After that, the boat will have to tilt back too far to reach the river and the new nose will rip into the sawmill roof. The next day we try again. The boat won't move. Finally it slides into the river. Ba, Má, our partners and their kids, and a few workers walk on a plank to the boat.

Má asks me to check for leaks. The first thing I do is open the latch that leads to the space between our boat and the new nose. We sealed all the spaces between the boards by using a chisel and pounding rope fiber mixed with tar into the cracks. I even pounded it into the holes made by the nails attaching the new nose. I hope bending the nails over and filling the holes helps keep the water out. I stick my head in. Sunlight streams in, shining in a tight beam on a side wall. It's wet. The water must have leaked through the nail holes. I get a lantern and climb down the ladder to a ledge inside and step into water up to my knees. I find my parents on the deck. "There's a lot of water in there."

My parents send for the boat architect. He's working on another boat near the town hall. "I expected the water to go in there." He shrugs. "It's not really possible to keep it out."

Every new boat takes in water, but how much more can this one take on? I ask Nhiều and Trắng to help me bail the water out with a bucket and string so I can see how fast it refills. The next morning, I open up the hatch to check the water level. Overnight it went up to my waist.

"Bail it out until it stabilizes," Ba says.

I bail again. A day later, the water is up to my chest. The boat mechanic we hired sets up a pump, but the water keeps coming back to a little below the river level outside.

I find Ba. "I don't think the new nose will make it." Any wave could crack the old wood and we'd take on more water or the vibrations of engine could tear the boards.

"With all those nails, three sets, it will hold," Ba says.

Maybe. If we don't hit any big waves.

The workers start to add a cabin on top of the boat for the captain. People thinking of buying passage on the boat show up to tour. While they're on the boat, we keep the hatch to the water-filled nose locked. As the people touring the boat walk around, the mechanic tries to fit the truck engine in. "That doesn't look like a boat engine," someone says.

"It's a dump truck engine," the mechanic says, "very powerful and sturdy."

"We have two engines instead of one." Ba waves toward the original Yamaha. "We'll have a backup and won't get stranded on the ocean."

A few of the people touring nod. "Good idea." Ba sells all of the spaces on the boat.

The workers finish the cabin and put the propeller on. I help them paint the boat the gray color of the Navy's standing face boats. We hire a captain who brings a large map for navigating the ocean and a brass ship compass—two of the reasons we hired him, since they're hard to find. His payment is free passage. Ba, the captain, and our partner sit in our house in front of the map calculating how much fuel we'll need to get to Singapore or Indonesia. Out on the foot ferry dock, workers weld together a 2000-liter main tank and 600-liter spare tank. We can get all the fuel we'll need on the black market: freighters travel with the current so they can save their government allotment and sell it.

A few days after the meeting, a man stops by at dusk and tells Má that they're unloading the diesel we bought. Out on the river, two men in a small boat near the foot ferry dock roll metal drums to the bow and flip them overboard. The drums splash into shallow water near the dock and embed in the knee-deep muddy water. Má tells me to watch the barrels while she finds someone to roll them up to our house. The man who told Má about the diesel gets on the boat, and the men motor back to a waiting freighter. The men in the boat tie up behind it. The anchor raises and the freighter leaves.

Má comes back with my cousin Anh Chín Phát and Seven Dancer's oldest son, Long. Metal scrapes and bangs as my cousin and Long push a barrel full of diesel up the slope from the river to the concrete road. Neighbors step out to watch. Along the road, the flickering of lantern light starts to come from the open doors of houses. When my cousin and Long get to the alley next to our house, Má covers the barrel up with a tarp. She had a trench dug in the side yard so that we could hide the barrels there, but we'll move them down later. After the first three barrels are up, Má goes back inside to get another tarp. Even with the tarp, it's obvious what they are, but everyone has to buy fuel on the black market.

My cousin and Long go down to get the next barrel. Three police run down the street toward us, holding AK-47s out in front of them with both hands. I stand back. The police rush by me on their way down to the river edge.

My cousin and Long look up from the barrel they're rolling. The police wave their guns. "You are under arrest for illegal activity. Move that barrel up here. Then step over there."

Mr. Tư Hạnh comes down behind the police. Rở, the son of the tailor who killed himself, follows. He's always looking around. I'll bet he went and woke Mr. Tư Hạnh to tell him about this.

Ba runs out the open door to our house. "I'm the one who bought the diesel. They work for me."

"We're going to arrest you for this, Chú Tám," one of the policemen says.

Má rushes out to stand by Ba. "We need this fuel. Our boat doesn't run on water. You're blocking us from leaving."

My cousin and Long look over at my parents, gasping for breath as they push the barrel up the slope.

"I'll help. I know this area." Mr. Tư Hạnh takes out his notebook and starts writing in it. "I have responsibility here."

Ba usually smiles to hide his feelings, but he scowls at Mr. Tư Hạnh. "Whatever you're doing here, you're going to get yourself in trouble."

Anh Chín Phát and Long push the barrel onto the street and over to the side of the house. "We'll take the workers to jail and come back for you later," the police tell Ba. "We have to look into whether we can arrest the person who hires workers to do an illegal activity."

Mr. Tư Hạnh asks the neighbors who've come out of their houses to watch to roll the rest of the barrels up to the side of our house. One of the police stands guard over the barrels while Mr. Tư Hạnh and the other two policemen lead my cousin and Long away.

"We'll get you out," Má shouts after them. "Let us do the worrying."

"We have to get Ông Three Của," Ba says to Má.

My parents go to Mỹ Tho to find the director of the half-legal boat program. After a while, Mr. Tư Hạnh comes down with a government seal and tapes it on the barrels. The guard leaves. I keep expecting my cousin to come home with my parents, but it gets late so I go to bed.

The next morning, my parents are home, but not my cousin. Ba leaves to search for Three Của again. I'm glad Ba is standing up to the town hall. A while later, Mr. Tư Hạnh comes down to check that the drums are still there—that no one is siphoning off his evidence.

In the late morning, Anh Chín Phát and Long walk in the door. Má offers to buy them something to eat from the street vendors, but they just take their payment for the job and go home. My cousin comes back after eating and sits on the bed under the stairs.

Má sits at the kitchen table facing him. "What happened?"

"I was scared. They could do anything. I was so hungry... The mosquitoes bit me like crazy all night. Then in the morning, Chú Tám and a Brown Cow came with a letter saying that anybody interfering with the half-legal boat program would be punished. The police didn't want to let us go, but the Brown Cow shouted, 'Release them or I'll put *you* in jail.'"

A Brown Cow really came with Ba to help us?

～

The next day, the mayor and Mr. Tư Hạnh come down to our house. I sit in Chị Tư's desk on the other side of the room and pretend to work on something.

"Come in, have some tea." Ba motions the mayor to sit in a chair on one side of the door to the lean-to. The mayor takes a seat and Ba sits on the other side. There's no other chair, so Mr. Tư Hạnh stands next to the front door. We don't have a table in our front room anymore because there's a big crack in the concrete floor from the fill underneath settling.

"Thank you, I just had tea," the mayor says. "Did you know that yesterday I had to personally deliver a report to the governor's office for interfering in a national matter?" The mayor turns to Mr. Tư Hạnh. "Because of you, Tra." He uses Mr. Tư Hạnh's first name instead of family rank, the way Communists do. It seems disrespectful, but maybe nicknames like "Soybean" and "Dancer" aren't that respectful either.

Mr. Tư Hạnh's shoulders fall, but he keeps his eyes on the mayor.

"The governor let me sit there all day waiting," the mayor says. "I thought I wasn't going to come back."

Ba smiles. "Well, we needed to buy fuel to leave. There was nowhere else to get it."

The mayor looks at Mr. Tư Hạnh. "Leave now. Wait for me in the town hall."

~

Mr. Tư Hạnh comes back to our house a couple of days later. He stands a step inside the doorway. He doesn't have his big notebook with him, just a small one in his front shirt pocket along with a pen. Ba doesn't invite him in for tea.

"The mayor . . . was very upset," Mr. Tư Hạnh talks softly, the end of his words trailing off. "I spent the whole day in town hall . . ." He stops to wait for Ba to say something, but he doesn't. "I was hungry and thirsty waiting . . ."

The mayor should have made him sit in jail overnight and get mosquito bites like my cousin. Maybe it would clear his mind so he'd quit informing on us and help the neighborhood instead.

"The mayor must be busy," Ba says. "Perhaps he forgot about you?"

"No . . . the mayor was just . . . angry . . . All these people leaving are beyond his authority."

We're beyond his authority? Only a quarter of the half-legal boats leaving Việt Nam now are making it safely to another country, but it doesn't matter: we're already beyond his control.

~

Every time, I see Mr. Tư Hạnh walk by, he glances over at the barrels next to our house—the reminder of his disgrace.

"Why don't you put those barrels somewhere away from the main road?" he asks Má for the fourth time.

"We don't have anywhere else to put them," she says.

"When are you going to load them on your boat?"

"We're still building the tank."

We already finished the tank. Má just likes the barrels there to remind him.

~

The *Pearl Orchid* is the first boat to leave Mỹ Tho. Three of our passengers come from Sài Gòn to live with us. We should get permission to leave soon. I want to see Cồn Tàu one last time, so I hitch a ride down with one of Mr. Six Soybean's relatives. We turn into the stream that cuts through the island. Houses are perched everywhere. The pole bridges are bigger and the paths wider. It feels like the backyard of our house in Tân Long where so many people live crowded behind us.

When I get to Mr. Six Soybean's house, he talks about people I don't know or remember. He offers me fruit to eat and some to take back to my family. I feel touched by his offering. He doesn't have much. I pick a tangerine and ask about Lành and Quý.

"Lành is working on his farm," Mr. Six Soybean says. "He has some health problems, but he's doing well. Quý is sick and drunk."

I dig my nail in and peel the tangerine. "Where is Quý staying?" I thought he'd move-on and do something, but it seems like he's drinking himself to death.

Mr. Six Soybean shakes his head. "I don't know. He doesn't want to see anyone."

Quý might not know people are building boats—that he could leave. Maybe I can find him and tell him there's another way. Even Ngọc Anh, the oldest son of my favorite uncle, is coming with us. My uncle might still believe in Communism, but Má said his wife sure stopped believing.

The tangerine tastes sour. In the old days I'd toss it in the stream, but I eat it all before I leave to visit Ông and Ba Năm. I take the path along Mrs. Ten Sea's land. Someone's planted lemon trees right next to the edge of the strip.

"Ê! There's no path here. You're ruining our fruit." Ten Sea's relatives look at me like I'm doing something illegal.

This was a path before. I used to wander around free to cross the stream or someone's land wherever I wanted. Now people don't want you to even look at their fruit—the backside of Tân Long is freer. I turn to visit Chị Mộng's in-laws who bought the six strips of land. The soil seems packed and bare, with no worms or little crabs digging around. Only the tangerines Má planted grow well.

I get into the water downstream from where our hut used to be. I want to see my old hut, but I don't want to hear Mrs. Fourth Real screaming at me for eroding her stream bank. I sink into the water, and it rises up to my chest. It wasn't this high before. The water goes along at high speed along a deep, hard bottom. I poke my hands into the roots of water coconuts near my old hut feeling for hiding fish and shrimp. The bank underneath is undercut—about to fall away. The water coconuts Mrs. Fourth Real planted to prevent erosion narrowed the stream and made it worse.

I walk in chest high water to where we left the boat by Mr. Six Soybean's, searching for fish as I go. I grasp at one tiny fish and some water snakes. A small shrimp flicks away as I reach out to grab it. Nothing lives here anymore.

When I get back to the boat by Mr. Six Soybean's, the stream has become so narrow the water is over my head even though the tide is going down. I change into a dry pair of shorts and walk over to visit Aunt Curly and Chị Bảy Kim.

"Where's Quý?" I ask when I get there.

Aunt Curly and my cousin don't know. I'd like to see Quý, but I don't have enough time to find him, and I don't even know where to start. I look around for some fruit. "What's ours is yours," Aunt Curly says. She's still like Má—she doesn't care if you fill your belly with her fruit. It's the only thing here that feels the same.

"People here aren't the same as they were before," Chị Bảy Kim says. "Everyone's possessive about their land now. If there's no path— don't wander or they'll give you trouble."

I pick some green bananas to eat while I wait for lunch. I miss the old Cồn Tàu, but I won't miss this.

~

Mr. Seven Coal, a fruit farmer who has mango trees in the south part of Tân Long, greets me as he walks down the street in front of our house.

He's not tall, like Mr. Three East, but he's just as stern. No one wants to cross him. "I heard boats are sinking out in the ocean," he says to me.

"Which boats?" The *Pearl Orchid* made it, but by September most of the boats leaving are sinking. The fishing boat that was rotting by the town hall got fixed up and left with over a hundred people. It hit a sandbar at the river mouth and turned over on its side. Only thirty people survived. Another boat downstream fell on its side because the government makes boats leave in the dark, and no one saw that the anchor was still down. Everyone on it died.

"Boats from around here," Mr. Seven Coal says. All of the neighborhood boys come up to listen. He tells us about a boat that capsized near the river mouth. Fishermen say how tough it is to get in and out of the mouth—especially out. It seems like a horrible place full of sandbars, rocks, and big waves.

"Are you afraid of getting eaten by sharks?" Mr. Seven Coal asks.

"Drowning and being eaten is part of the deal," I say. We just want it to be our turn and take our chance. I'll make sure our anchor is up, and if we follow the government's lead boat out we won't hit the sandbars.

"You had better earn as much goodwill as you can," Mr. Seven Coal says. "You'll need looking over by a higher spirit."

I wish Mr. Seven Coal hadn't said anything because soon Trăng is saying things like, "You'd better be nice to me so I can give you good wishes. You don't want to end up eaten by sharks."

When I'm eating a banana, Trăng comes up. "I'm hungry, do you have a spare?"

I give Trăng a banana. I'll share if it's not a threat. He finishes it quickly. Everyone likes bananas because they fill you up and don't make you hungrier like most fruit.

"Give me another one," Trăng says.

"No."

"I'm going to curse you."

"I don't need your blessing. We'll take our chance and if we die, we die."

Trăng's eyes get big. "You don't know how terrible it would be to get eaten by a shark."

"If I were a shark, I'd eat my legs first, then my belly. Then I'd tear my face to shreds."

Trăng stares at me. "You don't know. It would be horrible."

"If I'm dead, I'm dead. It doesn't matter if sharks eat me or not. But if I make it, I'll laugh my head off when I have freedom and lots to eat while you starve to death."

Inside the house, I turn on the shortwave radio in my parent's bedroom and tune it to Voice of America. International people talk about boat people dying and pressure the government to stop allowing us to leave. All these countries interfered with the South trying to defend itself during the war, and now they want to pressure the Communists into not letting us leave? I want my chance at freedom. Why do they only tell us about people dying? Why don't they tell us something useful like the weather? There's no chance of our boat taking a storm. I feel that we're going to die. But I'd rather be dead than here.

Creeping through a Narrow Opening

While I wait for the foot ferry in Mỹ Tho, a man approaches. "Do you remember me?"

It's the man who stole our chickens. His face is less pulled in and his clothes aren't tattered. "Yes. You live in Giao Long."

"I heard you're leaving," Anh Tư Quân says. "I wish you a safe journey." He looks toward the half-legal boats anchored out in the river as he talks. "Thank you for giving me a chance. I'm a different person . . . I can provide for my family."

"It's not much. That's in the past."

He glances at me and then back at the river. "It could have been terrible if I didn't have the chance."

"It's the Communists that make it difficult . . . Hopefully things will improve and your family will have a better future."

"Well, good luck on your journey. When are you leaving?"

Boats registered to leave before ours sit anchored in the river in front of us. It's been months since a half-legal boat left. "I don't know. Hopefully we can have a chance. Everything is shut down."

He smiles. "You will. Good luck when it happens. If we meet again, I'll invite you over."

On the way home, I avoid greeting a neighbor from upstream. I've already said goodbye so many times. The neighbor sees me anyway. "What? You're still here? When are you leaving?"

"When I'm not around anymore, you'll know I left," I say.

The house is quiet. The boy and the two men that were staying with us went back to Sài Gòn to wait. People say the government halted departures because too many people were dying during the winter storms. It's hard to know what's real. The conflict with China over Cambodia is getting worse. What if the Brown Cows take us to the jungle for trying to leave? We watch to see if any of the other families building boats disappear, if any half-legal boats go missing without the noise of 400 people saying goodbye.

$\backsim$

After my younger sisters leave for school, I sit down to breakfast with my parents and Chị Tư. We're eating the dry Chinese noodles and sausages that we had loaded on the boat. I'm tired of eating noodles and feed them to Trắng and Nhiều when they come over.

Má looks up. "We can't be here," she says. "We don't know if we'll be rounded up and disappear."

"Well, what can be done?" Ba says. He sits deep in the corner with his back against the wall facing the shell curtain to the front room so he can see if anyone steps in. "We have to wait until we get permission."

"We might not get permission." Má's voice gets lower. "I've heard people are creeping through a narrow opening . . ."

"But we already paid all that gold for the boat and the deposit to the government," Ba says. "The people who bought seats on our boat depend on us. I don't know why the government won't let us go."

I hate sitting here and waiting, but we already have the half-legal boat. How else could we leave?

"The longer we stay the worse it's going to get," Má says. "We've already made it known we don't like this government."

Chị Tư sits eating quietly across from me. Ba whispers, "But doing this would be dangerous."

"People say you get a fishing boat captain and mechanic. Then you build a boat and leave."

"There are a lot of fisherman around. How do we know who's good?"

"We have to interview them," Má says. "I've already looked into getting past the guards at the mouth of the river. I went down to check out how they patrol."

Ba stops eating. "You went down to the ocean?"

"Yes."

"This is very risky. We have to make sure we don't enter prison."

~

Three weeks later, Má says, "Lượng, go across the river. We need to hire a fishing boat captain and a mechanic." She gives me a description of a house on stilts on the edge of the river. "If you sense anything that's not right, leave. If they seem legitimate, ask them to come over for a discussion in Tân Long."

"I understand." So we are going to leave illegally. Instead of hiring a ferry, I walk out to Mr. Five Salt's house along the dock and ask if I can borrow his flat-bottomed canoe. People don't pay attention to small boats.

Mr. Five Salt's canoe is so old it's cracked. I paddle across to a row of houses on stilts and slide the canoe into a narrow space between two of them. I tie it near the river bank and walk up to a concrete road. As far as I can see in either direction, houses crowd the road on one side and sit over the river on stilts on the other side. The house Má described is on the river side. I walk up to one with two wood panel doors swung open on their hinges. Inside, an older couple and a young woman sit talking.

"*Chào, Chú. Chào, Cô,*" I say. "Is this the house of Mr. Five Ocean and Mr. Six A?" The children scatter and leave.

"Who are you? Why are you asking?" says the old man.

"I live across the river. I canoed here." There's not much in the house. A dull-colored sheet folded in half separates the front room from the bedrooms and kitchen in back. "I want to talk to these two men so they can tell me stories about fishing and fixing engines."

"Why? You don't know these men."

"I've been sent here to talk to them. No one but them."

"You don't know them, so what is there to talk about?"

"Well, I know Mr. Five Ocean was in reeducation camp. He's a little more than a fisherman. Is that right?"

The man glances at the two women. "Can someone make tea?" Then he looks back at me. "Let's talk."

"I'm sorry, but I can't be here unless I talk to Mr. Five Ocean and Mr. Six A. I'm sorry that I came and interrupted you. I'll leave."

A tall, thin rough-looking man steps out of a back room. "Are you looking for me?"

I'm surprised anyone was back there. Usually people step out when visitors come by. "Are you the ex-Army who distance fishes? Can you tell me about fishing for tuna on the ocean?"

"I wasn't a tuna fisherman." He has a big jaw and a tough voice. "We went way out, but on a smaller type of boat, not the big ones that go into international waters."

"What size of boat? What kind of engine did it have?" I try to look past the sheet into the back room. "Where is Mr. Six A?"

"My brother lives in Tây Ninh."

"Can I see some paper that says who you are?"

He puts his eyebrows together and glares at me. "Who are you to ask this?"

"It's very important." I walk to the side and point to the crack where the canoe is. "I canoed across the river to find you. I need to know it's you."

"What's your name?"

"Kiệt," I lie. "I'm sorry I seem rude. I know more about you than you know about me. If you prove it's you, I'll tell you about me and the next step." I turn toward the door and step out on the porch.

Five Ocean talks to the old man, addressing him as uncle. Then he comes out to the door. "Here's the paper."

I step back inside. The name and picture on the paper match. I hand it back. "My name is Lượng. I'd like to hear more about your fishing stories over at my house in Tân Long. The address is 35/1."

"I haven't been fishing because I can't get diesel," Five Ocean says. "I can't afford to go around."

"We'll repay you more than your trouble. Get your brother and come to the address I gave you. Ask for me." No one can find work anymore—they'll come.

～

The next day, Chị Tư calls for me. I walk up to the front door. Five Ocean stands half inside and half outside the open panels.

I walk past him into the house. "Come inside. Have some tea."

Five Ocean steps inside and looks at the hole in the concrete floor where it's collapsing into the sand beneath. I open the lid of the coconut husk warmer and check the teapot inside. "I'll make more tea."

"Don't trouble yourself. I drank coffee before I came."

"Did you bring your brother?"

He doesn't answer.

"We need to see your brother."

"It costs a lot of money to bring someone from Tây Ninh down here."

"Why don't you get him? I'll pick you up at your uncle's house in two days around dinner." I stand up and walk toward the door.

He follows me. "I'd have to pay the bus fare up and then two fares down—"

I start walking upstream with him. "I said we'll repay you." After seeing our half-empty house falling apart from termites, he probably wonders if we have any money. I finger the bills in my pocket Má gave me for taking care of this. "You might get some mixed information if you ask around about us, but I trust that you're not going to say anything." I reach out and shake his hand and slide the money into it. "We want to talk to you and your brother together or the conversation ends."

He puts his eyebrows together and squints. Then he takes the money and puts it into his pocket.

Two days later, I borrow Mr. Salt's canoe again and paddle up to the house on stilts. Five Ocean comes out. He has a smile on his face. "You came. Come in for dinner. We're waiting for you."

He waves toward a whole chicken worth of dishes on the table: salty chicken with lemongrass, chicken and vegetable stir-fry, chicken rice soup. His aunt and uncle and the young woman and her kids sit around on wood stools and orange square plastic buckets. They've just started eating.

A shorter man with a smooth, handsome face stands near Five Ocean. I look straight at Five Ocean. "Where's your brother?"

"This is my brother."

The man doesn't look anything like him. "May I see his papers?"

"Show him your papers," Five Ocean says.

The smooth-faced man hands me his papers.

I look at them and hand them back. "I'll have one bowl of rice. Then we leave."

The young woman looks at the kids and tilts her head. They pick up their bowls and go behind the sheet to the kitchen in back. She quickly sets up a stool and bowl and chopsticks for me.

"Why hurry?" the uncle says. "We haven't had a meal like this for a long time."

"Where's this meal from?" I ask.

"Your money," Five Ocean says. "My brother took the cheap way down, so we could have this dinner."

"I'll have one bowl of rice and wait for you in the canoe. I don't want to make too much noise." They get a little money and they're already acting like this? The neighbors are going to know something is going on. I sit down on one of the orange buckets and push a bowl of rice and a few bites of chicken down without dipping it in any sauce. I get up to leave with the rice still sticking in my throat.

I move the canoe away from the river bank and busy street and tie it to one of the coconut pillars behind their house. Waves splash against the river bank. A few minutes later, Five Ocean and his brother come out of the back door scowling. They walk down the washing platform to the water. "We haven't eaten a good meal in a long time," Five Ocean says.

"You should enjoy the chicken quietly later on. Hopefully you won't bring attention to yourself. Otherwise our relationship ends here."

"You're just a boy. Why are you so serious?"

"We got this far and these are the terms. If not, I'll pay for your brother to go home." If they can't hold themselves in, they could mess up the plan for the half-legal boat, too.

The uncle and aunt stick their heads out the back door. "Why are you still there?" the uncle asks.

I look at Five Ocean. "Do we agree?"

"Alright."

Five Ocean and his brother step onto the boat. I tell them to sit on the beams in the corner of the boat to balance the weight. "If it sinks you have to swim."

"No problem," they both say.

I untie the canoe and go slowly across. I start asking Six A how to fix certain types of engines. I know a little from watching the mechanic of the half-legal boat.

After a few questions Six A says, "I can fix anything. Any engine."

I let the canoe drift so I have more time to talk.

Five Ocean says, "Isn't your house over there?"

"I want to hear stories," I say.

"Aren't we going to meet your parents?" Six A turns from me to his older brother.

"Well, if he doesn't like the stories, we're going back to our house." Five Ocean looks at me. "Right?"

"That's right."

Five Ocean pushes his eyebrows together. "When I know you better, I'll strangle you."

"I'm not that easy to strangle," I say.

When we get back to the dock, I return the canoe. Five Ocean and his brother walk ahead and stand near Vũ's house waiting. "Follow me." I lead them into the house and back to the kitchen.

Má looks at them. "Let me see your papers."

Five Ocean meets my eyes and smirks.

~

Má says we're going to build an illegal boat and hires Five Ocean as the captain and Six A as the mechanic. My parents plan to leave the owner of the Vĩnh Sương Hardware in charge of the half-legal boat when we escape. Three Của should let our partner take over—he already has the deposits. Still, nothing the government does makes sense.

A week later, the framing on the illegal boat starts in a shipyard downriver from our house. Má said it's better to build it farther away, where there aren't as many eyes and ears around. She tells the officials that we're building the boat for her sister and puts Dì Bảy's name on the papers. Dì Bảy's husband was a martyr to the cause—no one will question her wanting a boat.

Five Ocean oversees the construction, and Six A works on the engine. When I go down to see it, I'm surprised. The boat looks like one of the long buoys on a fishing net. I expected it to look like a fishing boat, but Má says this shape will ride waves and punch through them.

On the way home from the shipyard, I walk near Mr. Three East's house. He's still in reeducation. His family is redlisted. They've sold everything but their house, so they can eat.

"Lượng?" Lệ, the younger sister of the widow Chị Dung, comes outside when she sees me coming home. "When can you introduce me to Mr. Six A?" Lệ came to live with her sister a while ago, and she's the prettiest girl around. Her body is so full for someone so poor. She doesn't wear anything revealing, just an *áo bà ba*, but you can still see what's right there underneath when she moves.

"Please bring me to meet him, Lượng." Even her voice is beautiful. Every time Five Ocean and his brother come for dinner, Lệ stares out the door of the widow's house across the street hoping to meet eyes with Six A when he leaves. She asks me about him every day, but no one is supposed to know anything about the two men working on the illegal boat.

She smiles. "Please, Lượng."

"Alright." With her and Six A asking me to introduce them every day, I give up. "I'll take you tonight."

I walk her down to the shipyard in the evening. Lệ and Six A sit next to each other in a dark corner. I stay in the boat to make sure they only talk and hold hands. It's alright to have love, but I don't want anything to keep Six A here. And I don't want Lệ to get hurt since he's leaving, and he's already twenty-four. She should know that men that old usually have a family.

～

In the heat of the afternoon, when there's nothing to do for the boat, Five Ocean and I play chess. Five Ocean unfolds the paper board between us on the flat-top of the concrete foundation where Sơn's house used to be. We bought Sơn's old house when the woman who lived there left. We wanted to replace our crumbling house, so we thought we'd rebuild on their foundation. Five Ocean and I set up the wooden disks on our sides of the board in the shade of the coconut-leaf roof over the foundation. The roof is the only thing that got built—once we registered to leave we stopped working on building a new house.

Five Ocean is winning the game, as usual. Then he makes a bad move. I could take his car—the best piece besides the general. But usually when people make that bad of a move they take it back. "It looks like you're trying to corner me?" I say.

"Come on, kid."

"What do these Chinese words in the middle mean?" I point at the paper spread between us to four characters printed on the river that divides the two sides of the board.

"Gentlemen never withdraw a move. That's the essence of the game—you never take back your move."

I smile and take his car.

"I can't believe it." He stands up. "I promised to strangle you. This is the time I'll do it."

I laugh.

"I'm going to tell your father you're being tricky."

Five Ocean doesn't strangle me, but he complains to both of my parents. In the evening, I go with him to check on the boat. I try to avoid Lệ so she won't ask me to take her to see Six A. The boat frame and boards are up, but they haven't built the roof or put the aluminum sheeting on. I check the nails to make sure they're using the right size. All the joints look tight. There aren't any loose nails. "This boat will last a long time," the workers say. "Everything is stronger than normal. You don't see boats built this tough."

This boat will be able to withstand anything. It has rib after rib right next to each other and it's made of teak. Even the seams are designed to handle the expansion and contraction of the wood. Later, Five Ocean and I will put a stabilizer on it to make it ocean worthy. Right now it's just a river boat.

～

When the boat is almost ready to launch, Six A asks if he can take Lệ over to Mỹ Tho for ice cream.

"Take her for ice cream, but only ice cream," I say.

When they come back, I stop by the widow's house. "How was the ice cream with Mr. Six A?"

Lệ steps out. "Why do you know everything? You're more than just someone who introduced us. I don't understand. Why not tell me?"

"I just know. He works for my aunt, we oversee his work."

"There's something a little secretive going on. Mr. Six A won't tell me anything."

"So is there something else you did besides eat ice cream?"

She gives me a funny laugh and glares at me.

～

The illegal boat is done. I've been camping out in it for a week with Five Ocean on the backside of Tân Long where it faces the Coconut Monk's Phoenix Island. There's only one house nearby. It's just the two of us. When Five Ocean found out that Six A took Lệ for ice cream, he sent his brother to stay with their uncle.

Five Ocean and I get along pretty well. In the evening, we listen to the radio and cassettes, or he tells stories about serving in the Army. Sometimes we play chess in the heat of the afternoon. Today, Five Ocean wants to see how fast the boat can go in case we get chased by the river mouth patrol. We try to find a boat to measure our speed against, but all the large boats move slowly to save diesel.

The big car ferry going from Mỹ Tho to Bến Tre speeds around the head of the island. We're a couple hundred meters behind it. We run both motors at once trying to catch up. I stand in back guiding the outboard motor. Five Ocean is in front next to the top, steering using cables that connect to the rudders in back. He increases the speed, but the front of the boat lifts. We can't keep up. Five Ocean stops and turns around.

We spend the rest of the day fitting a rectangle piece of wood on the tail to keep the front from lifting. The next day we race the ferry again. The passengers onboard watch us pass by. I don't know what they think about a long boat that's all black, but there's no other way to know how fast we can go. We wait until the ferry is out of sight before we take the boat back to our hiding place.

When we come back to the house for dinner, I check to see if Lệ is looking out of her sister's house across the street. I try to avoid her because every time she sees me she asks if I know where Six A is. She doesn't ask Five Ocean, though. He looks too tough for most people to talk to.

We wait until after dinner, when we can talk to Má alone, before we tell her about the speed test. We have to be careful what we say around my younger sisters. "We modified the boat so it can outrun the ferry," Five Ocean tells her.

"That's unnecessary attention," Má says. "Are you sure the change you made won't be a problem in the ocean?"

"We only need it to outrun the police," Five Ocean says. "Once we get to the ocean, we can saw the damper off."

Over the next few days, Five Ocean and I nail all the windows shut and repaint the gaps with tar so the boat is a dark, dull black. The last task is reinforcing the roofline. We wake up early and cook some rice and Chinese sausages on the open back of the boat. Five Ocean drinks coffee and smokes while we talk. Then, we go inside the boat to work on bracing the roof with pieces of wood.

A group of people shout in the distance. It sounds like they're coming closer. I go up to the front of the boat and look out. Brown Cows with AK-47s run down a path straight toward us. A group of people follow behind.

I come back down. "Brown Cows."

Five Ocean's eyes open wide. He reaches for the pistol he keeps near the engine. "I'm not going to enter prison."

I can hear the footsteps on the dry dirt. "Stay down. Let me handle this," I say. I don't trust Five Ocean not to get crazy and shoot.

I jump off the front of the boat and run as fast as I can toward the Brown Cows. If I can get up to them, I can cut them off from coming toward the boat.

"What's going on?" I ask the Brown Cows, gasping for air. "What are you looking for?" I hope my breathlessness hides the tremble in my voice. We're too far away for them to notice that our boat is abnormally long and painted all black. It's pointed straight back so all they can see is the nose. And they can't see that we've nailed shut all the windows.

The first Brown Cow stops and looks around. A second man in the same golden-brown uniform runs up. "We're looking for a robber that ran this way. Did you see anybody?"

"No." I pant. "I've been here all morning and I didn't see anyone." Bellfruit and tall mango trees run along each side of the path, but the trees are easy to see through. The only place to hide is the canal.

A third officer comes up. He's older than the other two, maybe their leader. He glances behind me, seeming to calculate that if I ran from the water edge, the robber's probably not there. He steps to the side where a canal blocks the way and looks down to see if any mud has been stirred up.

The first Brown Cow runs the opposite direction along the shore, toward the only house. "Did you see anything?" he shouts. The old woman who lives there doesn't answer or open the door.

"Can I help you look?" I say. I want to make sure they stay away from our buoy-shaped boat, jet black with a fresh coat of tar.

The leader says, "Go back to your boat, kid."

A crowd comes down the path. The kids run ahead toward me. I stay in the middle of the path to block them from coming closer. "But they're helping you." I point to the people behind the officer.

"Get back to your boat now." He turns to face the crowd. "This is a dangerous situation. You could get hurt. Everyone get back to where you came from. Now."

Most of the group turns back, but a few kids stay. The officer heads up the island and starts crossing canals to the right. I go back a little ways toward the boat and stand around watching. If they see me in the path, maybe they won't come down this way. "I want to chase the robbers, too," I say loudly to no one, hoping Five Ocean will hear and know what's going on.

The leader crosses the canal back toward me. It's high tide. He's up to his waist in the water and all muddy. He gets out and heads toward the old woman's house. She steps out. "I didn't see anyone," she says.

The leader and the other Brown Cows head downriver. Voices drift back. It sounds like they've picked up the trail.

I walk back toward my boat. The kids on the path wander away.

"I think the robber went downstream," I mutter as I head to the boat. I keep talking to myself so Five Ocean will know it's me. I don't want to enter the boat and have him shoot me.

When I get back inside, Five Ocean is clutching his gun. "I was going crazy hearing voices, not knowing what people were saying." He has one of our two grenades next to him. If you cut his face no blood would come out.

We set the boat up so it can drift toward some empty islands if the Brown Cows come back. After a while, we move it downriver close to where Sơn moved after he came back. It doesn't seem like a good place, but we don't know where else to anchor.

"I was ready to fight for my life," Five Ocean tells Má when we go back to the house for dinner.

"Where is the boat now?" Má asks.

I tell Má it's near Sơn's house. I haven't been friends with him since he asked me to beg for a raisin, and I haven't talked to him since we got in trouble for playing on their land when they first moved to the backside of the island.

"It's alright to have it near them," Má says. "His family is blacklisted. Even if they see something wrong they won't say anything."

After a few days, Má says, "Word is already out about a long, black boat—too many people saw it when they were chasing after the robber. The Brown Cows might wonder why it's tied up by Sơn's house and investigate. Bring it down here and tie it next to the half-legal boat."

Won't that be suspicious? I don't say anything, though, because I don't know where to hide it.

∾

The next day, Mr. Tư Hạnh comes to the door. "There's a long boat out there. It looks like someone tied it up to yours."

Ba steps out of the lean-to. "That's my wife's sister's boat.

"Why is it here?"

"She's going to help make money ferrying people for the half-legal boat when we leave. Then, she'll use it to buy rice in Bến Tre and sell in Mỹ Tho. You probably remember her from when she was here visiting?"

"Ô, yes, her. But you shouldn't have other boats associated with these half-legal boats."

"You could ask Ông Three Của."

"Ô. I just wanted to know what's going on." Mr. Tư Hạnh leaves. I'm sure he remembers the last time Three Của got involved. The mayor ended up being transferred.

Later, some of the neighbors come by and ask about the long, black boat. Ba says, "Well, you can ask Tư Hạnh about it. He seems to have taken an interest in this."

∾

In February, we hear on Voice of America that the Chinese have invaded the northern border. We don't get a lot of information, but we know China hasn't gotten all the way down to Hanoi. I hate the Communists, but everyone in our family is proud when we hear they've pushed the Chinese out. No one talks about it on the streets, though. The government doesn't want anyone to know what happened.

Má says only half of the family will leave on the black boat. She and Ba will stay with the rest of the family to see if the government will let the half-legal boat leave. My parents worry that if they don't stay the government might confiscate the half-legal boat. Then the people who already put down deposits would be stuck. I thought we'd all go together, but with all the people dying on the ocean, it makes sense to double our chances. Má doesn't say who will go on the black boat, but I know I'll be one of them. I know that boat inside and out.

The lean-to is packed with canteens of water, dried bread and noodles, and plastic buoys in case the boat sinks. No one has said anything, but I know we'll be leaving soon. Five Ocean and the other fisherman around say that there's an Old Lady in the ocean in the spring. Toward the end of March, Má tells us who will go: my two oldest sisters, my brothers, and two of my little sisters. Not me.

"I know the boat well," I tell Má. "I should be able to help." I spent so much time building this boat. I want to take care of it all the way to the ocean.

"You need to help watch the house and take care of the half-legal boat."

It's my boat. I want to be on it. "Mr. Five Ocean's not going to be happy." He knows I'd do battle with him to fix anything on that boat and keep it afloat. I'd bail water out on the ocean if I had to.

"Your brothers can help him. We need you here."

I'm not going? Am I ever going to get a chance to leave?

Around eleven the next night, Má tells my brothers and me to load the black boat. Why make it look suspicious by doing it at night? I could have loaded it daytime and no one would have paid attention. It's parked right next to the half-legal boat and I load and unload that boat all of the time, cycling the roast rice and noodles so they don't get wormy while we wait to leave.

We borrow Aunt Curly's flat-nosed farm boat to bring out supplies to the illegal boat. We're loading fruit, water, and cooked rice packed in aluminum canisters—fisherman say rice will last a week that way. I step into Aunt Curly's boat carrying a basket in both arms. Rở, the tailor's son, comes down the dock. He stands at the boat edge looking down at me and the canisters of water and baskets of supplies. "*Ê!* You're loading fresh food?"

Vân steps out from our house onto the dock with a basket. He sees Rở and runs back inside. "You're loading something illegal," Rở yells. Why didn't Má let me load during the day?

Neighbors start to look out their doors. Vũ's father looks out the door of his house near the dock, then steps back in.

Má comes out onto the dock with Vân. "The neighbors are sleeping."

"I caught you doing something illegal." Rở talks loudly trying to get neighbors to come out.

"I don't want to go through the hassle of talking to officials," Má says. "We have to load some supplies. You're welcome to tell Tư Hạnh, but then you'll have to answer to someone a lot higher."

My brothers and I load the boat while they talk. We could have avoided this if they had let me take care of it.

"Why don't you stand around and tell us if someone is coming?" Má says. She holds out some money for Rở. "For your work."

He looks at the money in her hand, but doesn't take it.

"Well, do what you have to do then," Má says.

Rở walks back toward his house. I'm sure he's going to tell his neighbor, Mr. Tư Hạnh. As soon as he leaves, Vân paddles Aunt Curly's boat out. Five Ocean must have heard the noise because he lets the illegal boat drift down toward the sawmill with the outgoing tide. It's black so no one can see it out in the river.

Rở comes back with Mr. Tư Hạnh. "Rở told me there's some illegal activity going on," Mr. Tư Hạnh says.

I can't stand people like them who just make things harder for everyone.

Ba points to Rở. "Ask him. He knows something we don't know."

"Which boat are you loading? Are you leaving?" Mr. Tư Hạnh asks.

"Someone dropped off supplies for the half-legal boat," Ba says. "They've already left."

"They're loading fresh food," Rở says. "I saw the whole thing."

"Look, we have to rotate the supplies. We don't know when we might need to be ready."

"They're sneaking around," Rở says.

Ba looks at Mr. Tư Hạnh. "So you'd prefer us to load during the daytime? You could ask Ông Three Của, but I think he prefers not to have everything done in public."

"They tried to bribe me."

Ba glares at Rở. "Rather than waking up the neighbors and interrupting our work?" Ba turns back to Mr. Tư Hạnh. "You had better get him out of here before I have to ask the authorities to send him to jail—maybe he needs some mosquito bites to wake him up."

Rở looks like he wants to jump up and down. "You're letting illegal activities go on," he says to Mr. Tư Hạnh.

"Go home and go to sleep, Rở," Mr. Tư Hạnh says. "They have to load their supplies. Sometimes you do it in the evening. Stop meddling or you might get yourself in trouble."

Rở leaves muttering. Mr. Tư Hạnh turns to Má and Ba. "It looks like your family, since you are Chinese, can leave . . . I think the political system here no longer applies to you. There's nothing for me to report."

I feel gratified to hear him admit this. That he's finally been defeated. "Thank you," Má says.

I say good luck to my brothers and two of my sisters before they leave to board the black boat. Then Má takes Aunt Curly's boat to pick up my other two sisters and the rest of the passengers in Mỹ Tho and bring them to An Hóa. The black boat will drift down tonight to meet them.

Rở might go up to the town hall to get someone else, but even if he does, the black boat will already be on its way out of the country with half of my family on it.

~

In the morning, Má comes back in Aunt Curly's boat. "Watch the boat and return it to Aunt Curly." She hands me a roll of large bills. "Here's money for taking care of things. I'll be gone for a while. The boat left, but I have to go and make sure it got past the checkpoint at the river mouth."

She starts to give me more money. "That's enough," I say.

Má leaves on a foot ferry to Mỹ Tho. She'll go down the river on land to check all the jails and stations, carrying all that money so she can bribe the guards if the black boat gets stopped. Half of my family is already on their way. When will it be my turn?

The tide is too low to tie it to the dock with the short rope I have, so I stick a pole in the mud and tie it to that. I'll have to come out move it in to the dock when the tide comes in.

The house is dark and empty. Ba left to meet someone, so I'm alone. It's already stifling in the late morning. I walk out to the front step to look around and get some air. The tide's still not high enough for me to tie the boat up.

Rở stands near the foot ferry dock leaning against a post. "Where's the boat you loaded the other day?" He walks over to me. "Where are your brothers? Where is everyone?"

"The boat's tied up in Mỹ Tho." I point. "Up near the ferry dock. Ông Three Của said to put all the small boats together until we use them."

"I know it's gone."

"I just told you where it is. Go and check."

"I will."

That will keep him busy. I go back inside and work on rigging up a hidden string so that I can lock and unlock the door bolt from outside. Then, I remember. Aunt Curly's boat. I need to retie it. I step outside and look at the mud bank. It's gone.

I use the string to pull the bolt lock on the front door. Then I run upstream toward the market. "Have you seen a boat? Have you seen a boat?"

It's late morning. The market is closed, but some people living nearby stand around talking. "Someone found a boat floating up past the town hall," a few people say. They point to the third house on stilts on the edge of the river.

I walk down a narrow path behind the row of stilt houses. Aunt Curly's boat rocks against tires nailed to the post it's tied to. I knew it would be floating around here somewhere. If it wasn't, I would have rented a boat and chased it.

A man pokes his head out of the third house.

"I'm the son of Chan La," I point to the boat. "My boat floated away. I can see it tied up down there." I tell him the type of engine and the kinds of baskets that are in it.

He steps out of his house. "That boat was floating upstream with the tide. It would have been lost forever if I hadn't swam out there."

"Where did you find it? I had it tied to a pole."

He steps behind the row of stilt houses. I follow him along a path back to the market to a concrete dock for unloading goods from the ferry. He points up to a gas depot on the edge of Tân Long. "Past that, about a hundred and fifty meters out."

The people living near the market come up to listen. They make a noise of agreement and talk among themselves. "We just saw him get the boat tied up there." "I don't know how he got a boat."

"It had no owner, so it's mine," the man says.

I turn to the people behind me. "It's my boat." I start walking with the man away from the market back to the path behind the row of stilt houses. "A boat's not something you can just find and pick up. If you hadn't gotten it, it would have floated farther up. But I would have found it because it's my boat."

Two boys follow us on the path, the older one wearing a T-shirt, the other just shorts.

"Stand back," I say to them. "This is a private talk." The grown-ups in the market glare at the kids, but they don't go back.

"You have to buy it back if you want it." He whispers the price, so the two kids standing behind me don't overhear.

I laugh. He wants 50,000 *đồng*? A fourth of the price of the boat? "Your work was swimming out there and paddling it in, but it's still my boat. I'll give you 10,000." That's about two months' worth of work—if he could get it.

He stares down at me. "This boat is worth a lot more."

"Let me talk to the mayor about this." I look at the older boy. "Go and get the mayor. Tell him Lượng needs him to mediate something." The new mayor lives a few houses up.

"I've swam across the river before," I say while we wait. "How long did it take you to get the boat? Ninety minutes?"

"It was very difficult to get. The current was pulling it away. Then, it didn't have the starter in it, so I had to paddle against the current to get back."

"You don't have the starter because I have it."

The mayor walks toward us with a smile on his round, broad face. "Lượng, how are you?" He's a big man with some gray hair and a lot of extra flesh. "I haven't seen your father for a while. What can I do for you?" He knows me because I pass him bribes from my father. The cost of permits for building the illegal boat was the price of fixing a leak in the cement wall of his house.

"The rope came loose on my boat and this man swam out and got it for me. Looks like I owe him some work for getting the boat back. What would be reasonable?" The man looks between the mayor and me. His eyes seem to shrink.

The mayor turns to the man. "This would be a day's worth of labor? You're not usually working are you?"

The man looks pale. He makes a garbled noise. I look straight at him. "Thanks for swimming out and getting my boat. I'll come back and give you the amount I told you before. Are you happy with this?" I'll pay him what I said I would, but I don't want everyone to know. I turn to the mayor. "How about pay for two days of work and enough for coffee and a meal. Is this settled?"

"Yes. Yes. Lượng you should come to lunch more often." The mayor pats me on the shoulder and leaves.

I go home to get the starter and the money. When I come back, the man tells me how difficult times are for his family. He hasn't had work for a long time, they're hungry. He's scared he's only going to get a few hundred *đồng*, the two day's work I told the mayor I'd give him.

"Here's the coffee money." I hand him 15,000 *đồng*—more than I promised.

He takes my hand in both hands and shakes it. "I'll remember this."

"Don't." I don't want my parents to know. "If anyone hears about this, I'll get the mayor again."

∼

A few days later, while I'm standing in front of my house waiting for a street vendor to come by so I can buy some food, Rờ sees me. The house is empty except for me and Ba. Má is still checking jails all the way along to the river mouth, making sure there weren't any arrests. "Where did you say that boat went?" Rờ says. "I was looking over in Mỹ Tho."

"How do I know? Ask the Brown Cows. They're the ones keeping the boats."

He looks at me. I stare at him.

"Where are your brothers?" he asks.

"Do you see them here much? They live above the beauty shop."

"You're doing illegal things."

"We're leaving. There's nothing illegal about it. Don't be a fart flower, stinking up this area." My parents won't let us swear, but this saying fits him perfectly. He's just like those smelly flowers that grow along the road. "What do you get out of this, anyway?"

Ba comes out onto the porch. "Leave, Rờ, or I'll have you arrested for interfering."

"I didn't do anything," Rờ says.

"You can explain that to the police."

"I know you're doing something illegal," Rờ says as he leaves.

I go back into the house to wait. That's all we can do.

Chapter Thirty-nine (March–May 1979)

Waiting for My Chance

I'm supposed to watch the house, but I haven't had breakfast and there's no food around. Since the black boat left a week ago, I've hardly seen Má. Once she came back, cooked coconut shrimp, and left. Nhiều and Trắng came over and begged for some, and I gave them a bowl of rice and some shrimp to eat on the front steps.

I decide to quickly walk to Mr. Three Thẻ's house and buy some fried bananas or sticky rice wrapped in banana leaves that his wife sells. When I open the door, the younger brother of the Eight Talent family is waiting outside for me. "My mother wants to talk to you," he says.

"Later." What could she want? I don't let him inside. To keep our neighbors from finding out half of our family is gone, we tell everyone they can't come in because the floor has a huge crack in it, and they might get hurt.

I wait until two o'clock before heading down the alley and across the stream behind our house. I walk around the fishpond outhouse by their house trying to throw dirt to the other side, glancing toward the Eight Talent's house between tosses. The outhouse is unused now that so many people have moved away.

Mrs. Eight Talent sticks her head out of her house. I walk toward her, then back to the side of the fishpond farthest away from any of the houses. She walks over to me. "Where are your brothers and sisters?"

"Ô, they're around." It's hard to keep them being gone secret. We already had my older sisters' supervisor come to our house looking

460 . *Waiting for My Chance*

for them when they didn't show up for work after a nursing trip to another village. Má accused him of not being able to keep track of her daughters and no one's come back. Hopefully, he saw that they were on the list to leave half-legally and gave up.

"My oldest son said he saw them in Indonesia," Mrs. Eight Talent says.

I feel an instant of relief—I need to tell Má they're safe, but in Indonesia, not Singapore like we planned. Still, I can't let Mrs. Eight Talent tell everyone about my siblings leaving illegally. "What? Your son is in Indonesia?" I say.

"No. No. That's not it. I'm talking about *your* family. My son sent a telegram and said he saw six of your family."

I look at her. "He must have seen someone else. My brothers and sisters are in Mỹ Tho. They'll come by soon."

"I know that you don't accept all this . . . but I got the telegram. Do you want to see it?"

"I believe you got a telegram, but it must be a mistake. When my sisters and brothers are around I'll ask them to stop by. The two oldest are working as nurses far from here."

Mrs. Eight Talent looks bewildered. "The information is accurate—"

"I'm glad that your son is safe, but he's mistaken." I turn and leave. I don't know what her son said in the telegram about my family, but by now everyone in the town hall will have read it. I spend the rest of the day watching the back of the house to see if anyone comes down to push Mrs. Eight Talent for information. No one does. Someone stops Mrs. Eight Talent on the street and asks where her children have gone. "They went to the New Economic Zone to try to find a living," she says.

A few days later Má gets a telegram. I'm surprised the government even lets us have it. The message is two lines about my sisters going to school in a nearby village. Má says it means they're in Indonesia. They made it. Half of our family made it.

Má is joyous. She sends a telegram back asking about the weather and waves and telling them to try to go to Australia. We've heard America isn't taking many refugees, only small families with skills. But Australia has a lot of land and not that many people—since we won't know the language we can farm. I'm happy they're safe, but I wish it were me that had made it.

~

Má brings me outside the front of our house and points to a boat tied up in the shade of a cheap tree. It's a small-covered boat, the same type as Cậu Năm Lộc's ferry boat.

"What's that boat for?" I ask.

She bends her head toward the boat and motions with her hands toward it. She raises her eyebrows and looks at me as if I should understand something. This is the new illegal boat? How's this small boat going to go out on the ocean?

I step onboard into the covered area with Má. It's piled with baskets. A small man with white hair welcomes us with a smile. Colonel Nửu? Why is he here? I only met him a few days ago when he stopped by our house. He got out of reeducation camp early for a colonel.

When we get in the house, Má tells me the Colonel will live on the boat to make it look like a houseboat. The baskets make it look like he's a fruit wholesaler. "Take care of everything for this boat like the last one," Má says. "Prepare it, load it, get the Colonel anything he needs—"

"How can this boat possibly go out on the ocean?"

"People sometimes take these kinds of boats out to the ocean," Má says.

"They probably go on the ocean when it's calm. I don't think it will handle big waves."

"Well, people say the next few months the ocean will be calm. If we don't get permission from the government to leave before the rainy season, we'll go in this boat."

I'd prefer the half-legal boat. At least it's bigger and higher up.

At night, I help carry the baskets up from the boat to the house. In the morning, I carry them back down filled with cooking utensils and food. Everyone is always carrying baskets around—people probably think we're watching them for the Colonel so they don't get stolen.

The Colonel tells me he's living in the cracks, not registered with any household. He has to stay out of sight. I tell him to wait until the evening to cook and shower, so people don't see his pale skin and know he doesn't belong here where the men take off their shirts in the heat and everyone is brown.

The boat has to be reinforced with aluminum sheeting on the bottom, so we pull it to a shipyard by Mr. Three East's house. He's back from reeducation camp early too, but he hasn't come out of his house.

People say the government let him out because he's ill. I look in the window when I'm near the shipyard so if he sees me he can call out. I'm disappointed that he doesn't.

One day I see Mr. Three East through the open front door. He's in the back room, hunched over, leaning on things as he moves around. I want to talk to him, but everyone says he's about to die and won't see visitors. He used to walk around like he was in charge of everything. Now, life is ending for him—the government reduced him to this. And here I am planning to cross the border with empty hands into a strange land where everyone says I'll be mute like the Chinese here trying to speak Vietnamese. But I think I'll be able to learn a new language like Grandfather Lưu and Ba did.

There's not much to do about the Colonel's boat, so most of the time I stay inside. When I come outside to get some food from a street vendor, Lệ walks out of her house and over to me. She shows me a letter she says is from Five Ocean's brother. "Anh Six A is in Indonesia. Do you want to read it?"

"Ô, so that's where he went." I look away from the letter—I don't want to acknowledge knowing anything about who he went with. Lệ doesn't know anyone in my family is gone.

"I need to talk with you. There's something important I want to know. Let's go swimming and talk there." She wades out into the river in her *áo bà ba*. I follow her. She tries to get closer and whisper in my ear. My heart pounds and my body's hard to control. I can see her breasts through the thin fabric.

"He says he loves me and wishes we had more time together. Why didn't you tell me he was leaving?"

I move away. I'm so afraid she might get close to me and feel something. "It wasn't his choice or mine to say anything." I notice she didn't say he made any promises.

"Why don't you tell me what you know?" She moves close to me again.

"There's only so much information you're going to find out." I swim away from her and go back to the shore.

"What's going on between you and Lệ?" the widow Chị Dung asks me later that day. "She was crying after she talked with you. What did you do?"

"Broken heart."

"Is it that other man?"

"Yes."

"Ô, so that's who wrote the letter."

～

Cousin Hai Thăng sticks his head in the one open panel of our front door and walks in. He's still dressed for work in a short-sleeve white shirt, long pants, and a belt even though his barber shop doesn't have any customers. He looks into my parent's bedroom as he walks to the kitchen. "Where are the rest of your brothers and sisters?"

"They're busy working," I say. He always comes around dinner and talks until we invite him to eat. Now that we have money from selling seats on the first illegal boat, we have enough food to share. There's not much at his house.

"Where are your little sisters? School's not over yet?" He looks over at the clothes hanging to dry on the line between the kitchen and bathroom. None of Young's or Hằng's clothes are there. If someone really wanted to find out they were missing it wouldn't be hard.

Má sets a dish on the table. "Ô, you just missed the younger ones, they went to Mỹ Tho. Now that they're older, they like the city more."

Hai Thăng's eyes search the room as he sits his tall body down slowly at the table. "I stopped by the beauty shop today. I didn't see anyone there either. What about Thượng and Vân?"

"The boys quit school, they're probably off somewhere," Má says.

"If they were around, I would run into them." His eyes glance around as he talks. Even relatives can't know that half of our family is gone and the rest of us will leave illegally soon too. Someone's mouth might get happy and spurt something out.

"Did you go straight here from Mỹ Tho?" Má asks.

"No." Hai Thăng shakes his head and squints at us. Má says he asks all these questions because he's *ba trợn*—someone kind of crazy who talks a lot. Still, he's my oldest cousin from my oldest aunt.

"Why don't you go over there right now, you'll see them. Then you can stop asking."

"Maybe in a couple days." He stays at the table talking while Má does the dishes.

"We close the doors early," Má says. The front room is already dark. "You'd better get back to your children."

"My kids won't have eaten yet—"

"Just a minute." Má scoops the rice leftover from dinner into a plastic bag and hands it to him.

"Also, my wife probably hasn't eaten . . . times are tough."

Má goes to the rice vat and gets a small bag of uncooked rice. "Take this."

~

"Is anyone home?" a man's voice calls into the front door.

I follow Ba out from the kitchen into the front room. Mr. Seven Coal stands sternly in the entrance. I think he still suspects it was me who led the neighbor boys to steal mangoes from his trees.

Ba smiles broadly and shakes his hand. "Sit down, have some tea."

Mr. Seven Coal gives a small smile. "I just stopped by." He sits down in one of the chairs set on either side of the lean-to door. The chair on the other side of the doorway tilts, so Ba sits on a small stool near the teapot. I stand close to him and look at the termite holes in the beams. Everything in our house is falling apart.

"Did you hear any news about leaving?" Mr. Seven Coal asks. He has the same type of job on the neighborhood watch that Ba used to have, except for the area south of us. But he's not a Communist—just a fruit farmer who also raises pigs and fish.

"Well," Ba says, "we still have to be ready to leave whenever they give us the news."

"Being in a holding pattern can be difficult." Mr. Seven Coal's face sets into seriousness, and his voice drops into a low monotone. "You should be aware that there are reports from inside eyes and ears."

"Is that true? Well, we're leaving, there's not much to report," Ba says.

"There is no reason for these kinds of reports at all," Mr. Seven Coal says.

I know exactly who the inside eyes and ears are. My cousin should protect the family, not say things behind our back.

That night at dinner, Ba tells Má about Mr. Seven Coal's visit.

"Anh Hai Thăng is the person poking us," I say.

"That's probably true," Má says.

Ba finishes and puts down his rice bowl. "Thăng is always eating here and then talking with his big mouth. Instead of taking care of his family, he worries about what the people at the market think."

"Well, he's a little *ba trợn*," Má says. "Be careful what you say around him."

I wonder what my parents will do to my cousin the next time he comes.

～

In the morning, Má tells me to open up the front door panels. She steps out to stand near the road and talk. The neighbors haven't seen her for a while, so she wants to make sure everything seems normal.

"*Chào*, Dì Tám," Cousin Hai Thăng calls from the street.

"Thăng," Má says. "Where are you going?" I wait for Má to say something about his reports to Seven Coal.

"I just came up this way and stopped by." Cousin Hai Thăng steps around Má into the front room and starts walking back toward the kitchen.

Why doesn't Má stop him? Is she scared of upsetting her older sister? Well, he's my cousin, not my elder. I step in front of him. "Anh Hai, you're a dead dog. You don't come into our house and then report on us."

"No, no. I didn't."

"Get out and don't come back. You're not welcome anymore."

He turns sideways toward Má. "Tell Lượng to stop."

Má looks away.

"You eat here and then you poke us from behind?" I walk toward him, pushing him out the door. "Get out now."

He steps away from me, still pleading with his eyes to Má. "That's not how you treat your cousin."

Má doesn't turn. He steps around her to the street.

When he leaves, Má comes back inside.

"He's been telling Mr. Seven Coal everything he sees and hears," I say. "I won't allow him to step foot in this house again."

For a moment, Má doesn't talk. Then she says, "Yes. He shouldn't have done that."

～

Half-legal boats start getting permission to leave. A few days later, we get our date: May 9th. Three weeks away. My parents look happy and relieved—they don't have to worry anymore about what would have happened to the half-legal boat and our partner if we left illegally. Má's youngest sister and some non-Chinese relatives will go on the second illegal boat with the Colonel.

Ba has to register everyone leaving on the half-legal boat with Three Của. Chị Năm's husband says he doesn't want to go. His family wants them to stay because she just had a baby. I don't like my sister's husband. He's scrawny, his skin is scaly, and he looks like he's wearing lipstick. I thought she shouldn't get married to him in the first place— she was only eighteen. Má doesn't give Chị Năm a choice—her husband can either stay here alone or get on the boat. When Ba turns in the list his name is on it.

Then, the Chinese partner comes down and says we have to change the number on the half-legal boat from 014 to 041.

"But we've already registered with the other number," Ba says.

The partner insists. "This way the number is balanced—light in the front, not too heavy in the end."

When he leaves, Má laughs. "As if we don't have enough to do." But Ba sends someone to paint the new numbers on. Then he and the captain mount the large brass compass on the boat.

~

"Finally," the neighbors say when they hear we have a date. "But where are your other brothers and sisters to say goodbye to?"

"They're in Indonesia already." I tell the story my parents decided on. "They traded places and left on another half-legal boat. You know what happens . . . crossing the ocean a lot of people die."

They nod. "It's smart to divide the family."

Mrs. Eight Talent insists that my brothers and sisters left before. I won't admit anything. What good can come of people knowing they left illegally?

All the men I run into—Mr. Three The, my cousin's husband, Trắng's older brother, and most of our neighbors—come up to me and say, "Smoke a package of cigarettes for me when you get there, one that smells good and has filters."

"I will," I promise. They name Salem, Dunhill, Pall Mall, and the thick ones with a picture of cats on the box. I just remember they want expensive ones with filters.

A few of the men ask me to "drink a beer or two for them or some good cognac."

"Sure, when I come across some." I hope I don't. I tasted Hennessey at Chị Năm's wedding, and I didn't like it.

Everyone says, "Don't forget about us." I don't say anything. I plan to forget everything. How could I survive leaving if I didn't?

Cậu Năm Lộc, the ferryman, comes to say goodbye. "Do you want to seek a route to leave?" Má asks. The Colonel and I just nailed the windows shut on the illegal boat. We have one space left on it.

The ferryman talks about sending his oldest son. "But if he gets caught. The government will take our land, everything . . . It's too much risk."

"You have to save some money so you can bail him out of jail," Má says, "But yes, you could lose everything."

"I'll think about it more."

He needs to take the chance. It looks like Communism is going to be around for a long time—there's nothing worth staying for. Nothing. Even Phượng, the girl I liked, moved with her parents back to the countryside.

~

I spend my time working with the Colonel on the illegal boat and getting the half-legal boat ready. I talk with the new mechanic about the half-legal boat's engine. It's still not running as well as it was before our boat partners made us replace our first mechanic with him. When I come home, I overhear Mr. Seven Coal saying to my parents. "There are a lot of things happening that I don't know."

"There probably are," Ba says.

"You could be the person making things happen as well," Má says. "Look around."

He walks away lost in his thinking. It's clear he wants to leave. He should figure it out and do something.

~

Mr. Tư Hạnh calls from the front door. I come out of the backyard and walk into the front room carrying some *bánh*. He stands in the doorway watching me eat. "Don't forget us when you have a lot to eat," he says. "Don't forget how hard it is here."

I give him a piece of the *bánh* I'm eating. "I won't forget a lot of things," I say. "Especially unpleasant ones."

He looks old from years of not having enough to eat. "Is there anything you're going to leave behind that I can have?" he asks.

"Ask my parents." We don't have much left. Just old clothes and worthless electronic equipment. Anything of value is already gone. My parents have already given the mayor our pots and pans, desks, and bicycle parts.

"Tư Hạnh keeps asking us to give him things," Má says when I tell her. "Just seeing him makes me upset." She blames Mr. Tư Hạnh and the Communist meetings for my brother dying. His shadow is enough to make her angry.

Mr. Tư Hạnh comes again and asks Ba for something, anything that we're leaving behind. "The government already did a checklist of the house," Ba says. "If anything is missing, we won't be able to leave."

There's no list.

∽

I tell Vũ, Trắng, Nhiều and some other boys to tell their families I'm taking them to Mỹ Tho for a sugarcane drink at the cart Chị Năm and Chị Châu run in front of the beauty shop. The beauty shop is closed, so my sister and cousin bought the cart to stay busy while waiting to leave. They say they're playing anti-Communist music on the reel-to-reel stereo we hid after April 30th, and that all of Mỹ Tho is coming. I want to see if it's true.

We cross the river in a foot ferry boat. On the other side, I get into a cyclo with Nhiều and the other boys pack into another. "Go to the roundabout where there used to be a fountain," I tell the cyclos.

The boys act like they're riding a car, wanting people to see them, standing up in the seat trying to look around. The sun is just going down and the lights in people's houses haven't come on yet. The roundabout is full of people standing outside talking. Music blares from speakers setup in the street. It's pro-South Vietnamese music by Duy Khánh and others.

> *You leave your home and your youth*
> *to defend your country.*

You could return dead or on crutches
no longer the person who left,
your sweetheart may not recognize you,
but we will always honor your sacrifice.

People wait in line at the sugarcane cart or sit on plastic tables and chairs in the street with their drinks. Some sit on the edge of the sidewalk. My sister said she was busy, but I didn't think it was anything like this.

We hop off the cyclo, and I pay. "I come here in the evening and wait for customers," one of the cyclos says, "but no one wants to leave until after the curfew." Ex-officers, cyclos, everyone in Mỹ Tho seems to know about our sugarcane drink stand. How am I going to get any drinks for my friends with this crowd?

Men who look like they're former Army stand around. My friends cling to me. "Are you sure this is the right place?" Nhiều says. "Is this Army music?"

"Yes."

Nhiều points across the street, "Are the police there?"

I nod. Sweeter than hearing the music is knowing what's on the other side of the roundabout. "That's the police station right there."

"Is this music legal?" Vũ asks.

"Yes. For us it is." The rules don't seem to apply to us anymore.

We sit on the curb of the sidewalk in front of a neighbor's house. The lights and loud music remind me of when I came to Tân Long from the countryside and saw electric lights and people in cafés at night for the first time. I haven't felt this kind of energy and excitement for so long—it's how the flower markets used to be on the eve of *Tết* with rows of color and everyone talking, haggling, and carrying things home. Now there's not much to buy and fewer people to buy it.

"We're thirsty, let's have some sugarcane drinks." I leave my friends and go behind the cart.

Chị Châu washes plastic glasses in an overflowing tub on the cart. Customers crowd in front asking for drinks, saying if they want orange or kumquat with the sugarcane. My sister squeezes a stick of cane and slice of orange out of the machine into a plastic bag, sticks in a straw, and twists a rubber band around.

"I need some drinks for the neighbor kids."

"Wait a little." Chị Năm hands the bag to a customer who doesn't want to wait for a clean glass. "My hands are wet—help us collect money."

I toss the money I collect into the eight-liter can next to the drink cart. Then, I start sticking it into my pocket so I don't have to go through the crowd to get to the container. My sister and cousin take whatever people have—they don't have time to make change. One man gives me a bill five times the value. "It's too much." I start looking through my pockets for change.

"It's worth it," he says. "Don't bother. It's worth it."

I go back and get drinks in bags for my friends. I grab some *bánh* off the cart and take it over too. One of the cyclos didn't leave. He's parked by the tailor's house next door because he can't get any closer. I hand him a drink in a plastic bag.

"It feels like the old days," he says.

When my friends finish I give them each some money for the ferry. I tag two cyclos and tell them to take my friends to the ferry dock at Lạc Hồng Garden. Then I go back and help my sister and Chị Châu until they close at eleven. I'll stay in our house in Mỹ Tho tonight. I'm exhausted cleaning up and putting all the chairs away. I don't know how they can do this every night.

The next day, I stop along the river for lunch on the way home to Tân Long. I have money in my pocket from the profit we made on the illegal boat. Ever since we found out we could leave, I've been trying all the restaurants I couldn't afford to eat at before. This one is bad, just like the others. While I eat, I imagine the meals I'll have when I leave, how much better the food will taste.

On the way back to the ferry, I pass the line of tractors along the side of the street. The tractors have been sitting there for four years, a broken promise full of dust and rust.

∼

A week later, my sister and cousin sell their drink cart and our stereo and all the music reels to the café across the street—they're exhausted. The café plays the pre-1975 music softly indoors. After two days, the police confiscate the drink cart, stereo, and music.

Half-legal boats begin leaving again. All around us we hear people saying goodbye. Every two nights a boat anchored out in the river leaves from a boarding area north of the Bến Tre ferry. With the boats leaving, my parents get bolder about what they say.

I take a look around at the river and the trees. I'll miss this place. But I hate the Communists so much I'll never come back. I'm going to go on a journey to a new land, away from where I grew up. I'm so angry at everyone in the South for losing and at the Communists for taking away everything I ever cared about. The only way I can manage is to forget everything and leave it behind as if it didn't exist.

I go over to the shipyard where the Colonel's boat is anchored. He's painting it with tar. People might laugh at a black boat in a hot country, but at least this boat doesn't look as suspicious as the buoy-shaped boat my siblings left on. Tar is cheap—people will think that's all he can afford.

On the way home, I run into Mr. Seven Coal near his house.

"Hai Thăng and other people are reporting happenings I don't understand," Mr. Seven Coal says. "Do you know anything?"

My cousin is still making reports? He couldn't have found out about the Colonel's boat. He must be talking about someone else or what he saw at our house before I told him to leave. It doesn't matter what he says about half of my family already being gone—it's too late now. "You can create your own happening," I say.

"All the available boats have been bought already."

I tell him more than I normally would dare. "There are a lot of boats left. A boat only has to be ten meters to handle the ocean in this weather." Mr. Seven Coal has access to a bigger boat than the one he chased me with when we stole his mangoes. "If you want something it's up to you. You have land on the front river and on the back river. The gas station next to you has a good dock."

He stares at me.

"If you look you might see it. A lot of non-Chinese around here are missing."

"I'll try to figure out what I can do."

"Ask questions if you have them. We're leaving. We don't like the government."

Maybe we can help him leave. We tried to help the ferryman. Má told him he should use his boat to take his whole family—it's bigger than the Colonel's boat—but he said it was too much of a risk.

≈

A girl who lives below the sawmill comes up to my house to talk. We walk out to the dock. "I want to leave," she says. "How can I go?"

"You need ten ounces of gold and papers to show you're Chinese." I smile at her. "Unless we do something and I marry you, then it's free."

I expect her to say, "That's not going to happen," like most girls would, and quit bothering me. Instead she looks thoughtful. We talk a little longer. Then she leaves.

An hour later, the girl runs up to me and says that her father wants to talk to me. I'm dead. His house is on stilts on a canal across from the sawmill. I sit at a table across from her father. His wife serves us tea and biscuits, and then stands nearby listening. There's no sign of the girl.

"I heard that you were talking about what it would take for my daughter to go with you," the father says.

"I was joking."

"If it's possible, I would like to have that happen. You have my permission."

"I'm too young to get married." I can't believe this is happening. "The timing is too close to leaving anyway. But there are ways . . ." There's a dry space between the old head of the boat and the new nose that could probably hide twenty people. "I could hide her on the boat, but she'd be on her own when we get there."

"She has to be with somebody. Someone has to take care of her."

I look down at my tea. "No, I can't do that. She'd be on her own."

He talks about how he has no future here. "I hope you can work it out somehow. If you need me to come and talk to your father—"

"If you talk to my father, then this opportunity will close."

He stares at the wall and then looks at his wife. "I can't have my young girl leave like that. We have to see if there's another way."

When I leave, the girl comes out of the house and follows me.

"It was a joke. Why did you do that?" I say.

"My father says I have to find a way to leave, that there's no future for our family."

She follows me back to the house trying to talk with me.

I turn around at the door. "Well, if we're going to get married, then let's go inside and practice."

She looks at me. "We have to be engaged."

I shouldn't have said anything.

The next day, her father finds me near my house and talks about moving forward with the marriage plan. How did a joke start this? "It won't happen no matter what," I say. "Even if I got engaged to your daughter, I'd still have to sneak her on board—there's no paperwork."

He nods. "Yes, then she'd become an in-law."

"Not when I'm young. I can't take care of another person."

I turn and walk into the house. Only Chị Tư and Ba are home. "Who was that person talking to you so seriously?" Chị Tư asks.

"He lives downstream. I joked about marrying his daughter, and he thought it was real."

Chị Tư laughs at me.

The girl comes back. "My parents think it's too dangerous for me to go alone . . ." She looks down at her feet and glances up at me. "But we still could get married."

I have to end this. I smile. "I'm only fifteen. I hardly know you. I already told your father that if you really want to go, I can hide you, but you'll be on your own."

I go to find her father and tell him what I told Mr. Seven Coal. "Look around at all the houses where people were but aren't anymore. They didn't go to the New Economic Zone, they left. And they left on small boats."

He stares at me intensely. "Thank you for telling me this. Best wishes for your trip."

"Best wishes for *your* trip," I say.

～

Má decides that the Colonel's boat is going to leave the day after the half-legal boat. We'll have to rush to get it ready. I go with Má upstream to the salt processing place in Tân Long owned by Mr. Five Salt's relatives. A family who lives nearby on a stilt house will let us use their house to store supplies. They serve us tea and whisper about relatives in West Germany.

The next day, Chị Châu runs away with her boyfriend. He doesn't want her to leave with us. We try to find my cousin, but we can't. "How could she do this stupid thing? How could she listen to her boyfriend?" Má huffs her words out as she complains to Ba. "He's older. He lured her away."

The boyfriend is the cousin of Chị Năm's husband. Má goes to their house and demands they find Chị Châu and her boyfriend. They send someone to get them from Tây Ninh.

I come over to see Lệ. I want to make sure she forgets Six A.

"Have you heard from Anh Six A," she asks as soon she sees me. "Why doesn't he write to me?"

"He didn't write to us—but he'd contact you if he wanted to. I don't know much about him, but it's better off for you to forget." I feel bad he made her love him, but he was a handsome man from out-of-town . . . What did she expect?

"I'm going to write back."

"Forget about him. Don't waste two weeks of work on a stamp."

"Does he have a family?"

"I didn't meet his family, but he's handsome. And he's not young."

"Ồ! He's married . . ." Tears flow to her eyes. "Does he have any children?"

"I don't know. I didn't see any of them."

"You know everything, Lượng, but you don't tell me everything."

"I tell you what you need to know."

"Why didn't you tell me about Anh Six A?"

"I told you that his life is complicated and he's gone. That's all you needed to know."

She puts her hands over her face and tears run down.

"If I meet him again, I'll tell him what happened here." I'll tell him he broke her heart.

∼

When Chị Châu comes back, Má insists on talking to her alone to ask her if she really wants to stay. Má comes back upset. My cousin told her she's confident in her decision. The next day my cousin and boyfriend have disappeared. She's stupid for running off. Má's scared Chị Năm's husband will convince her to run away, too. She won't let my sister out of her sight.

I hope Chị Năm won't do anything stupid, but I'm too busy loading the Colonel's boat to think about anything else. This time, we load in the daylight. I carry baskets with food and twenty-liter plastic containers of diesel from our house out to the boat. The next day, we move the illegal boat up to the salt processing place. I go over the map with the Colonel and the captain and give them one of our spare compasses so they have a better one. I worry that we're too rushed, that we're not helping them enough. I like my chance better on the half-legal boat.

But the ocean is calm, even small boats should make it.

On May 9th, my parents leave at five in the morning to do paperwork and get ready. Chị Tư leaves a little later. Everyone is in Mỹ Tho where we'll load tonight. Only my favorite uncle's oldest son, Ngọc Anh, and I are left in the house in Tân Long. Our boat will be the fifth to leave this year. The boat the Sài Gòn Chinese were fixing next to ours in the sawmill will be the sixth.

There's nothing left in the house but the faded cloth bag full of my clothes sitting on the floor in the kitchen. It's quiet. The neighbor kids are all in school. I feel a little sad looking over the house and the yard and saying goodbye to it. I see some neighbors and say goodbye.

A man waits across the street near the widow Chị Dung's house, ready to take over the house when I leave. Ngọc Anh and I take showers to use up the water in the rain barrel. Then I take my cousin out to the boat. I come back to check the house to make sure there's nothing left behind. When I step out, the man comes over and tapes a government seal on the door. I laugh to myself. Our house has cracked floors and termites eating the posts. It's about to fall down. What are the Communists going to do with it?

As soon as I get on the boat, Ngọc Anh says he forgot his underwear hanging on the line outside the house. "I'll go back," I say. It's only ten, and we have to wait until late afternoon before the boat leaves to Mỹ Tho to pick up the other passengers.

I get in the canoe and go back. Sơn stands in the alley on the side of our house in a light brown uniform. I knew he was training at the town hall, but I'm surprised to see him standing here with an M-16.

"I just want to get my shorts from the line." I hop up onto the bellfruit tree and up onto the roof of the lean-to.

Sơn points the M-16 up at the roof. "Get down."

What is he doing? "I just need to get these shorts. Don't point the gun at me."

"You're not allowed here anymore." He's clutching his rifle. "It's not your house anymore."

It's not our house anymore, but those are still my cousin's shorts. "Look." I wave my hand toward the clothes line on the balcony. "I won't even go inside the door. I'll just climb up the side and get them."

"This belongs to the government, and I have to protect it. Leave now." He clicks the safety off.

He's threatening to shoot me? I jump down from the tree and turn like I'm going to leave. Sơn lowers the M-16. I'm not going to let him get away with doing this to me. I grab the gun out of his hands, throw it, and punch him in the side of the face. The rifle lands in the trench on the side of the house Má had dug for the diesel barrels. Sơn turns and heads toward the trench to go after the gun. I kick him in the ribs. He lunges into the trench. I jump in and knock him into the muddy water in the bottom.

Sơn gets up and reaches for the rifle. I punch him down and straddle him in the mud. "I'm going to kill you if you point that gun at me again." I hold his face in the mud. He's not stopping me from leaving. Sơn thrashes trying to get up. I lean down on him. When he goes unconscious, I'll tie him up and leave.

"Lượng, stop!" Mr. Three The comes up from the alley and looks down at us. "Sơn, get out of there."

I push Sơn away. I'll see what Mr. Three The has to say. But if he doesn't help, I still have to stop Sơn. I find the gun, pull out the ammunition, and push the barrel into the mud. Sơn won't be able to use it now.

Mr. Three The pulls Sơn out. Sơn screams, "I'm going to get you arrested for destroying the gun."

I didn't destroy it. He can probably clean it. I look at Mr. Three The. "I was just trying to get my shorts, and he pointed a gun at me."

Sơn's frantic. "You're going to be punished for destroying the gun."

If I'd wanted to, I could have hit the barrel on the dirt to bend it, but I didn't want to get Sơn in that much trouble.

Mr. Three The locks Sơn's arms behind his back. "Go, Lượng, I've got him."

I look at Mr. Three The and Sơn, then up at the shorts hanging on the line. How did the Communists get Sơn to point a gun at me over this? I motion toward the line. "I want to get my shorts first."

Mr. Three The shakes his head. "Go."

They both look at me, Sơn worried, Mr. Three The on high alert. I hesitate. I didn't get what I came for. It feels unfinished.

"I'll tell the authorities," Sơn says. He's no longer yelling or struggling to get away. But I'm still so mad. How could he pull a gun on me?

"Go," Mr. Three The says. "Your future is in front of you, not back here."

None of the neighbors has come out of their house and there's no sign of the police. He's right. I can leave. It can end this way. I turn and walk toward the foot ferry dock to the canoe. I don't look back until I'm on the river. By then, houses block the shore, and I'm too far away to see anything. When I get to the half-legal boat, I listen for a commotion on shore. If Sơn's stupid enough to come out to the boat, I'll take a flare gun to him.

There are too many people helping the Communists, turning on neighbors for a little bit of credit from the government. But there are still people like Mr. Three The, who could have informed on everyone but didn't. There are just too few of them, and I'm not sure who to trust.

No one comes out from shore. An hour later, Aunt Curly steers her small boat up to ours and Mr. Six Soybean and his wife and some other people from Cồn Tàu call out. Aunt Curly hands a basketful of fruit up to me. They came to say goodbye to Má. They're disappointed when I explain that she's waiting with Ba and everyone else at the loading station—we'll pick them up when we're cleared to leave. They give their wishes from their family to ours for a safe journey across the ocean and a prosperous future. I try to remember each message to tell Má.

While we wait to leave, I eat soursops and jackfruit and jump in the river to cool off. It's hot and there's no breeze. Around three in the afternoon, a government boat full of Brown Cows comes by and signals to the captain. It's time. Our old neighbors hear the engine and come out to the foot ferry dock to wave. I wave back as I help the captain pull up the anchor and loop the rope. As we start moving, more people come out to the dock to say goodbye. People in boats wave. I climb on top of the captain's cabin to sit. I'm finally on my way.

Epilogue

Third Country

After four days at sea, Lượng's family ended up not in Indonesia as planned, but in Malaysia. The Colonel's illegal boat left a day later and made it to Indonesia. Using telegrams and letters, his parents made plans to reunite with the brothers and sisters who left before them. After eleven months in refugee camps, Lượng left for his third country—the United States—in April of 1980.

He wanted to forget. As the airplane went from Hong Kong to Japan and then Seattle, he stayed up watching the clear skies and ships below traveling the Pacific, wanting to see what going halfway around the earth meant, trying to erase the memories of what he was losing. But he didn't forget. No one in his family did. Whenever they gather together, they tell stories. And laugh. Especially Má.

My husband never imagined he'd have a wife born in America listening to his stories, asking: how did it look, smell, sound—how did he feel? He put on old thoughts again like discarded clothes found in the attic. When he slept, he'd relive the past, seeing where every mango tree grew, feeling how every stream ran. Some stories were fun to recall, unpleasant edges hidden at first—others hurt. I felt guilty, but he told me: "Everything I tell you makes me a little bit freer."

Author's Note

Putting together a story from memory is like putting together a puzzle. I worked with my husband and his family to capture events as accurately and in as correct a timeline as possible. Lượng made sure to take me and our children back to the Mekong Delta to walk through the scenes from his boyhood.

Still, there were surprises. More than forty years after it happened, Lượng found out that it wasn't his uncle who was burned and carried through town. It was his uncle's older brother. The uncle and his older brother were both called Chú Bảy, Uncle Seven, and died around the same time. But overall, Lượng's childhood memories have proved to be reliable. When trying to determine the order of events, I thought dates carved in stone would be correct. But family graves were moved and relabeled with incorrect conversions to and from the lunar calendar, requiring old pictures and multiple interviews to sort out. Lượng's memory that his Grandfather Lưu died on a hot day in 1972 turned out to be correct even though the new grave lists Grandfather's death as a year earlier.

My husband and his family must have wondered at my asking them to retell the same stories again and again as I tried to fill in the details. I'm grateful to Lượng and Má and everyone in my extended family for their patience during the many years it took to complete this book and their generosity in sharing their story.

Glossary

AK – Slang for AK-47, a rifle used by the Việt Cộng.

anh – Older brother or man.

Army – The South Vietnamese Army or Army of the Republic of (South) Việt Nam (ARVN), allies of America.

áo bà ba – Peasant shirt.

áo dài – Traditional long dress worn by women.

ăn cơm – Eat rice.

ba – Father. Also the number three.

bác – Man or woman your grandparents' age.

bánh – Rice or tapioca flour pastries.

bà – An older woman.

bellfruit tree (cây mận) – A tree with bell-shaped fruit. The thin-skinned, watery fruit are also called wax or water apples.

bo bo – Job's Tears or Chinese pearl barley, a grain substituted for rice.

bố – Father (in northern Vietnamese).

bún – Vermicelli rice noodles.

caterpillar helicopter – A Chinook, a helicopter with two rotors used for transporting troops and heavy lifting.

cậu – Uncle.

cháo – Rice soup.

chào – Hello.

cheap tree (cây bần) – A type of cork tree called a mangrove apple in English.

chè – Desserts made of sweet rice or drinks made with beans and coconut milk.

chị – Older sister or woman.

Chúc mừng năm mới – Happy New Year.

Civilian Self-Defense (Nhân Dân Tự Vệ) – Local militia for neighborhood defense.

cold room – Intensive Care Unit (ICU) in a hospital.

cô – Aunt.

cyclo – A cycle rickshaw or the driver of one.

dép – Flip-flop sandals.

dì – Aunt on the mother's side.

dượng – Uncle (husband of mother's sister).

Đảng – The Politburo of the Communist Party.

đần – Mentally slow.

đi – To go.

ê mầy (or ê) – Hey there.

five-ten – Hide-and-seek (kids count by fives).

Hộ Khẩu book – A head count book the Communists gave each family to track food purchases and travel.

lì xì – Lucky money given to children during the New Year.

M-16 – Assault rifle used by the U.S. and South Vietnamese Army.

mai – Yellow flowering bush that blooms around Tết.

mắm – Pickled anchovies.

mẹ – Mother (in northern Vietnamese).

mướp – Luffah squash.

Mùa Hè Đỏ Lửa – The Summer of Red Fire (or as the kids misheard it, Mùa Hè *Đổ* Lửa, The Summer of *Pouring* Fire) the Vietnamese term for the Easter Offensive, an invasion of the South by the North between 30 March and 22 October, 1972.

mứt – Dried fruit candy often bought at New Year's.

mysterious misters (mấy ổng)– What the villagers called Việt Cộng soldiers to avoid naming them directly.

nón lá – Conical hat made of water coconut leaves.

nước mắm – Fish sauce, a condiment made of pressed anchovies.

old queen (máy bay đầm già) – Villagers name for the two-seat reconnaissance plane (L-19) used by the Americans.

ông – Mister or man your parents' age.

ơi – Term of endearment.

paper gold and silver – Fake money for burning on the altar.

phèn – Iron-contaminated water.

rau – Vegetable greens.

shoulder pole seizures – Tetanus.

standing face boat – A troop carrier with a metal ramp in front that lowers for unloading.

stick of gold – Equivalent to a Chinese metric ounce of gold (50 g) or 1.6 troy ounces.

sweet water – Soda pop.

Tết – The Lunar New Year. To "eat Tết" means to celebrate the New Year.

thầy – Teacher.

thiếm – Aunt (wife of father's younger brother).

thưa – Respectful greeting of child to an elder.

trốn lính – Men hiding from Army recruitment.

Việt Cộng – Communist guerillas in the South. They called themselves the National Liberation Front (NLF) or the Front.

water spinach (rau muống) – Also called water morning glory, a tropical leafy vegetable that grows in water and wet soil.

Neighbors and Relatives

Common Vietnamese Titles

Ông – Grandfather or man your grandfather's age.

Bà – Grandmother or woman your grandmother's age.

Dì – Aunt (mother's sister).

Dượng – Uncle (husband of mother's sister).

Chú – Uncle (father's younger brother).

Thiếm – Aunt (wife of father's younger brother).

Cậu – Uncle (mother's brother) or man your uncle's age.

Cô – Aunt (wife of mother's brother) or woman your aunt's age.

Thầy – Teacher.

Quới Sơn

Ba – Lượng's father, Chan La, also called Chú Tám or Anh Tám.

Bà Bảy – The widow who lives across the street.

Captain Can – South Vietnamese Army Captain of the local fort.

Chinese doctor – Neighbor from China married to a Vietnamese woman. He's like a godparent to Lượng and his siblings. His family moves to Tân Long after the Tết Offensive.

Dì Bảy – Má's seventh sister, a rice farmer in Quới Sơn.

Grandfather Lưu (Ông Nội) – Lượng's paternal grandfather from China.

Má – Lượng's mother, Rở Thị Lê, also called Thiếm Tám, Dì Tám or Chị Tám.

Mr. Three Xuyên – A well-off next-door neighbor.

Mrs. Từ Ba – A mentally-ill woman with three sons.

Cồn Tàu

Bà Bảy – Mr. Six Soybean's adoptive mother who works cutting grass for Má.

Aunt Curly (Cô Ba) – A neighbor and the mother-in-law of Chị Bảy Kim. She also has a house in Tân Long.

Dì Hai Temple – An older woman who follows Buddhism and lives near the area of the island controlled by the Việt Cộng.

Five One-Eye and Fort Hag – Việt Cộng squad leaders.

Mr. Fourth Post – Neighbor who sells fish he catches with a net on posts across the river.

Lành – An Army captain who builds a fort on Cồn Tàu. He seeks revenge for the Việt Cộng's execution of his father.

Ông Năm and Bà Năm (Ông Bà Năm) – The old couple who live next door.

Quý – A local Việt Cộng who collects taxes. Best friend of Lành until the Communists force him to execute Lành's father as part of his recruitment.

Mr. Six Soybean – Close neighbor who farms with his wife and children.

Six Stone Brave (or Six Gecko) – The Việt Cộng regional leader.

Mrs. Ten Sea – A woman who farms next door.

Yến – A teenage girl living alone for the summer, studying for a test.

Tân Long

Bà Ba – The medium who lives next door to Lượng's family.

Cậu Tám Tranh (Nurse Tranh) – A nurse who lives with his family close to Lượng's house.

Chị Ba Dung – Widow living across the street next to the ferry dock.

Five Ocean – The captain of the illegal boat.

Mực – A dog named "ink" for his black coat. Mực belongs to Mr. Five Salt's son but lives with Lượng.

Nhiều, Trắng, Vũ, and Six Chicken – Neighborhood kids.

Rở – The son of a tailor who committed suicide.

Mr. Seven Coal – A farmer who is on the neighborhood watch in the south part of Tân Long.

Mr. Six A – Mechanic for the illegal boat.

Mr. Six West – The medium's helper.

Sơn – Neighbor boy with an American father who lives with his Vietnamese mother.

Tây – Mr. Five Salt's son, and the owner of the black dog, Mực.

Mr. Three Belt – Neighbor who owns the shipyard across the road.

Mr. Three East – A former Army officer and leader of the local Civilian Self-Defense.

Mr. Three The – The medium's adult son and a former Army soldier.

Mr. Tư Hạnh (also Cậu Tư Tra) – A neighbor who reports everyone's activities to the Communists.

Vũng Tàu

Chú Tư (Thạch) – Lượng's favorite uncle, his father's younger brother, who lives in Vũng Tàu.

Ngọc Anh – Chú Tư's oldest son.

Giao Long

Cậu Năm Lộc (the ferryman) – A farmer in Giao Long who runs a ferry between Giao Long and Tân Long.

Dũng – Former Việt Cộng assassin given a small plot of land next to the teacher after the war for his contribution to the cause.

Nguyên – The ferryman's daughter.

Phèn – Cousin Lượng's age. The son of Dì Bảy.

Thầy Giáo Bi (Thầy Bi) – Teacher who lives on the land across the stream.

Thiệu – The ferryman's son.

Mỹ Tho

Dũng, Mến, Nhả, and Phục – Lượng's school friends.

Ông Three Của – Head of the half-legal boat program in Mỹ Tho.

Tuyên – Leader of the Red Scarf group at school.

Children of Oldest Aunt (Dì Hai)

Hai Thăng – The oldest child of Lượng's oldest aunt, a barber who lives in Tân Long.

Children of Missing Aunt (Dì Ba) & Dượng Ba

Chị Ba Chẳng – The oldest daughter of Lượng's missing aunt. She lives in Giao Long.

Chị Năm Hộ – Cousin whose husband, Anh Năm Nô, worked for the Việt Cộng and defected. Anh Năm Nô joined the Army, but was discharged after losing half of his foot in an accident.

Anh Sáu Triệu – Cousin working for the Việt Cộng who defected.

Chị Bảy Kim – Cousin helping on the farm.

Chị Thủy – Cousin helping on the farm.

Chị Mộng – Cousin helping on the farm.

Chị Châu – Cousin helping on the farm.

Trực – Cousin Lượng's age.

Dearest – Youngest cousin who has a speech problem.

Children of Fourth Aunt (Dì Tư)

Cousin Fourth Triều – Cousin in the Army on the front.

Chị Năm Gương – Lives in Sài Gòn and owns an exercise gymnasium.

Chị Bảy Ký – Cousin helping on the farm.

Anh Chín Phát – Cousin helping on the farm and later fixing electronics.

Made in the USA
San Bernardino, CA
03 November 2015